CHILD DEVELOPMENT: THEORIES AND CRITICAL PERSPECTIVES

Child Development: Theories and Critical Perspectives provides an engaging and perceptive overview of both well-established and recent theories in child and adolescent psychology. This unique summary of traditional scientific perspectives alongside critical postmodern thinking will provide readers with a sense of the historical development of different schools of thought. The authors also place theories of child development in philosophical and cultural contexts, explore links between them, and consider the implications of theory for practice in the light of the latest thinking and developments in implementation and translational science.

Early chapters cover mainstream theories such as those of Jean Piaget, B.F. Skinner, Sigmund Freud, Eleanor Maccoby and Lev Vygotsky, while later chapters present interesting lesser-known theorists such as Sergei Rubinstein, and more recent influential theorists such as Esther Thelen. The book also addresses lifespan perspectives and systems theory, and describes the latest thinking in areas ranging from evolutionary theory and epigenetics, to feminism, the voice of the child and Indigenous theories.

The new edition has been extensively revised to include considerable recent advances in the field. As with the previous edition, the book has been written with the student in mind, and includes a number of useful pedagogical features including a glossary, discussion questions, activities and websites of interest.

Child Development: Theories and Critical Perspectives will be essential reading for students on advanced courses in developmental psychology, education, social work and social policy, and the lucid style will also make it accessible to readers with little or no background in psychology.

Rosalyn H. Shute is an Adjunct Professor in the School of Psychology, Flinders University, Adelaide, Australia, and Federation University, Ballarat, Australia. Her research expertise lies broadly in clinical child psychology and paediatric psychology/child health and wellbeing, and she is an experienced teacher of developmental psychology and clinical child/paediatric psychology.

Phillip T. Slee is a Professor in Human Development in the School of Education at Flinders University, Adelaide, Australia. He is a trained teacher and registered psychologist. His main areas of interest include childhood bullying/aggression, conduct disorders, stress and teacher education, and he has a particular interest in the practical and policy implications of his research.

International Texts in Developmental Psychology

Series editor: Peter K. Smith, Goldsmiths College, University of London, UK.

This volume is one of a rapidly developing series in *International Texts in Developmental Psychology*, published by Routledge. The books in this series are selected to be state-of-the-art, high level introductions to major topic areas in developmental psychology. The series conceives of developmental psychology in broad terms and covers such areas as social development, cognitive development, developmental neuropsychology and neuroscience, language development, learning difficulties, developmental psychopathology and applied issues. Each volume is written by a specialist (or specialists), combining empirical data and a synthesis of recent global research to deliver cutting-edge science in a format accessible to students and researchers alike. The books may be used as textbooks that match on to upper level developmental psychology modules, but many will also have cross-disciplinary appeal.

Each volume in the series is published in hardback, paperback and eBook formats. More information about the series is available on the official website at: http://www.psypress.com/books/series/DEVP, including details of all the titles published to date.

Published Titles

The Child at School: Interactions with Peers and Teachers, 2nd edition
By Peter Blatchford, Anthony D. Pellegrini, Ed Baines

Aging and Development: Social and Emotional Perspectives, 2nd edition
By Peter Coleman, Ann O'Hanlon

Childhood Friendships and Peer Relations: Friends and Enemies, 2nd edition
By Barry Schneider

Children's Literacy Development: A Cross-Cultural Perspective on Learning to Read and Write, 2nd edition
By Catherine McBride-Chang

Child Development: Theories and Critical Perspectives, 2nd edition
By Rosalyn H. Shute and Phillip T. Slee

CHILD DEVELOPMENT: THEORIES AND CRITICAL PERSPECTIVES

Second edition

Rosalyn H. Shute and Phillip T. Slee

Routledge
Taylor & Francis Group

LONDON AND NEW YORK

First published 2015
by Routledge
27 Church Road, Hove, East Sussex BN3 2FA

and by Routledge
711 Third Avenue, New York, NY 10017

Routledge is an imprint of the Taylor & Francis Group, an informa business

© 2015 Rosalyn H. Shute and Phillip T. Slee

First edition published by Hodder Education 2003

British Library Cataloguing in Publication Data
A catalogue record for this book is available from the British Library

Library of Congress Cataloging in Publication Data
A catalog record for this book has been requested

ISBN: 978-1-84872-451-8 (hbk)
ISBN: 978-1-84872-452-5 (pbk)
ISBN: 978-1-315-76798-7 (ebk)

Typeset in Bembo
by Keystroke, Station Road, Codsall, Wolverhampton

CONTENTS

FIGURES, TABLES AND BOXES

Figures

Tables

Boxes

PREFACE

Our intention in this second edition of our 2003 book is to advance thinking about theories of children's psychological development still further. Some theorists take a lifespan perspective, others a shorter-term one, while still others maintain that we are too concerned with children's 'becoming', to the neglect of their 'being'. Although theories are the main focus, their contribution to policy and practice is certainly not neglected. As well as being academic psychologists, we have strong professional interests. Phillip, a registered psychologist with a background in teaching, educates student teachers and has produced internationally utilized materials to address school bullying and young people's mental health. Rosalyn for many years coordinated and taught on professional postgraduate psychology courses and provided paediatric psychology services to children and families. Most of our publications address applied issues.

At first sight, then, it is perhaps a little curious that a book on theories of child and adolescent development should be written by two people whose primary interests are applied. However, we take a holistic approach to our work, and see theory as underpinning all aspects of it, including research, teaching and professional practice. We therefore considered it important to include material on the implications of theory for practice, especially given the primary readership of the book (higher-level undergraduates, Honours students and postgraduates), who are at the stage of considering the connections between their undergraduate education and future career plans. In fact, we have expanded and updated this applied coverage in the final chapter.

We also considered it important to have some empirical basis for decisions about structuring the book. As well as drawing upon the developmental literature, our own experience with writing texts and guidance from the series editor and book proposal referees, for the first edition we held a focus group of Honours psychology students to ask them what they would like to see in a book such as this. One of their main wishes was to gain an overall picture of various theories and how they fitted together, in contrast to the fragmented image they felt they had taken away from their undergraduate studies. In addition, they felt that the university culture of critique left them with only a sense of 'what was wrong' with various theoretical approaches, and they also wanted to know 'what was right' with them. They asked to see examples of the implications of theory for practice and reported being put off by too much abstract writing without examples and too many pages of unbroken text. Within the constraints of the series, we have again aimed to address all these issues. In particular, making some explicit historical and theoretical links between different schools of thought remains a strong feature. We have attempted to avoid the type of text described by Jones:

> dry, distanced monologues bereft of the warm breathing human being who wrote them ... obscure and difficult ... simply commodities in the academic marketplace ... 'valuable' perhaps for the students forced to wade through their pages and reproduce their arguments in return for grades.
>
> *(Jones, 1991: 9)*

For this second edition we asked two early-career lecturers in psychology to review the first edition and the proposal for the second. They noted that the original book was very readable and liked the stories, poems and metaphors, and the historical context, background and detail of the various theories, which they felt really enabled students to understand developmental psychology and how it has evolved. We have aimed to retain these features.

Other texts provide a detailed exposition of many of the classical theories of child development. In the present volume, we have focused in the main upon more recent critiques and trends, including issues of epistemology – theory of knowledge. However, we have also sought to provide a sense of historical development of various schools of thought, and have included information about some theorists whose work is less well known today.

While the early chapters cover mainstream theories, later chapters consider the contributions of postmodern thinking to theorizing about child and adolescent development. In preparing the first edition, we felt that it was important to include postmodern critiques, as they were generally found in journal articles and specialist books but not in child development textbooks, which instead tended to adopt a standard scientific perspective; this situation has hardly changed. This decision meant we were confronted with the tensions that characterize current modern and postmodern debate concerning the nature and role of developmental theory. This, in turn, raised for us the significant question of whether one is able to articulate a middle ground for developmental theory. Is there a position that absorbs the best that modernism has to offer while also accommodating postmodern views of human development, and the theory and practice surrounding it, as inhabiting a historical time and culture? We are hopeful that, as the story of this text unfolds, readers will be challenged and encouraged to consider such issues in addition to the more familiar ones about nature–nurture and continuity–discontinuity in development.

We begin the book with an overview of some of the historical, cultural and philosophical influences on theorizing about children's development, followed by a chapter on biological explanations for development, with expanded coverage of epigenetics. Chapters follow based on organismic, psychoanalytic and mechanistic theories, dialecticism and contextualism. In updating the second edition we have expanded the coverage of systems thinking, believing that it now deserves its own chapter. The postmodern influence becomes apparent as we move into a consideration of sociocultural and feminist theories. Many texts on child development still fail to include the 'voices of young people' themselves, and we have attempted to address this imbalance with a new chapter. Having considered these diverse schools of thought, we examine the prospect of a more integrated approach to developmental theorizing, followed by a discussion of implications for practice, including new material on translational research, concerning the emerging issue of how evidence-based practice and programmes aimed at promoting children's healthy development are enacted in the 'real world' setting of organizations such as schools.

We have provided ideas for further study at the end of the book rather than integrating them into the chapters. We did this to avoid creating an 'undergraduate' feel, and to enable those wishing to simply read the book to do so (this is in line with the wishes of our focus group students and reviewers). However, we felt it important to provide some exercises and ideas for further study for those students or lecturers seeking them, hence their inclusion in a Student Resources section. This also includes references to some relevant websites.

The first edition was well reviewed and we received unsolicited positive comments from our readers (especially on the postmodern aspects), which buoyed us up on those lonely nights spent finalizing the text. We thank our Routledge editor Russell George and his colleagues for support and encouragement in proceeding with this new edition, as well as all the reviewers, whose feedback was enormously helpful in shaping the new content. They asked for some additional areas to be covered and we have been able to incorporate most, but not all, of their ideas, given the space constraints, and of course we take responsibility for those editorial decisions. We thank Routledge for allowing us some extra space in this edition, but we make no claim to be comprehensive. Much important material and many influential names have been omitted (if yours is one of them, please forgive us!), and we can provide only a few examples of empirical studies relevant for the various theories. We have tried, however, to select these (including some from our own work) to illustrate some important themes and trends in the developmental path of theorizing in the field, as well to create the sense of connection between different theories that had been requested by our students. We hope the fact that we are writing from the Antipodes has helped to give a broader perspective than is found in many texts; we have included examples from Australia, other Pacific nations and the Asia-Pacific rim.

We thank Peter Smith for his invitation to write the original text and for his helpful comments on drafts of both editions. We also thank Wilhelmina Drummond for permission to use her illustration of the Maori model of human development. Finally, Phillip thanks Elizabeth for her support, and their sons (Matthew, Nicholas and Christopher), who helped to maintain some balance in his life by distracting him with invitations to kayak and snorkel. Rosalyn has achieved her own life balance, as this book is one of her retirement projects. She is most grateful for Jason's help in proofreading the final draft, and Elen's assistance with Figure 1.1.

Rosalyn Shute and Phillip Slee

Adelaide, June 2014

Reference

Jones, A. 1991. *'At school I've got a chance.' Culture/privilege: Pacific Islands and Pakeha girls at school.* Palmerston North, NZ: Dunmore Press.

1

WAYS OF KNOWING
ABOUT DEVELOPMENT

Introduction

Some of our readers may be habitual 'preface-skippers', and if you are one, we do encourage you to turn back to the Preface so that the rationale for this book and our general approach to this second edition are clear. We further set the context in this introductory chapter. After considering the nature of developmental psychology, we devote the main body of the chapter to discussing some ways of knowing about children: knowing them from various philosophical and theoretical perspectives, knowing them in a cultural sense and knowing them as beings placed in historical contexts. As such, the chapter reflects David Kennedy's view that 'characterizations of children function symbolically as carriers of deep assumptions about the construction of human subjectivity, about the ultimate meaning of the human life cycle, and about human forms of knowledge' (Kennedy, 2000: 514).

Developmental psychology

Psychology is a relatively young discipline, which has wholeheartedly embraced a positivist philosophy and the scientific method. The field of study in psychology that is concerned with how the individual grows and changes from conception until death is known as developmental psychology, and has its own distinctive history (Cairns, 1998). Within this field, child development is one special avenue of interest. We use the word 'child' here generically to include all stages of development from conception through infancy, childhood and adolescence. We have laid out some historical 'milestones' in developmental psychology on p. 269, but it is in the body of the text that the underlying theoretical cross-fertilizations and debates are expounded. One current challenge is to consider whether theoretical diversity or integration is the way of the future. Another is whether to embrace a more critical outlook regarding the theories and assumptions underpinning the field. We are not sure that the polarization of thinking in terms of a modern–postmodern dichotomy is a helpful trend, and we hope to encourage some informed debate on the issue.

Several broad questions are addressed in this text:

1. How do children change as they develop?
2. What factors influence the developmental changes?
3. What individual differences exist in growth and development?

In each of the chapters we encourage readers to return to these questions as a way of reviewing the nature of the theories presented, as well as using the discussion questions, activities and websites listed on p. 272.

What is development?

Although it is a more than reasonable question to ask, 'What is development?', it is not so easy to answer. Broadly, human development is about the totality of changes that a person undergoes over time. 'Ontogeny' is a more biological term that similarly encapsulates the developmental history of an individual organism, human or otherwise. Willis Overton (2006) has identified two broad types of developmental change:

1. *Transformational change* is really morphological change that involves the emergence of novelty. An example is that of the single celled zygote differentiating and emerging into ever more complex forms.
2. *Variational change* describes the individual differences that occur in development – e.g. the age by which a child walks in relation to the norm.

Overton sees these as reciprocal and complementary, arguing that 'transformational systems produce variation and variation transforms the system' (Overton, 2006: 28). For detailed consideration of what constitutes developmental change, and what it is that changes, see Paul Baltes (1987) for an early examination of the issues and Overton (2006) for more recent writing.

The positivist view so wholeheartedly embraced by developmental psychology tends to see development as a linear unfolding of potential, although this view is challenged by those who see development as being often very non-linear and in a continual state of flux. For example, Mark Howe and Marc Lewis (2005: 248) suggest that 'ontogeny cannot be considered hard-wired in any sense, but rather emergent, unpredictable, and always coupled with environmental events'. This idea will be considered further in later chapters, especially Chapter 10, where we discuss systems theories of development. Also relevant is Baltes's (1987) lifespan approach, which views development as a change in adaptive capacity, potentially meaning loss as well as gain. A push to include the environment in defining development also comes from non-western perspectives, with A. Bame Nsamenang defining developmental psychology as 'the science of human development in context' (Nsamenang, 1999: 163). We can throw further spanners into the definitional works by observing that the western focus on 'the individual' as the subject of change is alien to some societies, while certain scholars are critical of developmental science's 'future focus', to the neglect of the here and now (see Chapters 9 and 12).

The question of how to define development is inextricably linked with two further questions: what is it that develops, and how? The 'what' can be considered relatively narrowly, as in the case of Jean Piaget's schemas, or more broadly, in terms of different facets of development. For example, attachment theorists focus on emotional development and ethologists on evolved innate behaviours, while for others cognitive development is central.

As for the 'how' of change, this is extensively considered in the chapters that follow. For example, Piaget focused on how developing children construct their own knowledge as a largely solitary activity, while the Russian psychologist Lev Vygotsky theorized that children's cognitive abilities develop through interaction with others, although these theories may be better seen as complementary rather than in opposition (Lourenço, 2012).

Lifespan development

Our subject matter of the early years is where the major focus of developmental psychology lay for many years. Sigmund Freud, for example (see Chapter 5), emphasized the significance of the first years as the formative ones in human development, which implies that the study of adults is of little relevance to developmental psychology; that is, while it may be acknowledged that individuals continue to change past adolescence, such changes might be viewed as largely cultural and not the result of 'gene expression', and lacking the age-linked and universal qualities that often characterize developmental theories.

By contrast, other theorists such as Erik Erikson (see Chapters 3, 5 and 8) emphasized that human development continues across the life-cycle. Simplistically, lifespan development is 'the study of the development of living organisms from conception to the end of life' (Overton, 2010: 4) but, as Overton further notes, a more considered examination highlights the underpinning complexities. Typically, lifespan theories consider age-related areas of study (e.g. infancy) in the context of various dimensions (e.g. biological and cognitive) against the background of the various systems within which the individual develops, such as family and school.

Such systemic views characterize development in a number of important ways (Shanahan *et al.*, 2000). First, they emphasize lasting malleability: 'the prominent place of plasticity in many theories acknowledges that change can occur at any level of organization in the ecology of human development and that intra-individual variability is possible across the entire life-span' (Shanahan *et al.*, 2000: 421). Indeed, in relation to the structure and functions of the human brain, there is now 'compelling evidence in favor of structural plasticity throughout life' (Leuner and Gould, 2010: 112). Second, in adopting a more contextual 'life-history' view of development, account can be taken of secular trends such as changes in the onset of girls' puberty and the health status of children. Third, the greater appreciation of individual differences afforded by systems approaches has restricted the degree to which developmental psychology is looking for generalizability. Finally, the understanding of the impact of multiple contexts and multi-directional influences on development has contributed significantly to an appreciation of life-cycle development. We see a lifespan view as offering a broader context against which to view children's development and we will refer to this perspective from time to time, particularly in Chapter 8.

Why study child development?

A dominant theme, as verified by an examination of the contents pages in significant journals, is that of raising children. This ongoing concern arose from the writings of early philosophers such as John Locke and Jean-Jacques Rousseau, and religious writers such as John Wesley.

It is also recognized that through the study of children we may come to under-stand adult behaviour better. As John Milton commented in *Paradise Lost*, 'The childhood shows the man as morning shows the day' (Milton, 1671/2007: Book IV, 220–1). Gabriel Compayré, a nineteenth-century French educationalist, also believed that information concerning the child's early years would serve to illuminate later development: 'If childhood is the cradle of humanity, the study of childhood is the cradle and necessary introduction to all future psychology' (Compayré, 1896: 3).

From a somewhat different perspective, Charles Darwin believed that the child was the link between animal and human species. The birth of his son (nicknamed 'Doddy') prompted Darwin to begin a diary description of Doddy's development – a 'baby biography'. By observing the development of the infant, Darwin believed some understanding could be reached about the species itself. For example, in *The Expression of the Emotions in Man and Animals*, Darwin argued that emotional expression was basically a physiological matter and that expressive gestures were largely universal and innate:

> Everyone who has had much to do with young children must have seen how naturally they take to biting when in a passion. It seems instinctive in them as in young crocodiles, who snap their little jaws as soon as they emerge from the egg.
> *(Darwin, 1872/1965: 241–2)*

Gene Medinnus (1976) identified four main reasons for studying children, which remain pertinent:

1. An intellectual curiosity concerning natural phenomena.
2. The need to gain information to guide children's behaviour.
3. To increase our ability to predict behaviour.
4. The need to understand our own (adult) behaviour.

We contend strongly that the study of development does not occur in a historical, cultural or philosophical vacuum. It is a salutary point to consider that the very words 'child' and 'childhood' have changed their meaning in recent western history and have different meanings in different cultures. The historical element is highlighted when, with the benefit of hindsight, we note that Darwin's observations were designed to explore the links between animal and human species. The infant was essentially depicted as a biological organism influenced and shaped to a greater or lesser degree by the environment. A surge of interest in the study of children along with the study of so-called 'primitives' arose as the perceived key to an improved understanding of the development of 'normal' behaviour. The concept of 'recapitulation' – the idea that 'ontogeny recapitulates phylogeny', or that individuals in their lifetime demonstrate the patterns and stages exhibited in the development of the species – underpins the writing of many early theorists, such as G. Stanley Hall (see Chapter 3). The identification of children's stages of development and the obsession with minutely recording normal growth and development characterized much early research, such as that of Arnold Gesell (see Chapter 4).

A postmodern outlook points out that the conduct of this science went hand in hand with the development of an empirical methodology that clearly separated the observer from the observed, in the best interests of the scientific endeavour. The child was objectified, in the spotlight of this critical gaze. The exercise involved a gendered division of labour, with men viewed as having the necessary credentials to conduct objective, verifiable observations: 'Women were excluded from the investigative enterprise because they were declared constitutionally incapable of regarding their children with the requisite objectivity' (Burman, 1994: 12). So, in a postmodern context, our attention is drawn to the various factors impacting on and shaping the study of child development, which is also related to how we conduct science. Some of these issues facing contemporary psychology are examined in more detail in the later chapters.

Three factors shaping views of development

Writers have identified a number of factors that have shaped our views of children and families over the centuries (Ariès, 1962; Clarke-Stewart, 1998; Elkind, 1987; Schorsch, 1979; Volk, 2011). As Philippe Ariès (1962) reminded us, little, if anything, escapes history or culture, not even the central elements of life itself for women, men and children. A third factor is the philosophy of science. We begin our discussion by examining the child in a historical context.

History

It is important to appreciate the view expressed by Ariès (1962): that childhood, as it is understood today in western society, is a relatively recent phenomenon. Following Ariès's pioneering work on the history of childhood, a number of writers have supported his views. For example, Anita Schorsch observed that 'thinkers of the 16th century, and of the preceding centuries as well, agreed that the child is nothing more than a lower animal – "the infant mewling and puking in the nurse's arms" as Shakespeare put it baldly but succinctly' (Schorsch, 1979: 11). Kennedy later observed, 'Looking back to the foundations of the Western philosophical tradition, the child does not fare particularly well in adult male construction (we do not hear from the females)' (Kennedy, 2000: 518). Ariès's thesis is not without its shortcomings, and there also exists the idea that, at various times throughout European history, the infant has been revered as an embodiment of New Testament depictions of 'sinlessness'. For examples of this ideal, consider the representations of infants and young children by Renaissance painters.

David Elkind (1987) captured some of the complexity of the changing views of childhood from antiquity to the late twentieth century. In Ancient Greece the stress was upon educating children into the laws and cultural mores of the time. Children in Babylon went to school at the age of six, while Roman children started to attend school at around seven to acquire reading and writing skills. However, children in medieval Europe fared far less well. During this time the prevailing image was of the child as chattel or property of the parent and state. All in all, during the medieval period the child did not count for much in the eyes of society, as a sixteenth-century rhyme indicates:

> Of all the months the first behold,
> January two-faced and cold
> Because its eyes two ways are cast
> To face the future and the past.
> Thus the child six summers old
> Is not worth much when all is told.
>
> *(Cited in Schorsch, 1979: 23)*

History shows that for centuries children have been looked upon as property, particularly of their fathers, with paternalism and patriarchy playing a significant role in parent–child relationships. Some basis for understanding the contemporary status of children in western societies is found in the writings of the Greek philosopher Aristotle. In Bertrand Russell's description of Aristotelian ethics, he noted that, while Aristotle considered human beings as 'ethically equal', 'the justice of a master or a father is a different thing from that of a citizen, for a son or slave is property, and there can be no injustice to one's own property' (Russell, 1974: 186). Law elaborated between CE 1300 and CE 1800 prescribed the relationship between parent and child in terms of trust. The parent's rights came from the state, and the state reserved the right to intervene and protect children's rights and interests. However, while the court would protect children's interests, it could not present their grievances and had no guarantee of independent representation (Fraser, 1976).

Further insight is gained from philosophers such as Thomas Hobbes, John Locke and John Stuart Mill. Hobbes, writing in the seventeenth century, argued that children were cared for solely because they were capable of serving their father and should be assigned a position of complete dependence. 'Like the imbecile, the crazed and the beasts over ... children ... there is no law' (Hobbes, 1651/1931: 257). The implication is that children have no natural rights and no rights by social contract, because they lack the ability to make formal contracts with other members of society and cannot understand the consequences of such contracts.

English philosopher John Locke (1632–1704), arguing from a different perspective, considered children to be under the jurisdiction of their parents until they were capable of fending for themselves. Until then, children were thought to lack understanding and therefore they could not assert their will (Russell, 1974). Unlike Hobbes, Locke believed that both adults and children possessed certain natural rights, which needed protection. Parental benevolence was believed to be sufficient to ensure that children's rights were protected. Locke's outlook replaced the proprietary aspect of parenthood with the concept of children as God's property. Locke's description of children as lacking in understanding reflected the view that children need to develop adult capacities for reasoning and understanding. Until such time, parents were under a God-given obligation to care for children. By implication, where parents failed to fulfil their obligation to children, the state would be empowered to do so.

The late eighteenth and nineteenth centuries in Europe were witness to the dramatic social and economic changes wrought by the Industrial Revolution. In large part, children fared very poorly in the face of these changes. Schorsch noted that young children worked in the cotton mills of England:

> A child over seven worked from sunrise to sunset six days a week with two and a half days off a year; children between six and sixteen earned slightly more than half a woman's wages and only a fourth of a man's.
>
> *(Schorsch, 1979: 143)*

The nineteenth-century French novelist Emile Zola, in his novel *Germinal* (1885/1979) depicts 12-year-old children working alongside their fathers and older siblings in the mineshafts of France.

Eventually, child labour laws were enacted, first in Britain in 1833, to protect children from the excesses and exploitation of the Industrial Revolution. The nature of childhood as viewed by western society was beginning to change. New emphasis was given to education and recognizing the special needs of young children. Childhood was gradually acknowledged as a distinct stage in human development. Box 1.1 illustrates how views about children and their relationship to adults are reflected in such behaviours as corporal punishment.

Most recently the field of developmental psychology has contributed to the recognition of divisions in the concept of childhood itself. Beyond infancy, at least four stages of child development are commonly identified in western societies today: early childhood, middle childhood, late childhood and adolescence. Overall, the status of children, attitudes towards children and the value society attaches to children are best understood in historical context. For example, Kim Collard has

---

BOX 1.1 CHILDREN AND PUNISHMENT

There was an old woman who lived in a shoe;
She had so many children she didn't know what to do.
She gave them some broth without any bread;
Then whipped them all soundly and sent them to bed.

In Australia and other western countries, the notion of the iniquitous child as reflected in the use of corporal punishment still continues to elicit controversy. Sweden became the first country in the world to ban corporal punishment of children. Internationally, 23 countries have prohibited corporal punishment in all settings, through legislation (Holzer and Lamont, 2010). In Australia, all states have banned the use of corporal punishment in public schools but it is still lawful in private schools in some states and territories. What does the view we hold about corporal punishment say about how we understand young people as 'experiential', 'iniquitous', 'virtuous', 'competent' or 'postmodern'?

---

emphasized the role of history in providing Australian Aboriginal people with a sense of belonging: 'in considering the present it is important to look at the past, particularly an Aboriginal account of history, which has either been conveniently ignored or omitted from the official history of Australia' (Collard, 2000: 22). It is a sad reflection on Australian society and culture that Collard's point remains relevant today.

Japan is another culture where a historical perspective has been found valuable (Kojima, 1996). For example, in the late seventeenth century Confucian moral teachings were used to advise parents, but this later expanded to include advice on childcare, health and education, at a time when the rulers were making an effort to produce 'an obedient and productive working class' (Kojima, 1996: 377).

Culture

A second important factor shaping the way we understand children and adolescents is that of culture. William Kessen (1979) even described children and child psychology as 'cultural inventions', highlighting that we cannot easily separate the influence of culture from any discussion of the nature of children and families. The ideas of the US anthropologist Margaret Mead help us to appreciate the role played by culture (see Chapter 8). In her book *Culture and Commitment* (Mead, 1970) she called upon knowledge gleaned from studying children in Manus, Bali and New Guinea, following their lives into adulthood.

An example from China is the portrayal of the twentieth-century child in literature as a sign of national hope and prosperity, and (commodity-like) as a bearer of national and political messages (Jones, 2011). Similarly, in mid-nineteenth-century USA the cultural construction of the child was embodied in child actors and actresses and reflected in their role in national theatre, which 'became a marketplace for national esteem, and child actresses became marketable signifiers of what the country needed · to escape or deny' (Mullineaux, 2012: 284). As the same author observes, the popular press of the time proclaimed the talents of the child actors as markers of 'national integrity, sophistication and spirit' (Mullineaux, 2012: 283).

The issue of culture in child-rearing is exemplified by considering again the case of Australian Aborigines. In traditional Aboriginal communities, the values stressed included sharing, mutual cooperation, kinship obligations and personal relationships (Jenkins, 1988). Aboriginal children were largely brought up by their mother and her sisters, with boys' education later taken over by the father, 'learning by emulating adults rather than by formal instruction' (Lippman, 1970: 21). Each society had rich oral, spiritual traditions, which conveyed knowledge about local lands and seasons; upon initiation at puberty, the amount of learning and community responsibility expected for the Aboriginal child greatly increased (Collard, 2000). Traditional child-rearing values and practices still exist in many indigenous Australian communities (see Chapter 9).

The mix of the population should be taken into consideration when examining the effect of culture on child development. For example, around 44 per cent of all Australians were either born overseas or have at least one overseas-born parent (Australian Bureau of Statistics, 2006), raising specific developmental issues. Cynthia Leung (2001) compared the adaptation of Chinese migrant adolescents in Australia and Canada, pointing to the significance of social support, as did a study by Lydia Kovacev and Rosalyn Shute (2004) of resettled adolescent refugees from the former Republic of Yugoslavia. Des Storer (1985) reported that male migrant workers from Mediterranean countries earned less than Australian-born or English-speaking migrants and had higher unemployment rates. These factors have an obvious impact on the family in terms of social and human capital. Migration also sets the scene for some conflict between parents and children in terms of values, attitudes and morality, as with South European girls tending to be more restricted and supervised in their activities than their Australian-born counterparts (Storer, 1985).

In summary, contemporary developmental thinking increasingly recognizes the central role of culture in shaping the way children grow and develop and, indeed, in shaping our very views of children and childhood. Jerome Bruner and Helen Haste captured this idea in the sentence, 'It can never be the case that there is a "self" independent of one's cultural-historical existence' (Bruner and Haste, 1987: 91).

Philosophy of science

While developmental psychology has never hesitated to draw upon disciplines such as biology, anthropology and sociology, recent developments in the philosophy of knowledge have been largely ignored (Teo, 1997). This rather curious omission has occurred despite the fact that influential writers and researchers in the field, such as Piaget, had epistemology as the basis for their work. Thomas Teo suggested that the primary reason for this neglect concerns the rise and dominance of empiricism, particularly as reflected in mainstream North American psychology.

The philosophy of science has significant ramifications for the theoretical and conceptual foundations of developmental psychology, shaping the very way we view the subject. 'In the broadest sense of the term a world view helps people interpret, understand and bring some order to their lives' (Slee, 1987: 8). Worldviews help to shape how we use terms like 'knowledge', 'information' and 'science'. That is, they help to specify the types of theory used in research, and identify problems worthy of study and the methodology to be employed in investigating a problem (Lerner, 1986).

'Common sense' has often initially prompted and informed the interpretation of behaviour, as demonstrated by Darwin's observations regarding the emergence of emotions in children (cited earlier), or Piaget's careful recording of the behaviour of his children in relation to their use of senses and motor activity to acquire knowledge about the world (see Chapter 4). These scientists attempted systematically to bring some order and coherence to their observations, for example by gathering further evidence or performing experiments in an attempt to reproduce the initial findings. As Overton (1998: 155) noted, 'This issue – the route from common sense to science – constitutes the methodology of science'.

Presently, the dominant western model of 'reality' draws heavily upon belief in a particular view of the scientific method as the only valid approach to the acquisition and understanding of a systematic body of knowledge. The basis for the prevailing scientific method is drawn from the worldview of empiricism, a philosophy of science that has exerted a powerful influence on scientific practice. In a very direct way, it has shaped how we have conducted the science of child study. Thus, in modelling itself upon the natural sciences such as physics and chemistry, the empirical method of child study has placed a great deal of importance on a search for causes of behaviour, with an emphasis on reducing the complexity of behaviour to its basic components. In 1974, Urie Bronfenbrenner drew attention to the fact that some 76 per cent of child development research was of an experimental laboratory nature, contrasting with only 8 per cent that used naturalistic observation (Bronfenbrenner, 1974).

While the empirical method eschews interpretation, at the beginning of the twentieth century psychology struggled with the practice of *Verstehen*, or understanding, as a methodology. Ultimately, the method drowned in the sea of empiricism, which became the dominant scientific discourse in developmental psychology. Presently, the role of interpretation is undergoing a re-examination in relation to understanding human development, in light of the contribution that postmodern and feminist thinking is making to the field, along with a reappraisal of the role of philosophy.

What is a theory?

In current popular discourse, we often hear the word 'theory' used disparagingly, as when climate change deniers say that 'climate change is only a theory', as though to suggest that theory has no necessary relationship to facts. As defined by *The Macquarie Dictionary*, a fact is 'what has really happened or is the case; truth; reality; something known to have happened' (Delbridge, 2001: n.p.). Research into child development is uncovering facts at a rate that sometimes outstrips our ability to integrate them into a coherent framework. Facts are very important as building blocks of science. However, just as a pile of bricks does not make a house, a collection of facts does not make a science: 'A theory may be considered as a way of binding together a multitude of facts so that one may comprehend them all at once' (Kelly, 1963: 18).

But to backtrack a little …

The word 'theory' has its origins in the Greek *theoria* – contemplation, spectacle, mental conception. Jerry Harvey (in Williams, 1976) relates theory to 'fantasy', suggesting that it is quite inferior to practice. As noted by Jill Morawski (2001), though, any understanding of the concept of 'theory' should look to embed it in historical context. In relation to psychology, theory has held a rather troubled and uneasy place. From a logical-positivist perspective, 'a judiciously crafted theory, sparse and logically pristine, could be submitted to hypothetico-deductive method; that is, it could yield tidy hypotheses for laboratory testing', although theory unrestrained has frequently resulted in 'profligate claims about human nature' (Morawski, 2001: 434–5). Moreover, theory has existed uneasily alongside practice. Francis Bacon distinguished theory from 'practice' (Bacon, 1626), while 'praxis' is practice informed by theory (Williams, 1976: 268). We will consider such issues further in the final chapter.

In the first edition of this book, we drew attention to the notion of 'metatheory', and this is a concept that has increasingly been referenced in the child development literature as applying to broad groupings of theories with similar core assumptions. Other terms used for much the same idea include theoretical 'approaches', 'traditions' or 'orientations'; they are often 'isms', as in organicism and behaviourism. They are sometimes seen as metaphors, as we discuss later. Metatheories are similar to 'paradigms', while 'worldviews' can be seen as even broader, and concern ways of knowing (epistemology) and issues of reality (ontology) (Overton, 2007). More specific theories, sometimes called mini-theories, can be located within broader metatheoretical frameworks, and it is from these that specific, testable propositions can be derived.

This approach is based upon the philosophy of science articulated by Imre Lakatos (Ketelaar and Ellis, 2000), which provides a broad framework for making decisions about whether to accept or reject a theory. The Popperian view that science proceeds by falsification of hypotheses remains widely accepted in psychological research. However, Lakatos proposed that falsification should not be used to reject a theory, only to reject specific statements derived from the theory. For Lakatos, a metatheoretical core is surrounded by a 'protective belt' of middle-level theories and auxiliary hypotheses that give rise to specific, testable statements. In this way, competing statements derived from the same basic metatheory may be tested. Rather than experimental results leading to wholesale acceptance or rejection of the basic metatheory, they contribute to evaluation of the performance of the protective belt – to a decision about whether the metatheory is generally progressive or degenerative.

An area where the theory–metatheory distinction has been sharply drawn is in certain feminist critiques of evolutionary psychologists, with some of the latter accused of confusing 'research theories' with higher-level metatheories in a way that muddles conceptual discussions about the conclusions to be drawn from research evidence. Another area where the distinction arises is in considering the issue of diversity versus integration in developmental theorizing. We will consider these matters further in Chapters 11 and 13.

Various other writers have suggested criteria for evaluating developmental theories (e.g. Gewirtz and Pelaez-Nogueras, 1992; Green, 1989; Kelly, 1963; Lerner, 1983; Thelen and Smith, 1994), but we can identify little consensus. We suggest that readers might apply a number of criteria concerning change, based on the key points raised earlier in this chapter.

- How well do the theories explain how children change as they develop? What empirical support is provided for their explanations?
- How do the theories account for the various factors, such as culture, that influence developmental change?
- How well do the theories account for individual differences that exist in children's growth and development?
- Is the explanation parsimonious (Gewirtz and Pelaez-Nogueras, 1992)?

How do children change as they develop?

We now consider the nature of change in the light of the following frequently debated questions in development. These key concepts, listed below, are identifiable in various theories and provide a useful heuristic for understanding development.

- Heredity versus environment.
- Continuity versus discontinuity of development.
- Similarity versus uniqueness.
- Stability versus instability of behaviour.
- Activity versus passivity of behaviour.
- Thinking versus feeling.

Heredity versus environment

The role that these play in shaping the person is a major issue not only in psychology, but also in education, sociology, politics and related disciplines. Everyday observations reveal similarities and dissimilarities between people, such as in their physical appearance, mental capacity or emotional make-up. Are such characteristics innate or are they shaped by environmental forces after birth (or even before

---

BOX 1.2 CAN BABIES LEARN LANGUAGE BEFORE BIRTH?

Babies begin to hear as the third trimester of pregnancy begins. They are able to discriminate between different vowel sounds, but until recently it was not known whether they could *learn* about vowel sounds prenatally. Newborn babies from the USA and Sweden were presented with: a) vowels from the language to which they had been exposed before birth; and b) unfamiliar vowel sounds from a different language. They could control the presentation of the sounds by sucking faster on a dummy (pacifier). They sucked faster on presentation of the novel vowels, demonstrating their greater attentiveness to them. The results suggest that 'birth is not a benchmark that reflects a complete separation between the effects of nature and those of nurture on infants' perception of the phonetic units of speech' (Moon *et al.*, 2012: 159).

---

birth – see Box 1.2)? The discussion engendered by this question is often referred to as the nature–nurture debate. At various times in history, one or another view has held sway. The nature–nurture debate raged inconclusively for some years, but now it is generally accepted that heredity and environment must interact in order to produce behaviour. The issue is becoming less about how far each contributes to an individual's development, and more about how they combine. Recent research in epigenetics is especially relevant here (see Chapter 2).

Continuity versus discontinuity

The second important issue is whether an individual's development is gradual (continuous) or occurs in sudden leaps (discontinuous). The continuous viewpoint emphasizes slow methodical changes over time. An analogy here is that of a tree growing from a small seedling, whereby growth from seedling to sapling and finally mature tree is steady, with no apparent 'sudden' transformations or changes into another form. Some psychological theories and praxis, such as behaviourist theories and behaviour therapy, draw heavily upon the notion of continuity to explain human growth (see Chapter 6). An alternative viewpoint emphasizes discontinuity. The analogy here would be a caterpillar changing into a butterfly. Theories such as those proposed by Piaget (cognitive-developmental theory) and Freud (psycho-analytic theory) emphasize a stage-like or discontinuous view of human development (see Chapters 4 and 5).

Joachim Wohlwill argued that 'The usefulness of the stage concept remains an open question today and its potential promise unfulfilled' (Wohlwill, 1973: 236). The concept of stages in the psychological literature has proved difficult to define, despite the observations made by parents, teachers, social workers and others that not all functions are present at birth and that some do appear in most children at a particular time in their development.

Moreover, the use of the concept of stages differs from theory to theory. Thus, in Erikson's psychosocial theory of human development the concept of stages is broad, descriptive and evocative in nature and does not 'refer clearly to anything definite or measurable in behavior' (Meadows, 1986: 19), whereas the use of the term 'stage' in relation to other psychological theories is more specific. In Piaget's cognitive-developmental theory, during the child's 'sensori-motor stage', for example, it is generally possible to identify clearly observable aspects of a child's thinking. For instance, a favourite toy hidden from a six-month-old child under a handkerchief will not elicit a search reaction, the child acting as though 'out of sight is out of mind'. More particularly, some stages are associated with clearly defined behaviours, such as crawling in an infant of ten to twelve months. So it appears that the use of the word 'stage' varies along a continuum from less to more specific in terms of associated behaviours.

In order to enhance the descriptive and explanatory power of stage theories it is desirable to achieve the following.

- Clearly establish the relationship between structure and behaviour at any one stage (Kagan *et al.*, 1978).
- Account for or explain the factors contributing to the child's movement from one stage to the next (Meadows, 1986), such as through biological maturation or environmental input.
- Clearly relate the structure of one stage to the succeeding stage (Kagan *et al.*, 1978).
- Specify the behaviours subject to age changes that make up the stages (Meadows, 1986).

Similarity versus uniqueness

One view is that people are essentially similar despite superficial differences. Much of developmental psychology concerns the search for general principles. Carl Jung (1923), however, was particularly interested in 'individuation' or the development of differences in people's preferred ways of attending to the world and making decisions. His thinking about psychological 'types' has led to more recent work identifying the 'Big Five' personality traits (extraversion, agreeableness, conscientiousness, neuroticism and openness to experience); this framework has been used, for example, to examine how personality differences are related to wellbeing in Indian adolescents (Singh and Lal, 2012).

Stability versus instability

Freud's psychoanalytic theory suggests that an individual's personality is largely shaped during the early years of childhood (Wollheim, 1974). An alternative outlook is that an individual's characteristics are constantly changing. Erikson's theory (1963) is in accord with this outlook. Erikson proposed that an individual continues to develop throughout his or her lifespan, as a result of being faced with certain normative crises that must be addressed and dealt with, thereby allowing the person to proceed to the next stage. For example, following the dismantling of apartheid in South Africa, norms changed so that Black youths became more confident of their cultural identity than did White adolescents (Thom and Coetzee, 2004).

Activity versus passivity

One view presents individuals as agents: they take responsibility for their own behaviour; are understood to be capable of acting for certain purposes or goals; they attach some freedom of choice to their acts; and they may cite reasons for their behaviour, reasons that are often guided by values (Battye and Slee, 1985). Arguments were mounted as the twentieth century progressed that such a view of child development was gaining sway in the psychological literature (Bruner, 1986; Gauld and Shotter, 1977; Harré and Secord, 1972).

Alternatively, development can be considered as shaped by powerful forces that are largely beyond the individual's control. In this view, the individual is seen as essentially a passive / reactive organism. Writers such as Alan Gauld and John Shotter (1977) argued that this view of human behaviour was promulgated by lines of thought such as learning theory.

Thinking versus feeling

Writers such as Piaget emphasized the study of children's thinking, while theorists such as Freud and Erikson focused on emotional or affective development. The complex interplay between thinking and feeling in governing behaviour was revealed in a famous experiment by Stanley Schacter and Jerome Singer (1962). It showed that how people reacted to a 'vitamin' (actually, adrenaline) injection depended on the behaviour of the experimenter's collaborator, who had supposedly received a similar injection: as participants experienced hand tremors and rapid breathing, they acted in accord with either the angry or the euphoric behaviour they observed in the collaborator, thus demonstrating that emotional responses are influenced by cognition and are not, as Darwin thought, purely physiological.

A commentary on these controversies about developmental change

These various controversies suffer from a number of limitations (Overton, 1998). Their either–or nature suggests that one or the other represents the 'right' or 'real' nature of development. This in turn suggests that empirical inquiry will soon uncover the correct answer. 'The simple empirical observation that generations of empirical observations have failed to resolve any of these issues demonstrates the inadequacy of this assumption' (Overton, 1998: 113). Instead, the focus may best be shifted away from 'which one' questions, to the nature of functioning of the ends of the continuum and their relationship (Overton, 1998). For example, continuity and discontinuity may not be mutually exclusive, but depend on how fine-grained the analysis is.

Despite their 'either-or' nature, the classical developmental theories do have their advantages. Samuel Rose and Kurt Fischer suggested that a strength of theories 'such as those of Freud (1933), Piaget (1983/1987) and Heinz Werner (1948), has been their sense of the richness and complexity of human beings, in contrast to the oversimplifications that are often evident in more narrowly empirical research' (Rose and Fischer, 1998: 123). A contrasting, postmodern, perspective decries the value of theory: 'Theory is taken to be a conceit of modernist knowledge seekers who imagine (and can only imagine) an epistemology of truth – of foundational, transhistorical knowledge. Theory in such a postmodern view resembles its earlier depiction as fantasy' (Morawski, 2001: 436).

Images of children

As we have outlined, history, culture and the philosophy of science play significant roles in shaping how we view children and adolescents. It is possible to draw out a number of 'images' of children influenced by one or more of these factors, including the experiential child, the iniquitous child and the virtuous child (see Figure 1.1).

The experiential child is a mainstream view identifiable in the psychological literature. Inherent in this view is the notion that at birth the infant is a *tabula rasa* or blank slate, a concept that developed from the worldview of empiricism, which relied heavily on the work of John Locke. Empiricism did much to replace scholasticism, a worldview of a God-ruled static cosmos. Empiricism advocates that all knowledge is derived from experience.

> Let us suppose the mind to be, as we say white paper, void of all characters, without any ideas; how comes it to be furnished? Whence comes it by that vast store, which the busy and boundless fancy of man has painted on it with an almost endless variety? Whence has all the materials of reason and knowledge? To this I answer in one word; from experience: in that all our knowledge is founded, and from that it ultimately derives itself.
>
> *(Locke, cited in Russell, 1974: 589)*

Scottish philosopher David Hume (1711–1776) further developed Locke's view. He focused specifically on sensation, advocating that research drawing directly upon experience through the senses was the means by which we acquire knowledge of the world.

Empiricism became the building block of science in the nineteenth century. Science triumphed over philosophy as the means for gaining knowledge about the world. As viewed by the French philosopher Auguste Comte (1798–1857), science referred to the natural sciences such as biology, chemistry and physics. However, the

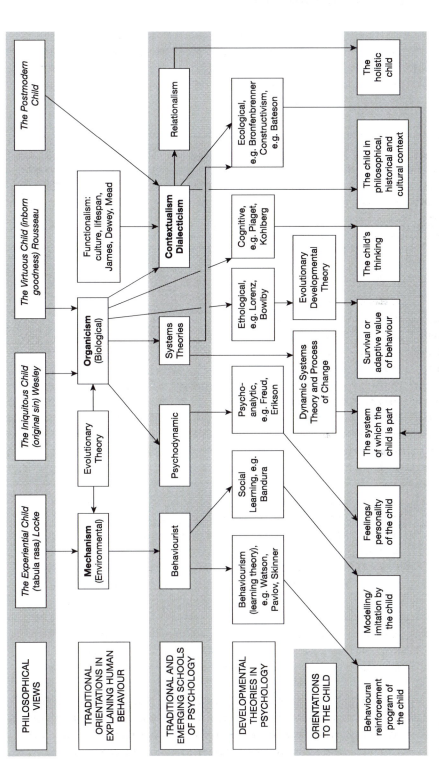

FIGURE 1.1 'Images' of children as influenced by history, culture and the philosophy of science (adapted from Slee, 2002)

Note: Pepper's (1942) root metaphors (excluding Formism) in bold.

implication for the social sciences was that human behaviour could be investigated and studied by applying the methods and principles of the natural sciences. Comte had identified three ages of thought, namely: the early theological; a metaphysical age that during his time was, in his view, just finishing; and an era of positive science (Gadamer, 1993). During the twentieth century positivism was further refined in relation to the influential philosophical writings of the Vienna Circle. Logical positivism focused on reduction and induction, which complemented causal explanation.

Empiricism, as reflected in positivism, has firmly established itself in developmental psychology as the predominant means of gaining knowledge about the world (Battye and Slee, 1985). Underpinning this worldview are four propositions regarding the nature of science, and these have had significant implications for the development of psychology as a science (Evans, 1979). They may be placed under two headings: scientism, and the unity of science thesis. Scientism maintains the following.

- Science gives us the whole truth about the nature of reality.
- Science gives us the ultimate truth about the realities it deals with.

The unity of science thesis holds the following.

- There is one method that all the genuine sciences employ.
- This one method consists of giving deterministic causal explanations that are empirically testable.

In its most basic form, positivism is concerned with establishing causes and with predicting events or behaviours. Overton noted two features of logical positivism. First, there is the reduction of all scientific theories and propositions to words whose meaning can be directly observed, requiring a '... neutral observation language – completely objective, and free from subjective or mind–dependent interpretation'; second, '... to be scientifically meaningful, any universal propositions (e.g. hypotheses, theories, laws) had to be demonstrably nothing more than summary statements of the pristine observations themselves' (Overton, 1998: 158).

This outlook presented humans as passive or inert organisms whose behaviour is shaped by external forces. That is, at birth the infant is a *tabula rasa* and the environment determines all that the child becomes. A modern exponent of this view was Burrhus Skinner (see Chapter 6).

A second view of children, as iniquitous, accepts the proposition regarding the inherent sinfulness of the human race (see Figure 1.1). Because the child is thought to be born into original sin, the task of the parents becomes that of breaking the child's will. This may be accomplished by teaching children to submit to the will of their parents and of God (see Box 1.1). In the Puritan tradition of seventeenth-century and eighteenth-century England and the USA, educators and the establishment generally understood the child as inherently sinful. The English churchman John Wesley wrote forcefully:

Break their wills betimes, begin this work before they can run alone, before they can speak plain, perhaps before they can speak at all . . . Let a child from a year old be taught to fear the rod and to cry softly; from that age make him do as he is bid, if you whip him ten times running to effect it. If you spare the rod you spoil the child; if you do not conquer you ruin him.

(Wesley, 1703, cited in Southey, 1925: 304)

Wesley's views were incorporated into regulations for running a girls' boarding school. Faint-hearted parents intending to enrol their children were warned off. The girls' daily life included a 4 a.m. rise, an hour of religious instruction followed by public worship, breakfast and then the school day, which ended at 5 p.m., with no time for play (Cleverley and Phillips, 1976). A more contemporary exploration of the iniquitous view of the child is found in William Golding's novel *Lord of the Flies* (1954), in which a group of children is stranded on a desert island; free of the restraint of traditional culture and adult supervision, the iniquitous nature of the children comes to the fore.

Contrast this with the idea of the virtuous child (Figure 1.1). An exponent of this ideal was the eighteenth-century Swiss philosopher Jean-Jacques Rousseau. He took issue with Locke's ideas about children, proposing instead the concept of an innocent child whose development was powerfully directed by nature. He thereby affirmed the inherent goodness of children. Rousseau also rejected Locke's notion of the rational child, arguing that the capacity for reasoning does not develop until around 12 years of age. In his novel *Emile*, Rousseau applied his ideas to education: 'God made all things good; man meddles with them and they become evil' (Rousseau, 1762/1914, Book 1: 5). He believed that in educating the innocent and amoral child, it made no sense to punish wrongdoing: 'Before the age of reason we do good or ill without knowing it, and there is no morality in our action' (Rousseau, 1762/1914, Book 1: 34).

Rousseau's views were reflected in the later thinking of the educator Alexander S. Neill (1968), who also rejected the idea of original sin or evil and advocated non-interference in the education of children. He believed in some innate driving force that would lead children to make the best decisions if left to their own devices. We will see something similar in an Australian Aboriginal perspective, explored in Chapter 9.

David Elkind (1987) presented an arguable case for a fourth contemporary outlook: the 'competent infant'. This view presents 'infants and young children as having much more capacity to learn academic skills than children, regardless of background, actually have' (Elkind, 1987: 8). Elkind argued that this view had been adopted by educators such as Jerome Bruner, with his now famous statement in 1962 that it is possible to teach any child any subject matter at any age in an intellectually responsible manner. Elkind believed that Bruner may not have appreciated how sincerely parents and educators would take up this statement as a rallying call. A new optimism was generated regarding the capabilities and competencies of the infant that, in Elkind's view, overstepped the mark.

BOX 1.3 CHILDREN AND MORAL PANIC

To highlight how views about children impact on society, consider the debate regarding the extent to which children are seen as 'out of control', 'in crisis' and 'at risk'. Fears are held for the safety of children (e.g. in relation to victimization) and regarding the risk that children present to others (e.g. in relation to school bullying and homicide). Phil Scraton (1997) and Michael Wyness (2000) have both raised questions about whether such a 'crisis' actually exists. One outcome of the perceived 'crisis' relates to the manner in which children have become the subject of both overt and covert regulation (James and James, 2001). For example, in relation to social networking, Sonia Livingstone (2008) has noted that media panics regarding the dangers of social networking sites often feed or amplify public anxieties. Such panics in turn often lead to adults calling for legislative or other means to control young people's access to mobile phones or social networking sites.

For Elkind, a second factor contributing to the image of the competent infant concerned Benjamin Bloom's (1964) idea that one should teach as much as possible to young children because their minds are growing so rapidly. In addition, Joseph McVicker Hunt (1961) held that intelligence is malleable and not fixed. Finally, Elkind (1987) argued that Ariès, in pointing out that the concept of childhood is a largely social invention, contributed to the idea that we have been ignoring children's true potential. According to Elkind, in over-emphasizing the competence of children we have distorted the true nature of young children and how they actually grow and learn.

To highlight how perceptions of children impact on society, we can consider the emerging debate in the literature and the moral panic generated in the media regarding the extent to which children are seen as 'out of control' and 'at risk' (see Box 1.3).

Metaphors, theories and metatheories

In considering different theoretical orientations to child development (e.g. Smith *et al.*, 1998), some writers have drawn upon the work of Stephen Pepper (1942) on metaphor. Rich discussions of metaphor exist in such diverse fields as anthropology, philosophy, sociology, linguistics and psychology (see also Chapter 11). While metaphors can be nonlinguistic (e.g. ritual or gestural), it is the linguistic metaphors that have gained most attention. The literature on metaphor has a long history in western civilization, e.g. Aristotle's *Rhetoric* and *Poetics*. More contemporary writing on the topic is found in works by Max Black (1962) and George Lakoff and Michael Johnson (1980). Paul Rosenblatt held that 'A metaphor is a figure of speech in which a word or phrase that ordinarily applies to one kind of object or idea is applied to another, thus suggesting a likeness or analogy between them' (Rosenblatt, 1994: 12). He gives the example of an individual exclaiming, 'My love is like a red, red rose,' which transfers all the meaning we attach to a red rose (such as passion, colour and delicacy) to the loved one, thereby clearly communicating why the person is loved. Lakoff and Johnson (1980) have argued that metaphor is a common everyday facet of language that guides our thinking regarding a wide variety of topics.

Two traditional orientations to behaviour that flow from the experiential, iniquitous and virtuous views of children are the mechanistic and organismic orientations (Figure 1.1). Pepper (1942) identified these as two of four 'root metaphors' influencing various schools of thought in developmental psychology. Following Pepper, Roger Dixon and Richard Lerner (1992) identified these as two metatheoretical traditions in developmental psychology.

Theories within the mechanistic tradition, such as behaviourism, use a machine analogy and emphasize that the environment is all-important in shaping what we become and how we develop. Notions of classical science or 'Newtonianism' in the seventeenth and eighteenth centuries highlighted an image of a 'world in which every event was determined by initial conditions that were, at least in principle, determinable with precision. It was a world in which chance played no part, in which all the pieces came together like cogs in a cosmic machine' (Toffler, 1984: xiii).

The organismic tradition encompasses a wide range of theories, such as that of Piaget, drawing upon the notion of the iniquitous or virtuous child, or the competent child, or a mixture of these. The organismic view does not consider the newborn as a blank slate: for example, infants may differ in temperament. Organicism draws heavily upon the image of the growing organism, unique in its own right, but whose development is significantly shaped by mutual influence and the patterning of its parts. Although humanistic theory can be considered to belong to this tradition, we do not cover it in this book because its proponents did not focus upon child development. However, ethological, psychoanalytic, cognitive and constructivist theories are considered here. In addition, dialectical theories (such as Vygotsky's) can be seen to belong to the organismic tradition, although they can also be seen as providing a bridge between mechanistic and organismic theories, with the organism and the environment in mutually influential interaction. Dixon and Lerner (1992) categorized dialectical theories separately from organicism.

Systems approaches to development could be considered as part of the organismic tradition, although, like dialecticism, they emphasize mutual interaction between organism and environment. In fact, the notion of systems should perhaps be considered as an additional metaphor to those suggested by Pepper. Emphasizing holism, systems theories focus on the organization of and relations among systems, and how these are transformed over time. The writings of Gregory Bateson (1972), deriving principally from cybernetic theory, significantly shaped the development of systems theories. So too did the writing of Paul Watzlawick *et al.* (1974) in distinguishing between first- and second-order change: first-order change represents a western positivist ideal of change as orderly, predictable and progressive; second-order change can be sudden and spontaneous, resulting in the emergence of unpredictable new patterns and behaviours.

Pepper's other root metaphors are contextualism and formism. Contextualism is concerned with placing the developing child within a historical time and culture, and Dixon and Lerner (1992) identified it as a separate metatheoretical tradition. Contextualists such as John Dewey and George Herbert Mead (see Chapter 8) laid some of the groundwork for more recent sociocultural and Indigenous approaches. For example, for Dewey the essential problem is 'to understand the relation between universal aspects of human nature and its different forms of expression in different social circumstances or arrangements' (Cahan, 1992: 207).

Formism concerns classification. It draws upon the metaphor of the similarity of objects and highlights their classification into discrete and hierarchical categories. The world is seen to consist of 'things' or 'entities' that can be classified using some scheme or system, as in psychiatric diagnostic systems. The notion of formism does not appear to link with any particular theoretical tradition, and thus does not appear in Figure 1.1. However, attempts to classify theoretical approaches are in themselves expressions of formism. In reality, while groupings of theories are convenient, they are not always clear-cut. We do not expect all readers to endorse the scheme in Figure 1.1 but we offer it as a useful heuristic for conceptualizing theories in developmental psychology.

Pepper's root metaphors have been subject to very little investigation in terms of research and measurement, with the possible exceptions of Charles Super and Sara Harkness (2003) and David Shwalb and colleagues. (2010). It is perhaps sufficient to use them to help us understand the various lines of thought and the distinctions between them that have informed our theoretical understanding of child development.

Dixon and Lerner (1992) identified evolutionary theory, especially Darwinian theory, as playing a seminal role in the five metatheoretical traditions they identified (organicism, mechanism, contextualism, psychodynamic and dialectical). Discussions of evolutionary theory and Darwin's contribution appear at various points in this book. Also missing from this list is 'relationalism': we consider it in this book alongside dialecticism, though it can be considered as a metatheory in itself.

A postmodern view of knowledge and children

Finally, we acknowledge the very different philosophical framework embodied in postmodernism, to which we have alluded at various points in this chapter. Influential postmodern philosophers include those in the German critical-theoretical tradition (Jürgen Habermas and Klaus Holzkamp), the French postmodernists (Jean-François Lyotard, Jacques Derrida and Michel Foucault) and a broad range of feminist and ethnic theorists (Teo, 1997). William Tierney (2001) has identified five attributes underpinning postmodern thinking. The first relates to the conceptualization of knowledge, which is not understood as something that is 'discovered' as though it is there somehow waiting to be unearthed; rather, knowledge is understood as being constructed. Social constructionists (or constructivists) argue that knowledge is produced by people working in groups, and is thus a social product with a political basis (Tierney, 1996). Tierney has commented that it is therefore no accident that science has been a largely male enterprise, which has ignored women's concerns or interpreted them in a patriarchal manner (Tierney, 2001).

The second attribute of postmodernism relates to the challenge that it directs at modernism's faith in science and the efforts that it expends in analysing underlying assumptions and frameworks. The epistemological position of modernism, with its positivist assumptions, has been contrasted with postmodernism's 'critical questioning, and often outright rejection, of the ethnocentric rationalism championed by modernism' (Cooper and Burrell, 1988: 92, cited in Tierney, 2001). Central to this attribute is the idea of 'power' and that knowledge is not something neutral but is part of the scientific endeavour.

The third attribute relates to the contrasting identities of the modernist and postmodernist scientist. Contrast the popular image of the nameless and faceless scientist labouring away in a laboratory with what Tierney calls the 'fractured nature of the postmodern identity' (Tierney, 2001: 362). We consider the notion of developmental psychology as a fractured discipline in Chapter 13.

A fourth attribute of postmodernist knowledge relates to the chaos, uncertainty and disorganization that a great deal of postmodern thinking encourages. This is in direct contrast to the causal, linear modernist thinking searching for certainty and predictability. Tierney suggests that the political and cultural underpinnings of postmodern thinking are significantly broadening our understandings about the nature of knowledge.

Finally, Tierney has suggested that what we witnessed in the latter part of the twentieth century was globalization and the death of the 'nation state', wherein the university is no longer seen as the sole arbiter, producer and purveyor of knowledge. We will return to this point in the final chapter of the book.

What would a 'postmodern child' look like? We suggest that this child is one understood in philosophical, historical and cultural context; one who is listened to and valued for himself or herself rather than simply as a means of understanding the adult condition; one whom the researcher strives to understand without exploitation, and whom the practitioner seeks to help in a full understanding of the social and historical contexts within which the child, practitioner and other relevant parties operate. The very structure of this chapter implies that we are indeed open to such reflection on our theory and practice. Critiques of traditional schools of thought in developmental psychology appear especially in our considerations of cultural and Indigenous psychologies, feminism, children's voices and implications of theory for practice.

Conclusions

This chapter has set the scene for those that follow. While acknowledging the positivist tradition of developmental psychology and its western roots, we have also deliberately embedded theoretical thinking in the context of history, culture and philosophy. In contextualizing theory in this manner we believe that it provides a richer account and understanding of influential theories in this postmodern era. We are hopeful, in presenting such material, of engendering debate regarding this very point.

References

Ariès, P. 1962. *Centuries of childhood*. New York: Vintage Books.

Australian Bureau of Statistics. 2006. *Census of population and housing: nature and content* (cat. No. 2008.0).

Bacon, F. 1626. *History of philosophy*. New York: Dover Publications.

Baltes, P.B. 1987. Theoretical propositions of life-span developmental psychology: on the dynamics between growth and decline. *Developmental Psychology*. 23 (5): 611–26.

Bateson, G. 1972. *Steps to an ecology of mind*. London: Ballentine.

Battye, P. and Slee, P.T. 1985. The demise of the person in social work. *Australian Social Work*. 38: 23–31.

Black, M. 1962. *Models and metaphors: studies in language and philosophy*. Ithaca, NY: Cornell University Press.

Bloom, B.S. 1964. *Stability and change in human characteristics*. New York: Wiley.

Bronfenbrenner, U. 1974. Toward an experimental ecology of human development. *American Psychologist*. 32: 513–31.

Bruner, J. 1986. *Actual minds, possible worlds*. Cambridge, MA: Harvard University Press.

Bruner, J. and Haste, H. 1987. *Making sense. The child's construction of the world*. London: Methuen.

Burman, E. 1994. *Deconstructing developmental psychology*. London: Routledge.

Cahan, E.D. 1992. John Dewey and human development. *Developmental Psychology*. 28: 205–14.

Cairns, R.B. 1998. The making of developmental psychology. In R.M. Lerner (ed.), *Handbook of child psychology. Theoretical models of human development*. Fifth edn, Vol. 1. New York: Wiley, 25–107.

Clarke-Stewart, A.K. 1998. Historical shifts and underlying themes in ideas about rearing young children in the United States. Where have we been? Where are we going? *Early Development and Parenting*. 7: 101–17.

Cleverley, J. and Phillips, D.C. 1976. *From Locke to Spock*. Melbourne: Melbourne University Press.

Collard, K. 2000. Aboriginal culture. In P. Dudgeon, D. Garvey and H. Pickett (eds), *Working with Indigenous Australians: a handbook for psychologists*. Perth: Centre for Aboriginal Studies, Curtin University of Technology, 21–6.

Compayré, G. 1896. *The intellectual and moral development of the child*. New York: Appleton.

Darwin, C. 1872/1965. *The expression of the emotions in man and animals*. Chicago, IL: University of Chicago Press.

Delbridge, A.S. 2001. *The Macquarie dictionary*. Cambridge: Cambridge University Press.

Dixon, R.A. and Lerner, R.M. 1992. A history of systems in developmental psychology. In M.H. Bornstein and M.E. Lamb (eds), *Developmental psychology: an advanced textbook*. Third edn. Hillsdale, NJ: Erlbaum, 3–58.

Elkind, D. 1987. The child yesterday, today and tomorrow. *Young Children*. May: 6–11.

Erikson, E.H. 1963. *Childhood and society*. Harmondsworth: Penguin.

Evans, C.S. 1979. *Perceiving the person: a look at the human sciences*. Westmont, IL: InterVarsity Press.

Fraser, B.G. 1976. The child and his parents: a delicate balance of rights. In R. Helfer and C.H. Kempe (eds), *Child abuse and neglect*. Cambridge, MA: Ballinger, 315–33.

Freud, S. 1933. *New introductory lectures on psychoanalysis*, trans. W.J.H. Sprott. New York: Macmillan.

Gadamer, H.G. 1993. *Über die Verborgenheit der Gesundheit*. Frankfurt am Main: Suhrkamp.

Gauld, A. and Shotter, J. 1977. *Human action and its psychological investigation*. London: Routledge and Kegan Paul.

Gewirtz, J.L. and Pelaez-Nogueras, M. 1992. B.F. Skinner's legacy to human infant behaviour and development. *American Psychologist*. 47: 1,411–22.

Golding, W. 1954. *Lord of the flies*. Boston, MA: Faber and Faber.

Green, M. 1989. *Theories of human development. A comparative approach*. Englewood Cliffs, NJ: Prentice Hall.

Harré, R. and Secord, P.F. 1972. *The explanation of social behaviour*. Oxford: Blackwell.

Hobbes, T. 1651/1931. *Leviathan*. Oxford: Blackwell.

Holzer, P. and Lamont, A. 2010. *Corporal punishment: key issues*. Melbourne: National Child Protection Clearinghouse, Australia Institute of Family Studies.

Howe, M.L. and Lewis, M.D. 2005. The importance of dynamic systems approaches for understanding development. *Developmental Review*. 25: 247–51.

James, A.L. and James, A. 2001. Tightening the net: children, community and control. *British Journal of Sociology*. 52: 211–28.

Jenkins, H. 1988. Annotations: family therapy – developments in thinking and practice. *Journal of Child Psychology and Psychiatry*. 31 (7): 1015–26.

Jones, A.F. 2011. Developmental fairy tales: evolutionary thinking and modern Chinese culture. Cambridge, MA: Harvard University Press.

Jung, C.G. 1923. *Psychological types*. London: Kegan Paul.

Kagan, J., Kearsley, R.B. and Zelazo, P.R. 1978. *Infancy: its place in human development*. Cambridge, MA: Harvard University Press.

Kelly, G.A. 1963. *A theory of personality*. New York: Norton.

Kennedy, D. 2000. The roots of child study: philosophy, history, and religion. *Teachers College Record*. 102: 514–38.

Kessen, W. 1979. The American child and other cultural inventions. *American Psychologist*. 34: 815–82.

Ketelaar, T. and Ellis, B.J. 2000. Are evolutionary explanations unfalsifiable? Evolutionary psychology and the Lakatosian philosophy of science. *Psychological Inquiry*. 11 (1): 1–21.

Kojima, H. 1996. Japanese childrearing advice in its cultural, social, and economic contexts. *International Journal of Behavioral Development*. 19: 373–91.

Kovacev, L. and Shute, R. 2004. Acculturation and social support in relation to psychosocial adjustment of adolescent refugees resettled in Australia. *International Journal of Behavioral Development*. 28 (3): 259–67.

Lakoff, G. and Johnson, M. 1980. The metaphorical structure of the human conceptual system. *Cognitive Science*. 4: 195–208.

Lerner, R.M. 1983. *Concepts and theories of human development*. New York: Random House.

Lerner, R.M. 1986. *Concepts and theories of human development*. Second edn. New York: Random House.

Leuner, B. and Gould, E. 2010. Structural plasticity and the hippocampus function. *Annual Review of Psychology*. 61: 11–113.

Leung, C. 2001. The sociocultural and psychological adaptation of Chinese migrant adolescents in Australia and Canada. *International Journal of Psychology*. 36: 8–19.

Lippman, L. 1970. *To achieve our country: Australia and the Aborigines*. Sydney: Cheshire.

Livingstone, S. 2008. Taking risky opportunities in youthful content creation: teenagers' use of social networking sites for intimacy, privacy and self expression. *New Media & Society.* 10 (3): 393–411.

Lourenço, O. 2012. Piaget and Vygotsky: many resemblances, and a crucial difference. *New Ideas in Psychology.* 30: 281–95.

McVicker Hunt, J. 1961. *Intelligence and experience.* New York: Ronald.

Mead, M. 1970. *Culture and commitment.* New York: Doubleday.

Meadows, S. 1986. *Understanding child development.* London: Hutchinson.

Medinnus, G.R. 1976. *Child study and observation guide.* New York: Wiley.

Milton, J. 1671/2007. *Paradise regained.* London: John Murray.

Moon, C., Lagercrantz, H. and Kuhl, P.K. 2012. Language experience *in utero* affects vowel perception after birth: a two-country study. *Acta Paediatrica.* 102: 156–60.

Morawski, J. 2001. Gifts bestowed, gifts withheld: assessing psychological theory with a Kochian attitude. *American Psychologist.* 56: 433–40.

Mullineaux, N. 2012. Our genius, goodness, and gumption. Child actresses and national identity in mid-nineteenth century America. *Journal of the History of Childhood and Youth.* 5 (2): 283–308.

Neill, A.S. 1968. *Summerhill.* Harmondsworth: Penguin.

Nsamenang, A.B. 1999. Eurocentric image of childhood in the context of the world's cultures. *Human Development.* 42: 159–68.

Overton, W.F. 1998. Developmental psychology: philosophy, concepts, and methodology. In R.M. Lerner (ed.), *Handbook of child psychology. Theoretical models of human development.* Fifth edn, Vol. 1. New York: Wiley, 107–89.

Overton, W.F. 2006. Developmental psychology: philosophy, concepts and methodology. In R.M. Lerner (ed.), *Handbook of child psychology. Theoretical models of human development.* Sixth edn, Vol. 1. New York: Wiley, 18–88.

Overton, W.F. 2007. A coherent metatheory for dynamic systems: relational organicism-contextualism. *Human Development.* 50: 154–9.

Overton, W.F. 2010. Life-span development: concepts and issues. In W.F. Overton and R.M. Lerner (eds), *Handbook of life-span development. Cognition, biology, and methods across the lifespan.* Vol. 1. Hoboken, NJ: Wiley, 1–29.

Pepper, S. 1942. *World hypotheses: a study of evidence.* Berkeley, CA: University of California Press.

Piaget, J. 1983/1987. *Possibility and necessity. The role of necessity in cognitive development,* trans. H. Feider. Vol 2. Minneapolis, MN: University of Minnesota Press.

Rose, S.P. and Fischer, K.W. 1998. Models and rulers in dynamical development. *British Journal of Developmental Psychology.* 16: 123–31.

Rosenblatt, P.C. 1994. *Metaphors of family systems theory.* New York: Guilford Press.

Rousseau, J.J. 1762/1914. *Émile, or education,* trans. B. Foxley. New York: Basic Books.

Russell, B. 1974. *History of western philosophy.* London: George Allen and Unwin.

Schachter, S. and Singer, J.E. 1962. Cognitive, social and physiological determinants of emotional state. *Psychological Review.* 69: 379–99.

Schorsch, A. 1979. *Images of childhood.* New York: Mayflower.

Scraton, P. (ed.). 1997. *Childhood in 'crisis'?* London: Routledge.

Shanahan, M.J., Sulloway, F. and Hofer, S.M. 2000. Change and constancy in developmental contexts. *International Journal of Behavioral Development.* 24: 421–7.

Shwalb, D.W., Shwalb, B.J., Hyun, J.-H., Chen, S.-J., Kusanagi, E., Satiadarma, M.P., Mackay, R. and Wilkey, B. 2010. *Maternal beliefs, images, and metaphors of child development in the United States, Korea, Indonesia, and Japan.* Hokkaido: Research and Clinical Center for Child Development, Hokkaido University.

Singh, S. and Lal, R. 2012. A study of subjective wellbeing of adolescents in relation to Big Five factors of personality. *Journal of Psychosocial Research*. 7 (1): 33–42.

Slee, P.T. 1987. *Child observation skills*. Beckenham: Croom Helm.

Slee, P.T. 2002. *Child, adolescent and family development*. Second edn. Melbourne: Cambridge University Press.

Smith, P.K., Cowie, H. and Blades, M. 1998. *Understanding children's development*. Third edn. Oxford: Blackwell.

Southey, R. 1925. *The life of Wesley*. Vol. 2. London: Humphrey Milford.

Storer, D. 1985. *Ethnic family values in Australia*. Sydney: Prentice Hall.

Super, C.M. and Harkness, S. 2003. The metaphors of development. *Human Development*. 46: 3–23.

Teo, T. 1997. Developmental psychology and the relevance of a critical metatheoretical reflection. *Human Development*. 40: 195–210.

Thelen, E. and Smith, L.B. 1994. *A dynamic systems approach to the development of cognition and action*. Cambridge, MA: MIT Press.

Thom, D.P. and Coetzee, C.H. 2004. Identity development of South African adolescents in a democratic society. *Society in Transition*. 35: 183–93.

Tierney, W.G. 1996. The academic profession and the culture of the faculty: a perspective on Latin American universities. In K. Kempner and W.G. Tierney (eds), *The social role of higher education: comparative perspectives*. New York: Garland Publishing, 11–26.

Tierney, W.G. 2001. The autonomy of knowledge and the decline of the subject: postmodernism and the reformulation of the university. *Higher Education*. 41: 353–72.

Toffler, A. 1984. *Future shock*. London: Random House.

Volk, A. 2011. The evolution of childhood. *Journal of the History of Childhood and Youth*. 4 (3): 470–93.

Watzlawick, P., Weakland, J.H. and Fisch, R. 1974. *Change: principles of problem formation and problem resolution*. New York: Norton.

Werner, H. 1948. *Comparative psychology of mental development*. New York: International Universities Press.

Williams, R. 1976. *Keywords: a vocabulary of culture and society*. New York: Oxford University Press.

Wohlwill, J.F. 1973. *The study of behavioral development*. New York: Academic Press.

Wollheim, R. 1974. *Freud: a collection of critical essays*. New York: Doubleday Anchor Books.

Wyness, M. 2000. *Contesting childhood*. London: Falmer Press.

Zola, E. 1885/1979. *Germinal*, trans. L. Tancock. Harmondsworth: Penguin Books.

2

FROM DARWIN TO DNA

Biologically based theories of development

Introduction

Human behaviour today is frequently examined through a biological lens. This has been described as psychology's most recent paradigm shift, succeeding the cognitive approach that in turn took over from behaviourism (Campbell, 2012). The core assumption of a biological approach is that explanations for human behaviour and development are to be sought through an understanding of genetics, brain function, hormones and the like, although biology by no means excludes environmental influences; for example, environmental changes are central to processes of natural selection.

In this chapter we consider some theoretical frameworks for development that place a heavy emphasis upon biology. Unsurprisingly, these have often emanated from fields such as biology, medicine and pharmacology. We first question how far Charles Darwin (1809–1882) really influenced various theoretical traditions in developmental psychology, then we consider more recent applications of evolutionary theory, including ethology, sociobiology and evolutionary developmental psychology. We also discuss behaviour genetics and neurological perspectives on development, and how the nature–nurture debate is being revolutionalized by recent research in epigenetics. We end by addressing the medicalization of children's behavioural and emotional problems.

How far was Darwin really the forefather of developmental psychology?

Darwin's impact on the discipline of biology was, of course, profound. He has been described as 'having attained sainthood (if not divinity) among evolutionary biologists' (Gould and Lewontin, 1979: 589). As we observed in the previous chapter,

Darwinian evolutionary theory has been seen as the precursor of five major families of developmental theory: mechanism, organicism, contextualism, psychodynamic theories and dialecticism (Dixon and Lerner, 1992). Developmental psychologists in the late twentieth century often claimed that Darwin had a revolutionary effect on the child development field, with one popular child development text, for example, crediting him as the 'forefather of scientific child study' (Berk, 2000: 12).

Historians of psychology have identified the strong impact of Darwin on the field of psychology in general, especially in emphasizing continuity between human and animal minds, the importance of individual differences, adaptation to the environment and a broadening of investigative methodologies (Charlesworth, 1992). However, William Charlesworth contended that, in the specific area of developmental psychology, Darwin's influence was 'weak, indirect and somewhat distorted' (Charlesworth, 1992: 7), and that Darwin had no significant influence on developmental psychology's empirical research or theorizing. In particular, he concluded that the most distinctive feature of Darwin's theory – natural selection – was missing.

Charlesworth suggested three reasons for this actual lack of influence. One is a conceptual issue concerning the differentiation of phylogeny (changes over evolutionary time) and ontogeny (individual life histories). Developmentalists focus on the latter, and 'evolutionary speculation about different ancestors fighting it out in different environments now long gone is viewed as having little utility in guiding research' (Charlesworth, 1992: 11). A second reason concerns methodology, with developmentalists attracted to studying readily available, proximate factors rather than the ultimate factors stretching back across evolutionary time. A third reason concerns moral values: the Darwinian perspective that 'less fit' organisms do not survive implies a harsh fate for infants and children born into disadvantaged circumstances. Charlesworth suggested that this perspective is sharply at variance with the underlying motivation of many developmental psychologists to improve the lot of the world's children – a 'melioristic' ideology.

Nevertheless, Charlesworth observed that at the time he was writing (the early 1990s) the implications of evolutionary theory for developmental psychology were just beginning to be recognized. Indeed, by the turn of the millennium evolutionary developmental psychology was being hailed as an emerging field of interdisciplinary inquiry. Forerunners can be identified, however, in the fields of ethology and sociobiology.

Ethology

During the mid-twentieth century, the work of two European Nobel Prize-winning zoologists, Konrad Lorenz and Nikolaas Tinbergen, became highly influential in the understanding of animal behaviour and, later, human development (e.g. Lorenz, 1981; Tinbergen, 1973). The ethologists studied innate behaviours (instincts) that fitted animals for survival, examining these both in the natural environment and the laboratory. A particularly important ethological concept was that of the 'critical period' (later modified to the more flexible 'sensitive period'): a time early in life when it is crucial for certain environmental conditions to be present for an instinct to be properly realized (Sluckin, 1970). For example, newly hatched chicks normally become attached to, or imprinted upon, their mother over the first day, but if they are exposed instead to a suitable alternative, they become imprinted on that (readers will doubtless be familiar with the famous photographs of Lorenz being followed around by goslings). Imprinting is a clear example of gene-environment interactions at work. Such ethological concepts influenced researchers into early parent–child relationships, such as England's John Bowlby (see Chapter 5) and Robert Hinde. Ethology values observation and description of natural events, and developmental psychology's neglect of this approach in favour of theory-derived hypothesis testing is perhaps detrimental (Hinde, 1992a). For example, Bowlby's influential research on attachment arose from observations that disturbed adolescents had disrupted early childhood relationships; this key area of research would not have happened if it had relied solely on existing theory to drive it. Nicholas Blurton Jones (1972), a former student of Tinbergen's, was particularly influential in promoting the application of ethological methods to provide objective descriptions of children's behaviour. While acknowledging the pioneering nature of this work, Hinde (1982) suggested that Blurton Jones had gone too far in rejecting alternative data-gathering methods, such as rating scales and parent interviews.

Although ethologists, like evolutionary biologists, were interested in innate behaviours subject to natural selection, they (like developmental psychologists) were nevertheless more interested in proximate behaviours than ultimate factors (Charlesworth, 1992).

Sociobiology

In the mid-1970s, a far more radical view about the role of biological heritage was proposed: that human beings, and their behaviour, exist merely to provide the means for their genes to survive and reproduce. This new discipline – sociobiology – was initiated by US biologist Edward O. Wilson (1975). The notion that human behaviour is subservient to genes (which compete with other genes for survival) was encapsulated in the title of English ethologist Richard Dawkins's (1976) book *The Selfish Gene*. This perspective has profound implications for our understanding of human reproduction and child-rearing. Sociobiologists based their arguments on sexual selection theory: that, in addition to 'survival' (natural selection) as an influence on evolution, 'sexual selection' would also confer an evolutionary advantage (competition for mates with same-sex members and selective mating with opposite-sex members). More specifically, what came to be known as 'sexual strategies theory' concerns the human psychological processes involved in sexual selection, particularly differences in strategies between males and females. Sociobiologists argued that, since males can produce numerous gametes (sperm) the best strategy for their genes to survive would be to impregnate as many females as possible, with a low subsequent investment in personally parenting these many off-spring. By contrast, females, with their smaller reproductive potential, would best ensure their genes' survival by being very choosy about their children's father and investing heavily in raising their small number of offspring. Hence greater male promiscuity and the primary role of females in parenting were seen as biological imperatives. Furthermore, aggression between males was seen as a natural conse-quence of male competition for females. It was even proposed that if a man discovered that his spouse had had sexual relations with another man, then being jealous to the point of murder (whether of the woman or her lover) could be seen as biologically legitimate (Freedman, 1979). Not surprisingly, feminists were out-raged at such biological apologies for sexist and violent behaviour (see Chapter 11) and theorists (whether feminist or not) mounted various arguments against socio-biology. Notably, Richard Lerner and Alexander von Eye (1992) critiqued three of its major tenets.

First, they took issue with sociobiologists' use of the notion of homology – the idea that if behaviours of separate species can be described similarly, this implies an evolutionary connection. For example, arguments for an evolutionary impetus for human male promiscuity and even rape were based on fruit fly and monkey behav-iours. Yet similarities in observed behaviours provide no proof at all of evolutionary connectedness, and are more appropriately seen as analogies. Neither do such simi-larities provide any evidence for how far the behaviours in question are genetically constrained or produced.

Second, Lerner and von Eye critiqued the notion of heritability as used by sociobiologists. Heritability estimates, which vary between zero and one, represent an estimate of the *variation in genetic inheritance between individuals*. However, socio-biologists and others have sometimes used the term to imply that the higher the heritability estimate, the more the behaviour in question is determined by genes. In fact, heritability estimates say nothing about how genes or the environment deter-mine the behaviour of individuals. Lerner and von Eye provided the following clear example to illustrate how heritability estimates can be misinterpreted in this way. Imagine a law permits men, but not women, to be elected to government office. A person's eligibility for office could then be absolutely predicted by their genes (possession of an XX or XY pair of chromosomes) – giving a perfect heritability estimate of one. Clearly, this is not evidence that eligibility for office is genetic, yet this is exactly how heritability estimates of various behavioural traits are often inter-preted. Conversely, traits which are universal, such as the capacity for language, have zero *heritability* but are clearly *inherited*, a point often overlooked even in texts about the nature–nurture debate (Wells, 2000).

A third contentious principle of sociobiology is the assumption that what exists is necessarily an adaptation – that observed physical features and behaviours represent ideal outcomes of evolution. Darwin himself noted that sutures (gaps) in the skulls of infants are a perfect adaptation to childbirth, giving flexibility to the skull as the child descends the birth canal, but how is their existence to be explained in baby birds, which simply have to escape from shells (Lerner and von Eye, 1992)? Some features may develop for no particular purpose or become co-opted for a purpose for which they did not originally evolve. This point had previously been made by biologists Stephen Jay Gould and Richard Lewontin (1979), who used a now famous architectural analogy. Cathedrals and churches may have rounded arches in their ceilings with triangular spaces between them containing designs that fit the space perfectly; while no one would argue that the arches were placed there *in order to* provide the spaces for the designs, biologists frequently make similar arguments for the evolutionary origins of animal structures and behaviours. Similarly, it has been argued that post hoc explanations for the evolutionary pressures that may have determined various forms and functions may be no more scientifically valid than a Rudyard Kipling *Just So* story (see Box 2.1: a distinctly Lamarckian evolutionary theory is apparent, which today's epigenetics research suggests may not be so far-fetched after all!).

Lerner and von Eye concluded that the problems with sociobiological explanations are so great that this theory is not relevant for understanding human development or sex differences. While powerfully argued, this view is perhaps extreme. Hinde (1992b), however, found Lerner and von Eye's critique valuable in helping to balance the more extreme sociobiological views. He agreed that a primary role for genes should be rejected, that homologies should not be confused with analogies and that heritability estimates should not be misinterpreted. He nevertheless suggested that their criticisms were too sweeping; for example, analogous behaviours might provide evidence that similar selection pressures have been at work.

Hinde also pointed out that Lerner and von Eye focused on aggression rather than cooperation – something also given considerable attention by sociobiologists. Altruism posed a challenge for 'selfish genes', though that metaphor has been said to muddle thinking in this area by confusing biology (genetics) with morality (selfishness); it has been suggested that biological altruism should be distinguished from psychological altruism (although one may promote the other; see Okasha, 2013). Biologically, altruism occurs when an organism reduces its own survival chances by helping others, such as by giving an alarm call or sharing scarce food resources. Wilson's early explanation that such behaviour benefited the group (*group selection theory*) was undermined by the argument that non-altruistic individuals would have greater survival chances so that genes favouring altruism would soon be wiped out. *Kin selection theory* was then proposed, whereby individuals are most likely to show altruism to close relatives. This theory is well supported, although it does not explain the common human practice of adopting and raising non-related children. It also fails to explain humans' frequent cooperation with non-relatives, therefore *reciprocal altruism theory* has been proposed, whereby assisting others may yield benefits through having favours returned (Okasha, 2013). This requires the ability to monitor interactions with others in order to calculate the likelihood of later reciprocity, and whether the benefits of helping another individual will, in the long run, outweigh the costs. Support for this theory includes a recent experimental

---

BOX 2.1 THE ELEPHANT'S CHILD

> Then the Elephant's Child put his head down close to the Crocodile's musky, tusky mouth, and the Crocodile caught him by his little nose, which up to that very week, day, hour, and minute, had been no bigger than a boot, though much more useful . . . Then the Elephant's Child sat back on his little haunches, and pulled, and pulled, and pulled, and his nose began to stretch . . . and at last the Crocodile let go of the Elephant's Child's nose with a plop that you could hear all up and down the Limpopo . . . he . . . wrapped it all up in cool banana leaves, and hung it in the great grey-green, greasy Limpopo to cool . . . The Elephant's Child sat there for three days waiting for his nose to shrink, but it never grew any shorter . . . the Crocodile had pulled it out into a really truly trunk same as all elephants have today.
>
> *(Kipling, 1902/1975: 45–6)*

---

study, which found that, by about five and a half years of age, the degree to which a child is prosocial towards an unrelated classmate depends on how prosocial that child has previously been towards him or her (House *et al.*, 2013).

Ethology and sociobiology were valuable in adding a focus on function and evolution to considerations of biological structures and behaviours (Hinde, 1992b). The potential for sociobiology to inform developmental psychology was identified by Smith (1987), who discussed several relevant sociobiological concepts, such as viewing the whole human lifespan as an evolved strategy for replicating genes. Such notions are increasingly being given attention under the rubric of 'evolutionary developmental psychology'.

Evolutionary developmental psychology

Despite the backlash against evolutionary approaches sparked by sociobiological theory, evolutionary theory has gained new influence in psychology since the turn of the millennium. It has been described as a metatheory, or broad perspective, which may vary in its usefulness (Tate, 2013) and within which more specific theories can be developed and tested (Buss and Schmidtt, 2011), as we discussed in the previous chapter. If we accept Anne Campbell's (2012) suggestion that a biological perspective constitutes a paradigm (similar to a metatheory), then this is at a broader level of generality than the evolutionary metatheory. That there may be different levels of metatheories has been discussed by Willis Overton (2010).

The goals of evolutionary *developmental* psychology are 'to identify the genetic and ecological mechanisms that shape the development of . . . phenotypes and ensure their adaptation to local conditions' (Geary and Bjorklund, 2000: 57). The interplay between genetic and ecological conditions to determine the phenotype (physical and behavioural characteristics) is known as epigenetics: imprinting, as described by ethologists, is a good example. (Note that, as discussed later, a narrower definition of epigenetics is often used by biologists today.) Like sociobiology, evolutionary developmental psychology draws upon evidence from other animal (especially primate) species, from fossil records of ancestors of *Homo sapiens* and from a consideration of modern hunter-gatherer societies.

In a manner reminiscent of Robert Havighurst's notion of developmental tasks (see Chapter 3), evolutionary developmental psychologists divide the lifespan into a number of stages defined by differences in physical development, social dependence and social goals, for example, infancy, childhood, juvenility, adolescence and adulthood (Bogin, 1997, cited in Geary and Bjorklund, 2000). An important function of the extended pre-adult period of development in humans is said to be the provision of the opportunity for the practice of skills needed for survival and reproduction (for example, competition for mates), through play, social interactions and exploration of the environment. Social and cognitive immaturity may themselves serve adaptive functions concerned with the shorter-term survival of the young individual rather than being a preparation for adulthood. For example, children's short auditory memory span might aid language comprehension by reducing the amount of information to be processed (Geary and Bjorklund, 2000).

In infancy and childhood, attachment to parents is seen as the central social relationship, functioning to keep the young organism alive by keeping it close to parents and increasing the level of parental investment in offspring (see Chapter 5). The existence of individual differences in quality of attachment (e.g. Ainsworth and Wittig, 1969) is taken as evidence that attachment is an epigenetic process. However, an exclusive focus on parents overlooks the potential evolutionary role of others, especially grandmothers, in helping to raise children, as highlighted by anthropologists (see Box 2.2).

As children grow older, the shift away from parents towards peers, especially same-sex peers, is seen as preparatory for adult reproductive activities. For example, boys' social relationships are concerned with status and dominance, which can be interpreted as preparatory for competition for mates, while girls' more intimate relationships with each other can be seen as fostering a supportive network for later parenting activities (Geary and Bjorklund, 2000). This traditional sex-typed interpretation (competing males but cooperating females) required modification considering research (e.g. Crick and Bigbee, 1998) that broadened the definition of aggression from physical and verbal types to social forms more typical of girls, such as spreading rumours about others and keeping them out of friendship groups. Thus David Geary and David Bjorklund acknowledge that girls also compete, proposing that perhaps upsetting the social networks of competitors lays the groundwork for later competition for mates. Our own research does show that competition between teenage girls over boyfriends is one (of several) triggers for social aggression (Owens et al., 2000). Evolutionary theory has recently been used to provide a framework for understanding adolescent bullying as often being adaptive rather than dysfunctional,

BOX 2.2 THE GRANDMOTHER HYPOTHESIS

It is often assumed that the steady increase in life expectancy over the past century and a half has resulted in a larger proportion of older people than ever before . . . But . . . it is levels of fertility, not life expectancy (mortality) that shift the proportion of elders in a population . . . [In contrast to other primates, in] both historical and hunter-gatherer populations a third or more of women are usually beyond the age of 45 . . . Developments in evolutionary life-history theory suggest that, instead of help *for* older members of the population, it is help *from* postmenopausal grandmothers that accounts for the age structure of human societies . . . In an ancestral population that was shifting from chimpanzee-like feeding [at weaning] to hard-to-handle foods, the more vigorous elder females could help more, thereby increasing the representation of their vigour in descendant generations, shifting rates of ageing, and lengthening average adult lifespans.

(Hawkes, 2004: 128)

drawing upon evidence supporting the idea that it serves both boys' and girls' physical, sexual and dominance goals (Volk *et al.*, 2012).

The evolutionary framework has been applied to cognition as well as to social development. In 1983, Jerry Fodor expounded a 'modularity of mind' theory – an exemplar of Stephen Pepper's (1942) formism metaphor in that it was based upon dividing the mind into separately functioning cognitive categories. Evolutionary psychologists further developed this idea, proposing that there are hierarchically organized modules of the mind that have evolved to process both social and nonsocial (ecological) aspects of the world (see Table 2.1) (Geary, 1998, cited in Geary and Bjorklund, 2000). This is an example of a 'core-knowledge' theory of development. Modules related to the social world are divided into those concerning different social groups and those that are individually based, such as theory of mind. Ecological modules are divided into the biological and the physical. While their underlying neural structures are seen as inherent, they develop as children initiate activities and gain competence in 'folk psychology, folk biology and intuitive physics' (Geary and Bjorklund, 2000: 62). In other words, epigenetic processes are responsible for phenotype, although the mechanisms involved are poorly understood. The notion of sensitive periods is incorporated, with the additional suggestion that these may be related to the position of modules / submodules in the hierarchy, being shorter and earlier for lower-level than higher-level modules.

A goal of evolutionary developmental psychology is to understand how biases and constraints on behaviour determined by evolutionary pressures are relevant for the modern world (Geary and Bjorklund, 2000). For example, while children the world over are biologically predisposed to learn language, reading is a cultural

TABLE 2.1 Evolutionary developmental theory: evolved domains of mind

Domain of information	Social		Biological	Physical
Subdomain	Individual	Group		
Function of information-processing modules	Online monitoring of dyadic interactions; maintaining interpersonal relationships	Parsing social universe into kin, friends and competitors	Categorizing and representing behaviour / growth patterns of flora and fauna, e.g. food sources	Guiding / representing movement in three-dimensional space; using physical materials
Examples of information-processing modules	Language Theory of mind	Ingroup Outgroup	Flora Fauna	Movement Representation

Source: Based on information in Geary and Bjorklund, 2000.

expression of language (Snowling, 2000) and thus inherently more difficult to learn. Similarly, Geary and Bjorklund suggest that while deadly male-on-male violence is an understandable result of evolutionary pressures to compete, this could be channelled more safely into alternative competitive activities, such as athletics (a view, incidentally, that would be strongly challenged by some sociologists concerned with gendered aspects of education, who would see this as encouraging harmful 'macho' attitudes; see Gilbert and Gilbert, 1998).

While many theories of development focus on specific aspects, the above over-view makes clear the breadth of coverage afforded by evolutionary developmental theory, implying that it could play an important role in integrating otherwise diverse theories (see Chapter 13).

The evolutionary perspective carries some dangers, however, some of which we have alluded to already. Hinde (1992b) warned against drawing simplistic and anthropomorphic parallels between animal and human behaviour, providing the example of the removal of an infant from its mother in both humans and rhesus monkeys. While in both cases, the greater the disruption to the mother-infant relationship, the more the infant's behaviour is disturbed, the dynamics differ: human children are more disturbed by spending the separation in a strange environment, while monkey infants are more disturbed by remaining in the familiar group environment. Thus, rather than simply drawing parallels, animal data should be used to suggest principles that can be tested in humans. In a similar vein, John Archer (2001) has argued that the value of evolutionary psychology lies in suggesting novel, testable hypotheses. However, Lynne Segal (2001) suggests that evolutionary-based tales of wicked step-parents (with their lack of genetic investment in their stepchildren), competitive men and nurturing women are simply clichés repackaged as new insights. Other opponents of the evolutionary approach maintain that, while our evolutionary history clearly empowers and limits our behaviour, this is at such a level of generality as to be unhelpful in considering most specific human behaviours (Rose and Rose, 2001).

Even more seriously, Alice Eagly and Wendy Wood (2013) draw attention to the considerable evidence *against* predictions based on sexual selection theory regarding matters such as mate preferences, and suggest that proponents of evolutionary theory ignore such evidence in favour of the few confirmatory studies. They suggest that science writers' keenness nevertheless to favour evolutionary explanations of sex differences and attraction is due to psychology's current biological metatheory. David Buller (2005) offers another critique, based upon illogical interpretations of empirical results in the interests of 'reverse-engineering' today's human mind to fit our imagined Pleistocene past. For those wanting to pursue this controversy further, good starting points are David Bjorklund and Anthony Pellegrini's (2002) overview of evolutionary developmental psychology, the critical papers by Eagly and Wood and by Buller already cited and an article by Timothy Ketelaar and Bruce Ellis (2000) on the question of whether evolutionary explanations are unfalsifiable.

Behaviour genetics: a focus of the nature–nurture debate

Evolutionary theory focuses upon characteristics of the human species in general. However, evolution (at least by natural selection) depends upon the existence of individual differences. Individual differences in behaviour and development are the subject matter of behaviour genetics, which has become an important focus of the familiar nature–nurture debate. Genetic explanations for human phenomena are very much in the public eye as a result of the Human Genome Project, which mapped the genes on human chromosomes and discovered the complete sequence of nucleotides on each gene. Sequencing was declared complete in 2003 (Schmutz et al., 2004).

The notion that genes set limits on development has existed for some time, with the 'reaction range' being bounded by the upper and lower limits of possible developmental outcomes (Gottesman, 1974). Imprinting again provides an example, with chicks only becoming imprinted on objects if they possess certain characteristics in terms of size and movement, which under normal circumstances would be fulfilled by the mother. More recently, however, genes have come to be seen as playing a much more active role in development. US psychologist Sandra Scarr (1992) built a theory which drew upon the finding of behaviour genetics research that similarity in genetics correlates with similarity in behaviours. She acknowledged the role of the environment in promoting phenotypical behaviours, but pointed out that in reality the environment is very similar for many individuals, and that the genes, in effect, rely on the existence of that environment for their expression. She promoted the notion of the 'average expectable environment' whereby, assuming a 'normal' environment, genes will express their potential. Variations of environment within the normal range are functionally equivalent. Provided the environment is indeed 'normal', environmental changes such as extra stimulation will have no effect. Only if the environment is outside the range of normality – for example, in abusive families – will such environmental change significantly change behavioural outcomes.

Furthermore, the phenomenon of 'niche-picking' is introduced, whereby organisms shape their own environments, with genotypes driving experiences. Acknowledging that this notion ran counter to mainstream developmental theory, Scarr (1992) presented various kinds of evidence that individuals are active shapers of their own environment (which accords with organismic theories of development, as discussed in Chapters 3 and 4). Overall, she argued that '*genotype-environment correlations*, rather than gene-environment interactions, predominate in the construction of experiences' (Scarr, 1992: 8, original emphasis). Scarr saw the effect of genes becoming stronger as children grow older and become increasingly able to select environments that suit their genetic make-up.

Similar in many ways to Scarr's model was that of another US psychologist, Robert Plomin, who referred to his work as environmental genetics (e.g. Hetherington *et al.*, 1994). He introduced the notion of the 'nonshared environment'. This can be exemplified by siblings. Behavioural differences between siblings are often very apparent despite their sharing 50 per cent of genetic material and being raised in the same family. Plomin maintained that being raised in the same family does not constitute being raised in an identical environment: the 50 per cent of genetic material that differs between siblings causes children to respond to similar events differently, and also evokes differing responses from parents. This nonshared environment creates different outcomes, while the shared environment is thought to have little effect.

Theories such as these have given genetics a more predominant place than previously in explaining behavioural differences between individuals. For example, Scarr's theory implies that children could be raised by different families and they would turn out much the same anyway. Such interpretations lead to profound conclusions. For example, differences in parenting style are seen to matter little: as long as parents are 'good enough' children will develop as their genes dictate. Furthermore, provided the environment is not very deviant, early enrichment programmes for families would be a waste of resources.

Such conclusions have certainly not gone unchallenged. Diana Baumrind (1993), who undertook seminal research in the USA on the effects of parenting styles on children's development, strongly took issue with Scarr's notions of average expectable environments and 'good enough' parenting. She maintained that the heritability estimates used by Scarr suffered from implausible basic assumptions, underdeveloped constructs, inadequate measures of family environment and unrepresentative populations. For example, the populations in which heritability estimates have been made are extraordinary, being mainly studies of twins and adoptees. Scarr did not specify what constitutes a 'good enough' environment, which appears to be any environment other than abusive. Baumrind cited evidence to support her counter-proposition that '[a]ll nonabusive environments above the poverty line are not equally facilitative of healthy development' (Baumrind, 1993: 1,299). Scarr accepted that her theory depends on children having a broad range of environments from which to choose, and excluded individuals with disadvantaged circumstances or restricted life choices. Baumrind suggested that such 'excluded' individuals are in fact the norm worldwide, the absence of disadvantage not being the same as access to a rich environment. She disputed Scarr's assumption that the same ontological principles apply within all cultures: 'What is "normal" or "expectable" in one culture frequently is anathema in another' (Baumrind, 1993: 1,301). For example, parents from diverse cultural backgrounds rear their children very differently because of different values; this necessarily limits the generalizability of heritability indices. Baumrind maintained that negative social or genetic factors can be attenuated by parents, but that parents will not be open to interventions if they accept Scarr's position and believe the situation is genetic and unmodifiable.

A detailed critique of the interpretations of behaviour genetics research by Gert-Jan Vreeke (2000) questioned the assumption that behaviour genetics studies are relevant for matters of development. Echoing the critiques of sociobiology, Vreeke observed that the main statistical technique used by behaviour geneticists, analysis of variance, is a correlational technique. Although, as every undergraduate psychology student knows, correlation does not imply causation, in the field of behaviour genetics providing developmental interpretations of analysis of variance became standard practice. If, say, the heritability of IQ in a population is 80 per cent, this is understood to mean that genetics play a major causal role in intellectual ability. Vreeke argued that there are several weaknesses in this logic. For example, as in Baumrind's earlier critique, the nature of the sample is seen as crucial – if the study participants were from a selected background (e.g. college students) one might find a very different heritability estimate than if they were from a sample representative of the broader population. Assuming one does, in fact, succeed in taking such population effects into account, an assumption of analysis of variance is that the variables are additive, whereas the evidence is that developmental processes are interactive, and analysis of variance is arguably not sensitive enough to detect this.

A counter-critique by behaviour geneticists argues, on the basis of Mendel's laws of inheritance, that additivity is the biological reality, as reflected by additive effects of different genes to produce those phenotypes which are determined by multiple genes. However, Vreeke argued that Mendel's laws mention interaction, as well as additivity, between genes, so that taking multiple genes as a model for gene–environment relationships is not a basis for supporting the additivity assumption. A further argument made in support of additivity is that it is adaptive. Yet, using evolutionary theory in this way can be seen as inappropriate: it relies on a consideration of the *outcomes* of development (phenotypes) upon which evolutionary processes operate, and ignores the actual gene–environment relationships that determine the phenotypes of individuals. Although various researchers have defended the additivity principle, this stance flies in the face of evidence from molecular biology and animal research, that genotypes are translated into phenotypes by 'complex, dynamic and nonlinear' processes (Vreeke, 2000: 40).

Vreeke maintained that Scarr's and Baumrind's interpretations can be reconciled if we accept that genes and the environment have an interactive relationship: shared environmental effects demonstrated in experimental social research may not show up in a behaviour genetics study if the research design does not allow for the possibility that individuals with different genotypes may respond differently to the same environment. Thus 'it cannot be deduced from percentages of explained variance that an intervention cannot be successful. An interactive logic predicts that it is a matter of finding the right key to the right lock, the environment that fits an individual genotype' (Vreeke, 2000: 43).

Others have also criticized behaviour genetics as giving too much importance to genetic influences on behaviour, an extreme view being that the role of genes ceases at conception, with epigenetic processes then taking over, so that phylogeny and genetics add little of significance to an understanding of phenotypes. The neuroscientist Steven Rose maintains that 'heritability estimates are simply meaningless when applied to complex human behavioural traits' leading to 'implausible claims such as a significant heritability for "religiosity" or "job satisfaction"' (Rose, 2001: 144).

A framework for understanding gene-environment interactions which gave a more important place to environmental influences on development was the bio-ecological model (Bronfenbrenner and Ceci, 1994; Bronfenbrenner and Morris, 1998). Urie Bronfenbrenner's (1979) earlier ecological model was highly influential in drawing attention to the multiple and interacting social and environmental systems influencing children's development (see Chapter 8). The later bioecological model took issue with the view that individual and group differences in developmental outcomes are mainly genetically driven, proposing instead that it is appropriate and ongoing interactions with the environment which enable genes to exert their potential to a greater or lesser degree (see Chapter 13). It is thus these proximal processes that drive development, and their quality will affect heritability estimates.

Recent research and theorizing (e.g. Boyce and Ellis, 2005) has focused on this notion of gene-environment interactions with regard to individual differences in sensitivity to context. It addresses Vreeke's point that those with differing genetic inheritance might respond differently to the same environment. Children differ in how they react to being raised in adversity, some being vulnerable and suffering long-term ill effects but others demonstrating greater resilience. The diathesis–stress or dual-risk theory (e.g. Sameroff, 1983) holds that children who have a genetic or constitutional vulnerability will have poorer outcomes in the face of adverse developmental circumstances. Drawing upon both human and animal studies, and using a Swedish metaphor, W. Thomas Boyce and Bruce J. Ellis (2005) propose that the situation is more complex than this, and that children can be characterized as 'dandelions' or 'orchids'. Dandelions thrive quite well in good or poor conditions, but are never stunning. Orchids, by contrast, suffer badly in the wrong conditions, but bloom magnificently in the best ones. Similarly, it seems that some children have especially *good* outcomes in very supportive conditions, but particularly *poor* outcomes if they grow up in adverse circumstances. These individuals are said to be more 'biologically sensitive to context'. The level of sensitivity is long term, and seen as an outcome of the interaction between genetic predisposition and rearing environment, which either 'tunes up' their sensitivity to context (orchids) or 'tunes it down' (dandelions). Furthermore, it is seen as adaptive, evolutionarily speaking, to possess a stress system that can be matched to the environment. Accumulating evidence supports the biological sensitivity to context theory, which shifts the focus from psychopathology alone to a consideration of thriving – something that may be motivating for parents receiving help in raising children who seem to be vulnerable (Pluess and Belsky, 2012).

Brain, behaviour and epigenetics in development

Brain–behaviour relations were relatively neglected by developmental psychologists during most of the twentieth century, but an explosion of new information occurred after the development of non-invasive technologies for studying brain functioning (van der Molen and Ridderinkhof, 1998). In the limited space available here, we will restrict ourselves to a few basic theoretical issues, including an increased role for epigenetics.

It is often assumed, and promulgated in populist literature, that genes determine brain structure, which in turn determines behaviour. Differences in brain structure – for example, between males and females or between those diagnosed and not diagnosed with ADHD – may be interpreted as providing evidence of fundamental, inherited individual differences in neurology that underlie observed behavioural differences. Such findings may be favoured for publication over failures to replicate them or over cultural explanations for the observed behavioural differences, so that the evidence for such differences may be much weaker and more contradictory than at first apparent (e.g. Fine, 2010; Gilbert and Gilbert, 1998). Thus, the nature–nurture controversy is again evident in the field of brain-behaviour relations.

In fact, there is good reason to believe that the structure of the human brain is determined epigenetically. The young child has many more synaptic connections in the cerebral cortex than in adulthood; therefore it seems that experience determines which are retained and which lost. Furthermore, it is difficult to explain the great complexity of interconnections in the human brain as being determined purely by a limited number of genes (van der Molen and Ridderinkhof, 1998).

Animal studies have also established that brain structures can be changed as a result of early experience with environments that are especially stimulating (e.g. Rosenzweig, 1996) or that deprive the young animal of normal experience, such as normal visual experience (e.g. Tees, 1986). This is also apparent in human infants with uncorrected squints (strabismus), whereby a lack of normal visual input in the early months affects neurological functioning permanently, resulting in low acuity in the affected eye and a failure to develop normal binocular vision (e.g. Westall and

---

BOX 2.3 PERRY'S THEORY OF EARLY TRAUMA AND BRAIN DEVELOPMENT

Child trauma specialist Bruce Perry was influential in the 1990s in drawing attention to how abuse might affect the developing brain and result in later psychopathology. He stressed that humans evolved as social animals, with the survival of the individual dependent upon nurturing by the clan. The majority of the brain has evolved to subserve necessary social relationships, and the early caretaking experience is instrumental in determining how the brain becomes organized, from the more primitive brainstem and midbrain, through the limbic system and up to the complex cortex. The cortex becomes increasingly able to modulate the functions of the more primitive parts of the brain. However, he proposed that certain experiences in the early years disrupt the development of the lower parts of the brain, which in turn influence the development of the higher parts, given the brain's hierarchical structure. The result of disruption to early nurturing (such as exposure to neglect or violence) can be that the modulating effect of the higher influences is reduced, resulting in effects such as increased anxiety and a predisposition to violence.

Shute, 1992). Human and animal studies therefore indicate that while the young brain is plastic, or malleable, this plasticity is constrained by external factors, such as exposure to a normal environment, and internal factors, such as the progressive development of the brain from deeper to more superficial areas (van der Molen and Ridderinkhof, 1998).

These issues are illustrated by Bruce Perry's (1997) theory of the neurodevelopmental aspects of violence (Box 2.3). He argued that biological markers (such as certain blood chemicals) associated with violent behaviours should not mislead us into assuming that these must reflect genetic differences between individuals which are causing the behaviours. Rather, they reflect the biochemical *outcomes* of brain structures and processes determined by early experience. However, genes are not irrelevant: it was later shown that whether a child raised by abusive parents becomes a violent youth depends on whether he or she has a particular gene variant (Caspi *et al.*, 2002). This accords with the diathesis–stress theory. Perry's view is compatible with the hierarchical nature of Geary's evolutionary theory of development (outlined previously) and incorporates the notion of sensitive periods emphasized by ethologists and demonstrated by human and animal studies of brain development.

More recent theorizing about brain development has made explicit reference to epigenetics, definitions of which vary. Following the biologist Conrad Waddington (1942), developmental psychologists have used the term for decades in a broad way to refer to development as a function of gene-environment interactions, with a sense that although development is plastic, options become increasingly narrowed as development proceeds down particular channels, or is 'canalized' (another term coined by Waddington). With increased understanding of genetics, and a recent 'explosion' of biological epigenetics research (Miller, 2010), narrower definitions have been adopted, although these are debated. Animal studies have shown that genes in various cells of the body can be 'switched on', 'switched off' or expressed more or less strongly, as a result of early experiences. The switching may occur in networks of interacting genes, it may occur only in certain types of cell or more widely through the body and it may be brief or long-lasting, with brief or long-lasting effects. The genetic changes may even be passed on to subsequent generations, with the DNA sequence unaltered (that the changes should be heritable underpins one strict definition of an epigenetic trait, though in practice whether this is the case is not always known). In a seminal paper by Michael Meaney and Moshe Szyf and their team (Weaver *et al.*, 2004) it was shown that rat pups' stress response systems can be 'tuned up' or 'tuned down' in response to their early environment, an idea we saw previously in discussing 'orchid' and 'dandelion' children. In the case of rats, the quality of mothering they receive (more or less attentive) does the tuning, with more attentive mothers producing less reactive offspring. Furthermore (and this is where the brain comes into it), these effects seemed to be mediated by changes to the neural structure that forms part of the complex web of bodily systems involved in responses to stressors. In addition, an evolutionary perspective has been proposed. Long-term effects of being raised in adverse circumstances, such as anxiety, used to be viewed as pathological remnants of (presumed) prehistoric conditions of greater physical threat, when high reactivity would have been useful. A newer suggestion is that it is, in fact, adaptive, to possess a stress response system that is plastic and changeable by early experiences: an individual raised in a stressful environment would be well served by having a stress response system that can be 'tuned up' to detect and respond readily to stressors, while one raised in a 'normal' (moderate-stress) environment would benefit from having a 'tuned-down' system that is responsive enough to stressors, but not over-responsive.

Szyf's team (Labonte *et al.*, 2012) has also shown that brains from suicided people with a history of early abuse differ epigenetically from those who suicided without such history, specifically in an area of the brain concerned with mood regulation. Although limited by its correlational nature, the study offers a starting point for increasing understanding of the epigenetic changes that might underlie Perry's theory of the effects of early abuse.

Neural epigenetics has also been invoked in the case of cognitive development, by Annette Karmiloff-Smith (2012). She has contrasted *domain-general* with *domain-specific* theories of cognitive development. A prime example of a domain-general theory is that of Jean Piaget, with assimilation, accommodation and equilibration underlying all aspects of cognition, such as language development and appreciation of space (see Chapter 4). This theory raises the question of what causes strengths and weaknesses in children's cognitive profiles. An example of a domain-specific theory is Geary and Bjorklund's evolutionary theory, discussed previously, which sees the evolved neural substrates for the various domains as being 'fleshed out' in interaction with experiences. Karmiloff-Smith proposes an alternative to this, with a difference that is both subtle and profound: that the inherited brain mechanisms are not *specific* for the various domains, but are *relevant for* them or *biased towards* them. This neuroconstructivist approach holds that, depending on the environment, the neural systems develop (epigenetically), and localization of form and function gradually emerges as neuronal pruning occurs and the developing neural systems compete with one another through means such as the selection of cell types, and variety in their density and interconnectedness. The brain is therefore seen as a self-organizing entity, with domains as end-points, not starting-points, and it is therefore perfectly possible for a child to show strength in one area, such as numerical understanding, but weakness in another, such as language. That there exists a degree of brain plasticity necessary for such a model is most strikingly demonstrated by the fact that, if done early enough, removal of the entire left hemisphere allows the right one to take over its usual language functions (although it must be appreciated that the long-term outcome of early brain damage is not always good and depends very much on its nature and timing; see Anderson *et al.*, 2011).

There has been recent marked progress in understanding early brain development with the discovery of two genes that are instrumental in determining the migration of neurons from the middle of the brain to form the outer cortical layer in the first 18 months of life (Cappello *et al.*, 2013). More broadly, epigenetic processes are increasingly seen to lie at the heart of neural development and functioning: 'The billions of neurons in a single brain have the same DNA sequence yet are differentiated for their diverse functions through epigenetic programming during pre- and postnatal development and possibly throughout life' (Murgatroyd and Spengler, 2011). While epigenetics is increasingly influencing developmental theorizing, some have called for caution. Human brains for studying the detailed mechanisms involved are understandably hard to come by, and enthusiasm for applying epigenetics to a broad range of human traits may be outstripping knowledge (Miller, 2010).

The medical model

Why are we considering a perspective on children's behaviour that is not a theory, not developmental and not based in the psychological tradition? We consider this approach essential to address, given the real impact a medical perspective has on the lives of many children whose behaviour is considered problematic. Undergraduate and postgraduate students may be introduced to a medical diagnostic approach to children's behavioural and emotional problems, and indeed clinical psychology course accreditation may require that students learn psychiatric diagnosis. However, in our experience, the specific issue of how such an approach accords (or otherwise) with psychological theories of child development (and indeed, with the scientist-practitioner model frequently espoused by professional psychology courses) is rarely addressed. Students, new practitioners (and perhaps many not so new practitioners!) are left to try and make sense of the professional dilemmas this can cause.

For example, one of us (RS) has worked as a paediatric psychologist in an Australian hospital, conceptualizing cases within theoretical frameworks such as systems theory and learning theory. However, the official hospital summary records did not reflect this at all, requiring cases to be described in terms of medical (psychiatric) diagnoses that were irrelevant to how the case was actually conceptualized and managed. Recording of contextual causes was actively discouraged, in favour of an individual diagnosis (implying that the problem was inherent in the child).

The pervasiveness of the medical model in western societies may encourage certain behaviours to *become* seen by the public as problematic and needing medical attention. For example, parents who have difficulty in managing their children's behaviour frequently present their children (and even themselves) as suffering from ADHD (Searight and McLaren, 1998). This illustrates the application of medical diagnosis to children's (and adults') behaviour, as laid out in various editions of the *Diagnostic and Statistical Manual of Mental Disorders* (*DSM*) of the American Psychiatric Association (American Psychiatric Association, 2013) – another example of Pepper's (1942) 'formism' metaphor.

The *DSM* manual was drawn up as a descriptive taxonomic system; it was explicitly claimed to be atheoretical, to enable it to be used by practitioners favouring different theoretical orientations. However, it is not possible to devise an explanatory system devoid of underlying theoretical assumptions. Those underlying the *DSM* project include viewing mental disorder as a subset of medical disorder, with each illness defined by certain behavioural criteria endowed with biological significance, and removed from any broader contextual considerations. Peter Butler claimed that 'despite the cool neutrality of its language, the diagnostic project was *intended* from its inception to lead to a progressive exclusion of non-biologically focused systems of explanation (psychological, psychosocial, psychoanalytic) from authoritative psychiatric discourse' (Butler, 1999: 21). He and others have argued that successive changes to *DSM* classifications, rather than being driven by scientific evidence, as claimed, have been heavily influenced by sociocultural factors – the modification and eventual removal of homosexuality as a mental disorder, in the face of changing societal attitudes, being a prime example.

The phenomenon of ADHD also provides a good illustration of the ongoing trend to view children's problematic behaviours through a medical lens. It is often 'uncritically accepted as a neurobiological condition' (Reid and Maag, 1997: 13), with children's problematic behaviours regarding attention, impulsivity and high activity levels attracting a medical label and a drug-based solution (usually the psychostimulant methylphenidate). The diagnosis of ADHD has long been contentious, with proponents finding it necessary to draw up an international consensus statement confirming its acceptance as a neurobiological condition (Barkley *et al.*, 2002). This statement in turn was critiqued by Sami Timimi and 33 co-endorsers (2004), who pointed out the lack of any biological marker for ADHD, any effect of medication specific to those diagnosed with it or any effect of medication beyond four weeks. In the USA, 11 per cent of children and adolescents had at some time been diagnosed with ADHD by 2011, with the majority still currently diagnosed and on medication; this represented a 28 per cent increase in medicated ADHD since 2003 (Visser *et al.*, 2014). Although the presenting problems are behavioural, most children diagnosed with ADHD are seen solely by general medical practitioners, with no psychological evaluation (Searight and McLaren, 1998). The wide acceptance of this medical perspective has sidelined the expertise of other professionals, including child psychologists, whose very area of expertise is children's behaviour (Atkinson and Shute, 1999). Furthermore, increased demands that some countries place upon children for educational achievement, together with declining education and mental health budgets, increase the pressure for children's behaviour problems to be treated medically (Searight and McLaren, 1998). Consequently, children are more likely to receive drugs than a careful assessment and intervention in terms of the contextual factors maintaining their behaviour; this also means that little consideration is given to the role of broader public policy and funding to tackle ADHD (Prosser *et al.*, 2002).

Even ADHD policy documents in which psychologists have played a leading role use the medical term 'diagnosis' rather than the psychological term 'assessment', and may grant precedence to the medical profession in assessment and intervention (Atkinson and Shute, 1999). In fact, some psychologists argue strongly that it is vital for psychologists to be excellent diagnosticians. On the other hand, expert psychological evidence has been ruled inadmissible in court with regard to behaviours codified within *DSM*, since such behaviours are judged to be within the domain of medicine (Australian Psychological Society, 1998). This is part of a general pattern of 'medicalization' of non-disease states that has been identified in western societies, with relief sought for discomforts and distress which would have been tolerated in the past (Searight and McLaren, 1998). In the case of ADHD, its wide acceptance as a neurobiological condition treatable by medication has led to a neglect of possible environmental causes, a lack of concern about the side-effects of medication and the promotion of a culture in which a pill is the solution to life's problems (Timimi *et al.*, 2004; see also Box 2.4).

If indeed the intention of the *DSM* project was to sideline alternative theoretical perspectives on mental and behavioural problems, it has succeeded very well; it can be difficult in practice for the alternative perspectives on child development considered in this book to be brought to bear effectively to address children's behavioural and emotional problems, in accord with melioristic values. However, this situation might be changing. The production of the *DSM-5* in 2013 coincided with a rash of critical books as new diagnostic criteria were set to cast an even wider net; for example, continuing to grieve for a loved one could be seen as pathological within weeks of the death, leading to accusations that *DSM-5* medicalizes normal sorrow. The credibility of the project has been further undermined by the finding that most of the various panels involved in the revision had a majority of members with a financial interest in the pharmaceutical industry (Cosgrove and Krimsky, 2012). There have even been rumblings from the USA's National Institutes of Mental Health that alternatives to the *DSM* might be considered as more suitable for underpinning future research efforts. The British Psychological Society has

---

BOX 2.4 ADHD: TWO VIEWS OF THE SOCIAL CONTEXT OF BIOLOGICAL EXPLANATIONS

ADHD is a potent and desirable label of forgiveness because it attributes troubling behaviour to physiological forms (i.e., neurobiological) outside an individual's control . . . the ADHD label legitimizes parents' concerns that children do, in fact, manifest problems and that those problems are recognized, common, and socially palatable. Problem behaviour now can be portrayed as an inability to respond appropriately to an underlying disorder, rather than unwillingness, lack of motivation, or poor parenting . . . the ADHD label allows parents to 'externalize the disorder' thereby separating the 'good' child from the 'bad' behaviour . . . a diagnosis of ADHD may be the most powerful route for parents to secure services for children.

(Reid and Maag, 1997: 15)

In [Australian pre-service teachers'] view [of ADHD] the 'label' and 'the teacher as labeller' was distinct from the diagnosis and the diagnostician. Moreover, labelling was viewed as school-based and negative, whilst diagnosis was viewed as clinic-based and positive or, at the very least, 'neutral' . . . [This] understanding . . . leaves a neutral space in which diagnosis, itself, rests uncontested. I contend that this lack of debate or questioning surrounding the actual diagnosis of ADHD represents an acceptance of truth about ADHD. It is suggestive of an unquestionable, scientific authority of the diagnosis and diagnostician. Perhaps this is not surprising. Biologically based discourses of behaviour imbue 'school' and 'teacher education' contexts with a dominance that is evident across several countries.

(McMahon, 2012: 261)

---

gone much further, comprehensively repudiating the *DSM* and similar diagnostic systems as a basis for clinical practice, favouring broad-based case formulation instead (British Psychological Society, 2011). Perhaps the *DSM* project has finally overreached itself. For an account of the *DSM-5* disputes placed in a complex historical context, see David Pilgrim (2014).

Conclusions

Biological influences on theorizing about child development have been apparent ever since the discipline emerged. With the advent of new technologies for studying genes and brain function, biological approaches to psychological development are gaining further credence, while epigenetics research is giving impetus to the reconciliation of genetic and experiential approaches to development. Biologically plausible theorizing about development is to be welcomed. However, the ongoing tendency to conceptualize children's behavioural and emotional problems as medical conditions raises concerns.

A major attraction of evolutionary and other biological approaches to behavioural development may be that they provide psychology with a yearned-for basis in the physical sciences (Miller, 1999). Miller noted that such approaches sideline culture, which does not just *contribute* to psychological processes, but is a qualitative *determinant of the patterning* of those processes. Criticisms of evolutionary approaches that see the mother–child attachment relationship as an 'inherent glue' have also been raised, as divorcing the reproductive experiences of women from oppressive historical and political realities (Franzblau, 1999). We will meet such critical approaches later in the book. Other aspects of biological approaches we discuss or revisit elsewhere include the attempt to develop a systems theory of development that is biologically valid (see Chapter 10) and the notion that evolutionary theory has the potential to play an integrative role in developmental theorizing (see Chapter 13).

References

Ainsworth, M.D.S. and Wittig, B.A. 1969. Attachment and exploratory behaviour of one-year-olds in a strange situation. In B.M. Foss (ed.), *Determinants of infant behaviour.* Vol. 4. London: Methuen, 111–36.

American Psychiatric Association. 2013. *Diagnostic and statistical manual of mental disorders.* Fifth edn (*DSM-5*). Arlington, VA: American Psychiatric Association.

Anderson, V., Spencer-Smith, M. and Wood, A. 2011. Do children really recover better? Neurobehavioural plasticity after early brain insult. *Brain.* 134: 2,197–221.

Archer, J. 2001. Evolving theories of behaviour. *The Psychologist.* 14 (8): 414–19.

Atkinson, I. and Shute, R. 1999. Managing ADHD: issues in developing multidisciplinary guidelines. *Australian Journal of Guidance and Counselling.* 9 (1): 119–27.

Australian Psychological Society. 1998. Society argues the case for PTSD assessment. *In Psych: The Bulletin of the Australian Psychological Society Ltd.* 20: 5.

Barkley, R. *et al.* 2002. International consensus statement on ADHD. *Clinical Child and Family Psychology Review.* 5 (2): 89–111.

Baumrind, D. 1993. The average expectable environment is not good enough: a response to Scarr. *Child Development.* 64: 1,299–317.

Berk, L. 2000. *Child development.* Boston: Allyn & Bacon.

Bjorklund, D.E. and Pellegrini, A.D. 2002. *The origins of human nature: evolutionary developmental psychology.* Washington, DC: American Psychiatric Association.

Blurton Jones, N. 1972. *Ethological studies of child behaviour.* Cambridge: Cambridge University Press.

Boyce, W.T. and Ellis, B.J. 2005. Biological sensitivity to context. I. An evolutionary developmental theory of the origins and function of stress reactivity. *Development and Psychopathology.* 17: 271–301.

British Psychological Society. 2011. Response to the American Psychiatric Association: *DSM-5* development. London: British Psychological Society.

Bronfenbrenner, U. 1979. *The ecology of human development: experiments by nature and design.* Cambridge, MA: Harvard University Press.

Bronfenbrenner, U. and Ceci, S.J. 1994. Nature–nurture reconceptualized in developmental perspective: a bioecological model. *Psychological Review*. 101: 568–86.

Bronfenbrenner, U. and Morris, P.A. 1998. The ecology of developmental processes. In R.M. Lerner (ed.), *Handbook of child psychology. Theoretical models of human development*. Fifth edn, Vol. 1. New York: Wiley, 993–1,027.

Buller, D.J. 2005. Evolutionary psychology: the emperor's new paradigm. *Trends in Cognitive Sciences*. 9 (6): 277–83.

Buss, D.M. and Schmidtt, D.P. 2011. Evolutionary psychology and feminism. *Sex Roles*. 64: 768–87.

Butler, P. 1999. Diagnostic linedrawing, professional boundaries, and the rhetoric of scientific justification: a critical appraisal of the American Psychiatric Association's *DSM* project. *Australian Psychologist*. 34 (1): 20–9.

Campbell, A. 2012. The study of sex differences: feminism and biology. *Zeitschrift für Psychologie*. 220 (2): 137–43.

Cappello, S. *et al.* 2013. Mutations in genes encoding the cadherin receptor-ligand pair DCHS1 and FAT4 disrupt cerebral cortical development. *Nature Genetics*. 45 (11): 1,300–8.

Caspi, A. *et al.* 2002. Role of genotype in the cycle of violence in maltreated children. *Science*. 2 August: 851–4.

Charlesworth, W.R. 1992. Darwin and developmental psychology: past and present. *Developmental Psychology*. 28 (1): 5–16.

Cosgrove, L. and Krimsky, S. 2012. A comparison of *DSM-4* and *DSM-5* panel members' financial associations with industry: a pernicious problem persists. *PLOS Medicine*.

Crick, N.R. and Bigbee, M.A. 1998. Relational and overt forms of peer victimization: a multiinformant approach. *Journal of Consulting and Clinical Psychology*. 66: 337–47.

Dawkins, R. 1976. *The selfish gene*. Oxford: Oxford University Press.

Dixon, R.A. and Lerner, R.M. 1992. A history of systems in developmental psychology. In M.H. Bornstein and M.E. Lamb (eds), *Developmental psychology: an advanced textbook*. Third edn. Hillsdale, NJ: Erlbaum, 3–58.

Eagly, A. and Wood, W. 2013. Feminism and evolutionary psychology: moving forward. *Sex Roles*. 69: 549–56.

Fine, C. 2010. The battle of the sex differences (interview with J. Sutton). *The Psychologist*. 23 (11): 900–3.

Fodor, J.A. 1983. *Modularity of mind: an essay on faculty psychology*. Cambridge, MA: MIT Press.

Franzblau, S.H. 1999. Historicizing attachment theory: binding the ties that bind. *Feminism and Psychology*. 9: 22–31.

Freedman, D.G. 1979. *Human sociobiology: a holistic approach*. New York: Free Press.

Geary, D.C. and Bjorklund, D.F. 2000. Evolutionary developmental psychology. *Child Development*. 71 (1): 57–65.

Gilbert, R. and Gilbert, P. 1998. *Masculinity goes to school*. St Leonards, NSW: Allen and Unwin.

Gottesman, I.I. 1974. Developmental genetics and ontogenetic psychology: overdue entente and propositions from a matchmaker. In A. Pick (ed.), *Minnesota symposium on child psychology*. Vol. 8. Minneapolis, MN: University of Minnesota Press, 55–80.

Gould, S.J. and Lewontin, R.C. 1979. The spandrels of San Marco and the Panglossian paradigm: a critique of the adaptationist programme. *Proceedings of the Biological Society of London*. 205: 581–98.

Hawkes, K. 2004. The Grandmother Effect. *Nature*. 428: 128–9.

Hetherington, E.M., Reiss, D. and Plomin, R. (eds). 1994. *Separate social worlds of siblings: the impact of nonshared environment on development*. Hillsdale, NJ: Erlbaum.

Hinde, R. 1982. *Ethology: its nature and relations with other sciences*. Oxford: Oxford University Press.

Hinde, R.A. 1992a. Developmental psychology in the context of other behavioral sciences. *Developmental Psychology*. 28 (6): 1,018–29.

Hinde, R.A. 1992b. Commentary. *Human Development*. 35: 34–9.

House, B., Henrich, J., Sarnecka, B. and Silk, J.B. 2013. The development of contingent reciprocity in children. *Evolution and Human Behavior*. 34: 86–93.

Karmiloff-Smith, A. 2012. Perspectives on the dynamic development of cognitive capacities: insights from Williams syndrome. *Current Opinion in Neurology*. 25: 106–11.

Ketelaar, T. and Ellis, B.J. 2000. Are evolutionary explanations unfalsifiable? Evolutionary psychology and the Lakatosian philosophy of science. *Psychological Inquiry*. 11 (1): 1–21.

Kipling, R. 1902 / 1975. *Just so stories*. London: Piccolo.

Labonte, B., Yerko, V., Gross, J., Mechawar, N., Meaney, M.J., Szyf, M. and Turecki, G. 2012. Differential glucocorticoid receptor Exon 1B, 1C, and 1H expression and methylation in suicide completers with a history of childhood abuse. *Biological Psychiatry*. 72: 41–8.

Lerner, R.M. and von Eye, A. 1992. Sociobiology and human development: arguments and evidence. *Human Development*. 35: 12–33.

Lorenz, K.Z. 1981. *The foundations of ethology*. New York: Springer Verlag.

McMahon, S.E. 2012. Doctors diagnose, teachers label: the unexpected in pre-service teachers' talk about labelling children with ADHD. *International Journal of Inclusive Education*. 16 (3): 249–64.

Miller, J.G. 1999. Cultural psychology: implications for basic psychological theory. *Psychological Science*. 10 (2): 85–91.

Miller, G. 2010. The seductive allure of behavioral epigenetics. *Science*. 329: 24–7.

Murgatroyd, C. and Spengler, D. 2011. Epigenetics of early child development. *Frontiers in Psychiatry*. 2 (16).

Okasha, S. 2013. Biological altruism. In E.N. Zalta (ed.), *The Stanford encyclopedia of philosophy*. Available at: http://plato.stanford.edu/archives/fall2013/entries/altruism-biological/. Accessed 19 August 2014.

Overton, W.F. 2010. Life-span development: concepts and issues. In W.F. Overton (ed.), *The handbook of life-span development. Part 1. Cognition, biology and methods*. Wiley Online Library.

Owens, L., Shute, R. and Slee, P. 2000. 'Guess what I just heard . . .' Indirect aggression among teenage girls in Australia. *Aggressive Behavior*. 26: 67–83.

Pepper, S. 1942. *World hypotheses: a study of evidence*. Berkeley, CA: University of California Press.

Perry, B.D. 1997. Incubated in terror: neurodevelopmental factors in the 'Cycle of violence'. In J.D. Osofky (ed.), *Children in a violent society*. New York: Guilford, 124–48.

Pilgrim, D. 2014. Historical resonances of the DSM-5 dispute: American exceptionalism or Eurocentrism? *History of the Human Sciences*. 27 (2): 97–117.

Pluess, M. and Belsky, J. 2012. Prenatal programming of postnatal plasticity? *Development and Psychopathology*. 23: 29–38.

Prosser, B., Reid, R., Shute, R. and Atkinson, I. 2002. Attention deficit hyperactivity disorder (ADHD): special education policy and practice in Australia. *Australian Journal of Education*. 46 (1): 65–78.

Reid, R. and Maag, J.W. 1997. Attention deficit hyperactivity disorder: over here and over there. *Educational and Child Psychology*. 14 (1): 10–20.

Rose, H. and Rose, S. 2001. Much ado about very little. *The Psychologist*. 14 (3): 428–9.

Rose, S. 2001. DNA is important – but only in its proper place. *The Psychologist*. 14 (3): 144–5.

Rosenzweig, M.R. 1996. Aspects of the search for neural mechanisms of memory. *Annual Review of Psychology*. 47: 1–32.

Sameroff, A.J. 1983. Developmental systems: contexts and evolution. In W. Kessen (ed.), *Handbook of child psychology. History, theory and methods*. Vol. 1. New York: Wiley, 237–94.

Scarr, S. 1992. Developmental theories for the 1990s: development and individual differences. *Child Development*. 63: 1–19.

Schmutz, J. *et al.* 2004. Quality assessment of the human genome sequence. *Nature*. 429 (6,990): 365–8.

Searight, H.R. and McLaren, A.L. 1998. Attention-deficit hyperactivity disorder: the medicalization of misbehavior. *Journal of Clinical Psychology in Medical Settings*. 5 (4): 467–95.

Segal, L. 2001. Main agendas and hidden agendas. *The Psychologist*. 14 (8): 422–3.

Sluckin, W. 1970. *Early learning in man and animal*. London: Allen and Unwin.

Smith, M.S. 1987. Evolution and developmental psychology: toward a sociobiology of human development. In C. Crawford, M. Smith and D. Krebs (eds), *Sociobiology and psychology: ideas, issues and applications*. Hillsdale, NJ: Erlbaum, 225–52.

Snowling, M. 2000. *Dyslexia*. Second edn. Oxford: Blackwell.

Tate, C.C. 2013. Addressing conceptual confusions about evolutionary theorizing: how and why evolutionary psychology and feminism do not oppose each other. *Sex Roles*. 69: 491–502.

Tees, R.C. 1986. Experience and visual development: behavioral evidence. In W.T. Greenough and J.M. Juraska (eds), *Developmental neurobiology*. New York: Academic Press, 317–61.

Timimi, S. and 33 co-endorsers. 2004. A critique of the international consensus statement on ADHD. *Clinical Child and Family Psychology Review*. 7: 59–63.

Tinbergen, N. 1973. *The animal in its world: explorations of an ethologist, 1932–1972*. Vols 1 and 2. Cambridge, MA: Harvard University Press.

Van der Molen, M.W. and Ridderinkhof, K.R. 1998. The growing and aging brain: life-span changes in brain and cognitive functioning. In A. Demetriou, W. Doise and C. van Lieshout (eds), *Lifespan developmental psychology*. Chichester: Wiley, 35–100.

Visser, S., Danielson, M., Bitsko, R., Holbrook, J., Kogan, M., Ghandour, R., Perou, R. and Blumberg, S. 2014. Trends in the parent-report of health care provider-diagnosed and medicated attention-deficit/hyperactivity disorder: United States, 2003–2011. *Journal of the American Academy of Child and Adolescent Psychiatry*. 53: 34–46.

Volk, A.A., Camilleri, J.A., Dane, A.V. and Marini, Z.A. 2012. Is adolescent bullying an evolutionary adaptation? *Aggressive Behavior*. 38: 222–38.

Vreeke, G.J. 2000. Nature, nurture and the future of the analysis of variance. *Human Development*. 43: 32–45.

Waddington, C.H. 1942. Canalization of development and the inheritance of acquired characters. *Nature*. 150: 563–5.

Weaver, I.C. *et al.* 2004. Epigenetic programming by maternal behavior. *Nature Neuroscience*. 7: 847–54.

Wells, A. 2000. Subtle interplay (book review). *The Psychologist*. 13 (12): 624–5.

Westall, C. and Shute, R. 1992. OKN asymmetries in orthoptic patients: contributing factors and effects of treatment. *Behavioural Brain Research*. 49: 77–84.

Wilson, E.O. 1975. *Sociobiology: the new synthesis*. Cambridge, MA: Harvard University Press.

3

A RAINBOW IS MORE THAN THE SUM OF ITS COLOURS

Beginnings of organicism

Introduction

Organicism draws upon the image of the growing organism whose development is significantly shaped by mutual influence and the patterning of its parts (Pepper, 1942). It is not the uniqueness of the individual child, but the universal features of children that are important. Theories in this tradition emphasize internal regulation and organization, and the ability of the organism to organize and reorganize itself at different levels.

Organismic theorists have addressed a number of different features underpinning development. First, children generally share some common features in relation to behaviours and capabilities; for example, children crawl before they walk. One of the principles of organicism is that the properties at one level of complexity (for instance, tissues) cannot be ascribed directly to their component parts but arise only because of the interactions among them, giving rise to *emergent properties*. Emergence can be considered as the spontaneous occurrence of something new as a result of the dynamics of the system. Second, there is commonality in the timing of the emergence of behaviours and abilities; for example, children generally start to crawl at around the same time. Third, while deviations from the general path of development may occur, they tend to be short-lived. Fourth, new abilities and capabilities of quite a different nature emerge out of early behaviours; thus, walking is a very different activity from crawling.

The organismic tradition has drawn heavily upon biological writings, including evolutionary theory (see Chapters 2 and 13). Human development is conceptualized in terms of the interaction between genetic maturation and experience. Development unfolds according to a purpose or design – a teleological view – and is frequently conceptualized in terms of discontinuous stages. Human beings are understood to be relatively active in seeking out and responding to a more or less passive environment. Generally, organismic theories espouse the idea that the organism is different from the sum of its parts, and the structural arrangement of the parts is quite significant.

The nature of organismic thinking is better understood in the light of some historically influential ideas. We will outline these before considering the views of a number of early organismic theorists.

Background ideas in Ancient Greek philosophy

Many central questions concerning child development theories are deeply rooted in philosophy. Of particular relevance for this chapter are vitalism and organicism, which we can contrast with atomism.

Vitalism proposed that the processes of life are not explicable by the laws of physics and chemistry alone and that life is in some part self-determining. Aristotle (384–322 BCE) argued that if there is something distinctive about living entities it resides in the 'soul', which all living things (as opposed to non-living things) possess. What is particular about human beings is the rational part of the soul enabling us to think as we behave. To understand life, Aristotle held that we have to understand purposefulness and we cannot understand the nature of parts without reference to the whole. He argued that wisdom is the understanding of the 'why of things', and to understand purposefulness he identified several kinds of cause, including final, or teleological, ones. These have two underpinning features: they explain things in terms of their ends and not their beginnings; and they incorporate the notion of 'goodness'. An activity is therefore understood by reference to its end point, which is considered to be beneficial (or not) for the agent whose activity is to be explained.

A reading of Greek philosophy also identifies organicism as an underlying theme: that the universe is alive and functions in an orderly manner. Plato's *Timaeus* describes the world (*kosmos*) as a living being created by the 'demiurge' (*ho demiourgos*), who follows an 'eternal pattern'. One important aspect of organicism is to see a fundamental unity in all things – to see beneath all diversity an unchanging one-ness. Another aspect is to see the whole as somehow different from its constituent elements. Following the Greek Stoic philosophers, the Roman emperor Marcus Aurelius captured the essence of organicism:

> What happens next is always intimately related to what went before. It is not a question of merely adding up disparate things connected by inevitable succession, but events are logically interdependent. Just as the realities are established in tune with one another, so in the world of sense, phenomena do not occur merely in succession, but they display an amazing affinity with one another.
>
> *(Marcus Aurelius, c. CE 167, in Collier, 1904: Book IV, 45)*

As a contrast, we can turn to atomism. Democritus, born around 460 BCE, argued that the universe is populated by two kinds of things: atoms and void. He considered atoms to be infinite in number, solid, indivisible and of varied shape. The objects of the world come into being through collision of the atoms in the void. Derived from this belief is the idea that the universe is divisible into simple and similar particles and that all wholes (forms) are fundamentally made up of these particles. The different concrete wholes, such as rocks, trees, planets and air, are simply different configurations of these particles; and change in a whole object, such as the growth of a rose from seed to flower, is the result of changes in the configuration of particles. This is the antithesis of organicism; its modern-day manifestation is mechanism, and – in psychology – behaviourism (see Chapter 6).

Background ideas from the nineteenth and twentieth centuries

Prompted by the thinking of the German scientists Kurt Koffka (1925) and Wolfgang Köhler (1927), Gestalt psychology holds that the whole experience of a person is more than just the sum of its parts: it is a phenomenon in its own right. The Gestaltists pointed out, for example, that red, green and blue light combine to produce white, but experiencing these colours is not the same as experiencing white. From his famous experiments with apes, Köhler (1927) argued that animals and humans learn through 'insight' (and not just through trial and error, as maintained by behaviourists). That is, in Köhler's terms there is a tendency to focus on the relationships between parts and not just the parts themselves. Gestaltists argued for the study of relationships, form and pattern, and were vehemently opposed to the reductionist claims of physiological psychology and the 'structuralist' psychology of Edward B. Titchener. This claimed that mental experiences could be analysed into elementary units, such as sensations, feelings and thoughts, and if we could only objectively examine our experience we would discover that what come to the forefront are sensations (strong), images (fainter than sensations) and affect. Gestaltists, by contrast, argued that the basic units of consciousness are 'things', not sensations: thus, we see cars and people and buildings because of our innate perceptual equipment; we do not construct them from sensations, images and affects and behaviourist 'laws of association' (see Chapter 6).

Another influence on organismic theorizing was 'functionalism', a school of thought founded by leading US psychologist William James (1890/1950). James was severely critical of structuralism (behaviourism) because he considered its outlook on human behaviour as narrow and artificial. He had been influenced by the thinking of Charles Darwin, who emphasized, through the mechanism of natural selection, the functional nature of the characteristics of animals. James argued that human consciousness similarly had a function, namely to enable people to make rational choices. Through the 1940s, the views and research of a number of psychologists belonging to the functionalist school (e.g. Ames, 1951) gained attention. Adelbert Ames experimented with striking visual illusions such as the Ames room (Figure 3.1), which tricks the human visual system into misapplying shape and size constancy. Perception is therefore seen to occur as a result of the relationship between the observing person and the observed object. Context is the critical functional factor in helping us to interpret the world around us. Ames and other functionalists argued against the idea that we can ever know anything as it 'really is': we can know things only in their relationship to us.

The work of US psychologist Eleanor J. Gibson (1910–2002) also provides some key concepts that will broaden our understanding of organismic theories of cognitive development. Gibson is well known for her elegant experimental

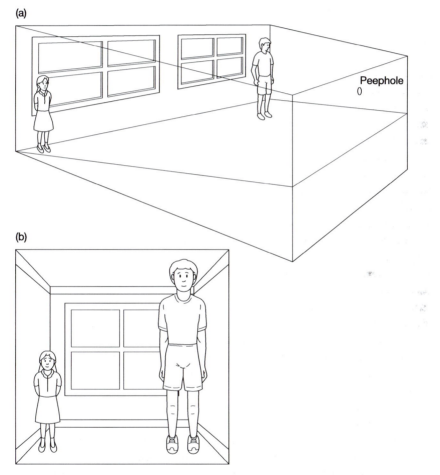

FIGURE 3.1 The visual illusion of the Ames room (adapted from Slee, 2002)
Because the left-hand corner of the room shown in (a) is almost twice as far away from the viewer as the right-hand corner, the girl standing in the left-hand corner projects a smaller retinal image than the boy in the right, even though both figures are the same height in reality. When viewing the room through a peephole (b), we assume that we are looking at a normal room and that both children are the same distance: hence the illusion of the impossibly different relative sizes of the children.

studies examining perception, such as the 'visual cliff' studies (Gibson and Walk, 1960). This experiment with infants tested whether depth perception is innate or learned. Another classic experiment conducted by Gibson and her husband James Gibson (Gibson and Gibson, 1955) provided a foundation for the introduction of a different way to understand learning. Study participants had the opportunity to compare and contrast a series of graphic 'scribbles' against a standard 'scribble'. Viewers became aware of variations in the nature of the scribbles, their performance improving with the number of trials allowed. Unlike the learning described in Chapter 6, which is seen to involve the forming of associations, the Gibsons' research suggested that the simple opportunity to improve perception permitted learning. Furthermore, there was no reinforcement, as behaviourism demands (Pick, 1992). An important concept for the Gibsons was 'differentiation': 'Our perception improves because we come to detect or differentiate more of the aspects, features, and nuances of the tremendously complex stimulation that impinges upon us' (Pick, 1992: 788).

Another central element was 'affordance'. James Gibson (1979) applied this term to the particular perceptual arrangements an organism possesses, such that the properties of any sensed object are perceived so as to optimize the species' survival. Thus, how objects are perceived depends on their meaning to the organism (Johansson et al., 1980). Box 3.1 addresses the child's search for meaning in stories.

BOX 3.1 THE CHILD'S SEARCH FOR MEANING IN STORIES

The idea that perception involves 'meaning-making' was an important element of Eleanor Gibson's thinking and research. This idea is well demonstrated in the process by which children learn to read. One challenge faced by the various theories is their ability to explain the very rapid growth in word learning such that, by six years of age, an English-speaking child will have a vocabulary of approximately 6,000 words (Anglin, 1993). It appears that direct teaching cannot easily account for such a rapid rate of word acquisition, so attention has been given to the means by which children learn words incidentally from their environment. Research (e.g. Wasik and Bond, 2001) suggests there is a positive correlation between reading storybooks to children and vocabulary development. Furthermore, a more interactive adult storybook reading style, using open-ended questions and praise, can positively influence language development. Research by Monique Sénéchal (1997) indicates that pre-school children make more gains in vocabulary after repeated readings of a storybook than after a single reading. Repeated exposure to the storyline and pictures appears to facilitate their memory search for novel labels. Sénéchal (1997) and Barbara Wasik and Mary Bond (2001) also found that asking labelling questions during repeated readings of a book was a very powerful means for encouraging the acquisition of expressive language.

Another prominent thinker influencing later versions of organicism was the biologist Ludwig von Bertalanffy. Psychology in the first half of the twentieth century was dominated by a positivistic-mechanistic-reductionistic approach, epitomized as the 'robot model of man' (von Bertalanffy, 1968: 5–6). Von Bertalanffy was particularly interested in the application of systems theory to biological processes. He defined a system as a 'complex of interacting elements' (von Bertalanffy, 1968: 55). He was particularly interested in the relationship between parts and whole. An important contribution that he made was to identify 'open' and 'closed' systems. A closed system has no interaction with the surrounding environment (such as a chemical reaction in a closed container). An open system (such as a family) is one that interacts with the surrounding environment. Systems theory is a twentieth-century scientific paradigm that has been used in conjunction with physical, biological and social systems (Minuchin, 1985) (see Chapters 4 and 10).

We now turn to a number of prominent early theories that highlighted the 'stage-like' aspect of development that characterizes organicism, beginning with the work of Stanley Hall.

G. Stanley Hall (1844–1924) and adolescence

Hall was born in a small Massachusetts town in the USA. He became a seminarian, later studying theology and philosophy in Europe. In 1884 Hall was appointed as professor in psychology and pedagogy at Johns Hopkins University. Underpinning his psychology was a profound religious belief:

> The Bible is being slowly re-revealed as man's great text-book in psychology, – dealing with him as a whole, his body, mind, and will, in all the larger relations to nature, society, – which has been so misappreciated simply because it is so deeply divine.
>
> *(Hall, 1885: 239)*

After moving to Clark University, Massachusetts, Hall focused on the use of questionnaires to gather data in a broad range of areas, but he is probably best known for his writings regarding adolescent development. Under Darwinian influence, Hall developed a social-biological framework to explain human development. An important idea was 'recapitulation', drawing upon the work of Ernst Haeckel (1874), who argued that an embryo's ontogenetic progression mirrored phylogenetic history – the evolution of its species. Parenthetically, it is interesting that the British philosopher Herbert Spencer (1820–1903) also adopted the concept of evolution, advocating the idea that there takes place in the universe a continuous redistribution of matter and motion; evolution occurs when the integration of matter and motion are predominant, and devolution when the opposite occurs. Spencer had interpreted Darwin's theory to mean survival of the strongest individuals, although Darwin argued for *species*, not *individual*, survival. Spencer's 'social Darwinism' has been interpreted as justifying the use of force in the struggle for existence, but this was not the underlying feature of Darwin's theory. Hall's interpretation differed from that of Spencer: he argued that during childhood and until adolescence the child repeats through play and fear the evolution of human society, while environmental factors come to have a greater influence at adolescence (Hall, 1904).

In 1891 Hall initiated his child development research at Clark University (White, 1992) and produced *The Content of Children's Minds on Entering School* (1893), establishing a tradition for measuring and observing children and summarizing findings in terms of age-based averages. Normative descriptive investigations were used to highlight similarities and differences in development. White noted that Hall's two-volume *Adolescence: Its Psychology and its Relations to Physiology, Anthropology, Sociology, Sex, Crime, Religion and Education* (1904) went largely unread by the 1990s. The volumes were most often noted for popularizing views on three issues: recapitulation; the idea that adolescence is a time of 'storm and stress' (*Sturm und Drang*); and the claim for the twentieth century's invention of 'adolescence'.

The term adolescence is derived from the Latin *adolescere*, which means 'to grow up' or 'to grow to maturity'. John and Virginia Demos argued that 'the concept of adolescence, as generally understood and applied, did not exist before the last two decades of the nineteenth century' (Demos and Demos, 1969: 273), indicating that it was Hall's writing that promoted this view. The change, storm and stress in adolescence, as seen by Hall, are characterized by:

> lack of emotional steadiness, violent impulses, unreasonable conduct, lack of enthusiasm and sympathy ... previous selfhood is broken up ... and a new individual is in the process of being born. All is solvent, plastic, peculiarly susceptible to external influences.
>
> *(Hall, 1904: 26)*

However, examination of some early writings indicates that, in fact, the idea commonly attributed to Hall – that adolescence is a time of change – is not at all new. Early writers noted the impetuosity of youth. Eighth-century BCE Greek poet Hesiod's opinion would not be out of place today:

> I can see no hope for the future of our people if they are dependent on the frivolous youth of today for certainly all youth are reckless beyond words ... When I was a boy, we were taught to be discreet and respectful of elders, but the present youth are exceedingly wise and impatient of restraint.
>
> *(Hesiod, eighth century BCE, available online)*

Aristotle noted that:

> The young are in character prone to desire and ready to carry any desire they may have formed into action. Of bodily desires it is the sexual to which they are most disposed to give way, and in regard to sexual desire they exercise no self restraint. They are changeful too and fickle in their desires, which are

transitory as they are vehement: for their wishes are keen without being permanent ... They are passionate, irascible, and apt to be carried away by their impulses.

(quoted in Demos and Demos, 1969: 633)

Novelists have been particularly adept at picking up on the 'storm and stress' of adolescence, and such references certainly predate Hall. Claudio Violato and Arthur Wiley (1990) reviewed the images of adolescence in English literature through the ages from Geoffrey Chaucer (1342–1400) to Charles Dickens (1812–1870). They concluded that, in the main, literary works portray adolescence as 'a time of turbulence, excess and passion, which is consonant with Hall's (1904) depictions' (Violato and Wiley, 1990: 263). For example, in Shakespeare's *Romeo and Juliet*, the impetuous, passionate nature of youth is shown in the rapid betrothal of Romeo and Juliet and their respective suicides upon believing each other dead. The heightened sensitivity of adolescents is also vividly portrayed in the popular fiction writing of Sue Townsend in *The Secret Diary of Adrian Mole Aged 13¾*, still popular with schools:

The spot on my chin is getting bigger. It's my mother's fault for not having known about vitamins. I pointed out to my mother that I hadn't had my vitamin C today. She said 'Go buy an orange'. So typical! Nigel came around

---

BOX 3.2 ADOLESCENT STORM AND STRESS – MYTH OR FACT?

As a trained secondary school history teacher, one of us (PS) has a particular interest in the concept of 'storm and stress' as part of adolescence! The perception that adolescence is a particularly troubled time in the lifespan has a long history. Aristotle and Jean-Jacques Rousseau commented on the idea of the 'troubled adolescent' period and Gerald Stanley Hall promoted the idea particularly strongly. Jeffrey Arnett (1999) reviewed the evidence and concluded that there was evidence for a modified 'storm and stress' view in relation to the areas of conflict with parents, moodiness and increased risk-taking behaviour. Arnett concluded that this was less evident in more traditional cultures, and hypothesized that in mainstream western cultures it was associated with globalization and in an increased emphasis on individualism. Allyn Hines and Sharon Paulson (2006) compared parental and teacher views of adolescent storm and stress. Their findings indicated that while both held views consistent with the idea of adolescence as a particularly troubled time, teachers held these views most strongly. They concluded that stereotypical beliefs regarding adolescence are maintained in western cultures, which in turn may be associated with parenting and teacher practice.

today. He hasn't got a single spot yet. My grandma came by today. She squeezed my pimple. It has made it worse. I will go to the doctors on Saturday if the spot is still there. I can't live like this with everybody staring.

(Townsend, 1982: 21)

Nancy Galambos and Bonnie Leadbeater (2000), in a review of trends in adolescent research, have noted an ongoing tendency to think of adolescence in terms of risks and opportunities. 'Challenges' concern adolescents' engagement in risky behaviours, and issues with poverty, homelessness and unemployment (Baumgartner *et al.*, 2010). Young people take more risks than children or adults do, but understanding the reasons for this is not straightforward (Slee *et al.*, 2012). Despite the popular conception of adolescence as a period of *Sturm und Drang*, the validity of this idea is still questioned (Box 3.2).

Heinz Werner (1890–1964) and the orthogenetic principle

Werner arrived from Germany to teach at Clark University some 50 years after Hall had begun his work there. Werner published in a diverse range of areas and was 'a very modern thinker whose theoretical views were so at variance with normal professional practices that his message is yet to be heard' (Glick, 1992: 558). While the work of his contemporaries, such as Jean Piaget and Lev Vygotsky, continues to be evaluated and interpreted (see Chapters 4 and 7), the writings of Werner have largely been overlooked.

Werner's views of development were influenced by Gestalt psychology and, more narrowly, by a particular school of Gestalt thinking emphasizing the 'developmental process of formation' (Glick, 1992: 559). Werner, with his strong background in biology and anthropology, argued that development was directional, underpinned by a basic survival drive and a desire to 'know'. While Werner shared an interest with Piaget in providing 'a developmental account of the a priori' (Glick, 1992: 559), he was more concerned with identifying growth principles or directions than with describing or discovering the nature of stages.

Werner elaborated his 'orthogenetic principle' in 1948 as follows: 'Man, destined to conquer the world through knowing, starts out with confusion, disorientation, and chaos, which he struggles to overcome . . .' (Werner and Kaplan, 1963: 5). While Werner's outlook in some ways reflects Hall's recapitulation theory and the views of earlier philosophers such as Spencer, suggesting a move from a primitive to an advanced state, his theorizing was more sophisticated in many ways. He saw some 'directiveness' associated with development; the organism is motivated by a drive to survive and master his or her fate, such that there is a movement towards ever greater differentiation. His research into human perception led him to conclude: 'We assume that organisms are naturally directed toward a series of transformations – reflecting a tendency to move from a state of relative globality and undifferenti-atedness towards states of increasing differentiation and hierarchic integration' (Werner and Kaplan, 1963: 7). The orthogenetic principle refers to establishing the correct ('ortho') development ('genetic') in both physical and psychological development. The orthogenetic principle 'has radical implications that served to make Wernerian psychology fundamentally different from other developmental views' (Glick, 1992: 560). Significantly, it resulted in greater confusion regarding the topic of study because, as Glick noted, Werner did not begin with a topic of development such as language, but rather focused on the entity of development itself.

Hierarchical integration captures the increasing organization, or 'articulation' of responses and skills; for example, a baby's development of eating skills. First, the baby needs to be able to sit and focus on the food. As the child develops there is a move from the 'syncretic' (global) to the discrete as the child is increasingly able to separate out the various components. Thus, perception is combined with physical reaching skills to grasp a biscuit (cookie) and then bring it to the mouth. Two further orthogenetic principles were that of development moving from a state of rigidity to greater flexibility in order to influence the environment (as when the older child is able to reach inside a box of biscuits) and that of 'stability' such that the older child can concentrate for ever longer periods.

There is some confusion regarding the status of Werner's theory, which may be better understood as a 'grand scale' theory (Glick, 1992). In this regard, it is not unlike dynamic systems theory, which also focuses on developmental processes in general rather than specific areas of development (see Chapter 10).

Arnold Lucius Gesell (1880–1961) and maturation

Gesell is a very significant figure in the history of developmental psychology. Having trained under Hall at Clark University, Gesell (1946) went on to use innovative film techniques to chart the course of normal human development.

Gesell was relieved to find Darwinian views of development superseding theological ideas such as original sin, thus rescuing children from 'gloomier ideas of fixity and fate' (Thelen and Adolph, 1992: 369). Drawing on Darwin's emphasis upon the maturational component of development (Darwin, 1888/1959), Gesell did much to advance the charting of the growth of children.

Working during the early twentieth century, Gesell embarked on the task of mapping the foetal, infant and early childhood behaviour of thousands of children. In the course of his work he established and standardized stages of development. His maturational view emphasized the natural unfolding of patterns of growth, which he believed was largely predetermined and self-regulated. His theory emphasized the 'lawfulness' of growth and consequently the ability to predict: 'Behavior is rooted in the brain and in the sensory and motor systems. The timing, smoothness and integration at one stage foretell behavior at a later age' (Gesell, cited in Knobloch and Pasamanick, 1974: 3). Gesell was well aware, however, of the multitude of factors impinging on a child and making accurate prediction a risky venture.

Gesell identified the following four major fields of behaviour.

- *Adaptive.* The most important field concerns the organizational component of behaviour, such as coordinating eye movements and reaching with the hand. Adaptive behaviour is the forerunner of later intelligence.
- *Gross and fine motor.* This includes sitting, standing, walking, using fingers and manipulating objects.
- *Language.* Gesell maintained that language also assumes distinct behaviour patterns and unfolds in a predetermined fashion, e.g. inarticulate vocalizations precede words.
- *Personal and social.* This incorporates the reaction of children to their social world. However, according to Gesell, personal and social behaviour are determined by intrinsic growth patterns. Thus, while toileting is a cultural requirement shaped by social demands, the child's attainment of bladder and bowel control depends upon neuro-motor maturation.

According to Gesell, then, 'a child's development proceeds stage by stage in orderly sequence, each stage representing a degree or level of maturity' (cited in Knobloch and Pasamanick, 1974: 7). The view that body growth is strongly influenced by physical maturation is widely accepted (but see our discussion of dynamic systems theory in Chapter 10). However, the assertion that other important aspects of human development, such as personality, are similarly determined still attracts criticism. Esther Thelen and Karen Adolph (1992) conclude their overview of Gesell's work by acknowledging his lasting contribution to developmental theory, while noting the contradictions – for example, in his emphasizing the importance of genetics in determining development while at the same time recognizing the importance of the environment.

Gesell was an extraordinary 'stage' theorist: 'Who before or since has had the tenacity to describe 58 stages of pellet behavior, 53 stages of rattle behavior, and so on …?' (Thelen and Adolph, 1992: 376). Gesell's maturational approach fell out of favour with the rise of Piaget, behaviourism and information-processing theories, but he probably laid the groundwork for the acceptance of Piaget's stage theory. The maturational approach is still apparent in clinical work with young children, where scales of developmental norms, based on work that Nancy Bayley began in the 1920s, continue to be used. For example, the Australian Council for Educational Research (ACER) publishes the Conners Developmental Milestones Scales (Conners, 2009) which, in the parent-completed version, provides an assessment of a young child's adaptive, communication and motor skills, play and pre-academic/cognitive skills.

Robert Havighurst (1900–1991) and developmental tasks

Another theorist who has made an important, if underrated, contribution to our contemporary understanding of child and adolescent development is Robert Havighurst. He described development in terms of 'developmental tasks', or 'those things that constitute healthy and satisfactory growth in our society' (Havighurst, 1953: 2). In his view, development is not one long slow uphill climb, but consists of steep gradients, where learning is difficult, and plateaus. One example is a child who must work hard to master the art of catching a ball, but who, having mastered the skill, can then 'coast' for years. Havighurst's theory addressed children's cognitive and other aspects of development. His views provide some contrast to cognitive-developmental and information-processing theories.

A question often asked of teachers or psychologists by parents, is 'How well is my child doing?' This is often answered in relation to developmental tasks. Evaluations generally reflect expectations based on pooled knowledge about child development that is transmitted from one generation to the next (Slee *et al.*, 2012). The expectations and concerns are often reflected in popular culture, such as the milestones provided in child-rearing books. Havighurst explained developmental tasks thus:

> A developmental task is a task which arises at or about a certain period in the life of the individual, successful achievement of which leads to happiness and to success with later tasks, while failure leads to unhappiness in the individual, disapproval by society, and difficulty with later tasks.
>
> *(Havighurst, 1953: 2)*

Havighurst proposed that three forces set up certain developmental tasks for the individual.

- The biology of the individual, involving physical maturation, such as learning to walk or learning to relate to the opposite sex during adolescence.
- Cultural forces, such as learning to read and write.
- The personal values and aspirations of the individual, such as aspiring to become a doctor or engineer.

He identified nine key tasks to be accomplished during early childhood, such as learning to walk, to eat solid food and to distinguish right from wrong. Nine tasks for middle childhood include learning the physical skills to play ordinary games and achieve personal independence. Havighurst identified ten developmental tasks during adolescence, including achieving mature relations with the opposite sex, achieving some economic independence and selecting and preparing for an occupation.

In a later development of Havighurst's theory, Robert Selverstone (1989) proposed that the ten developmental tasks during adolescence may be clustered into four main categories.

- *Identity.* This involves the determination of the question 'Who am I?'
- *Connectedness.* This includes establishing relationships with peers.
- *Power.* This concerns the development of a sense of control and power.
- *Hope/joy.* This is achieved via the accomplishment of the previous three tasks.

According to Havighurst (1953), there is a right, or opportune, moment for teaching or developing a task. He also adopted a broad outlook about the nature of tasks, believing that they extend beyond the individual to the cultural-historical context in which the individual is developing. Hence, his was not a universalist theory. This has enabled the notion of developmental tasks to be culturally adapted to Africa, with tasks being aimed at the child's systematic social integration there (Nsamenang, 2005).

At this point it is worthwhile revisiting the usefulness and validity of the concept of developmental stages such as 'adolescence' or 'youth'. As discussed earlier, organicism emphasizes the stages that help us identify and appreciate the nature of the challenges facing us as we grow and develop. However, alternatives to simple linear classification of the developmental process identified by normative transitions have been raised. For example, Johanna Wyn and Rob White emphasized that:

> the focus on youth is not on the inherent characteristics of young people themselves, but on the construction of youth through social processes (such as schooling, families or the labor market). Young people engage with these institutions in specific ways, in relation to historical circumstances.
>
> *(Wyn and White, 1997: 9)*

Thus, for example, historians such as Robert Enright and colleagues (1987) have specifically argued that adolescence is a life stage created to meet the demands of industry for a skilled labour force. Furthermore, the notion of developmental tasks has been criticized as being merely descriptive. However, overall, it provides a means of understanding human development in a way that reflects a popular understanding: at particular times in our lives, we must address important developmental issues, and how effectively we fulfil these tasks has implications for current and future functioning.

Conclusions

In this chapter we have provided some important background to the root metaphor identified as 'organicism' (Pepper, 1942). The basic metaphor is 'the organism, the living, organized system presented to experience in multiple forms' (Reese and Overton, 1972: 132). Organicism has a long history, as reflected in the earliest writings of Greek philosophers about concepts such as vitalism, though this idea of a 'vital force' is contentious: Jane Maienschein (1991) noted that, despite the admirable sentiment of organicism and its concern with the organism as a whole, it has come to be associated with somewhat fuzzy thinking and serious questioning regarding what constitutes the 'life-force' or 'soul' of vitalism.

The emergence of new phenomena at each new level of organization that are not commensurate with a reduction to a lower level of organization is a feature of organicism. Richard Lerner referred to the idea of 'epigenetic viewpoint', which:

denotes that at each higher level of complexity there emerges a new characteristic, one that simply was not present at the lower organizational level and thus whose presence is what establishes a new level as just that – a stage of organization qualitatively different from a preceding one.

(Lerner, 1983: 53)

To that end, organismic theorists would generally agree with the Gestalt position. Moreover, the whole is not only greater but 'different' in the sense that when one is experiencing a rainbow one is experiencing more than the sum of the various colours. Lerner (1983) has summarized the organicist outlook as comprising viewpoints that are:

- epigenetic;
- antireductionist;
- qualitative;
- discontinuous;
- multiple and interactionist in nature.

The organicist outlook also emphasizes that the individual's world moves through increasing levels of integration, that individuals are agents in constructing their reality and that there is some structural interdependence to the parts of development. A key feature concerns the universal features of human development, although Havighurst introduced a cultural-historical note. The notion of 'emergent properties' is not uncontested either, as it creates difficulty for the more deterministic organicists. In the following chapter we continue to pursue the organicism metaphor in considering constructivist theories of development.

References

Ames, A. 1951. Visual perception and the rotating trapezoidal window. *Psychological Monographs*. 65 (7): 234.

Anglin, J.M. 1993. Vocabulary development: a morphological analysis. *Monograph of the Society for Research in Child Development*. 58: 10.

Arnett, J.J. 1999. Adolescent storm and stress reconsidered. *American Psychologist*. 54 (5): 323–76.

Baumgartner, S., Valkenberg, P.M. and Jochen, P. 2010. Unwanted online sexual solicitation and risky sexual online behavior across the lifespan. *Journal of Applied Developmental Psychology*. 31: 439–47.

Collier, J. 1904. *The meditations of Marcus Aurelius*. London: The Walter Scott Publishing Company.

Conners, K. 2009. *Developmental milestones – parent scales*. Toronto: Multi-Health Systems.

Darwin, C. 1888/1959. *The life and letters of Charles Darwin*. Vol. 2. New York: Basic Books.

Demos, J. and Demos, V. 1969. Adolescence in historical perspective. *Journal of Marriage and Family*. 31: 632–8.

Enright, R.D., Levy, V.M., Harris, D. and Lapsley, D.K. 1987. Do economic conditions influence how theorists view adolescents? *Journal of Youth and Adolescence*. 16: 541–59.

Galambos, N.L. and Leadbeater, B.J. 2000. Trends in adolescent research for the new millenium. *International Journal of Behavioral Development.* 24: 289–94.

Gesell, A. 1946. The ontogenesis of infant behavior. In L. Carmichael (ed.), *Manual of child psychology.* New York: McGraw-Hill, 295–331.

Gibson, E.J. and Walk, R.D. 1960. The 'visual cliff'. *Scientific American.* 202: 64–71.

Gibson J.J. 1979. *The ecological approach to visual perception.* Boston: Houghton-Mifflin.

Gibson, J.J. and Gibson, E.J. 1955. Perceptual learning: differentiation or enrichment? *Psychological Review.* 62: 32–41.

Glick, J.A. 1992. Werner's relevance for contemporary developmental psychology. *Developmental Psychology.* 28: 558–65.

Hall, G.S. 1885. The new psychology. *Andover Review.* 3: 239–48.

Hall G.S. 1893. *The content of children's minds on entering school.* New York: Kellogg.

Hall, G.S. 1904. *Adolescence: its psychology and its relations to physiology, anthropology, sociology, sex, crime, religion and education.* Vols 1 and 2. New York: Appleton-Century-Crofts.

Haeckel, E. 1874. *The evolution of man. A popular exposition of the principal points of human ontogeny and phylogeny.* 2 vols. New York: AI Fowler.

Havighurst, R.J. 1953. *Human development and education.* New York: Longman.

Hesiod. Eighth century BCE. www.byrdseed.com/quote-problems-of-youth/. Accessed 27 June 2014.

Hines, A.R. and Paulson, S.E. 2006. Parents' and teachers' perceptions of adolescent storm and stress relations. *Adolescence.* 41 (164): 597–614.

James, W. 1890/1950. *The principles of psychology.* Vol. 1. New York: Dover.

Johansson, G., von Hofsten, C. and Jansson, G. 1980. Event perception. *Annual Review of Psychology.* 31: 27–63.

Knobloch, H. and Pasamanick, B. 1974. *Gesell and Amatruda's Developmental Diagnosis: the evaluation and management of normal and abnormal neuropsychologic development in infancy and early childhood.* New York: Harper and Row.

Koffka, K. 1925. *The growth of mind.* New York: Harcourt Brace and World.

Köhler, W. 1927. *The mentality of apes.* London: Routledge & Kegan Paul.

Lerner, R.M. 1983. *Concepts and theories of human development.* New York: Random House.

Maienschein, J. 1991. Morgan's regeneration, epigenesis, and (w)holism. In C. Dinsmore (ed.), *A history of regeneration research.* New York: Cambridge University Press, 133–49.

Minuchin, P. 1985. Families and individual development: provocations from the field of family therapy. *Child Development.* 56: 289–302.

Nsamenang, A.B. 2005. Human ontogenesis: an Indigenous African view on development and intelligence. *International Journal of Psychology.* April: 1–5.

Pepper, S. 1942. *World hypotheses: a study of evidence.* Berkeley, CA: University of California Press.

Pick, H.L. 1992. Eleanor J. Gibson: Learning to perceive and perceiving to learn. *Developmental Psychology.* 28: 787–94.

Reese, H.W. and Overton, W.F. 1972. On paradigm shifts. *American Psychologist.* 27 (12): 1,197–8.

Selverstone, R. 1989. Adolescent sexuality: developing self-esteem and mastering developmental tasks. SIECUS Report. 18: 1–4.

Sénéchal, M. 1997. The differential effect of storybook reading on pre-schoolers: acquisition of expressive and receptive vocabulary. *Journal of Child Language.* 24: 123–38.

Slee, P.T. 2002. *Child, adolescent and family development.* Second edn. Melbourne: Cambridge University Press.

Slee P.T., Campbell, M. and Spears, B. 2012. *Child, adolescent and family development.* Third edn. Melbourne: Cambridge University Press.

Thelen, E. and Adolph, K.E. 1992. Arnold L. Gesell: the paradox of nature and nurture. *Developmental Psychology*. 28: 368–80.

Townsend, S. 1982. *The secret diary of Adrian Mole aged 13¾*. London: Methuen.

Violato, C. and Wiley, A.J. 1990. Images of adolescence in English literature: the middle ages to the modern period. *Adolescence*. 25: 253–64.

Von Bertalanffy, L. 1968. *General system theory*. New York: George Brazillier.

Wasik, B.A. and Bond, M.A. 2001. Beyond the pages of a book: interactive book reading and language development in preschool classrooms. *Journal of Educational Psychology*. 93 (2): 243–50.

Werner, H. and Kaplan, B. 1963. *Symbol formation*. New York: Wiley.

White, S. 1992. G. Stanley Hall: from philosophy to developmental psychology. *Developmental Psychology*. 28: 25–34.

Wyn, J. and White, R. 1997. *Rethinking youth*. London: Sage.

4

THE CHILD AS PHILOSOPHER

Introduction

In continuing the presentation of theories associated with organicism we introduce the field of thinking broadly referred to as 'constructivism'. Some further background ideas include the philosophical notion of the 'world of ideas', George Kelly's personal construct theory and the psychological construct of 'cognition'. We then address in particular the theoretical contributions of Jean Piaget, Eleanor Maccoby and Jerome Bruner, and also consider the significant contributions that 'connectionism' and 'theory of mind' are making to our theorizing about human development. We also touch upon social cognitive theory and systems thinking, although these are both dealt with in more detail in later chapters.

Background ideas

Karl Popper proposed that the task of philosophy is to enrich our image of the world, arguing that the generally accepted picture involves a variation of mind–body dualism. He suggested that there are, in fact, three worlds:

> The first is the physical world or the world of physical states; the second is the mental world or the world of mental states; and the third is the world of intelligibles, or of *ideas in the objective sense*; it is the world of possible objects of thought: the world of theories in themselves, and their logical relations; of arguments in themselves; and of problem situations in themselves.
>
> *(Popper, 1972: 154, original emphasis)*

In 'World 1' we have physical reality, which we relate to with our five senses. 'World 2' is the inner world of thoughts, feelings and emotions, accessible through introspection. In 'World 3' we have the world that can be examined using the objective methods of logic and mathematics – similar to the Platonic realm of 'Ideas' (see Chapter 6). Writers such as Finn Tonnessen (1999) have argued that cognitive psychology is located in World 3, and in this chapter we will see the emergence of connectionism as reflecting mental structures and models derived from logical and mathematical reasoning.

The 1960s and 1970s were witness to a significant shift towards cognitive psychology. Behaviourism had been the dominant influence in the 1940s and 1950s, particularly in the USA. The early psychologists, including William James and Wilhelm Wundt (Chapter 6), were certainly interested in aspects of cognition, including attention and memory, but the dominance of behaviourism discredited the study of the 'mind'. The behaviourist John Watson confidently wrote that after psychology had accepted behaviourism, psychology could then be equated with the physical sciences: 'The findings of psychology . . . lend themselves to explanation in physico-chemical terms' (Watson, 1913: 177).

Despite Watson's prediction, the mid-twentieth century saw the emergence of a strong interest in cognitive processes, including an increasing interest in children's cognitive development, social cognition and cognitive therapy. Significant influences bearing on this shift included the work of George Kelly and his personal construct theory. Kelly posited two notions: '(1) that viewed in the perspective of the centuries, man might be seen as an incipient scientist, and (2) that each individual man formulates in his own way constructs through which he views the world of events' (Kelly, 1963: 12). This indicated that the personal constructs people hold lead them to understand and explain events in different ways, which in turn leads to different action. Personal construct psychology argued that individuals develop bi-polar dimensions of meaning, used to make sense of experience and anticipate the future. Each person psychologically constructs understandings of self, others and relationships, and continually evaluates whether these constructs effectively account for the world around them. Don Bannister and Fay Fransella (2003) have further elaborated on the application of the theory, including its implications for child development.

Beyond Kelly, methodological advances in the middle of the twentieth century meant that it also became possible to study cognition without resort to introspectionism. For example, a rat bar-pressing in the context of a certain stimulus, such as a green light, would indicate that the subject was attending to the stimulus. All in all, an increasing research effort was directed towards the understanding of cognitive development. Hans Kreitler and Shulamith Kreitler noted rather sceptically that 'the term "cognitive" has been used so widely that one might wonder whether there is anything in psychology that is not cognitive' (Kreitler and Kreitler, 1976: 4). Recognizing the plurality of cognitive science, George Miller presented a vision of a unified field concerned with 'the representational and computational capacities of the human mind and their structural and functional realization in the human brain' (Miller, 2003: 144). A number of the theoretical developments described in this chapter have received significant input from the field of artificial intelligence.

As Allen Newell and Herbert Simon noted, 'There is a growing body of evidence that the elementary information processes used by the human brain in thinking are highly similar to a subset of the elementary information processes that are incorporated in the instruction codes of . . . computers' (Newell and Simon, 1972: 282). In fact, cognitive psychologists have used the metaphor of the computer to compare with cognitive processes, highlighting at the same time the objectivity of their research (Tonnessen, 1999).

Jean Piaget (1897–1980) and cognitive developmental theory

Piaget is one of the most significant figures in twentieth-century developmental psychology. His theory came to prominence as the influence of behaviourism (see Chapter 6) was declining (Halford, 1989). For interested readers, Phillip Slee *et al.* (2012) have described the basic tenets of Piaget's theory in more detail. A number of early major reviews of Piaget's theory were provided by Harry Beilin (1992), Paul van Geert (1998) and John Flavell (1992), while Orlando Lourenço's (2012) reflections are more recent.

Piaget's theory of children's cognitive development was at heart an epistemological one – that is, a theory of how we know what we know. However, as we shall explain later, Piagetian theory also embodies constructivism. This maintains that meaning is constructed in our minds as we interact with the physical, social and emotional world of which we are part, with learning an active process unique to the individual. This is in sharp contrast to objectivist views of the world, which maintain that meaning exists in the world, to be discovered.

David Elkind (1974) identified three main phases in Piaget's theory.

1. From 1922 to 1928, Piaget was concerned with the ideas that children held about the physical world. In working with Alfred Binet on routine intelligence testing, Piaget's attention was caught by children's incorrect answers. Piaget developed and refined his clinical interview technique (*la méthode clinique*) and discovered that children reasoned differently from adults and had literally different philosophies about the nature of the world (Elkind, 1971). Piaget was also concerned with the apparent egocentrism of young children and their frequently observed inability to take in another's perspective.
2. The second period began in 1929, when Piaget undertook the study of children's mental growth, prompted primarily by curiosity about his own children's development (Elkind, 1971). Issues such as object permanence were addressed.
3. From the 1940s, Piaget dealt with children's understanding of concepts such as number, quantity and speed.

Piaget emphasized that children are actively involved in their own development. Some have maintained that Piaget regarded the child as a rather 'solitary' learner but, as we shall see, that understanding is not quite true. The child has a

---

BOX 4.1 HOLE-IN-THE-WALL COMPUTERS: CHILDREN TEACHING THEMSELVES

Children's natural curiosity and drive to experiment on the world has been drawn upon to bring computers and the Internet to children without access to formal education. Physicist Dr Sugata Mitra began his 'minimally invasive education' experiment by placing a hole-in-the-wall computer in a New Delhi street adjoining a slum in 1999. With no direction or assistance from adults, children experimented together and learned to operate the computer. Within days they could create documents, browse the Internet and paint pictures. The egg-timer icon they interpreted as 'Shiva's drum'. The project has been extended across India and to other nations such as Cambodia and Botswana. Further work (Inamdar, 2004) showed that rural children who used hole-in-the-wall computers scored only marginally lower on a Grade 8 computer science examination than children who had learned the material through the regular school curriculum.

---

multitude of ideas about the world, which may be quite different from an adult's understanding. The child in the course of education is always learning and unlearning ideas about the world, such as the concepts of space, time, quantity and number. Finally, 'the child is by nature a knowing creature' and as such 'is trying to construct a world view of his own, and is limited only by his abilities and experience' (Elkind, 1971: 108). For a recent example from India, see Box 4.1.

As described by Carol Honstead (1968), there are two components to Piaget's theory, a stage-independent and a stage-dependent component. In the former, Piaget addressed the issue of how cognitive development proceeds. He listed four factors to account for cognitive development (Honstead, 1968: 135), as follows.

1. *Maturation.* Piaget was a biologist by training and, from a biological perspective, viewed the developing child as maturing. At birth the immaturity of the infant's brain is a factor limiting cognition, but brain development (most rapid before birth) proceeds rapidly in the first two years after birth and continues to some extent for much longer.
2. *Experience.* Piaget argued that experience is of two kinds:
   (a) direct physical experience, such as playing with water and generally using the five senses to experience the world; and
   (b) mathematical experience, which occurs when the child reflects on the structure of experience and particularly on its logical and mathematical structure; according to Jean Piaget and Bärbel Inhelder (1969), logico-mathematical experience comes from the child's acting on the world rather than from the experience itself.

3. *Social transmission.* This least developed part of Piaget's model led some to conclude, as noted earlier, that he viewed children as rather solitary learners. While he certainly emphasized the dialectic between the child and the physical world, he 'included social interaction as a motivator of development, particularly through conflict of ideas between peers' (Meadows, 1986: 108).

4. *Equilibration.* This is probably the most basic of the four factors: it is the process of achieving equilibrium, of finding a balance between things that were previously understood and those that are yet to be understood. A child, encountering something new, actively works at relating it to something he or she knows. As the new object in its turn becomes familiar the child reaches a new level of equilibrium. The child has thus gone through the process of equilibration of self-regulation.

Piaget's theory is well known as a 'stage' theory of development. Four criteria for such theories were described by Inhelder (1975).

1. A period of formation and progressive organization of mental operations.
2. The progressive hierarchical development of one stage upon another.
3. Relative similarity on the attainment of each stage.
4. A directional and hierarchical nature.

As our readers will doubtless be aware, the stage-dependent component of Piaget's theory comprises four major stages, as described below. Each is identified in terms of the child's principal method of knowing.

1. *Sensori-motor period* (0–2 years). The child's primary method of knowing is through the actions he or she performs on the world in terms of the five senses.

2. *Pre-operational period* (3–7 years). The emergence of language, modelling and memory are key features. According to Harry McGurk, 'the child's internal, cognitive representation of the external world is gradually developing and differentiating but many serious limitations are also in evidence' (McGurk, 1975: 36–7). The child's thinking is dominated by perception rather than concepts (McGurk, 1975). For example, children make judgements in terms of how things look to them, not how they actually are. If shown two balls of clay of equal size and weight, and one is then squeezed into a sausage shape, the child is likely to say that the sausage has more clay because it looks longer (i.e. because the child cannot yet 'conserve'). The child's acquisition of language signals the beginning of symbolic thought. Egocentrism is another element of the child's thinking; thus a girl may tell you she has a sister but deny that her sister has a sister.

3. *Concrete operations period* (7–11 years). Children's thinking attains greater flexibility: 'grouping' of ideas comes about; logical deductive reasoning is possible. However, concrete operations are limited in that they are capable of operational groupings only with concrete objects such as blocks, sticks, clay,

liquids and marbles. Logical thought does not yet extend to verbal stimuli (Honstead, 1968: 139).

4. *Formal operations period* (11+ years). This is the final period of cognitive development. 'The hallmark of this stage is the child's ability to reason abstractly without relying upon concrete situations or events' (McGurk, 1975: 39).

Piaget's view of the process of cognitive development is that the individual moves from a less to a more mature level of functioning. The child is actively involved in pursuing information and attempting to understand the world. Piaget's theory has been labelled 'constructivist' (Gelcer and Schwartzbein, 1989) inasmuch as the child actively constructs the external world in acting upon it. Such a view contrasts with behavioural theories that emphasize the child's passivity. From a biological perspective, though, Piaget viewed development as progressive and directional. The invariant feature of his theory emphasized stage-like development, in which the manner of thinking at one level is qualitatively different from that at a later stage. Piaget exemplified the child's changing understanding with the response of Del, aged seven, when posed a question he himself had asked at six: 'It's silly to ask that when it's so easy. It's silly. It doesn't go together. It's so [silly] that I don't understand a word of it' (Piaget, 1959: 223).

A critique of Piaget's theory

Graeme Halford observed that if the 1960s represented a period of optimism regarding the application of Piagetian psychology to understanding children's cognitive development, then the 1970s produced a reassessment resulting in some disillusionment. This can be attributed to research that challenged many of Piaget's assumptions regarding the nature of cognitive development, and to the failure of Piaget's research to reap the anticipated rewards in some applied areas (Halford, 1989). The following represents an overview of some of the major criticisms of Piagetian theory.

A feature of Piaget's experimental method, *la méthode clinique*, was his careful interviewing of the child. His child-centred approach in his earliest work consisted of an open-ended discussion with the child. From an empirical perspective, Piaget's interview technique has been criticized as too subjective and value-laden. Criticism has also been directed at the reliance on verbal introspection of immature minds.

Another trenchant criticism is directed at the sequence of stages and the nature of children's behaviour within them (Gardner, 1979). Major concerns have been expressed that a universal age/stage approach overlooks the part played by individual differences in mental and environmental factors in shaping a child's behaviour.

A further criticism is that Piaget tended to treat other people in the child's life as objects. This neglects the social competence of infants and the role of others as *social partners*, with such partnerships promoting cognitive development (Eibl-Eibesfeldt, 1989; Xu and Kushnir, 2013). This was highlighted by theorists such as Lev Vygotsky (see Chapter 7), and Maccoby and Bruner (see below). Margaret

Donaldson's (1978) work was also influential. Her most famous piece of research, the 'Naughty Teddy' study, showed how children's cognitive performance is influenced by their understanding of the social situation: children who seemed unable to conserve number using the standard procedure (when the experimenter moves the counters out of line) were often able to do so when, instead, a 'naughty teddy' swooped in and messed up the line.

Piaget's theory has been said to fit 'the orderliness of development on a large scale' (Thelen and Smith, 1994: 21). However, Esther Thelen and Linda Smith argued that on a more detailed scale the theory fails to capture the 'complexity and messiness of cognitive development in detail' (Thelen and Smith, 1994: 21–2). In particular, they and others have challenged some central tenets of Piagetian theory, as follows.

1. *Children develop from an impoverished beginning state.* Research suggests that, in fact, the young infant is highly competent. The new view of the infant encompasses the notion of the infant as 'active, competent and in some ways, in control, of his/her own learning' (Trevarthen, 2010: 119).
2. *There are global discontinuities in cognition across stages.* In fact, there is evidence of early precursors to abilities, including advanced abilities of the newborn relating to processing emotional information and speech sounds (Huotilainen, 2010).
3. *Cognitive growth is monolithic.* In fact, there is wide individual variation in development and competences. Outcomes depend on a dynamic interaction between the child and others, including the infants' and caregivers' motivations to engage with and respond to one another (Brinck and Liljenfors, 2013).

Thelen and Smith concluded that 'Cognitive development does not look like a marching band; it looks more like a teeming mob' (Thelen and Smith, 1994: 22). Despite such criticisms, Piaget's theory remains influential educationally and has become one of the best-known theories of child development. It has also triggered much further research, one of the best-known neo-Piagetian theorists being Robbie Case (1998), who combined a Piagetian approach with an information-processing one (see Chapter 6). According to his theory, as the brain develops and schemas become more automatic with practice, working memory capacity increases, allowing more advanced processing of information. Thus, children become able to undertake more complex cognitive tasks. The uneven nature of cognitive development, as noted by Thelen and Smith, is accounted for in this formulation, as practice in one domain more than another would lead to uneven development across domains. See also our discussion about this point in Chapter 2, regarding Annette Karmiloff-Smith's epigenetic approach.

Despite these criticisms, the tremendous contribution of Piaget's theorizing must be acknowledged. Howard Gardner did so in the following terms:

> Whatever its ultimate scientific fate, Piaget's contribution has over the past
> few decades provided a major impetus for research in developmental

psychology. Before Piaget began research into the child's special cognitive and conceptual powers most work consisted of either sheer descriptions of objective features of the child's existence (physical milestones, preferred activities, motoric activities), anecdotal accounts of individual children, including ones displaying unusual abilities or difficulties, or broadly speculative interpretations of the course of growth.

(Gardner, 1979: 73–4)

Lourenço (2012) notes that while Piaget could be considered a figure of the past, his theory and writings continue to inspire developmental thinking. For example, Jaime Dice and Meghan Dove (2011) used Piagetian theory to examine referential behaviour in infants – behaviours generally understood in the social cognitive literature to indicate that infants realize they are sharing attention to an object with another person. A further recent legacy is Fei Xu and Tamar Kushnir's 'rational constructivism'. As they describe it, 'Rational learners integrate prior beliefs, knowledge, and biases with new evidence provided by the environment' (Xu and Kushnir, 2013: 28). In their terms, learning is then seen as rational, inferential and statistical, and they propose that this approach helps to explain why infants learn so quickly.

Connectionism

Connectionism first emerged as a force in the early 1980s and became a significant influence relating to research in language development, categorization and decision-making (Mahoney, 1993). Andy Clark wrote optimistically that connectionism 'promises to be not just one new tool in the cognitive scientist's toolkit but, rather, the catalyst for a more fruitful conception of the whole project of cognitive science' (Clark, 1993: ix). Connectionism is generally identified as a form of cognitive psychology, but there is no doubt that it also has much in common with behaviourism. Thus, neither distinguishes between the cognitive and the biological: 'Both emphasize that learning occurs primarily through changes to the nervous system' (Tonnessen, 1999: 391). Both are also able to explain gradual improvement through drill and repetition, trial and error and gradual adjustment. Where connectionism is linked to information-processing models is explored more fully in Chapter 6. Connectionism is linked to Popper's (1972) 'World 3', in that it is related to mathematical reasoning and the world of logic. The emergence of connectionism was associated with the development of supercomputers, and a number of models have been devised to account for developments in perception and cognition.

Connectionist models have also been influenced significantly by research relating to brain processing structures. Connectionist models, often termed neural networks, attempt to explain how the brain works. At the most basic level, the connectionist network contains many 'simple processing units, interconnected by unidirectional links that transmit activation' (Smith, 1996: 895), and the units are usually assumed to perform some simple computation. Athanassios Protopapas observed that the 'neural network comprises a number of interconnected units, or nodes, each of which is characterized by an activation value' (Protopapas, 1999: 414). As such, it is possible to identify the positive or negative sign of the input or output from a weighted algebraic sum of the units. The learning process is hypothesized to shape the weights on the interconnections among the units.

The description of neural networks in terms of 'units' and 'activation' 'leaves unanswered the question of what a unit represents semantically' (Smith, 1996: 898). A traditional conceptualization of memory invokes the metaphor of a filing cabinet wherein 'storage', 'search' and 'retrieval' represent 'inscriptions' that can be accessed, while connectionist models are very different: 'There is no discrete location for each representation. Instead, the whole network of connection weights is a single representation that contains information derived from many past experiences' (Smith, 1996: 898).

In relation to cognitive development, William Ramsey and colleagues (1991) noted that it was unquestionable that connectionism was already fostering major changes in how cognitive scientists conceived of cognition. Thelen and Smith (1994) saw it as intimately related to dynamic systems theory, but observed that connectionist models fail as developmental theories in not seriously considering a number of issues, such as how biology (including the brain) really works and how complex development actually is. Nevertheless, connectionism continues to be a force in the attempt to understand cognitive development. For example, it has been applied to preschoolers' ability to understand 'false beliefs' – what another person believes about the location of an object moved in her or his absence (Berthiaume *et al.*, 2013). A computer simulation based on a constructivist connectionist model successfully reproduced the transitions found in children's developing understanding.

Theory of mind

The previous example brings us to children's 'theory of mind' (ToM). David Premack and Guy Woodruff introduced this idea as part of their efforts to understand the cognitive and language abilities of chimpanzees: 'An individual has a theory of mind if he imputes mental states to himself and others' (Premack and Woodruff, 1978: 515). As we spend time with others we take into account their feelings, thoughts and behaviour in order to try and understand why individuals behave as they do. Indications of the existence of ToM awareness are found in everyday language usage, such as 'I think she was upset' or 'I'm sure you will like this'. To understand that children have a developing sense of others, researchers must first rule out the possibility that the child is: (a) not behaving egocentrically (e.g. indicating that another child wants something based not on their knowledge of the other's desire but on their own desire); or (b) not simply using past experience to infer something about another child. Autism is a prominent area in which ToM has been applied (Baron-Cohen *et al.*, 1985); see also Box 4.2, where ToM is applied to the issue of school bullying.

BOX 4.2 BULLYING AND THEORY OF MIND (ToM)

Claire Hughes and Sue Leekam, reviewing ToM and its link with peer relations, including bullying, concluded that, 'developments in theory of mind transform children's close relationships, but also highlight both the complexity of these socio-cognitive influences, and the need for more research in this area' (Hughes and Leekam, 2004: 296). Certainly, a common portrayal of students who bully others, particularly in fiction, is of the bully as a rather 'powerful, but "oafish" person with little understanding of others' (Sutton *et al.*, 1999: 117). Such a view is consistent with a social skills processing view, suggesting that individuals might be deficient at any one of the five stages of information processing, including: (a) social perception; (b) interpretation of cues; (c) goal selection; (d) response strategy generation; and (e) response decision. A bully might be thought of as lacking one or more of these 'social skills'. In contrast, Sutton *et al.* (1999) suggest that some bullies might be very adept at using ToM to understand other individuals in order to manipulate and organize them. This theoretical viewpoint has attracted some debate (e.g. Crick and Dodge, 1999) about whether bullying arose because the bully *lacked* social skills or because he or she *was* socially skilled.

In an early major review of the field, Flavell (1999) identified three main waves of research relating to children's knowledge about the mind. The first wave largely involved Piaget's theory and research. Piaget's argument concerning the essentially egocentric nature of children in the early stages of development indicated that children were restricted in their ability to appreciate the perspectives of others. Studies confirmed a gradual increase in children's perspective-taking abilities (Flavell, 1992).

A second wave of research related to children's metacognitive development, concerning knowledge about people as cognizers, the nature of different cognitive tasks, and possible strategies for solving problems (Flavell, 1999). How do children develop the capacity for 'thinking about their thinking'? Ingar Brinck and Rikard Liljenfors (2013) have examined the development of metacognition in infants from a dynamic systems perspective, arguing that it arises in infancy out of mutual and reciprocal dyadic interaction of infant and caregiver.

The third, and now dominant, wave of research relates to ToM development. A virtual avalanche of research began in the 1980s, the more recent studies suggesting that well below the age range of three to five (which has been the traditional focus of ToM research), even very young children possess such capacity, but fail to perform accordingly (Samson and Apperly, 2010). Nonverbal ToM tasks are easier for them than the verbal ones typically used in false-belief studies. The field has been reviewed by, among others, Hughes and Leekam (2004), and Ian Apperly and Stephen Butterfill (2009). The former have called for further research of a longitudinal nature that focuses on individual differences and that takes into account developmental features. Apperly and Butterfill concluded that the concept continues to make a major contribution to the field of child development, although they found that further research is warranted to improve understanding of the multifaceted nature of ToM, its developmental nature and the manner in which it is influenced by family and peer relations.

Several newer versions of ToM now exist (Gallagher, 2004). The original version, largely based on false-belief tests, has been called 'theory-theory (TT)', whereby a folk theory of the minds of others is either seen as developing with experience or as 'coming on-line' at specific ages. By contrast, 'simulation theory (ST)' holds that there is no 'theory', as such, but that we mentally simulate another's mind based on our own; this draws upon the discovery of mirror neurons that activate when we see another person performing an action, as well as when we perform that action ourselves. Finally, there is Gallagher's interaction theory (IT), which maintains that the use of TT and ST is rare, as we can mostly perceive another's intentions immediately by 'body reading'; both infants and animals are able to do this without any sophisticated cognitive apparatus.

Eleanor Maccoby (b. 1917): adding the 'social' to cognitive development

The extensive research interests of Maccoby placed her at a particular advantage in psychology to integrate various theoretical influences. In developing her own theoretical beliefs, Maccoby acknowledged the influence of cognitive–developmental theory in shaping her views (Maccoby, 1980), hence her inclusion in the present chapter. However, she expressed a concern echoed by others: that 'the theory is too "cold" and does not give enough weight to the role of emotions in social development' (Maccoby, 1980: 31). She was also critical of stage theory, arguing instead that there are 'decision points' in children's lives and at such points various influences, such as the family, can lead any two children to follow different developmental patterns.

Born in Tacoma, Washington, of parents with 'alternative' beliefs (Stevens and Gardner, 1982), Maccoby's adolescent rebellion against her parents' values was possibly reflected in an early interest in psychology and in her belief that human behaviour could be studied empirically according to the objective methods developed by positivist sciences. In 1950 she began teaching at Harvard University. Although she later reported receiving little gender discrimination, according to Gwendolyn Stevens and Sheldon Gardner (1982) she was unhappy in the rather patriarchal setting of that university (for instance, women were not permitted to enter the Faculty Club by the front door) (in Chapter 11 we will take a slightly more contemporary look at the lives of women in academia). She subsequently moved to Stanford University.

From an early stage in her career she was interested in studying children, including the effects of television on them. At various times her eclectic research interests also encompassed mother–child interaction, women's studies, gender, moral values, aggression, attachment and the relationship between intelligence and non-cognitive abilities.

In outlining her views of children's socialization, Maccoby acknowledged the influence of behaviourism and the particular contributions that the concepts of reinforcement and contingency have made to our understanding of how children's social behaviour is influenced (see Chapter 6). She also appreciated the contribution of Freudian theory to our understanding of the socialization process, particularly in relation to sex-role development. Perhaps most importantly, however, Maccoby identified a broad range of research influences shaping our understanding of children's social development, as follows.

• Research involving trait theory, which has highlighted not just consistency, but the inconsistency of children's behaviour in various situations.
• Cognitive-developmental theory, which has alerted us to the manner in which children's thinking shapes their perception of events.
• Ethological theory and the associated concept of instincts, which raises the possibility of the predisposition of children to learn certain things – for example, attachment.
• Temperament research, which has made us aware of the dissimilarity of infants at birth.
• Cross-cultural research, which has alerted us to the influence of social structures, such as the nature of the family unit, the economic basis of a society (e.g. agricultural or industrial), the role of men and women, and how a culture educates its members.

Broadly speaking, Maccoby's wide-ranging perspective reflected an awareness that the biology of the child should be taken into account, and that the child actively participates in the socialization process and also moves through various phases in developing a concept of the social self.

One important feature of Maccoby's thinking (Maccoby, 1980) concerned the parents' role in aiding the child's social development. She believed that children's social-psychological development will be fostered if parents:

• are interested in and responsive to their children's needs;
• have realistic, age-appropriate expectations of their children's behaviour;
• provide their children with some structure and predictability in their daily lives;
• are democratic in decision-making within the family;
• listen to their children's views;
• allow their children the opportunity to solve their own problems;
• are warm and affectionate towards their children;
• work at developing a set of values with their children.

In regarding the environment provided by parents as making a real difference to children's development, her perspective is more consistent with that of Diana Baumrind than with that of Sandra Scarr (see Chapter 2).

Jerome Bruner (b. 1915) and constructivism

Constructivism has its philosophical roots in the European tradition of thinking drawn from the philosophy of George Berkeley and Immanuel Kant, who emphasized the subjectivity of our perception, and it has been linked with the thinking of Piaget. Esther Gelcer and David Schwartzbein (1989) summarized two important assumptions of Piaget's theory: that there are different levels of knowing the same experience, and that the greater the level of abstraction, the more flexible is the individual's approach to problem-solving. Other key writers who have contributed to theory relating to constructivism include the Chilean biologist Humberto Maturana and his colleague Francisco Varela (1988), and the cybernetician Heinz von Foerster (1973). The systems thinking of Gregory Bateson, discussed later in this chapter, also had an impact.

The central assertion of constructivism is that reality cannot only be revealed to us in one true way. It is through the process of construing that we come to know reality, as in Kelly's theory: 'each organism creatively constructs its world within the limits of whatever biological or environmental context it encounters' (Gelcer and Schwartzbein, 1989: 440). Constructivism emphasizes a proactive view of the individual who, as an observer, participates actively in the process of observation. It is through this process of active participation that the co-creation of meaning occurs. Such a proactive view of the person contrasts with much of mainstream psychology, which views the individual as reactive. The theory of the US psychologist Jerome Bruner reflected a constructivist approach, and was greatly influenced by the thinking of Piaget and Vygotsky (see Chapter 7). While Bruner's theory is similar to that of Piaget in many respects, it also differs in crucial aspects. For Bruner, language is intimately related to a child's cognitive growth. In his view, thinking would not be possible without language. Bruner has also argued that the competencies of children are greater than Piaget's theory leads us to believe. He placed great emphasis on the child as a social being whose competencies 'are interwoven with the competences of others' (Bruner, 1987: 11). Bruner (1966) identified three major themes in understanding cognitive growth and the conditions that shape it. The first relates to how humans organize and represent their experience of the world. As detailed later, Bruner argued that children pass through three stages or modes of representing their world, each of which enables the child to represent the world in unique ways (Bruner, 1987).

A second theme relates to the impact of culture on growth. Bruner noted that cognitive growth is shaped as much 'from the outside in as the inside out' (Bruner, 1966: 13). We will take this idea further in later chapters. A third major theme relates to the evolutionary history of humans. Bruner believed humans to be particularly suited to adapting to their environment by social, rather than morphological, means (Bruner, 1986).

In reading Bruner's work, several basic assumptions are evident. One of these is that reality is constructed. Bruner placed a great deal more emphasis than Piaget on the notion that humans actively construct meaning from the world. In *Actual Minds, Possible Worlds* Bruner cited Goodman's notion of a constructivist philosophy:

> Contrary to common sense, there is no unique 'real world' that pre-exists and is independent of human mental activity and human symbolic language; that which we call the world is a product of some mind whose symbolic procedures construct the world.
>
> *(Bruner, 1986: 95)*

This is consistent with the postmodern philosophical ideas we encounter later in this book. Bruner argued that the idea that we construct the world should be quite congenial to developmental or clinical psychologists, who observe that humans can attach quite different meanings to the same event.

Another of Bruner's central assumptions is that development is culturally and historically embedded (Bruner, 1986; Bruner and Haste, 1987). In this way Bruner's outlook is closely aligned with that of Vygotsky. Culture is the means by which 'instructions' about how humans should grow are carried from one generation to the next (Bruner, 1987). That is, culture helps transmit knowledge and understanding.

Bruner also assumed that the child is a social being. Bruner and Helen Haste observed that 'we are now able to focus on the child as a social being whose competencies are interwoven with the competencies of others' (Bruner and Haste, 1987: 11). They were critical of the legacy bequeathed by Piaget, which suggested that while the child is active in the construction of the world, the picture that emerges is one of a rather isolated child working alone at problem-solving tasks. They emphasized that the child is in fact a social operator who, through a social life, 'acquires a framework for interpreting experience, and learns how to negotiate meaning in a manner congruent with the requirements of a culture' (Bruner and Haste, 1987: 1).

The first of Bruner's (1966) proposed stages is *enactive representation,* equivalent to Piaget's sensori-motor period. Bruner argued, as did Piaget, that the infant gains knowledge about the world not from mental images but rather from action. Comparing his enactive stage with Piaget's sensori-motor stage, Bruner noted that Piaget regarded the 'first part in sensori-motor intelligence as one in which things are lived rather than thought' (Bruner, 1966: 17; Piaget, 1954). Bruner likened this type of intelligence to an irreversible and fixed succession of static images, each connected to an action. The child seems able to 'hold an object in mind by less and less direct manual prehension of it' (Bruner, 1966: 17). During the enactive stage infants can perform actions but do not know how they perform them. To this extent, Bruner agrees with Piaget that the infant's intelligence is one in which things are 'lived rather than thought' (Piaget, 1954). These ideas can be linked with Vygotsky and with current thinking about 'embodied cognition' (see Chapter 7, Box 7.1).

Bruner's second stage of knowing, that of *iconic representation,* 'emerges when a child is finally able to represent the world to himself by an image or spatial schema that is relatively independent of action' (Bruner, 1966: 21). The word 'iconic' (today rather overworked) comes from the word 'icon' (from the ancient Greek word for likeness or image). A mental image is a genuine cognitive representation. It is representative of a body of information but takes a different form from that which it represents. In Bruner's (1966) view, iconic knowledge has a number of identifiable characteristics.

- It is inflexible.
- It focuses upon small details.
- It is self-centred in relation to having central reference to the child as an observer.
- It is subject to distortion because of the child's needs or feelings.
- Perception is closely tied to action or doing.
- Perception is unsteady in terms of the young child's unsteadiness of concentration.

Bruner and Piaget disagreed about the role of iconic representation in a child's thinking. In Bruner's theory the role of iconic knowledge is crucial to the explanation of conservation (the ability to understand that the physical attributes of objects, such as mass, do not vary when the object's shape is changed).

Bruner's third stage of knowing is *symbolic representation*: 'The idea that there is a name that goes with things and that the name is arbitrary is generally taken as the essence of symbolism' (Bruner, 1966: 31). Thus, while a picture of a beautiful landscape looks like a landscape, a written sentence describing it does not; the landscape is symbolized in the language describing it. In Bruner's (1966) theory, symbolic representation is enhanced through language acquisition in particular. Without the ability to symbolize, the child will grow into adulthood dependent upon the enactive and iconic modes of representing and organizing knowledge of the world.

By emphasizing the constructive nature of cognitive development and the influence of cultural factors, Bruner added a richer dimension to our contemporary understanding of the nature of children's thinking. For example, he proposed allowing students to 'discover' the connections between their learning and the relevance to themselves, thereby better remembering and making sense of information (Bruner, 1966). Used in Australian classrooms, 'guided discovery' scaffolded (appropriately supported) by the teacher provides students with greater autonomy in their learning (Reynolds, 2009).

Social cognitive theory as advanced by Bruner is further discussed in Chapter 6. He advanced the idea of the child's cognitive development in terms of agency, self-regulatory and self-reflective processes, which was in stark contrast to behavioural views. One application relates to how children and young people manage their 'on-line' behaviour, which can at times be 'risky' (Box 4.3).

Expressing similar sentiments to Bruner, Albert Bandura (2001) argued that nothing less than a paradigm shift occurred in psychological theorizing, supplanting

---

BOX 4.3 RISKY INTERNET USE BY YOUNG ADOLESCENTS: COGNITIVE AND PSYCHOSOCIAL EXPLANATIONS

Social networking is a relatively new type of communicative practice. It has swept the world, affording a seamlessly converging one-to-one, one-to-many and, especially, one-to-someone communication within a more or less permeable circle of peers on social networking sites (Livingstone *et al.*, 2013). Many Australian 10–12-year-olds use the Internet for between one and three hours per day, and by age 13, social media use has become the norm (Australian Communications and Media Authority, 2011). By age 15, use of the Internet has become an organic, integrated part of the everyday lives of Australian children. The increase in Internet time is associated with increased exposure to on-line risk (e.g. Byrne *et al.*, 2014). With risky behaviour peaking during adolescence (Baumgartner *et al.*, 2010), Laurence Steinberg has argued that recent advances in neuroscience suggest that this 'does not appear to be due to irrationality, delusions of invulnerability, or ignorance' (Steinberg, 2007: 51). The same author has argued that risk-taking in the real world is the product of cognitive reasoning and psychosocial factors. However, unlike logical reasoning abilities, which appear to be more or less fully developed by age 15, psychosocial capacities that improve decision-making and moderate risk-taking – such as impulse control, emotion regulation, delay of gratification and resistance to peer influence – continue to mature.

---

behaviourist theory with the view of the individual as an 'agent' with the capacity to make things happen intentionally by one's actions:

> Consciousness is the very substance of mental life that not only makes life personally manageable but worth living. A functional consciousness involves purposive accessing and deliberative processing of information for selecting, constructing, regulating, and evaluating courses of action.
>
> *(Bandura, 2001: 3)*

Social cognitive theory focuses upon transactions between cognition, behaviour and the environment (Bandura, 1997). A social cognitive view of motivation proposes that during the process of instruction, such as during school lessons, students access knowledge about earlier motivational states, outcomes and emotions, which influences their readiness and willingness to learn (Winne, 1991). In Philip Winne's view, this motivational knowledge influences task selection and shapes the quality of students' involvement with a task, including their expenditure of effort and level of interest, and affects task persistence.

Social cognitive theory has been applied in a range of contexts, such as the classroom, where it has been used to understand more about teachers' instructional strategies and students' knowledge about how to learn (Askell-Williams and Lawson, 2015).

Systems thinking and dynamic systems theory

In the previous chapter we mentioned that general systems theory is one of a number of influences on organismic developmental theories. While systems thinking, with its notion of self-organization, has clear connections with the organismic metaphor described by Stephen Pepper (1942), its novel emphasis on holism and non-linear causality suggests that it should be considered a new developmental metaphor in itself. We have devoted a later chapter to it (Chapter 10), but mention it briefly here given its organismic origins.

A number of developmentalists, including Arnold Sameroff (1983), recognized the implications of the work of Gregoire Nicolis and Ilya Prigogine (1977). It has been noted that 'Adoption of such a systems model, with its assumptions of wholeness, self-stabilization, self-organization, and hierarchical organization, has implications for every aspect of developmental psychology' (Thelen and Smith, 1994: 575). There has indeed been strong interest in the application of systems theory to the study of children and the family. During the 1970s, Gregory Bateson and colleagues developed and applied the ideas associated with general systems theory, in connection with research on families whose members had schizophrenia (Bateson, 1972; see Chapter 10). Later applications included work by Kenneth Kaye (1985), Scarr (1985), Patrick Tolan (1990), Ellen Wachtel (1990) and Ylva Parfitt *et al.* (2013).

With the advent of systems thinking, a change in theoretical focus was observed in the fifth edition of the *Handbook of Child Psychology*, edited by William Damon (1998). Lerner observed 'a burgeoning interest not in structure, function, or content per se, but in change, in the process through which change occurs, and thus in the means through which structures transform and functions evolve over the course of human life' (Lerner, 1998: 1). In many ways, this understanding captures significant features of a new developmental theory – dynamic systems theory (see Chapters 10 and 13). Increasingly, dynamic systems theory has being applied to various areas of developmental psychology (Pepler and Craig, 2000; Slee, 2001; Thelen and Smith, 1994).

Conclusions

In this chapter we have attempted to capture some of the vibrancy of the current debate in relation to organicism. Generally, the organismic worldview (Pepper, 1942) highlights the directional movement of the organism towards ever-increasing integration against the background of a dynamic, evolving context. All phenomena are interdependent. In this situation the child is an active constructor of reality and not merely responding passively. As an active individual, the child constructs interpretations of environmental events, and continually acts and interacts with his or her environment in order to construct and reconstruct experience. The child is viewed as a spontaneously active organism, and because some activities are not simply a response to external events it is not theoretically possible to predict all of an individual's behaviour. Acting like lay theorists, children are continually adapting their theories to fit ever-changing events in their world, altering the world in the process. However, the lay theories are by no means as neat and consistent as we might like to imagine (Basseches, 1989), and it is the very inconsistencies in children's theorizing that force them to act, so as to find a resolution.

While this approach takes into account the uniqueness of individuals and their active participation in their own development, two key limitations to organismic theories must be observed. One relates to the structural stage conceptions of development, which 'fail to reflect the complexity and diversity of individuals' meaning making' (Basseches, 1989: 189). The second limitation includes a lack of explanation for how internal regulation, organization and self-organization relate to the developmental process.

References

Apperly, I.A. and Butterfill, S.A. 2009. Do humans have two systems to track beliefs and belief-like states? *Psychological Review*. 116, 4: 953–70.

Askell-Williams, H. and Lawson, M. 2015. Changes in students' cognitive and metacognitive strategy use over five years of secondary schooling. In H. Askell-Williams (ed.), *Educational futures: translating research into visions for transformative practice*. Hershey, PA: IGI Global, 1–19.

Australian Communications and Media Authority. 2011. Communications report. Available at: www.acma.gov.au/webwr/_assets/main/. . ./comms_report_2011-12.pdf. Accessed 24 October 2014.

Bandura, A. 1997. *Self-efficacy: the exercise of control*. New York: Freeman.

Bandura, A. 2001. Social cognitive theory: an agentic perspective. *Annual Review of Psychology*. 52: 1–26.

Bannister, D. and Fransella, F. 2003. *Inquiring man: the psychology of personal constructs*. London: Routledge.

Baron-Cohen, S., Leslie, A.M. and Frith, U. 1985. Does the autistic child have a 'theory of mind'? *Cognition*. 21: 37–46.

Basseches, M. 1989. Toward a constructive-developmental understanding of the dialectics of individuality and irrationality. In D.A. Kramer and M. Bopp (eds), *Transformation in clinical and developmental psychology*. New York: Springer-Verlag, 188–210.

Bateson, G. 1972. *Steps to an ecology of mind*. London: Ronald Press.

Baumgartner, S.E., Valkenburg, P.M. and Peter, J. 2010. Assessing causality in the relationship between adolescents' risky sexual online behavior and their perceptions of this behavior. *Journal of Youth and Adolescence*. 39 (10): 1,226–39.

Beilin, H. 1992. Piaget's enduring contribution to developmental psychology. *Developmental Psychology*. 28: 191–204.

Berthiaume, V.G., Shultz, T.S. and Onishi, K.H. 2013. A constructivist connectionist model of transitions on false-belief tasks. *Cognition*. 126: 441–58.

Brinck, I. and Liljenfors, R. 2013. The developmental origin of metacognition. *Infant and Child Development*. 22 (1): 85–101.

Bruner, J. 1966. *Studies in cognitive growth*. New York: Wiley.

Bruner, J. 1986. *Actual minds, possible worlds*. Cambridge, MA: Harvard University Press.

Bruner, J. 1987. *Child's talk*. New York: Norton.

Bruner, J. and Haste, H. 1987. *Making sense. The child's construction of the world*. London: Methuen.

Byrne, S., Katz, S.J., Lee, T., Linz, D. and McIlrath, M. 2014. Peers, predators, and porn: predicting parental underestimation of children's risky online experiences. *Journal of Computer-Mediated Communication*. 19: 215–31.

Case, R. 1998. The development of central conceptual structures. In D. Kuhn and R. Siegler (eds), *Handbook of child psychology. Cognition, perception and language*. Fifth edn, Vol. 2. New York: Wiley, 745–800.

Clark, A. 1993. *Associative engines: connectionism, concepts, and representational change*. Cambridge, MA: MIT Press.

Crick, N.R. and Dodge, K. 1999. Superiority is in the eye of the beholder: a comment on Sutton, Smith and Swettenham. *Social Development*. 8: 128–34.

Damon, W. (ed.). 1998. *Handbook of child psychology*. Fifth edn. New York: Wiley.

Dice, J. and Dove, M. 2011. A Piagetian approach to infant referential behaviors. *Infant Behavior and Development*. 34: 481–6.

Donaldson, M. 1978. *Children's minds*. Glasgow: Fontana.

Eibl-Eibesfeldt, I. 1989. *Human ethology*. New York: Aldine de Gruyter.

Elkind, D. 1971. Cognitive growth cycles in mental development. *Nebraska Symposium on Motivation*. 19: 1–31.

Elkind, D. 1974. *Children and adolescents*. Second edn. London: Oxford University Press.

Flavell, J.H. 1992. Development of children's knowledge about the mental world. *International Journal of Behavioral Development*. 24: 15–23.

Flavell, J.H. 1999. Cognitive development: children's knowledge about the mind. *Annual Review of Psychology*. 50: 21–45.

Gallagher, S. 2004. Situational understanding: a Gurwitschian critique of theory of mind. In L. Embree (ed.), *Gurwitsch's relevancy for cognitive science*. Dordrecht, The Netherlands: Springer, 25–44.

Gardner, H. 1979. Developmental psychology after Piaget: an approach in terms of symbolization. *Human Development*. 22: 73–88.

Gelcer, E. and Schwartzbein, D. 1989. A Piagetian view of family therapy: Selvini-Palazzoli and the invariant approach. *Family Process*. 28: 439–56.

Halford, G.S. 1989. Reflections on 25 years of Piagetian cognitive developmental psychology, 1963–1988. *Human Development*. 32: 325–57.

Honstead, C. 1968. The developmental theory of Jean Piaget. In J.L. Frost (ed.), *Early childhood education rediscovered*. New York: Holt, Rinehart and Winston, 131–43.

Hughes, C. and Leekam, S. 2004. What are the links between theory of mind and social relations? Review, reflections and new directions for studies of typical and atypical development. *Social Development*. 13: 590–619.

Huotilainen, M. 2010. Building blocks of fetal cognition: emotion and language. *Infant and Child Development*. 19: 94–8.

Inamdar, P. 2004. Computer skills development by children using 'hole in the wall' facilities in rural India. *Australasian Journal of Educational Technology*. 20 (3): 337–50.

Inhelder, B. 1975. Some aspects of Piaget's genetic approach to cognition. In J. Gants and H.J. Butcher (eds), *Developmental psychology*. Harmondsworth: Penguin, 22–40.

Kaye, K. 1985. Toward a developmental psychology of the family. In L. L'Abate (ed.), *Handbook of family psychology and therapy*. Homewood, IL: Dow Jones-Irwin, 38–72.

Kelly, G.A. 1963. *A theory of personality*. New York: Norton.

Kreitler, H. and Kreitler, S. 1976. *Cognitive orientation and behaviour*. New York: Springer-Verlag.

Lerner, R.M. 1998. Theories of human development: contemporary perspectives. In R.M. Lerner (ed.), *Handbook of child psychology. Theoretical models of human development*. Fifth edn, Vol. 1. New York: Wiley, 1–24.

Livingstone, S., Kalmus, V. and Talves, K. 2013. Girls' and boys' experiences of online risk and safety. In C. Carter, L. Steiner and L. McLaughlin (eds), *Routledge companion to media and gender*. London: Routledge, 190–200.

Lourenço, O. 2012. Many resemblances, and a crucial difference. *New Ideas in Psychology*. 30: 281–95.

Maccoby, E. 1980. *Social development: psychological growth and the parent-child relationship*. New York: Harcourt Brace Jovanovich.

Mahoney, M.J. 1993. Introduction to special section: theoretical developments in the cognitive psychotherapies. *Journal of Consulting and Clinical Psychology*. 61: 187–93.

Maturana, H.R. and Varela, F.J. 1988. *The tree of knowledge. The biological roots of human understanding*. Boston, MA: New Science Library.

McGurk, H. 1975. *Growing and changing: a primer of developmental psychology*. London: Methuen.

Meadows, S. 1986. *Understanding child development*. London: Hutchinson.

Miller, G.A. 2003. The cognitive revolution: a historical perspective. *Trends in Cognitive Sciences*. 7 (3): 141–4.

Newell, A. and Simon, H. 1972. *Human problem solving*. Englewood Cliffs, NJ: Prentice Hall.

Nicolis, G. and Prigogine, I. 1977. *Self-organization in nonequilibrium systems*. New York: Wiley Inter-Science.

Parfitt, Y., Pike, A. and Ayers, S. 2013. Infant developmental outcomes: a family systems perspective. *Infant and Child Development*. 23 (4): 353–73.

Pepler, D.J. and Craig, W.M. 2000. Making a difference in bullying. *LaMarsh research report # 60*. Toronto, ON: York University.

Pepper, S. 1942. *World hypotheses: a study of evidence*. Berkeley, CA: University of California Press.

Piaget, J. 1954. *The construction of reality in the child*. London: Routledge & Kegan Paul.

Piaget, J. 1959. *Language and thought of the child*. London: Routledge & Kegan Paul.

Piaget, J. and Inhelder, B. 1969. *The psychology of the child*. New York: Basic Books.

Popper, K. 1972. *Objective knowledge. An evolutionary approach*. Oxford: Clarendon Press.

Premack, D. and Woodruff, G. 1978. Does the chimpanzee have a theory of mind? *Behavioural and Brain Sciences*. 1: 515–26.

Protopapas, A. 1999. Connectionist modeling of speech perception. *Psychological Bulletin*. 125: 410–36.

Ramsey, W., Stich, S.P. and Garon, J. 1991. Connectionism, eliminativism, and the future of folk psychology. In W. Ramsey, S.P. Stich and D.E. Rumelhart (eds), *Philosophy and connectionist theory*. Hillsdale, NJ: Erlbaum, 199–228.

Reynolds, R. 2009. *Teaching studies of society and the environment in the primary school*. South Melbourne: Oxford University Press.

Sameroff, A.J. 1983. Developmental systems: contexts and evolution. In W. Kessen (ed.), *Handbook of child psychology. History, theory and methods*. Vol. 1. New York: Wiley, 237–94.

Samson, D. and Apperly, I.A. 2010. There is more to mind reading than having theory of mind concepts: new directions in theory of mind research. *Infant and Child Development*. 19: 443–54.

Scarr, S. 1985. Constructing psychology: making facts and fables for our times. *American Psychologist*. 40: 499–512.

Slee, P.T. 2001. *The P.E.A.C.E. pack: a program for reducing bullying in our schools*. Adelaide: Flinders University.

Slee P.T, Campbell, M. and Spears, B. 2012. *Child, adolescent and family development*. Third edn. Melbourne: Cambridge University Press.

Smith, E.R. 1996. What do connectionism and social psychology offer each other? *Journal of Personality and Social Psychology*. 70: 893–912.

Steinberg, L. 2007. Risk taking in adolescence – new perspectives. *Annual Review Clinical Psychology*. 5: 459–85.

Stevens, G. and Gardner, S. 1982. *The women of psychology. Expansion and refinement*. Vol. 2. Cambridge, MA: Schenkman.

Sutton, J., Smith, P.K. and Swettenham, J. 1999. Bullying and 'theory of mind': a critique of the 'social skills deficit' view of anti-social behaviour. *Social Development*. 8: 117–27.

Thelen, E. and Smith, L.B. 1994. *A dynamic systems approach to the development of cognition and action*. Cambridge, MA: MIT Press.

Tolan, P.H. (ed.). 1990. *Multi-systemic structural-strategic interventions for child and adolescent behavioural problems*. New York: Hawarth Press.

Tonnessen, F.E. 1999. Options and limitations of the cognitive psychological approach to the treatment of dyslexia. *Journal of Learning Disabilities*. 5: 386–95.

Trevarthen, C. 2010. What is it like to be a person who knows nothing? Defining the active intersubjective mind of a newborn human being. *Infant and Child Development*. 20: 119–35.

van Geert, P. 1998. A dynamic systems model of basic developmental mechanisms: Piaget, Vygotsky, and beyond. *Psychological Review*. 105: 634–77.

von Foerster, H. 1973. Cybernetics of cybernetics (physiology of revolution). *The Cybernetician*. 3: 30–2.

Wachtel, E.F. 1990. The child as an individual: a resource for systemic change. *Journal of Strategic and Family Therapies*. 9: 50–8.

Watson, J.B. 1913. Psychology as the behaviorist views it. *Psychological Review*. 20: 158–77.

Winne, P.H. 1991. Motivation and teaching. In H. Waxman and H. Walberg (eds), *Effective teaching: current research*. Berkeley, CA: McCutchan, 295–314.

Xu, F. and Kushnir, T. 2013. Infants are rational constructivist learners. *Current Directions in Psychological Science*. 22: 28–32.

5

FROM OEDIPUS TO ATTACHMENT

The Freudian legacy

Introduction

Freudian theory is something about which commencing psychology students often expect to hear a great deal, but they find Sigmund Freud's work given only a minor place in psychology curricula, which instead emphasize the scientific method and evidence-based psychology practice. Freud's ideas were indeed developed in the absence of scientific support, during the first part of the twentieth century. Despite – and possibly because of – this lack of scientific support, Freud's concepts had great influence upon social science and the practice of psychiatry at the time: Freud may have tapped into ongoing desires to study subjective experience, which was being rejected by psychologists at the time as unscientific (Fisher and Greenberg, 1996). Even by the end of the twentieth century, Freudian ideas were described as having 'penetrated into the matrix of modern psychology and continu[ing] to exert formidable influence' (Fisher and Greenberg, 1996: 6–7). Recent appraisals variously declare him 'dead' (e.g. Kihlstrom, 2009), or 'the greatest psychologist since Aristotle' (Lothane, 2006: 285).

With the benefits of hindsight, Freud's psychosexual theory of child development, derived from his reflections on the early childhood recollections of his adult psychiatric patients, has to be seriously questioned. Nevertheless, as we will see in this chapter, empirical support has been found for some aspects of Freudian theory, and his thinking was inspirational to others who have greatly influenced our understanding of children's development, especially in infancy. These workers were in no way Freud's disciples, but reflected upon certain of his key insights and developed them in their own ways. Following a brief reminder of Freud's Oedipal theory of child development, we examine the scientific evidence for it and describe some of the later work in child development theory that built upon the Freudian tradition.

Freud's (1856–1939) child development theory

Austrian neurologist Sigmund Freud took a biological approach to development, seeing the child as coming into the world already equipped with basic instincts to survive and reproduce. These basic drives constituted the aspect of the psyche that he called the id. The ego was the part of the psyche in touch with reality, mediating between the id and the superego, or conscience. A continuity with earlier Darwinian theory can be observed in that Freud applied notions of phylogenetic evolution to intrapsychic development (ontogeny) (Emde, 1992). He proposed that the functions of current actions could be understood in terms of past history, placing great emphasis on early experience as laying the foundations, 'for a series of developmental stages – a notion later developed much further by Jean Piaget.

The stages of development delineated by Freud were the oral, anal, phallic, latency and genital. His theory is psychosexual, in that each stage is defined by the zone of the body that is the focus of pleasure for the child (the exception being the latency stage, when sexual instincts lie dormant):

> A child has its sexual instincts and activities from the first; it comes into the world with them; and after an important course of development passing through many stages, they lead to what is known as the normal sexuality of the adult.
>
> *(Freud, 1910/1974: 71)*

His emphasis upon the sexual nature of children was considered outrageous at the time. Although one of Freud's most enduring legacies is the recognition of the importance of early experiences for later development, it is important not to lose sight of the fact that Freud was a medical man who also emphasized the importance of hereditary and constitutional factors in development. It should be noted, however, that the word 'genetic' as used by Freud means ontogenetic or epigenetic rather than gene-controlled (Hilgard, 1962).

Although there are various aspects of Freudian theory with implications for child development, we will concentrate here on the Oedipal theory, 'the skeleton of the psychoanalytic model' (Fisher and Greenberg, 1996: 118). In fact, Seymour Fisher and Roger Greenberg conceived of Oedipal theory as a collection of mini-theories about a range of developmental issues, such as family dynamics, identification with parents, moral development and sexual development. Freud doubtless saw his theory as a 'grand theory', and the tendency to look back on it as a collection of mini-theories is perhaps reflective of later trends in theorizing.

From the vantage point of today's scientific psychology, it seems remarkable that a man who proposed a theory of child development undertook very little research or clinical work with children. Rather, he built his theory on the basis of the recollections of his (mainly female) middle-class patients diagnosed with psychological disorders such as hysteria. Freud originally took at face value their descriptions of childhood sexual experiences, attributing their adult psychological symptoms to repressed sexual trauma. However, he renounced this 'seduction theory' in 1897, coming to see these women as expressing childhood sexual fantasies. Although he worked mainly with women, Freud took the development of male children as the prototype for development (a reflection of his historical times), although we know today that, biologically speaking, the reverse is actually the case (Emde, 1992).

In describing the phallic stage of development, Freud drew upon the Greek myth of King Oedipus, who killed his father and married his mother. Freud theorized that the young boy, around the age of four or five, harbours sexual impulses towards his mother. This places him in direct competition with his father for her affections, and he fears that his father will castrate him as a punishment. To overcome this Oedipal conflict, the boy identifies with his father, in the course of which he internalizes his father's moral values and develops his own superego. Freud postulated that for girls, a parallel but necessarily somewhat different process occurs (the Electra complex), with the girl believing that she has already been castrated by her mother and moving towards her father as a love object; he has the potential to give her a baby in compensation for the presumed loss of her penis (the 'penis-baby equation'). Freud was less clear about how the female's conflict is resolved, but maintained that it is more gradual and results in a weaker superego for girls than boys. Freud saw normal adult psychological development as dependent upon the resolution of these early psychosexual conflicts, and theorized that adult neuroses and sexual dysfunctions result from a failure to resolve them adequately.

As we have noted, this theory was based on Freud's assumption that when his female patients described early sexual encounters with adult men, they were fantasies. John Bowlby later placed the emphasis back on reality, rather than fantasy, in investigating early childhood experiences (Andrews and Brewin, 2000), and writers increasingly began to suggest that Freud's earlier interpretations of his patients' recollections as actual abuse were correct (e.g. Masson, 1984). Even though there has been debate about the accuracy of childhood memories recovered in adult therapy, and prevalence is difficult to establish, international data suggest that around a quarter of girls and 8 per cent of boys experience sexual abuse (World Health Organization, 2001). As we write this chapter, an Australian Royal Commission into institutional responses to child sexual abuse is in train (with churches, particularly the Catholic Church, a focus of attention), illustrating increased public acceptance that such abuse of children is widespread and has long-lasting ill effects (Australian Broadcasting Corporation, 2014).

Putting aside the point that the Oedipal theory was probably based upon a false premise, it is nevertheless possible to examine how it stands up to scientific scrutiny. Fisher and Greenberg (1996) undertook two very detailed reviews of the scientific literature to determine how much empirical support there was for various aspects of Freudian theory. Was it appropriate to apply scientific standards, rather than alternative methods of inquiry such as those in a more relativist-subjectivist vein? Freud himself was ambivalent about this: he was pleased when science seemed to support his theories, but did not apply scientific principles to his clinical data collection. Fisher and Greenberg adopted the position that it is appropriate to evaluate Freud's theories from a scientific perspective, but to avoid trivial critiques of studies and look instead for overall trends across multiple studies.

Many studies were, in fact, specifically undertaken by experimental psychologists during the twentieth century to test propositions derived from Freudian theory. For example, the very basic proposition that infant experiences have enduring effects on adult behaviour was examined and supported by experiments during the 1940s and 1950s, demonstrating that adult rats' food-hoarding behaviour is influenced by early food deprivation (e.g. Albino and Long, 1951). With specific regard to Oedipal theory, Fisher and Greenberg found a considerable body of evidence supporting the basic notion of the 'Oedipal triangle' (the child favouring the opposite-sex over the same-sex parent). They also found evidence for children's concern about body experiences around the age at which Freud identified castration anxiety as occurring. They even found evidence supporting predictions derived from the controversial penis-baby equation theory; for example, an increase in phallic imagery during pregnancy. However, they found no evidence for the proposition that a boy identifies with his father and adopts his values as a result of fearing him. On the contrary, boys identify most strongly with fathers who are warm and nurturing. Evidence linking later sexual functioning with Oedipal notions is also lacking. Neither is there any evidence for the Freudian notion that boys develop stronger superegos than girls; Freud considered that this was so because of the depth of castration anxiety, with girls developing a weaker sense of justice and a greater tendency to be swayed by their emotions (Fleming, 2006). In this respect, Freudian ideas of morality development can be seen as male-centric, as has also been claimed to be the case for Piaget and Lawrence Kohlberg – see Chapter 11). Moral development has been found to be influenced by a range of factors other than the father-child relationship that was central to Freud's theory (Fisher and Greenberg, 1996).

Although they found support for particular aspects of the Oedipal theory, Fisher and Greenberg concluded overall that the empirical evidence for Freud's attempt to produce a grand theory of children's sexual and moral development was not strong. In a similar vein, Robert Emde (1992) pointed out that both gender identity and moral development can be observed well before the time when Freud saw the Oedipus complex as becoming resolved; also, rather than having an attachment to one parent disrupted later by the other, children usually develop ties of affection with both parents from an early age. Emde also made the more general theoretical point that Freud, in keeping with understandings of physics at the time, saw mental processes in terms of entropy (tending towards lower levels of organization, as in drive reduction), which contrasts with modern notions that development tends towards *greater* levels of complexity (see Chapter 10).

Despite its shortcomings, the influence of Freudian theory upon more recent developmental theories can easily be detected. A range of observations by Freud is echoed in later developmental theories (or, perhaps more appropriately, mini-theories), such as attachment theory, as discussed below (Emde, 1992). Such ideas were reflected in the work of later major developmental theorists such as René Spitz, Bowlby and Mary Ainsworth, and in the development of the psychoanalytic approach to child therapy (e.g. Melanie Klein, Donald Winnicott and the object relations school). Also, Piaget learned from Freud's open-ended approach to inquiry and, in particular, his attention to what an individual's errors can reveal about his or her cognitions, as Freud discussed in *The Psychopathology of Everyday Life* (Freud, 1914/1940). We will now consider a number of important twentieth-century child development theorists upon whom Freudian ideas had a particular influence.

Erik Erikson (1902–1994) and lifespan development

German-born US psychologist Erikson built upon Freud's theory, accepting his basic psychosexual framework, but developing the theory into further stages in adulthood. This promoted the notion of lifespan development, which has been particularly influential in US theorizing. Like Freud, Erikson saw development as resulting from conflicts; at each stage, the nature of their resolution could be more or less adaptive. Erikson's theory was a psychosocial one, which saw the ego not just as a mediator within the individual's psyche, but as an active promoter of development, under cultural influence. Erikson's influential works included *Childhood and Society* (1963) and *Identity, Youth and Crisis* (1968) (see also Chapter 8, Table 8.1, and Chapter 9).

Object relations

Melanie Klein (1882–1960) was an influential figure from the 1920s to the mid-twentieth century in the object relations school of psychoanalysis. She was involved in training therapists at the British Psychoanalytic Institute, and emphasized the potential of early loss for later psychopathology. An 'object', in the Kleinian sense, is a loved thing or, especially, person. Unlike Freud, she saw fear of death as being primary, not learned, and as the underlying cause of anxiety. However, she provided few observations of how infants actually behave in separation situations (Bowlby, 1975). She saw anxiety as being apparent right from the initial traumatic experience of birth, and internal conflict as the source of childhood emotional problems.

Others, such as Winnicott, later developed Klein's approach but gave more emphasis to external factors. Winnicott (1953) discussed the fact that young children often become attached to inanimate objects. For instance, a young relative of one of the present authors (RS) carried around a blue toy rabbit for several years until all that was left of it was a small piece of blue cloth. Linus's blanket in the *Peanuts* cartoons is another example. Winnicott termed such objects 'transitional objects', maintaining that they demonstrated the beginnings of symbolic thought. In representing a love object, such as the mother or her breast, they characterize the infant's journey from subjectivity to objectivity.

Object relations theory has been described as forming a bridge between Freudian theory, with its intrapsychic emphasis, and family therapy, which emphasizes interrelationships between family members (Gladding, 1998). The theory recognizes the influence of early object relations and the unconscious influence they may have on current relationships; these may lead to repeated dysfunctional patterns of interaction. Therapy aims to break these through assisting family members to gain insight into them.

Maternal deprivation

Important among the theorists whom Freud influenced was René Spitz (1887–1974), who emigrated from Europe to the USA in 1939, where he worked as a psychiatrist. Spitz is best known for his work on 'maternal deprivation' of babies in orphanages in the 1950s. Spitz had met Freud in 1911 and regarded him as a mentor (Emde, 1992). However, in contrast with Freud, his theorizing arose from direct observations of infants, and his (for the time) innovative use of film strengthened the impact of his work. Spitz also stressed a Darwinian influence, was a friend of the ethologist Konrad Lorenz, and told Emde that he wanted his final words to be remembered as 'survival, adaptation, and evolution' (Emde, 1992: 354). Therefore we could perhaps equally well have placed Spitz's contribution in Chapter 2 – a reminder of the multiple influences that impinge on any theorist's work – although it is certainly for his work on infant socialization that Spitz remains recognized.

Spitz was working at a time when unmarried motherhood was deeply shameful, and babies were often removed (sometimes forcibly) for adoption or institutional care. Spitz overturned notions that these institutionalized infants were sickly because their mothers were constitutionally morally inferior beings, and maintained instead that they failed to thrive because of a lack of mothering. His work on infant social smiling and on fear (more often now called wariness) of strangers around eight months of age remains well known. He also laid the foundations for a more recent thriving area of inquiry in proposing that reciprocity exists between infants and their caregivers – he recognized that a two-way flow of interaction occurs long before the child develops speech. In comparison with Freud, Spitz's research methods were exemplary, but in keeping with refinements in scientific methodology he was criticized even in his own time for poor reporting of experimental detail and lack of evidence for the reliability and validity of his measures. Nevertheless, his theory that maternal deprivation causes depression and apathy in infants was upheld by later work such as that of Bowlby, although further refinements remained to be made, such as the recognition that infants are typically attached not only to their mother (Emde, 1992).

Bill Goldfarb, a New York psychologist, was another researcher whose work was influential in this area (cited in Bowlby, 1953). He compared the development of two groups of adolescents, all of whom had been surrendered by their mothers in infancy. Those who had spent their first three years in institutions were delayed in development in comparison with those who had been taken straight to foster homes in infancy. For example, their speech and social skills were poorly developed. These findings demonstrated that early deprivation could have long-lasting effects, and suggested that there was a critical period for the development of such skills.

BOX 5.1 CATHERINE HELEN SPENCE (1825–1910), ATTACHMENT PIONEER

Spitz, Goldfarb and Bowlby are credited with establishing notions of infant institutionalization and maternal deprivation as developmentally damaging. Yet, in the nineteenth century, this issue was well recognized in South Australia, as recorded by a Scottish-Australian pioneer of women's rights and children's welfare, Catherine Helen Spence. She wrote a book in honour of Miss C.E. Clark, who had worked to establish a system of care for destitute children in family homes rather than institutions (Spence, 1907). At a time when unmarried mothers were vilified, legislation was enacted in 1881 to try and keep infants with their mothers: a woman entering the Destitute Asylum to have her baby would be contracted to stay with the baby for six months, 'giving it the natural nourishment', and Spence noted that 'affection grows strong during these six months' (Spence, 1907: 59). Where an infant could not be kept with its mother, it was boarded out to a foster mother: 'It is wonderful the love that grows up in the house where there is only one child placed' (Spence, 1907: 62). Efforts were also made to maintain the child's relationship with its natural mother: 'the foster mother shows to the real mother all its pretty ways, encourages it to crow and laugh . . . and sometimes is the means of reconciling the mother to her relatives' (Spence, 1907: 63). These images of happily attached nineteenth-century infants present a very different picture from those of the sickly infants observed in orphanages elsewhere in the world well into the twentieth century.

Although Spitz and Goldfarb are the names remembered for seminal work on maternal deprivation, the observations and practice of a South Australian woman pre-dated them by 70 years (Box 5.1).

The beginnings of attachment theory

Inge Bretherton's (1992) account has been informative in writing this section. John Bowlby (1907–1991), one of the originators of attachment theory, studied medicine and psychiatry, and also trained at the London Child Guidance Clinic and the British Psychoanalytic Institute. He disagreed with Klein's approach to child psychopathology, which emphasized internal conflict rather than external influences as the source of children's emotional problems. Later object relations theorists, such as Winnicott, were more in accord with Bowlby's views of the importance of early family relationships, although Bowlby preferred the term 'affectional bonds' to 'object relations' (Bowlby, 1975: 15).

Bowlby's interest in the importance of early attachment and loss developed originally from a couple of specific cases of children with emotional problems who had experienced early maternal loss (one of these used to follow him around the clinic, becoming known as his shadow). Later, he analysed over 40 case studies, concluding that the children's problems (including thieving) resulted from maternal deprivation. During the 1940s he began to put this area of research onto a more scientific footing when he developed some expertise in statistical analyses, which enabled him to add some numerical support to his case study approach. After World War II he became director of the Children's Department at London's Tavistock Clinic. Significantly, he renamed it the Department for Children and Parents and wrote one of the first papers on family therapy, about a method of his own devising (Bowlby, 1949).

Bowlby was commissioned by the World Health Organization to write a report on children displaced by the war, which appeared in 1951, and a later version of this report appeared as the well-known book *Child Care and the Growth of Love* in 1953. It is interesting to observe that in Bowlby's WHO report, a Freudian influence is obvious in the language used, but certainly not in the concepts expounded (Bretherton, 1992). His basic tenet was that healthy mental development of the young child was dependent upon an ongoing warm, intimate relationship with the mother (or permanent mother substitute). The mother acts as the child's ego and superego, the child gradually taking over such functions as he or she becomes capable – a very different scenario from the internal and interpersonal conflicts which characterize the Oedipal processes described by Freud (Box 5.2).

Bowlby's thinking was influenced by biological considerations and ethology, fruitful exchanges of ideas occurring between himself and ethologist Robert Hinde. He saw the organism's behaviour as controlled by a hierarchy of action plans, which, in more complex organisms, are determined by a combination of innate factors and those that are flexible in the light of environmental circumstances. This theorizing reflected a movement towards cybernetic, rather than drive-reduction, models of behavioural control (Bretherton, 1992). He likened the psychological development of the infant to that of an embryo: just as early interference in embryonic development will have widespread ill effects, so the failure to establish an attachment relationship to a single individual in the first year of life will be very difficult to make good, as 'the character of the psychic tissue has become fixed' (Bowlby, 1953: 59). Thus the notions of imprinting and critical periods in mother-infant relationships began to supplant the Freudian idea that the child is attached to the mother because she gratifies the child's oral needs. These ideas were later supported through animal research, such as Harry Harlow's well-known (but controversial, in terms of animal welfare) research with infant rhesus monkeys, who preferred to cling to a terry-cloth 'mother' than to a wire one that provided milk (Harlow and Harlow, 1966); however, as pointed out by Julie Robinson (1999), it is possible that the terry-cloth mother assisted temperature regulation and was therefore still meeting the infant's physical needs. Robert Hinde introduced Bowlby and Harlow to one another, and their work became mutually influential (Bowlby, 1969; van der Horst *et al.*, 2008).

BOX 5.2 DID BOWLBY'S IDEAS ANTICIPATE VYGOTSKIAN THEORY?

The Soviet psychologist Lev Vygotsky and later practitioners such as Jerome Bruner maintained that children develop through interaction with more capable individuals, who gradually withdraw support for activities as the child becomes independently capable of them. Vygotsky's work had not yet been translated into English when Bowlby wrote the following passage. While the language is Freudian, the notion is distinctly Vygotskian (Bretherton, 1992).

> It is not surprising that during infancy and early childhood these functions are either not operating at all or are doing so most imperfectly. During this phase of life, the child is therefore dependent on his mother performing them for him. She orients him in space and time, provides his environment, permits the satisfaction of some impulses, restricts others. She is his ego and his super-ego. Gradually he learns these arts himself, and as he does, the skilled parent transfers the roles to him. This is a slow, subtle and continuous process, beginning when he first learns to walk and feed himself, and not ending completely until maturity is reached ... Ego and super-ego development are thus inextricably bound up with the child's primary human relationships.
>
> *(Bowlby, 1951, cited in Bretherton, 1992: 761)*

Like Winnicott, Bowlby discussed infants' attachment to inanimate objects, but took issue with Winnicott's explanation in terms of a symbolic shift from subjective to objective existence. His more parsimonious explanation was simply that certain components of attachment behaviour become directed towards such objects because the 'natural' object, such as the breast, is unavailable. He suggested the term 'substitute object' rather than 'transitional object'. Bowlby's interpretation was supported by later research showing that in Mayan society in Guatemala, where infants sleep with their mothers and feed at will during the night, such objects are almost unknown (Morelli *et al.*, 1992).

Bowlby later expanded upon the notions of separation from, and loss of, attachment figures (Bowlby, 1975), drawing upon the work of Ainsworth, discussed below. An important theoretical advance in this connection was the introduction of the notion of 'working models' of the self and attachment figures. In other words, the child develops internal representations of the self and others, which guide his or her expectations about how others are likely to respond should he or she seek support from them. Bowlby suggested that this theory, taken together with Piagetian theory, provides a framework for understanding the psychoanalytic phenomenon of transference: the analyst is assimilated to the patient's pre-existing model, which has not yet accommodated to incorporate the way the therapist has actually behaved towards the patient.

In contrast with Freud, Bowlby's theorizing was supported thorough empirical observations of mothers and children. However, his ideas were received critically by influential members of the psychoanalytic movement at the time. Nevertheless, Bowlby's work has supplanted psychoanalysis in terms of its influence on modern child development theory, and his ideas about attachment have deeply influenced broader theorizing about grief and loss (Archer, 1999). Bowlby was concerned about the public policy implications of attachment and loss for children's welfare, and addressed issues such as adoption and the importance of mothers maintaining contact with their hospitalized children.

Someone else who proved to be an important figure in the development of attachment theory was James Robertson. He learned child observation skills working as a boilerman at a residential London nursery for children displaced by World War II, which was run by Freud's daughter Anna. The skills Robertson developed were later used to good effect when he worked for Bowlby collecting data about hospitalization of young children. Observing the plight of these children separated from their mothers, Robertson (1952, and later with his wife Joyce) made harrowing films that had the desired impact of bringing to public attention the hitherto unrecognized distress caused to young children through being separated from their parents, for example, through hospitalization or the mother's absence when giving birth to another child.

Mary Ainsworth (1913–1999) joined Bowlby's unit a little later; her name has become almost synonymous with attachment theory. As Mary Salter, she had completed a dissertation on secure dependence of the young child on parents, and moved from Canada to London in 1950, where she became familiar with Bowlby's work. She first studied mother–infant attachment in Uganda in the early 1950s, but did not publish the data for several more years, after moving to the USA and also renewing her intellectual collaboration with Bowlby.

Ainsworth made a very important contribution to attachment theory in two respects. First, she introduced the notion that the mother, or other attachment figure, provides a secure base from which the young child can explore the world. Second, she introduced the notion of parental sensitivity to child signals, paving the way for a later body of research on parent–infant communication. Ainsworth (e.g. Ainsworth and Wittig, 1969) is famed for developing an experimental protocol for examining infants' attachment to their mother, known as the 'Strange Situation'. The child is examined around the age of one, and is first observed playing with the primary caregiver, usually the mother. The child's behaviour is then observed in several different situations: when a stranger enters the room; when the mother leaves the room; when the mother returns and the stranger leaves; when the mother leaves; when the stranger returns; and when the mother returns. On the basis of studies using this procedure, Ainsworth proposed that infants vary in the degree of security of their attachment relationship. 'Securely attached' infants explore the room freely in their mother's presence, protest at her absence and reunite joyfully with her; this is regarded as the optimum type of attachment relationship, resulting from sensitive parenting. 'Insecure-avoidant' infants are less distressed at separation and avoid the mother on her return, while 'insecure-resistant' babies are distressed throughout the procedure and respond to the mother with a mixture of relief and anger on her return.

The sharing of ideas between those interested in infant development and attachment issues was not limited to Bowlby and Ainsworth: Bowlby was also influential in convening regular meetings between researchers from various backgrounds, including those interested in comparative psychology, such as Harlow and Hinde. The proceedings of these meetings appeared in *Determinants of Infant Behaviour* – a series of volumes edited throughout the 1960s by Brian Foss, whose own research interests lay in imitation and ethology. One of the present authors (RS) received undergraduate ethology lectures from Foss; on social occasions he would accompany himself on the piano and sing his own ditties on ethological themes, such as 'I'm a little fish' celebrating Niko Tinbergen's famous stickleback research.

Work by the psychiatrist Michael Rutter was later influential in examining more closely the mechanisms involved in 'maternal deprivation'. In his 1972 book, he concluded that there were two separate aspects to the reported ill-effects of separation: disruption of bonding with an attachment figure (not necessarily the mother); and privation of social, perceptual and linguistic stimulation (Rutter, 1972). The former might occur in short-term situations, such as hospitalization, while the latter was a crucial factor in the case of the institutionalized infants studied by Spitz and Goldfarb. A particularly important aspect of Rutter's work was to point out that not all children are similarly affected by separations. Variables modifying the long-term response include the child's age, the length of separation, whether there are other attachment figures available, whether the separation is a result of family discord and the temperament of the child. It was therefore becoming apparent that the developmental implications of attachment were much more complicated than previously supposed.

Later developments in attachment theory

Attachment theory became controversial as the twentieth century progressed, with increasing numbers of western women maintaining both careers and motherhood (Domenico and Jones, 2006). The issue was raised as to whether separation from their mothers would damage young children's development. Bowlby had always maintained that the attachment figure could be a mother substitute, and his position was supported by later research indicating that infants could be satisfactorily attached to a wider circle of caregivers, including fathers, grandparents and others (e.g. Schaffer and Emerson, 1964).

Sandra Scarr and Judy Dunn (1987), like Rutter, concluded that the psychological disturbance of institutionalized children was due to a lack of human contact and stimulation, not the lack of a mother per se. Despite early reports from horrified outside observers of children raised communally in Israeli kibbutzim, systematic research indicated that they were no more disturbed than children raised by their parents in the USA. Nevertheless, Ora Aviezer *et al.* (1994) concluded, on the basis of assessments of attachment with the Strange Situation, that communal sleeping arrangements were problematic, and too far removed from 'natural' parenting behaviour.

With regard to alternative (or, rather, supplementary) child care, Scarr and Dunn concluded that quality is what matters. This means that the parents and other carers should collaborate to provide a 'consistent and agreeable world for the child' (Scarr and Dunn, 1987: 187). Consistency involves having routines and not too many changes of carer. Children cared for consistently by others outside the family who are sensitive to their needs develop attachment relationships with them. Research indicating harmful effects of day care on infants mainly came from the USA, where the quality of such centres was not well regulated and was highly variable in comparison with some countries, such as Australia (Robinson, 1999), while attention was drawn to methodological criticisms of studies claiming negative effects and a tendency to make much of minimal negative findings (Ochiltree, 1994). We can add here that kibbutz-reared children actually experienced benefits, in terms of group skills and close peer relationships. With working mothers now commonplace in the West, the focus on quality care continues. For example, Jay Belsky and Michael Pluess (2011) found that adolescents with a history of experiencing low-quality child care had more behaviour problems if they had also been difficult-temperament infants. Interestingly, they did not find evidence to support a 'sensitivity to context' explanation (see Chapter 2), as these difficult-temperament children did not have especially *good* adolescent outcomes if they had experienced the *highest*-quality child care.

Robinson (1999) applied the notion of attachment to the 'stolen generations' of Australian Indigenous children removed from their families (see Chapter 9). She asked why many had such deep psychological disturbance if a child is capable of multiple attachments. For one thing, they experienced a range of stressors, such as racist attacks and various forms of abuse, as well as separation. Also, it is highly unusual for a child to simultaneously lose *all* attachment figures, as was usual in these cases. Even when siblings were removed together, there was often a deliberate policy to separate them. As Anna Freud found in studying World War II orphans, the peer group can provide attachment figures, and one of us (RS) has heard Indigenous people raised in institutions comment that other children were their lifeline. However, Robinson observed that many children may have received minimal support from other children because their peers were also psychologically injured. These children also generally experienced multiple placements; if we assume, as Bowlby did, that attachment 'blueprints' can be updated through experience, then we might predict that multiple placements would lead children to develop internal working models of relationships as temporary. It would hardly be surprising, then, if such children grew up with difficulties in maintaining interpersonal relationships.

Despite various challenges, attachment theory has remained an important guiding concept in developmental psychology. There has been continued use of the Strange Situation (with the addition of an extra type of attachment style – disorganized), although alternative, more naturalistic methods have also been developed. With the growing influence of lifespan approaches to development, attachment theory is also being increasingly adapted and applied to adults, under the assumption that early attachment schemas form a blueprint for other relationships. Mary Main and colleagues (1985) developed the Adult Attachment Interview as a means of assessing attachment style in older children and adults. This has opened up the issue of whether there is continuity in attachment. A recent longitudinal study, despite its rather misleading title, suggests not: while adopted children who experienced sensitive maternal support in both infancy and early adolescence were secure over the years, those who had experienced low maternal sensitivity in infancy but high sensitivity in adolescence shifted from low to high secure status (Beijersbergen *et al.*, 2012). This demonstration of plasticity presents an optimistic scenario in the face of less than ideal early parenting.

Freud's theory was that attachment developed *as a result of* the satisfaction of instinctual drives such as hunger, a view later supported by some biologically orientated writers (the 'cupboard love' theory of attachment – Archer, 1999). Freud's granddaughter, Sophie, has observed that, by contrast (and in line with the object relations school), some modern psychoanalysts have replaced this idea with the notion that seeking attachment is itself the primary 'wired-in' motivational force of human beings (Freud, 1998). This is consistent with the ethological tradition, and with the ideas of modern evolutionary psychologists that attachment theory can be seen as a major theoretical approach within the broader meta-theoretical framework of evolutionary theory (see Chapters 2 and 13).

Bowlby saw grief as having evolved in relation to attachment. Attachment theorists later came to use the term *attachment* to apply not only to the child's attachment to the caregiving figure, but also the caregiver's attachment to the child – so the term is used more broadly to apply to any affectional bonds (Archer, 1999). Viewed in this way, attachment theory assists in understanding grief reactions to all kinds of losses. Archer discussed the puzzling fact that, from an evolutionary perspective, grief appears maladaptive, resulting, for example, in immunosuppression and increased risk of ill health. However, it can be argued that temporary losses and separations from loved ones are much more common than permanent ones, and that humans have evolved behaviours that serve the purpose of attempting to become reunited with the missing person – typical grief reactions: searching, calling, preoccupation, etc. Thus grief becomes a by-product of the adaptive process of seeking to maintain important social relationships, and is the cost to be paid for the benefits of close relationships. As the UK's Queen Elizabeth II said in her condolence message with regard to the loss of life in New York's World Trade Centre on 11 September 2001, 'Grief is the price we pay for love'.

Attachment theory, like many other developmental theories, is open to the criticism that it has been developed within western societies and ignores alternative cultural perspectives (see Chapter 9), although we should recall that Ainsworth's early work was in Uganda. Japanese infants are much more likely than US children to show resistance; however, it has been questioned whether the Strange Situation is valid in Japan, as Japanese infants typically spend 24 hours a day with their mothers, so that the situation is especially strange for them (Miyake *et al.*, 1985). Furthermore, attachment theory is based on western notions of individuation, with the child being gradually 'weaned' from dependence towards independence (Ritchie and Ritchie, 1979); being expected to sleep alone at an early age is one manifestation of this. In most societies worldwide, the situation is different. In Polynesia, for example, a child is never required to identify with a single caretaking individual, but has multiple caregivers, including peers, and is expected to match her or his behaviour to various social environments, always having the choice to move from one to another.

Jane and James Ritchie observed that '[m]illions of human beings have grown up without [attachment]' and query what western child development experts would make of 'a New Guinea tribe where any lactating female will happily feed a hungry child or even a pig' (Ritchie and Ritchie, 1979: 155). Even in the West, children thrive under a variety of caretaking arrangements, as pointed out in a feminist critique of attachment theory (Birns, 1999). Indeed, being attached to a number of caregivers makes good evolutionary sense in case one attachment figure is unavailable for any reason (temporarily or permanently).

Rather than transporting western ideas to other cultures, it may be more meaningful to begin with understandings from other cultures themselves. In collectivist Japan, for example, the notion of *amae* (expectation of benevolence from others) might provide a more culturally appropriate framework than attachment for understanding social development (Rothbaum *et al.*, 2001). Nevertheless, findings from attachment research have been used to explain the abandonment of communal sleeping arrangements for children in Israeli kibbutzim (Sagi and Aviezer, 2001). A positive transportation of western grief and loss theory to another culture is that it has been adapted for use by Australian Indigenous people to provide a framework for understanding the effects of colonization (Wanganeen, 1990s, undated).

Critique of attachment theory has emanated from feminism as well as from sociocultural perspectives. Burman (2008) criticizes the whole 'project' of developmental psychology as focusing on mothers as providers of all that is best for their children, thereby acting to regulate women's lives. Interestingly, though, she values psychoanalytic theory more broadly as a counterpoint to positivist developmental psychology. Also from a feminist perspective, Beverly Birns critiqued attachment theory as follows: 'To believe that being a loving, sensitive mother to an infant can protect a child for life against the adversity of poverty, abuse, poor schools, uncaring neighborhoods and violent television, is both a theoretical and a practical mistake' (Birns, 1999: 19).

Finally, while attachment theory has been usefully applied to clinical practice, especially with young children, the evidence base is relatively small, and there has been a warning that 'popularized misconceptions' have led to the theory being inappropriately used, at times, in therapy (Zilberstein, 2014: 97). Specifically, research does not support the notion that conduct disorders such as aggression, lying and stealing result from attachment difficulties, and mislabelling a child's problems as an attachment disorder may have harmful results.

Conclusions

Writings about Freudian theory continue to appear, but they are largely from historical, philosophical or social perspectives, and not related to current developmental psychology. While some psychoanalytic practice continues, including with children, and has its own journals, it is not part of mainstream psychotherapy. Much has been written about what is wrong with Freudian theory. B.A. Farrell (1951), a philosopher, described it as 'unbelievably bad' as a theory. John Kihlstrom (2009), despite acknowledging Freud's cultural influence on the twentieth century as probably greater than that of Einstein, Lenin, Roosevelt, Picasso or the Beatles, saw Freudian theory as a 'dead weight' on that century's psychology.

Nevertheless, we should not finish this chapter without a reminder of some of its enduring legacies for understanding child development. Although there is a lack of evidence to support Freud's central Oedipal theory, his work continues to influence developmental theorizing via some of the paths we have attempted to chart above. Some influential 'guiding ideas' from the changing writings of Freud over the years include the notion of the continuity of development from infancy onwards, the idea that earlier influences on later behaviour occur at an unconscious level, and the suggestion that behaviour often results from attempts to resolve internal conflicts (Hilgard, 1962). Although the notion of 'the unconscious' is no longer considered tenable, there is a great deal of evidence for 'unconscious processes' (Westen, 1999). That these concepts remain broadly taken for granted in psychology is a measure of the depth of Freud's influence. His impact on the later development of attachment theory also remains as a major contribution to developmental psychology, and the notion of 'working models' of the self and others remains influential (Westen, 1999). Furthermore, attachment theory has been suggested as a potential integrating force underlying diverse schools of psychotherapy (Gold, 2011). Freudian theory also helped maintain some focus on emotional development in the face of radical behaviourism (Kihlstrom, 2009 – see Chapter 6).

Finally, it is of interest that, like Burman (2008), Freud's granddaughter Sophie made a connection between Freudian theory and postmodernism (Freud, 1998). Like Freudian theory, the overriding concern of constructivist theorists and narrative therapists is with the idiosyncratic meaning that individuals make of their experiences. So, while we noted earlier that Freud's theory was in many ways a reflection of its times, in this respect it can be said to have anticipated some later developments in psychological theorizing.

References

Ainsworth, M.D.S. and Wittig, B.A. 1969. Attachment and exploratory behaviour of one-year-olds in a strange situation. In B.M. Foss (ed.), *Determinants of infant behaviour.* Vol. 4. London: Methuen, 111–36.

Albino, R.C. and Long, M. 1951. The effect of infant food-deprivation upon adult hoarding in the white rat. *British Journal of Psychology*. 42: 146–54.

Andrews, B. and Brewin, C.R. 2000. What did Freud get right? *The Psychologist*. 13 (12): 605–7.

Archer, J. 1999. *The nature of grief: the evolution and psychology of reactions to loss*. London: Routledge.

Australian Broadcasting Corporation. 2014. Child sexual abuse royal commission: victims pleased with commission's progress after one year. ABC News. 11 January 2014. Available at: www.abc.net.au/news/2014-01-11/sex-abuse-victims-pleased-with-royal-commission-progress/5195450. Accessed 21 January 2015.

Aviezer, O., Van Ijzendoorn, M.H., Sagi, A. and Schuengel, C. 1994. 'Children of the Dream' revisited: 70 years of collective early child care in Israeli Kibbutzim. *Psychological Bulletin*. 116: 99–116.

Beijersbergen, M.D., Juffer, F., Bakermans-Kranenberg, M.J. and Van Ijzendoorn, M.H. 2012. Remaining or becoming secure: parental sensitive support predicts attachment continuity from infancy to adolescence in a longitudinal adoption study. *Developmental Psychology*. 48 (5): 1,277–82.

Belsky, J. and Pluess, M. 2011. Differential susceptibility to long-term effects of quality of child care on externalizing behavior in adolescence. *International Journal of Behavioral Development*. 36 (1): 2–10.

Birns, B. 1999. Attachment theory revisited: challenging conceptual and methodological sacred cows. *Feminism and Psychology*. 9 (1): 10–21.

Bowlby, J. 1949. The study and reduction of group tensions within the family. *Human Relations*. 2: 123.

Bowlby, J. 1953. *Child care and the growth of love*. Harmondsworth: Penguin.

Bowlby, J. 1969. *Attachment*. Harmondsworth: Penguin.

Bowlby, J. 1975. *Separation*. Harmondsworth: Penguin.

Bretherton, I. 1992. The origins of attachment theory: John Bowlby and Mary Ainsworth. *Developmental Psychology*. 28 (5): 759–75.

Burman, E. 2008. *Deconstructing developmental psychology*. London: Routledge.

Domenico, D.M. and Jones, K.H. 2006. Career aspirations of women in the 20th century. *Journal of Career and Technical Education*. 22 (2): 1–7.

Emde, R.N. 1992. Individual meaning and increasing complexity: contributions of Sigmund Freud and René Spitz to developmental psychology. *Developmental Psychology*. 28 (3): 347–59.

Erikson, E.H. 1963. *Childhood and society*. Harmondsworth: Penguin.

Erikson, E.H. 1968. *Identity, youth and crisis*. New York: Norton.

Farrell, B.A. 1951. The scientific testing of psychoanalytic findings and theory. *British Journal of Medical Psychology*. 24: 35–41.

Fisher, S. and Greenberg, R.P. 1996. *Freud scientifically reappraised: testing the theories and therapy*. New York: Wiley.

Fleming, J.S. 2006. Piaget, Kohlberg, Gilligan, and others on moral development. Available at: http://swppr.com/Textbook/Ch%207%20Morality.pdf. Accessed 12 August 2011.

Freud, S. 1914/1940. *The psychopathology of everyday life*. Harmondsworth: Penguin.

Freud, S. 1910/1974. *Two short accounts of psychoanalysis*. Harmondsworth: Penguin.

Freud, Sophie. 1998. The baby and the bathwater: Freud as a postmodernist. *Families in Society: The Journal of Contemporary Human Services*. September–October (79): 5.

Gladding, S.T. 1998. *Family therapy: history, theory and practice*. Second edn. Upper Saddle River, NJ: Prentice Hall.

Gold, J. 2011. Attachment theory and psychotherapy integration: an introduction and review of the literature. *Journal of Psychotherapy Integration*. 21 (3): 221–31.

Harlow, H.F and Harlow, M.K. 1966. Learning to love. *American Scientist*. 54: 244–72.

Hilgard, E.R. 1962. The scientific status of psychoanalysis. In E. Nagel, P. Suppes and A. Tarski (eds), *Logic, methodology and philosophy of science: proceedings of the 1960 International Congress*. Stanford, CA: Stanford University Press, 375–90. Reproduced in S.G.M. Lee and M. Herbert. 1970. *Freud and psychology*. Harmondsworth: Penguin, 29–49.

Kihlstrom, J.F. 2009. Is Freud still alive? No, not really. Available at: http://socrates.berkeley.edu/~kihlstrm/freuddead.htm. Accessed 21 January 2014.

Lothane, Z. 2006. Freud's legacy: is it still with us? *Psychoanalytic Psychology*. 23 (2): 285–301.

Main, M., Kaplan, N. and Cassidy, J. 1985. Security in infancy, childhood, and adulthood: a move to the level of representation. In I. Bretherton and E. Waters (eds), *Growing points of attachment theory and research. Monographs of the Society for Research in Child Development*. 50 (1–2, serial no. 209): 66–104.

Masson, J.M. 1984. *The assault on truth: Freud's suppression of the seduction theory*. New York: Farrar, Straus & Giroux.

Miyake, K., Chen, S.J. and Campos, J.J. 1985. Infant temperament, mother's mode of interaction, and attachment in Japan: an interim report. In I. Bretherton and E. Waters (eds), *Growing points of attachment theory and research. Monographs of the Society for Research in Infant Development*. 50 (1–2, serial no. 209): 276–97.

Morelli, G., Rogoff, B., Oppenheim, D. and Goldsmith, D. 1992. Cultural variation in infants' sleeping arrangements: questions of independence. *Developmental Psychology*. 28: 604–13.

Ochiltree, G. 1994. *Effects of child care on young children: forty years of research*. Melbourne: Australian Institute of Family Studies.

Ritchie, J. and Ritchie, J. 1979. *Growing up in Polynesia*. Sydney: Allen and Unwin.

Robertson, J. 1952. A two-year-old goes to hospital [film]. London: Tavistock Child Development Research Unit. Available at: www.robertsonfilms.info/. Accessed 21 January 2015.

Robinson, J.A. 1999. Update on attachment theory and research. Paper presented to Child and Adolescent Mental Health Service, Norwich House, Adelaide. April.

Rothbaum, F., Weisz, J., Pott, M., Miyake, K. and Morelli, G. 2001. Deeper into attachment and culture. *American Psychologist*. 56 (10): 827–8.

Rutter, M. 1972. *Maternal deprivation reassessed*. Harmondsworth: Penguin.

Sagi, A. and Aviezer, O. 2001. The rise and fall of children's communal sleeping in Israeli Kibbutzim: an experiment in nature and implications for parenting. *Newsletter of the International Society for the Study of Behavioral Development*. 1 (38): 4–6.

Scarr, S. and Dunn, J. 1987. *Mother care/other care*. Harmondsworth: Penguin.

Schaffer, H.R. and Emerson, P.E. 1964. The development of social attachments in infancy. *Monographs of the Society for Research in Infant Development*. 29 (3, serial no. 94): 1–77.

Spence, C.H. 1907. *State children in Australia: a history of boarding out and its developments*. Adelaide: Varolen and Sons Ltd.

Van der Horst, F.C.P., Leroy, H.A. and van der Veer, R. 2008. When strangers meet: John Bowlby and Harry Harlow on attachment behavior. *Integrative Psychology and Behavioral Science*. 42: 370–88.

Wanganeen, R. 1990s, undated. *Discussion paper: spiritual healing using loss and grief*. Adelaide: Sacred Site Within Healing Centre (now Australian Institute for Loss and Grief).

Westen, D. 1999. The scientific status of unconscious processes: is Freud really dead? *Journal of the American Psychoanalytic Association.* 47: 1,061–106.

Winnicott, D.W. 1953. Transitional objects and transitional phenomena. *International Journal of Psychoanalysis.* 34: 1–9.

World Health Organization. 2001. *Comparative risk assessment: child sexual abuse.* Sydney: WHO Collaborating Centre for Evidence and Health Policy in Mental Health.

Zilberstein, K. 2014. The use and limitations of attachment theory in child psychotherapy. *Psychotherapy.* 51: 93–103.

6

MECHANISM

The whole is equal to the sum of its parts

Introduction

Possibly no other theory of child development has been subjected to such scrutiny as behaviourism, the approach to development forming the core of the present chapter. In Chapter 3, we saw that William James was severely critical of this approach ('structuralism'), because he considered it to provide a narrow and artificial view of human behaviour. As Frances Horowitz observed, 'It has been declared obsolete, overthrown, and outmoded. Yet, paradoxically, this object of derision, behaviorism, has given us our most unassailable behavioral laws' (Horowitz 1987: 62). Not only has it stood the test of time, but its underlying principles have given rise to powerful behavioural technologies, such as those used to assist people with intellectual and physical impairments.

Here, we describe the work of a number of influential theorists, including Ivan Pavlov, John Watson, Burrhus F. Skinner and Albert Bandura, the root metaphor for their theories being 'mechanism' (Pepper, 1942). The mechanistic model 'represents the universe as a machine, composed of discrete pieces operating in a spatio-temporal field' (Reese and Overton, 1970: 131). Also relevant are three key metaphors identified by Richard Mayer (1996) in relation to theories of learning and instruction: learning as response strengthening (S-R); learning as information processing; and learning as knowledge construction. We can also note here that social cognitive and information-processing approaches share with behaviourism an underpinning deterministic outlook towards developmental theory; that is, whatever facet of development we are considering, for every effect there is an identifiable antecedent cause that can be discovered in terms of its constituent elements. We first consider the development and rise of behaviourism and then discuss how other theoretical views challenged its pre-eminence.

A mechanistic outlook

The philosophical issue of the relationship between the mind and the body is relevant for a consideration of mechanism. Plato (*c.*429–*c.*347 BCE) adopted a dualist position, arguing that the two were different entities. He considered the body as temporal but the mind as having greater permanence, as ideas live on through generations. In his book *Utopia*, the mind was to be cultivated by education in order to bring some reason and order into what are often seen as chaotic ideas. Plato's theory of 'Ideas' (or 'thoughts') was developed in *The Republic*. He was seeking to understand the essence of things – the distinction between reality and appearance. In the seventh book of *The Republic*, Plato relates a myth that represents, symbolically, the structure of reality.

> 'And now,' I said, 'let me show in a figure how far our nature is enlightened or unenlightened: Behold! Human beings living in an underground den, which has a mouth open toward the light and reaching all along the den: here they have been from their childhood, and have their legs and necks chained so that they cannot move, and can only see before them, being prevented by the chains from turning round their heads. Above and behind them a fire is blazing at a distance, and between the fire and the prisoners there is a raised way; and you will see, if you look, a low wall built along the way, like the screen which marionette players have in front of them, over which they show the puppets.'
>
> 'I see.'
>
> 'And do you see,' I said, 'men passing along the wall carrying all sorts of vessels, and statues, and figures of animals made of wood and stone and various materials, which appear over the wall? Some of them are talking, others silent.'
>
> 'You have shown me a strange image, and they are strange prisoners.'
>
> 'Like ourselves,' I replied; 'and they see only their own shadows, or the shadows of one another, which the fire throws on the opposite wall of the cave.'
>
> *(Plato, cited in Garvey and Stangroom, 2012: 72)*

In this myth, the cave represents the world perceived by the senses, and its shadows are the things of the world, of the senses. The outside world represents the true world perceived by the mind, or the world of Ideas. The difference is one of appearance and reality. Plato's identification of the mind–body split is indirectly linked to the rise of experimental science in the modern era, since the mechanistic approach rejects introspection as a method appropriate for a behavioural scientist. Subjectivism and speculation regarding entities that cannot be directly observed or measured are believed to have no place in an empirical behavioural science. As a rationalist, Plato sought to solve problems using deductive as opposed to inductive reasoning, with knowledge derived from reason, which he argued to be superior to that derived from sense perceptions alone. In articulating the mind–body split, Plato set the scene for an ongoing debate regarding the 'proper' subject of study of psychology.

The context in which behaviourism arose

Behaviourism developed in the context of the rise to prominence in the nineteenth century of Newtonian science, which replaced the medieval view of the world, as a living, organic, spiritual universe, with a mechanistic vision of reality. In the Newtonian view, the earlier interpretation of the world based upon introspection, revelation, reason and ordinary experience was abandoned in favour of rigid determinism and linear causality. Science delimited knowledge to a worldview constrained by statistical probability, value-free research and quantification. The presentation of science as the sole arbiter of knowledge has since come to be labelled scientism (see Chapter 1).

Another underlying factor associated with the development of behaviourism was 'materialism', a key feature being that scientific principles could be applied to the study of living organisms. To this end, physical and chemical laws were the basis of explanation – for example, physiology was reduced to chemistry. It was in this intellectual climate of scientism and materialism that pioneer psychologists such as Sigmund Freud (see Chapter 5) and Pavlov were educated.

Ivan Pavlov (1849–1936) and the conditioned reflex

Pavlov was born in a small town in central Russia, the son of a clergyman. He turned from theological studies to obtain degrees in natural science and medicine, after which he travelled in Europe and studied with other scientists. He founded the Institute of Experimental Medicine in St Petersburg in 1890 and became its lifelong director. In 1904 he was the first Russian scientist to be awarded the Nobel Prize.

Pavlov's discovery of classical conditioning as a way of viewing the functioning of the nervous system remains his greatest contribution to psychology. In the course of his physiology experiments Pavlov noted certain irregularities in the normal functioning of the digestive glands of dogs. Sometimes a dog would start to secrete digestive juices as soon as it saw the person who customarily fed it. Pavlov conducted his preliminary experiments by simply showing the dog bread and then giving the dog bread to eat. Eventually the dog would begin to salivate as soon as it saw the bread. Salivation when the bread was placed in its mouth was a natural reflex of the digestive system, while salivation at the sight of the bread was learned – that is, a conditioned reflex, or CR.

Further experimentation clarified the conditioning process. For example, a bell (conditioned stimulus) was repeatedly sounded before food (unconditioned stimulus) was placed in a dog's mouth to produce salivation (unconditioned reflex) until eventually the sound of the bell alone caused salivation (conditioned reflex) (for further detail, see a child development text such as Slee *et al.*, 2012). Pavlov grasped that the importance of his discovery of the CR lay in the potential it provided for reducing complex behaviour to basic elements. Thus, his work lay well within the prevailing empirical paradigm of the time. As Pavlov wrote:

> A conditioned reflex is formed on the basis of all unconditioned reflexes and out of all the possible agents of the inner and outer world both in their elementary form and in their largest complexes subject to only one limitation the cerebral hemispheres must be provided with the corresponding receptory elements.
>
> *(Pavlov, cited in Gantt, 1941: 171)*

Pavlov's concept of associative learning, or associationism, dated back to early Greek philosophy (Mackintosh, 2003). From a scientific, empirical point of view, the significance of the discovery of the CR lay in its potential to explain human behaviour, for:

> These lectures are concerned with the physiological analysis of human conditions shading from the normal to the definitely pathological, from the analysis of types, as artists and scientists, to a discussion of the mechanisms of hysteria, obsessions, functional paralyses to those of catatonia and that most common form of insanity, schizophrenia.
>
> *(Gantt, 1941: 9)*

Later in his career Pavlov worked to link the CR to an understanding of human neuroses.

New understandings regarding neurology have overridden Pavlov's theory that excitation and inhibition occur on the surface of the cortex: it is now understood that the transmission of neural impulses occurs along neurons and across synapses. Pavlov's theory has also been criticized for suggesting that all behaviour is the sum of accumulated CRs, but it does not appear that Pavlov made such a suggestion (Pavlov, 1932). Others, such as Watson, were certainly interested in such an idea.

John B. Watson (1878–1958) and behaviourism

Watson was born in Greenville, South Carolina, USA. His PhD in psychology was completed at the University of Chicago, where he subsequently lectured. Later he became a professor at Johns Hopkins University. Scandal led to his dismissal, and in 1920 he left for New York, moving out of the academic world to apply his knowledge very successfully to the world of advertising. However, he continued to write psychology articles for popular magazines, such as *Harpers* and *Cosmopolitan*. Watson strongly rejected introspection in favour of the principles of objective observation of behaviour, and placed emphasis on the importance of the environment in shaping human development.

The first psychological laboratories set up in Germany and the USA defined psychology as the study of consciousness, with introspection as the principal method of study. However, critics quickly identified that subjects could not agree with any reliability on the description of sensation, images and feelings. At the same time, Freud was arguing that important aspects of the mind were not in consciousness. In the USA a literal revolution was occurring in the study of human behaviour. Numbers of researchers were making a significant contribution to the understanding of human development, utilizing basic tenets of the scientific method. Watson called behaviourism a 'purely American production' (Watson, 1914: ix).

Briefly, Watson's method placed a great deal of emphasis upon objective observation. Drawing upon his experience as a student of animal behaviour, Watson claimed that the subject matter of psychology was not consciousness, but behaviour:

> Psychology as the behaviorist views it is a purely objective, experimental branch of natural science. Its theoretical goal is the prediction and control of behavior. Introspection forms no essential part of its methods, nor is the scientific value of its data dependent upon the readiness with which they lend themselves to interpretation in terms of consciousness. The behaviorist attempts to get a unitary scheme of animal response. He recognizes no dividing line between man and brute.
>
> *(Watson, 1913: 158)*

He emphasized environmental stimuli (such as a loud noise or praise from a teacher) and the response (such as a startle reaction or on-task pupil behaviour). For this reason, Watson's view of behaviour is often called stimulus–response (S-R) psychology. Watson argued that the only inherited features of behaviour were simple physiological reflexes (such as the knee-jerk reflex). Watson credited all else to learning, hence his claim:

> Give me a dozen healthy infants, well formed and my own specified world to bring them up in and I'll guarantee to take any one at random and train him to become any kind of specialist I might select – doctor, lawyer, artist, merchant-chief, and yes even beggar-man and thief, regardless of his talents, penchants, abilities, vocation and race of his ancestors.
>
> *(Watson, 1930: 104)*

We can see a similar Confucian belief in the importance of the environment for shaping a child, in the story of Mencius's mother (Box 6.1). Watson was heavily influenced by the work of Pavlov, and wanted to explain how all complex behaviours, both animal and human, were the result of conditioning by the environment.

One of the most frequently cited learning theory experiments in psychological literature was conducted in 1920 by Watson and his research assistant Rosalie Rayner (who was implicated in the scandal that led to his dismissal from Johns Hopkins University). They had already tested an infant, Little Albert, at nine months old, finding that he showed no fear reactions when confronted suddenly with a white rat, rabbit, dog, monkey masks, cotton wool and so on. That is, in learning theory terms, the stimuli were neutral. They discovered that, when a metal bar was struck with a hammer behind Albert, the loud sound (unconditioned stimulus)

BOX 6.1 THE MOTHER OF MENCIUS: A STORY IN THE CONFUCIAN TRADITION

It was said that Mencius was raised by his mother alone because his father died when he was little. Their first house was near a cemetery, so young Mencius imitated the performances of obsequies. His mother thought that this was not good for the child, so she moved to a place near a market. In this environment, Mencius thus imitated butchers' activities. His mother was again dissatisfied and moved to a place near a temple and school. Mencius thus learned to perform rituals and practise etiquette, for he often saw people doing so. By now the mother of Mencius was happy and decided to stay there permanently. This story illustrates a widely accepted belief in Chinese society that what children played typically reflected their surroundings and the things they encountered in their daily lives.

(Bai, 2005: 14 (this widely known story originated from Liu Xiang's Biography of Exemplary Women, *1922))*

---

made him cry. When Albert was 11 months old, a white rat was presented to him, and as he reached for it the bar was struck behind his head. Little Albert jumped and fell forward with his face in the mattress. When he reached for the rat again and his hand touched it, the bar was struck and again he fell forward and began to whimper. The experiment was stopped at this point. One week later, when the rat was presented he would not reach for it. When the rat was pushed nearer he reached for it very tentatively. Thus, Watson and Rayner demonstrated learning in infancy through a process of conditioning.

An interesting aside in Watson's biography is that he reported suffering from an anxiety attack while at the University of Chicago. He observed that this experience 'in a way prepared me to accept a large part of Freud when I first began to get really acquainted with him around 1910' (Watson, 1936: 274). Watson first used William James's habit theory to explain psychoanalysis, and later used Pavlov's notion of classical conditioning. He hoped ultimately to assimilate psychoanalysis into behaviourism (Rilling, 2000). Box 6.2 describes Watson's views about introspectionism and psychoanalysis.

Horowitz noted that evaluating Watson's contribution to developmental psychology is problematic given that many psychologists suggest that 'he was, at best, a psychologist concerned only with defining psychology as a natural science and, at worst, a dogmatist who went far beyond his data to popularize his beliefs about development' (Horowitz, 1992: 360). Watson certainly acknowledged the biological functions of the human organism (Horowitz, 1992), but his theory focused on learning as being almost entirely responsible for behavioural development. In sum:

BOX 6.2 WATSON TAKES AIM AT FREUD AND INTROSPECTIONISM

Watson wanted no competitors and took aim at his rivals. Both Freudian psychoanalysis and introspectionism came under his fire. He regarded psychoanalysis as a rather occult enterprise, and berated its reliance on untestable hypothetical constructs and mystical notions such as 'the unconscious'. Many of Freud's observations, he felt, could be rendered in more behavioural terms. For example, affection could be restated as an 'organic sensory response', and transference as 'stimulus generalization'. Introspectionism, which was more deeply entrenched in American psychology, had to be more forcibly rooted out. In a letter to Robert Yerkes, Watson wrote that he had been experimenting with conditioning in humans and was elated to find that 'it works so beautifully in place of introspection . . . that it deserves to be driven home; we can work on the human being as we can on animals and from the same point of view'.

(Magai and McFadden, 1995: 98)

Watson's developmental model was exceedingly simple, containing no discussion of stages and little of sequences; there was no consideration that learning principles were in any way influenced by the age of the child. Furthermore, the developmental progression, despite the nod to structural change as variable, was linear and cumulative.

(Horowitz, 1992: 361)

Watson's theory provided a basis for shaping the nature of psychological thought in the early 1900s, particularly in the USA. In fact, he was hailed as a 'second Moses' for achieving the 'promised land' of behaviourism (Magai and McFadden, 1995: 98). He also influenced parenting at the time, providing the following advice in a book on child care:

There is a sensible way of treating children. Treat them as though they were young adults. Dress them, bathe them with care and circumspection. Let your behavior always be objective and kindly firm. Never hug and kiss them, never let them sit in your lap. If you must, kiss them once on the forehead when they say goodnight. Shake hands with them in the morning. Give them a pat on the head if they have made an extraordinarily good job of a difficult task. Try it out. In a week's time you will be utterly ashamed of the mawkish, sentimental way you have been handling it.

(Watson, 1928: 81–2)

Watson himself was rather ambivalent towards parenthood, and did not display physical affection towards his own children. In Chapter 9 we will see a suggestion that Watson's cultural and personal background influenced his attitude to emotions. However, he did compare children favourably with the subjects of his comparative psychology experiments, commenting that a baby could be 'more fun to the square inch than all the frogs and rats in creation' (Buckley, 1989, cited in Magai and McFadden, 1995: 97).

Mary Cover Jones (1896–1987) and behaviour therapy

Mary Cover Jones has been described as 'one of the most remarkable people in the history of Psychology' (Krasner, 1988: 91). As a parent, educator, psychologist and researcher, she emphasized that children were individuals who benefited by educational opportunities suited to their needs. Like Rayner, Jones worked for Watson as a research assistant. She was not comfortable with the ethical aspects of Watson's work with Little Albert (although Watson had some reservations about it himself, this did not prevent him from joking that if Albert had problems later in life, some psychoanalyst would probably attribute it to a sexual neurosis) (Magai and McFadden, 1995). Jones was more interested in the question of whether Watson's procedure could be reversed – whether a child with a phobia could be cured using conditioning principles. Working with children aged three years, she published research in 1924 demonstrating that the fear of furry objects could be deconditioned, her study with 'Little Peter' becoming widely cited. Jones's work was seminal, representing the establishment of behaviour therapy. Her research provided the basis for Skinnerian operant conditioning, Wolpean desensitization and Bandurian modelling. Wolpe dubbed her 'the mother of behaviour therapy', and yet she is now less remembered than Watson (Magai and McFadden, 1995). Procedures she developed are still used, however. For example, Robert Zettle (2003) reports the successful use of systematic desensitization in the treatment of mathematics anxiety disorders. Despite Jones's enormous influence on behaviourism, she focused on longitudinal work for most of her career; she later said that she would no longer be satisfied with treating a child's phobia without considering his or her total complexity as a person, and without following up with his or her longer-term progress (see Jones, n.d.).

B.F. Skinner (1904–1990) and operant conditioning

Behaviourism as developed by US psychologist B.F. Skinner has come to be known as operant conditioning. One of the most basic differences between classical conditioning and operant conditioning is that the former applies to reflexes and the latter to voluntary behaviour. Reflexes are called respondent behaviour, in contrast with voluntary or operant behaviour. Thus, when a dog salivates in response to food the salivation is a reflex or a 'respondent'. Operants, in contrast, are said to occur voluntarily – they are emitted rather than elicited. Thus, operants operate on, or have an effect on, the environment, and are not necessarily associated with any particular stimulus. When you see a bird moving around in its cage, it is not necessarily responding to any stimulus. Similarly, the babbling of a young baby is operant behaviour. For detail of the basic elements of Skinner's theory, readers are referred to introductory child development texts, such as the one by Phillip Slee and colleagues (2012).

A key term relevant to operant conditioning is that of 'consequences'. Put simply, the consequences that follow a response may either increase or decrease the probability of (a) further response(s). If the consequence to a response produces a repetition of the response or an increase in the frequency of responding, the consequence is described as reinforcing or rewarding. Should the consequence to a response result in suppression or reduction of the behaviour, the consequence is described as punishing.

Reinforcement can be either positive or negative. With positive reinforcement the frequency of response increases because it is followed by consequences that the subject finds rewarding. For example, if a dog is given a biscuit for running to its owner when it hears a whistle, this increases the likelihood of a repetition of this behaviour when the owner whistles. With negative reinforcement the frequency of a response increases because the response removes, or enables the organism to avoid, a negative or painful stimulus. For instance, a child completes a homework assignment to avoid being kept in after school.

The analysis of operantly conditioned behaviour has its foundations in laboratory studies of animals such as rats and pigeons, in the famous cage-like apparatus known as a Skinner box. While moving around, the animal inadvertently depresses a lever, which releases food into a tray and turns on a light. The food serves as a reinforcer to the hungry animal, which will depress the lever again to obtain more food (reinforcement). The lever-pressing is an operant, since it does not occur in response to any known stimulus. The experimenter may shape the subject's behaviour by rewarding successive approximations to the desired behaviour.

Food is an example of a primary reinforcer. Secondary reinforcers are previously neutral stimuli (such as the light in the Skinner box) that acquire reinforcing properties when paired with primary reinforcers. Some reinforcers – general reinforcers – acquire the capacity to reinforce many behaviours; for humans, these include praise, social prestige and power.

Various schedules of reinforcement (e.g. continuous, intermittent) are available for conditioning behaviour and each has a different impact on establishing and maintaining the behaviour in question. Generally speaking, variable interval schedules tend to elicit a high response rate (watch individuals playing poker machines) because of the unpredictability of knowing when a reward will be given.

Skinner's interest in the environmental conditions surrounding an organism was reflected in how his daughter was raised in infancy (Box 6.3).

There are three essential principles associated with traditional behaviourism. As noted in Chapter 1, it is argued that the organism at birth is a *tabula rasa*, and little attention is paid to internal cognitive structures. Second, it is believed that the principles of learning and conditioning apply across all species. Finally, the learner is essentially passive in the face of the conditioning process.

BOX 6.3 PARENTING SKINNER STYLE

Skinner reported in some detail the raising of his daughter Deborah in a device he designed and called the baby tender.

> For our second child, Deborah, I built a crib-sized living space that we began to call the 'baby tender'. It had sound absorbing walls and a large picture window. Air entered through filters at the bottom and after being warmed and moistened, moved by convection upward through and around the edges of a tightly stretched canvas, which served as a mattress. [A small fan blew the air if the room was hot.] A strip of sheeting 10 yards long passed over the canvas, a clean section of which could be cranked into place in a few seconds.
>
> *(Skinner, 1979: 30)*

Deborah was introduced to the baby tender from the very first weeks of life and slept in it more or less regularly until she was two and a half years old. Skinner claimed that the tender's soundproofing enabled Deborah to sleep well and protected her from infection. Skinner's initial reporting of his invention in *The Ladies Home Journal* in October 1945 generated considerable controversy, including a comparison of the project with the Skinner box. Contrary to rumour, Deborah did not eventually suicide but grew up to become a successful artist.

Beginning with the writings of Watson, the central proposition of behaviourism is that a science of behaviour is possible. However, as promulgated by Skinner, radical behaviourism takes a further step and asserts that a science of behaviour can be a *natural* science (this is what makes radical behaviourism 'radical'; see Baum, 2011). William Baum further notes that behavioural events are natural events that have no agency – 'they just happen'. Moreover they can be explained by other natural events, and this does not require any reference to inner states or other variables intervening between stimulus and response.

Some researchers cast doubt on the extent to which the principles proposed in behavioural theory can be applied. For example, Elsie Bregman (1934) found that it was possible to condition a child with fear if the conditioned stimulus was a live animal – like a rat – but not if it was an inanimate object. Martin Seligman (1972) linked conditioning to evolutionary theory, noting that birds are more easily conditioned to visual stimuli and human infants to verbal stimuli, suggesting that we come into the world 'prepared' in some way. Seligman further suggested that this preparedness might have survival value, as in the innate fear of snakes. Similarly, research by R.C. Bolles (1980) found that pigeons do not 'simply peck' at a small, lighted key, but are actually pecking in an attempt to eat it. This raises the interesting question of whether many of the behaviourist experiments, such as that with Little Albert, have fortuitously tapped into elements such as the 'preparedness' of the organism to be conditioned. Such considerations led to the development of 'ecological learning theory', which focused not just on 'how' learning happens, but 'what' is learned, in an adaptive and evolutionary sense (Davey, 1989).

There is no doubt that the principles of operant conditioning remain influential in a range of applied fields. An examination of key journals, such as the *Journal of Applied Behavior Analysis* will highlight the ongoing assessment of aspects of behaviour theory. For example, Eric Murphy and colleagues (2003) have researched the effectiveness of reinforcers. Henry Schlinger (1992) pointed out that Skinner's theory evolved towards a more functional than mechanistic view of behaviour, in the sense that it was specifically intended to be applied, and there is no doubt that behaviourist principles continue to be used in practice. For example, stamps, stickers and time-out are part of the daily regime of classroom behaviour management. Applied Behaviour Analysis (ABA), previously known as behaviour modification, is the application of classical and operant conditioning to modify behavior, widely used, for example, in treatment programmes with autistic children (see Autism Speaks, n.d., and Raising Children Network, n.d).

Although R.J. DeGrandpre suggested that 'operant principles represent today only a marginal force in contemporary psychological science' (DeGrandpre, 2000: 722), their usefulness in studying child development should not be underestimated. For example, a recent analysis of studies on conditioned kicking responses in infants aged between two and four months has been used to show that socio-economic status does not affect infant learning at that early age (Gerhardstein *et al.*, 2012).

Albert Bandura (b. 1925) and social learning theory

Learning theorists have attempted to develop a theory to account for all learning, but to date this goal has proved elusive. Moving beyond classical and operant conditioning, a third possibility accounts for learning in terms of imitation – social learning theory, as described by Albert Bandura and associates (Bandura, 1986, 1971; Bandura and Walters, 1963). Bandura and Walters's *Social Learning and Personality Development* (1963) broadened the scope of social learning theory with the now familiar principles of observational learning and vicarious reinforcement:

> Learning would be exceedingly laborious, not to mention hazardous, if people had to rely solely on the effects of their own actions to inform them of what to do. Fortunately, most human behavior is learned observationally through modeling: from observing others, one forms an idea of how new behaviors are performed, and on later occasions this coded information serves as a guide for action.

> *(Bandura and Walters, 1963: 22)*

Their research called attention to the importance of imitation and role models in learning. Their classic 1963 study featured a laboratory situation where nursery school children watched a woman (the 'model') play with toys and a life-size plastic 'Bobo' doll. In the experimental condition, she played quietly with the toys for a minute and then began to hit, kick and sit on the doll, with accompanying vocalizations such as 'Pow!' and 'Sock him in the nose!' In the control condition she simply played quietly with the toys. Neither the woman nor the watching children were directly reinforced at any time. After the woman had left the room, each child in turn was left alone with the toys. Children who had observed the aggressive model were more likely than the control group to act aggressively. These results could not be predicted by operant conditioning theories since there was no apparent reinforcement for the children's behaviour. The reviews of research in this field suggest a possible causal link between exposure to violence and increases in aggressive behavior (e.g. Anderson, 2004). Of course, claims regarding causality in social science research are highly contentious. Nevertheless Kevin Browne and Catherine Hamilton-Giachritsis concluded that:

> There is consistent evidence that violent imagery in television, film and video, and computer games has substantial short-term effects on arousal, thoughts, and emotions, increasing the likelihood of aggressive or fearful behaviour in younger children, especially in boys. The evidence becomes inconsistent when considering older children and teenagers, and long-term outcomes for all ages.
>
> *(Browne and Hamilton-Giachritsis, 2005: 5)*

Generally, Bandura believed that existing models of learning theory were too mechanistic: 'Much of the early psychological theorizing was founded on behavioristic principles that embraced an input–output model linked by an internal conduit that makes behavior possible but exerts no influence of its own on behavior' (Bandura, 2001: 2). In this view, human behaviour is shaped and controlled automatically and mechanically by environmental stimuli. That is, behaviourism is seen primarily as a theory of performance control, rather than a theory of learning. While it can explain how learned imitative behaviour can be shaped by the prospect of a reward, it cannot explain how new response structures are developed as a result of observation. As such, the mechanistic approach undervalued the potential of individuals to affect their own behaviour. In Bandura's theory, psychological development is neither driven by inner forces nor shaped by external stimuli. Rather, symbolic, vicarious and self-regulatory processes play a significant role. For example, Kenneth Dodge and colleagues proposed that 'Social learning theory posits that the experience of physical abuse will lead to later aggression to the extent that it makes aggressive responses salient in one's response repertoire as efficacious in leading to positive outcomes' (Dodge *et al.*, 1990: 259).

By the 1970s Bandura was becoming aware that a key element was missing, not only from the prevalent learning theories of the day but also from his own social learning theory. In 1977 he published 'Self-efficacy: toward a unifying theory of behavioral change', in which he identified the important piece of that missing element – self-belief. With the publication of *Social Foundations of Thought and Action: A Social Cognitive Theory* (1986), Bandura advanced a view of human functioning that accords a central role to cognitive, vicarious, self-regulatory and self-reflective processes in human adaptation and change. People are viewed as agents who are proactive, self-reflecting and self-regulating, rather than simply reactive organisms shaped by environmental forces or driven by inner psychic impulses. Theoretically, human behaviour was viewed as the product of an interaction among personal, behavioural and environmental influences. For example, how people interpret the results of their own behaviour informs and alters their environments and the personal factors they possess, which, in turn, inform and alter subsequent behaviour. This is the foundation of Bandura's (1986) conception of *reciprocal determinism*. This is the view that behaviour, personal factors (in the form of cognition, affect and biological events) and environmental influences create interactions that result in a *triadic reciprocality*. Bandura altered the label of his theory from social learning to social *cognitive* theory, both to distance it from prevalent social learning theories of the day and to emphasize that cognition plays a critical role in people's ability to construct reality, self-regulate, encode information and perform behaviours.

Bandura has continued to develop his work and, as we observed in Chapter 4, elaborated on the idea of human consciousness: 'Consciousness is the very substance of mental life that not only makes life personally manageable but worth living' (Bandura, 2001: 3). He posits 'functional consciousness' means the individual is active in choosing, sorting, storing and accessing the information needed to make choices regulating everyday living.

Bandura has also focused on the concept of human agency:

> To be an agent is to intentionally make things happen by one's actions. Agency embodies the endowments, belief systems, self regulatory capabilities and distributed structures and functions through which personal influence is exercised, rather than residing as a discrete entity in a particular place.
>
> *(Bandura, 2001: 2)*

He refers to a substantial body of research supporting the view that perceived self-efficacy motivates and guides one's actions.

> Perceived self-efficacy is defined as people's beliefs about their capabilities to produce designated levels of performance that exercise influence over events that affect their lives. Self-efficacy beliefs determine how people feel, think, motivate themselves and behave. Such beliefs produce these diverse effects through four major processes. They include cognitive, motivational, affective and selection processes.
>
> *(Bandura, 2000: 75)*

Bandura (2001) has also been particularly concerned about what he calls the 'biologizing of psychology' and the overemphasis on evolutionism (see Chapter 2). He is further concerned that 'the geneticization of human behavior is being promoted more fervently by psychological evolutionists than by biological evolutionists' (Bandura, 2001: 19). Kay Bussey and Bandura (2004) have elaborated Bandura's theory in terms of the effects of culture in shaping gender role development.

Information processing

This approach to understanding human development and cognition draws on the metaphor of the human mind as a computer. As Bandura notes, the line of theorizing associated with behaviourist principles 'was eventually put out of vogue by the advent of the computer, which likened the mind to a biological calculator' (Bandura, 2001: 2). The theory draws on the thinking of earlier writers such as Edward C. Tolman (1932).

Tolman's theory, variously referred to by terms such as 'molar behaviourism', 'purposive behaviours', 'sign learning' and 'cognitive behaviourism' (Malone, 1990) is viewed by many as not receiving the acknowledgement it deserves in mainstream psychological thought. As we observed in Chapter 3, Gestalt psychology directly challenged structuralist views. Tolman stressed the purposive features of behaviour, and the 'cognitive aspects'. He stressed broader, molar descriptions of behaviour, analysing it in common-sense units such as 'cooking a meal' (Hill, 1963). Very importantly, he introduced the idea of the 'intervening variable' to psychology. Previously, behaviourists viewed anything intervening between stimulus and response as just another response, whereas Tolman introduced the notion of cognitions as intervening between the two. In doing so, he made the concept of cognition more 'respectable' within behaviourism (Hill, 1963). The notion of intervening variables is central to information-processing models, as will become apparent.

Information processing examines how animals and humans use information from their environment to direct their behaviour. For example, imagine you are a child at school, leaving the classroom at recess. You get up from your desk as the recess bell rings and jostle with several other children in the doorway to be first to the handball courts. As you run to the courts you decide to leave eating your snack until after the game. As you approach the courts you see they are already in use by some children you do not know very well. You drop to a walk, looking to see how far into the game they are. You notice their game is almost finished and decide to ask if you can play next. Like the computer, the human mind takes in and encodes information, acts on the information, stores it and is capable of retrieving the information and generating responses. A simplified model of information processing is shown in Figure 6.1.

For example, note that the young child is faced with a potentially infinite amount of information impacting on the sensory system as he or she leaves the classroom. The child must *select* the most significant information and then *interpret*

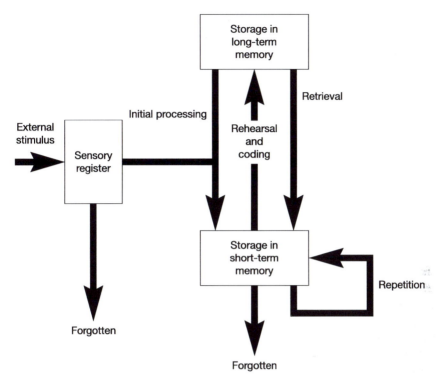

FIGURE 6.1 A simplified model of information processing (adapted from Slee, 2002)

it. The child must *infer* the motives and behaviour of the children already playing handball. Then the child must *match* or accommodate his or her behaviour to suit that of the other children, *selectively* attending to certain behaviours of the children and ignoring others. A number of critical claims by Jean Piaget regarding conservation and transivity problems have to do with the interaction of the *amount* of information a child receives with the *kind* of information (Bryant and Trabasso, 1971). For example, the likelihood of a child providing a correct response to a conservation problem is partly a function of how much information there is and how varied it is. The research of Daniel Keating and Bruce Bobbitt (1978) with children aged 9, 13 and 17 found 'evidence that late childhood and very early adolescence are a prime time for maturation of the information processing system' (Keating, 1980: 242).

Mayer (2003) has identified two main views on information processing – the classical view and the constructivist view – although there is a range of other information-processing models. Simply put, the classical view portrays the human mind using a computer-like analogy, with an input and an output and intervening processes involving encoding of information, storage and retrieval (see Figure 6.1). The analogy was developed to incorporate a 'multi-store model', involving three compartments of memory: sensory; working; and long term (Baddeley and Logie, 1999).

However, the early conceptions of information processing were introduced, in the 1960s and 1970s, largely in response to the response–strengthening metaphor (Mayer, 1996). With the development of theorizing around constructivism, the limitations of earlier information-processing models became apparent because they suggested that human cognition and understanding was a passive-reactive process that did not easily accommodate how individuals actively construe their under-standings and cognitions in a meaning-making manner.

The information-processing approach in psychology has been used to address such issues as the organization of thinking, cognitive strategies in problem-solving and the role of memory in learning. The general view of information-processing theorists is that, over time, a person develops an increasingly more complex and sophisticated 'computer' (mind) for solving problems, a computer that stores more and more knowledge and develops ever better strategies for solving problems.

Dodge et al. (1990) examined children's social adjustment using an information-processing approach. Thus the child is seen as confronting a particular problematic situation, such as solving an interpersonal conflict with another child, via serial cognitive processes that allow her or him to generate effective responses. Dodge proposed five sequential steps: encoding, which refers to the individual's ability to attend to and perceive social cues; interpretation, or understanding the meaning of the cues; response generation, in order to select from a repertoire of responses which response is most applicable; response evaluation; and enactment of the chosen response (refer back to Box 4.2). Elizabeth Lemerise and William Arsenio (2000) have reviewed the research relating to social information processing, noting that developments in the field have attempted to integrate the cognitive and social aspects of children's development in order to provide a better understanding of their behaviour.

In sum, information-processing theories have added another perspective to our understanding of children's cognitive development. In 1982 Keating expressed scepticism about the contribution of the approach, but arguably the use of information-processing theory and models to explain cognitive development (Halford, 2005), adult decision-making processes (e.g. de Wit et al., 2013) and children's learning (e.g. Snowling, 2000) has expanded. As we have also presented in this chapter, the field of social information processing has developed to improve the understanding of children's peer group behaviour.

Conclusions

Early philosophical thought regarding the mind–body problem set the scene for understanding the development of mechanism. There is little doubt that mechanism has elicited, and continues to elicit, strong and polarized opinion regarding its con-tribution to theoretical development and, more particularly, regarding its contribu-tion to understanding and explaining human development. There is certainly little doubt that the significant corpus of knowledge it has created continues to be applied in areas such as clinical psychology, health and education. However,

DeGrandpre has argued that behaviourism is being marginalized within the broad field of psychological science:

> although principles of operant psychology certainly are constrained in their ability to provide anything resembling a complete picture of psychological experience and action, psychological science has yet to exploit the full implications of basic operant principles, especially for a science of meaning.
>
> *(DeGrandpre, 2000: 721)*

While information-processing theories and Bandura's work both have their origins in the mechanistic school of thought, we have seen how these represent a move towards greater organicism. Furthermore, in emphasizing the notion of personal agency, Bandura has attempted to provide a fuller and richer account of human development.

References

Anderson, C.A. 2004. An update on the effects of playing violent video games. *Journal of Adolescence*. 27: 113–22.

Autism Speaks. n.d. www.autismspeaks.org/what-autism/treatment/applied-behavior-analysis-aba. Accessed 22 January 2015.

Baddeley, A.D. and Logie, R.H. 1999. Working memory: the multiple component model. In A. Miyake and P. Shah (eds), *Models of working memory*. Cambridge: Cambridge University Press, 28–61.

Bai, L. 2005. Children at play: a childhood beyond the Confucian shadow. *Childhood*. 12: 9–32.

Bandura, A. 1971. *Psychological modeling: conflicting theories*. Chicago, IL: Aldine-Atherton.

Bandura, A. 1977. Self-efficacy: toward a unifying theory of behavioral change. *Psychological Review*. 84 (2): 191–215.

Bandura, A. 1986. *Social foundations of thought and action: a social cognitive theory*. Englewood Cliffs, NJ: Prentice Hall.

Bandura, A. 2000. Exercise of human agency through collective efficacy. *Current Directions in Psychological Science*. 9: 75–8.

Bandura, A. 2001. Social cognitive theory: an agentic perspective. *Annual Review of Psychology*. 52: 1–26.

Bandura, A. and Walters, R.H. 1963. *Social learning and personality development*. New York: Holt Rinehart and Winston.

Baum, W.M. 2011. What is radical behaviorism? A review of J. Moore's *Conceptual foundations of radical behaviorism*. *Journal of the Experimental Analysis of Behavior*. 95: 119–26.

Bolles, R.C. 1980. Species-specific defence reactions and avoidance learning. *Psychological Review*. 77: 32–48.

Bregman, E.O. 1934. An attempt to modify the emotional attitudes of infants by the conditioning response technique. *Journal of Genetic Psychology*. 45: 169–78.

Browne, K. and Hamilton-Giachritsis, C. 2005. The influence of violent media on children and adolescents: a public-health approach. *The Lancet*. 365: 702–10.

Bryant, P.E. and Trabasso, T. 1971. Transitive inferences and memory in young children. *Nature*. 232: 456–8.

Bussey, K. and Bandura, A. 2004. Social cognitive theory of gender development and functioning. In A.H. Eagly, A.E. Beall and R.J. Sternberg (eds), *The psychology of gender.* Second edn. New York: Guilford Press, 92–119.

Davey, G. 1989. *Ecological learning theory.* London: Routledge.

DeGrandpre, R.J. 2000. A science of meaning: can behaviorism bring meaning to psychological science? *American Psychologist.* 55: 721–39.

De Wit, F.R.C., Jehn, K.A. and Scheepers, D. 2013. Task conflict, information processing and decision-making: the damaging effect of relationship conflict. *Organizational Behavior and Human Decision-making Processes.* 122: 177–89.

Dodge, K.A., Bates, J.E. and Pettit, G. 1990. Mechanisms in the cycle of violence. *Science.* 250: 1,678–83.

Gantt, W.H. (ed. and trans.). 1941. *Lectures on conditioned reflexes. Vol. 2. Conditioned reflexes and psychiatry,* by I.P. Pavlov. London: Lawrence & Wishart.

Garvey, J. and Stangroom, J. 2012. *The story of philosophy: a history of western thought.* London: Quercus Philosophy.

Gerhardstein, P., Dickerson, K., Miller, S. and Hipp, D. 2012. Early operant learning is unaffected by socio-economic status and other demographic factors: a meta-analysis. *Infant Behavior and Development.* 35 (3): 472–8.

Halford, G.S. 2005. How many variables can humans process? *Psychological Science.* 16: 70–6.

Hill, W.F. 1963. *Learning: a survey of psychological interpretations.* London: Methuen.

Horowitz, F.D. 1987. *Exploring developmental theories: toward a structural/behavioral model of development.* Hillsdale, NJ: Erlbaum.

Horowitz, F.D. 1992. John B. Watson's legacy: learning and environment. *Developmental Psychology.* 28: 360–7.

Jones, M.C. n.d. www.feministvoices.com/mary-cover-jones/. Accessed 5 May 2014.

Keating, P. 1980. Thinking processes in adolescence. In J. Adelson (ed.), *Handbook of adolescent psychology.* New York: Wiley, 211–46.

Keating, D.P. and Bobbitt, B.L. 1978. Individual and developmental differences in cognitive processing components of ability. *Child Development.* 49: 155–67.

Krasner, L. 1988. In memoriam: Mary Cover-Jones 1896–1982. *Behavior Analyst.* 11: 91–2.

Lemerise, E.A. and Arsenio, W.F. 2000. An integrated model of emotion processes and cognition in information processing. *Child Development.* 71 (1): 107–18.

Mackintosh, N.J. 2003. Pavlov and associationism. *The Spanish Journal of Psychology.* 2: 177–84.

Magai, C. and McFadden, S.H. 1995. *The role of emotions in social and personality development: history, theory and research.* New York: Plenum.

Malone, J.C. 1990. *Theories of learning. A historical approach.* Belmont, CA: Wadsworth Publishing Company.

Mayer, R.E. 1996. Learning strategies for making sense out of expository text: the SOI model for guiding three cognitive processes in knowledge construction. *Educational Psychology Review.* 8: 357–71.

Mayer, R.E. 2003. Memory and information processes. In W.M. Reynolds and G.E. Miller (eds), *Handbook of psychology. Educational psychology.* Vol. 7. New York: Wiley, 47–57.

Murphy, E.S., McSweeney, F.K., Smith, R.G. and McComas, J.J. 2003. Dynamic changes in reinforcer effectiveness: theoretical, methodological and practical implications for applied research. *Journal of Applied Behavior Analysis.* 36: 421–38.

Pavlov, I.P. 1932. The reply of a physiologist to psychologists. *Psychological Review.* 39: 91–127.

Pepper, S. 1942. *World hypotheses: a study of evidence.* Berkeley, CA: University of California Press.

Raising Children Network. n.d. http://raisingchildren.net.au/articles/applied_behaviour_analysis_th.html. Accessed 22 January 2015.

Reese, H.W. and Overton, W.F. 1970. Models of development and theories of development. In L.R. Goulet and R. Baltes (eds), *Life-span developmental psychology: research and theory*. New York: Academic Press, 116–50.

Rilling, M. 2000. John Watson's paradoxical struggle to explain Freud. *American Psychologist*. 55: 301–12.

Schlinger, H.D. 1992. Theory in behavior analysis. *American Psychologist*. 47: 1,396–410.

Seligman, M.E.P. 1972. Phobias and preparedness. In M.E.P. Seligman and J.L. Hager (eds), *Biological boundaries of learning*. New York: Appleton-Century-Crofts, 451–62.

Skinner, B.F. 1979. My experience with the baby-tender. *Psychology Today*. March: 29–40.

Slee, P.T. 2002. *Child, adolescent and family development*. Second edn. Melbourne: Cambridge University Press.

Slee P.T., Campbell, M. and Spears, B. 2012. *Child, adolescent and family development*. Third edn. Melbourne: Cambridge University Press.

Snowling, M.J. 2000. *Dyslexia*. Second edn. Oxford: Blackwell.

Tolman, E.C. 1932. *Purposive behavior in animals and men*. New York: The Century Co.

Watson, J.B. 1913. Psychology as the behaviorist views it. *Psychological Review*. 20: 158–77.

Watson, J.B. 1914. *Behavior: an introduction to comparative psychology*. New York: Norton.

Watson, J.B. 1928. *Psychological care of the infant and child*. New York: Norton.

Watson, J.B. 1930. *Behaviorism*. New York: Henry Holt.

Watson, J.B. 1936. Autobiography. In C. Murchison (ed.), *A history of psychology in autobiography*. Vol. 3. Worchester, MA: Clark University Press, 271–8.

Zettle, R.D. 2003. Acceptance and commitment therapy (ACT) *vs* systematic desensitization in treatment of mathematics anxiety. *The Psychological Record*. 53: 197–215.

7

DIALECTICISM

The child developing in a social world

Introduction

As we have seen, organicists such as Jean Piaget viewed development as arising from children's own actions as they experiment with the world, while mechanists saw the child as a passive recipient of environmental influences. Lev Vygotsky's theory is generally contrasted with these, as a *dialectical* theory (as are those of Sergei Rubinstein and Klaus Riegel), based on the notion that development occurs as a result of a tension and interaction between internal and external influences. Some writers, however, have also considered Piaget's theory as dialectical, as expressed in the tension between accommodation and assimilation (Lourenço, 2012).

Vygotsky was a Soviet psychologist who developed his ideas over just ten years between the two World Wars before he died at an early age from tuberculosis, leaving many unpublished manuscripts. He therefore had a very short time in which to elaborate his theoretical framework, in contrast with the long-lived Piaget, who spent decades revising his theory. Nevertheless, he ranks with Piaget as one of the two most influential developmental psychologists of the twentieth century (Lourenço, 2012). Vygotsky's focus was upon the development of cognition under social influence. In this chapter, we outline the dialectical approach to development (especially Vygotsky's) and some ways in which it has influenced recent theorizing in development, education and disability.

The German philosopher Georg Hegel (1770–1831) adopted Socrates' notion of the 'dialectic' (Feibleman, 1973). This is when two people arrive at the truth through a process of debate. Hegel proposed that reality is arrived at through a dialectic between three components: a beginning position, the 'thesis'; its opposite, the 'antithesis'; and the position arrived at in resolving the discrepancy, the 'synthesis'. The synthesis in turn becomes the next thesis, and so the process continues. Thus Hegel's philosophy concerned circular processes, with the whole greater than the sum of the parts. We will see these ideas reflected in the developmental theories of Vygotsky, Rubinstein and Riegel.

Lev Vygotsky (1896–1934) and dialectical theory

Vygotsky was a deep thinker who also founded and directed a number of research institutes, including the first Russian institute for the study of children with disabilities (Kozulin, 1988). Vygotsky was committed to Marxist doctrine but his interpretation of it led to a suppression of his writings until Nikita Krushchev denounced Stalinism in 1956. Despite this, his work had a great influence on psychological theory and practice in his own country, especially in terms of the education of children with disabilities. The work of the 'Institute of Defectology', in using his principles to foster the development of deaf-blind children – even enabling some to enter university – was beautifully illustrated in the documentary film *The Butterflies of Zagorsk* (British Broadcasting Corporation, 1990).

During his lifetime, Vygotsky had intellectual exchanges with Piaget, but his main influence on western developmental psychology has been much more recent, following the translation of his works into English. *Thought and Language* was published in English in 1962, with a foreword by Jerome Bruner (Vygotsky, 1934/1962). By the end of that decade, this text was set by Joan Wynn Reeves for one of the present authors' (RS) undergraduate classes at London University and, without doubt, had Reeves lived to produce a second edition of her book *Thinking about Thinking* (1965), Vygotsky would have featured prominently. In general, it was not for another decade, when an edited and translated body of his work appeared in 1978 as *Mind in Society*, that the broader psychological community began to take notice of Vygotsky's work. He now has a major place in undergraduate developmental textbooks, where his theory is typically compared and contrasted with that of Piaget. Possible reasons for his increased influence in the West include republications of his work in Russian and further translations into English, an increased exchange of ideas between US and former Soviet Union academics, and the relevance of his ideas for education (Wertsch and Tulviste, 1992). Also, his theoretical framework seems to have come at the 'right time' in terms of western scholars' thinking.

Central to Vygotsky's theory is the notion that human cognition has its beginnings in social life. This idea seems to have come from previous thinkers, such as Karl Marx and Pierre Janet (who was in turn influenced by Emile Durkheim, and also George Herbert Mead) (Wertsch and Tulviste, 1992). Vygotsky emphasized that the child develops cognitively through interactions with others; hence his theory is dialectical. He was critical of mainstream western views, where the emphasis was on individual development and where collective functioning was generally ignored.

In his preface to the English-language translation of *Thought and Language* in 1962, Bruner observed that Vygotsky's theory represented an enormous step up from understanding development in terms of classical Pavlovian conditioning. Vygotsky built upon Pavlov's notion of the 'second signal system', which 'provides the means whereby man creates a mediator between himself and the world of physical stimulation so that he can react in terms of his own symbolic conception of reality' (Bruner, 1962: x).

Vygotsky's theory was instrumental, cultural and genetic (Holaday *et al.*, 1994). His theory was instrumental inasmuch as it claimed that '[p]eople actively modify the stimuli they encounter and use them as instruments to control conditions and regulate their own behavior' (Holaday *et al.*, 1994: 16). As such, a feature of Vygotsky's theory (like Piaget's) was that individuals are active agents in creating their own development and learning. The cultural aspect (discussed further below) was expressed through the centrality he granted to language as a cultural tool in the development of thinking. The genetic aspect (in the same developmental sense we noted in connection with Freudian and Piagetian theory) was that, through interactions with others, higher-order mental functions develop from lower-order ones.

According to Vygotsky, child development is made up of periods of relatively stable growth, crises and transformation, which implies that development passes through qualitatively distinct stages. The development of an individual can come to a standstill or even regress. Based on Vygotsky's work, van der Veer (1986: 528) described five stages in child development: infancy; early childhood; the pre-school period; school age; and adolescence. Each is a so-called stable period, preceded and concluded by a period of crisis. At around 12 months of age the toddler faces a new period of crisis or transformation, which is associated with three new developments, namely, walking, speech and emotional reactions. For Vygotsky, the child's language development is paramount, and he made a distinction between thought and speech development in the first two years of life. However, at about two years of age the two curves – of development of thought and speech – come together to initiate a new form of behaviour. In Vygotsky's view this is a momentous time in the toddler's cognitive development: speech begins to serve intellect and thoughts begin to be spoken. The onset of this stage is indicated by two unmistakable objective symptoms: a sudden active curiosity about words, leading to questions about every new thing; and the resulting rapid increase in the child's vocabulary.

Vygotsky also articulated a number of stages in children's conceptual development, derived from experimental work on the sorting of blocks varying in colour and shape (Vygotsky, 1934/1962). Initially, objects are sorted into unorganized 'heaps', and later, in terms of functional, concrete uses, such as knife with fork and spoon (a kind of categorization that western adults also use). Then come chain complexes, with groups of objects sorted consecutively according to certain criteria (such as shape or colour), but the decisive criterion changes over time. Then come diffuse complexes, in which the selection criteria are fluid, and based on unreal attributes that would surprise an adult. These are followed by pseudo-concepts, which predominate in the thinking of the pre-school child: superficially, the child appears to be using true concepts, but deeper probing reveals 'flawed' reasoning; the development of pseudo-concepts is very much directed by adult language, which enables an adult and a pre-school child to communicate, but the underlying understandings may be quite different. True, abstract thought appears in adolescence, but earlier, more concrete, forms of thinking continue to operate. This latter point – that adolescents (and even adults) do not always, or even usually, operate at the highest level of abstraction, has also been demonstrated through studies designed to test Piagetian ideas about intellectual development. Piaget's stage theory has very much overshadowed the stage aspects of Vygotskian theory, which is acknowledged most for its emphasis on the social, language-driven nature of children's cognitive development, and has been identified by some (e.g. Berk, 2000) as a continuity theory.

Particularly influential has been Vygotsky's discussion of 'egocentric speech'. Initially, the child's behaviour is controlled by verbal instructions from others; later, the child talks aloud, especially when difficulties arise – in effect, instructing the self. Finally, these instructions 'go underground' (to use Vygotsky's phrase) and become internalized as thought. Vygotsky gave an example to illustrate how the child's self-directed speech performs a controlling function: a child was drawing a streetcar when his pencil broke; he said, 'It's broken', and, using another pencil, proceeded to draw a *broken* streetcar after an accident (Vygotsky, 1934/1962). Thus, egocentric speech (which Piaget saw as a by-product of thought) becomes an integral part of the developmental process in Vygotsky's theory. His pupil Alexander Luria and later researchers experimentally demonstrated the shift in children's development, from speaking aloud while performing tasks, to muttering, to silence (e.g. Frauenglass and Diaz, 1985). The term private, or inner, speech later became preferred. A summary of Vygotsky's view of the relationship between thought, language and action is captured in Box 7.1.

Although Vygotsky placed much emphasis on language, some activities (especially in certain cultures) are better learned by observation (Rogoff, 1990). Imagine, for example, trying to teach someone to knit through verbal instruction alone! Although Vygotsky certainly placed enormous importance on language, his theory did encompass all forms of cultural signs and symbols. Furthermore, he made special mention of the ability to imitate as being an important sign that the child is developmentally ready to understand the task at hand (Vygotsky, 1930/1978).

This idea of 'developmental readiness' brings us to another feature of Vygotsky's theory: the notion of the 'zone of proximal development'. He defined this as 'the distance between actual developmental level as determined by independent problem solving and the level of potential development through problem solving under adult guidance or in collaboration with more capable peers' (Vygotsky, 1934/1978: 86). Thus, a standard mental test, such as an IQ test, is a measure of independent problem-solving (completed development), but does not capture the entirety of a child's ability: two children with the same IQ might be able to reach different levels of performance under adult guidance. Furthermore, Vygotsky's perspective implies that a child's capacity to learn is not just a property of the child, but a shared property between the child and a particular guide (socially shared cognition). So, a child's zone of proximal development (ZPD) might be greater with a guide who is more sensitive to the child's developmental needs.

BOX 7.1 VYGOTSKY AND THE RELATIONSHIP BETWEEN THOUGHT, WORD AND ACTION

The relation between thought and word is a living process; thought is born through words. A word devoid of thought is a dead thing, and a thought unembodied in words remains a shadow. The connection between them, however, is not a preformed and constant one. It emerges in the course of development, and itself evolves. To the Biblical 'In the beginning was the word,' Goethe makes Faust reply, 'In the beginning was the deed.' The intent here is to detract from the value of the word, but we can accept this version if we emphasize it differently: in the *beginning* was the deed. The word was not the beginning – action was there first; it is the end of development, crowning the deed.

(Vygotsky, 1934/1962: 153)

Vygotsky was way ahead of his time here, as it is only recently that cognitive science has taken seriously the proposition that abstract concepts are built upon bodily interactions with the environment ('embodied cognition'). A recent study examined children's use of gestures to indicate spatial concepts (e.g. left, up) and the more complex metaphorical use of such spatial gestures to indicate time (e.g. now, tomorrow) (Iossifova and Marmolejo-Ramos, 2013). While sighted children made gestures that depended upon an appreciation of external landmarks, such as pointing ahead, blind children were more likely to use their own body as a reference point (e.g. touching the head or chest), especially for temporal gestures, which were much more difficult for them to produce. The study showed that children's development of abstract concepts depends on the type of bodily interactions they have experienced with the world. With his deep interest in 'defectology', Vygotsky would not have been surprised by these findings.

Two important dimensions of the ZPD are 'joint collaboration' and 'transfer of responsibility'. 'Joint collaboration' is best viewed as active, shared participation for the purpose of solving a problem. The adult, by virtue of greater understanding of the problem, actively facilitates or encourages the child in her or his own definition and redefinition of the problem to promote the achievement of a solution. 'Transfer of responsibility' refers to the adult's decreasing role in regulating and managing behaviour or task performance, with the child being given more opportunities to perform the task independently (Holaday *et al.*, 1994; Rogoff, 1986). While the notion of the ZPD has become influential in child development theory and education, it has also been criticized as circular; in other words, it cannot be defined a priori, but only in relation to the child's performance (it is not alone in this, however, with the behaviourist term 'stimulus' being criticized as only definable in relation to a response).

Despite its enormous influence on educational thinking, the ZPD was a relatively minor concept in Vygotsky's work. It has been elaborated, misunderstood and misrepresented. For example, the value of using peer collaboration as a learning method has been attributed to Vygotsky, although he only mentioned it as a method (pairing with a higher-IQ child) to assess the ZPD (Gredler, 2012).

Vygotsky compared with Piaget

It is often said that the Vygotskian child is a 'little apprentice', in contrast with the solitary 'little scientist' of Piaget. From a Piagetian perspective, while procedures can be learned from others, this does not represent true understanding, which is demonstrated by unassisted performance (Wood, 1988/1998). However, as we observed in Chapter 4, Piaget did maintain that social interactions between equals could be important for cognitive growth, especially with regard to the development of moral understanding. The European social psychologist Willem Doise (1990) took up the notion that social interaction can promote cognitive development under some circumstances, but based this on Piaget's theory, not Vygotsky's. He proposed (and demonstrated experimentally) that a child can develop cognitively if his or her schema comes into conflict with an alternative schema proposed by another person, provided circumstances permit the successful resolution of the cognitive conflict to produce a more advanced schema. For this to happen, the child must already have a certain level of competence; to translate this into Vygotskian terms, this would mean the task must be in the ZPD. Also, the nature of the social relationship must be one in which the cognitive conflict can be explored and resolved. Drawing upon ideas from Durkheim, Doise maintained that this can only happen in 'relations of cooperation' rather than 'relations of constraint'. In other words, if the other person uses authority to impose his or her perspective on the child, cognitive growth will not occur. It is often peer relationships that permit the necessary cooperation, rather than the relationships with adults that Vygotsky saw as important for cognitive development. There is no real antagonism between the view of Piaget / Doise and the Vygotskian perspective if we take into account that an adult who uses authority to impose his or her view upon a child would also be an adult who, in Vygotsky's view, was not operating within the child's ZPD – and again, no cognitive progress would be expected.

A crucial difference between Piaget and Vygotsky remains, however. While Piaget acknowledged that the speech of another person could spark thoughts leading to cognitive growth, the real driver of that growth is the child's own activity. For Vygotsky, however, cognitive processes are directly derived from speech. The autonomy of the Piagetian child, versus the heteronomy of the Vygotskian one, has been characterized as the most important difference between the theories – something that should not be lost sight of amidst a growing tendency to emphasize their similarities (Lourenço, 2012). Orlando Lourenço has observed that the

Piagetian view reflects a social democratic ideal in contrast to Vygotsky's Marxist one, and suggests that the two theories are complementary.

Scaffolding

The concept of sensitive guidance for development was taken up and elaborated by a number of workers, who applied the term 'scaffolding' to this (Bruner and Haste, 1987; Wood, 1988/1998; Wood *et al.*, 1976, 1978). These researchers were inspired by Vygotsky's theory to examine the tutoring of young children by adults on tasks that the children were unable to perform alone. They discovered, for example, that mothers provided different levels of support for their children's performance on a block construction task, ranging from full demonstration of the task, through verbal instruction on how to do it, to simply encouraging the child to perform the task. Not all such tutoring was equally effective: for example, children often became frustrated with full demonstration (an example of adult imposition of a solution) or were given verbal instructions that were too difficult. It was found that children's learning was best promoted by providing assistance as soon as the child became stuck, and refraining from intrusive assistance when the child was making progress. David Wood called such an instructional style 'contingent teaching'. 'These mothers ensured that the child was not left alone when he was overwhelmed by the task, and also guaranteed him greater scope for initiative when he showed signs of success' (Wood, 1988/1998: 79). Barbara Rogoff and William Gardner described scaffolding as occurring when 'a more competent or able adult or peer adjusts the learning situation or task conditions . . . to produce appropriate understanding of a particular problem for a learner at a particular level of ability' (Rogoff and Gardner, 1984: 109).

Rogoff suggested that the term 'guided participation' is more inclusive than scaffolding. Albert Bandura and others had previously used this term to refer to assistance provided by a trusted and encouraging companion to help children and adolescents to overcome fears, such as fear of snakes (Bowlby, 1975: 226). As used by Rogoff, it involves children with 'multiple companions and caregivers in organized, flexible webs of relationships that focus on shared cultural activities' (Rogoff, 1990: 98). This acknowledges that it is not just parents who participate in the process: in some societies, young children spend more time with older siblings and peers than with adults. Older siblings and peers can therefore play a particularly powerful role in younger children's development. An extreme view is that in all societies it is peers, rather than parents, who mainly influence children's development (Harris, 1995). This was not Vygotsky's own view, however.

In general terms, Rogoff suggested that the characteristics of guided participation are: the provision of a bridge between existing skills and knowledge and those needed to perform new ones; the provision of structure by the tutor; active learning; and transfer of responsibility to the learner. There need not be an intention on the part of the tutor to teach: learning can occur whenever children participate in helping more capable companions to perform everyday tasks (Rogoff, 1990).

These ideas have been applied educationally, and indeed Bruner observed that Vygotsky's theory is as much a theory of education as of cognitive development. We noted above how Doise used Piagetian theory as a basis for understanding how peer collaboration on a task can lead to cognitive growth. By contrast, Vygotsky's theory provides a theoretical framework for understanding peer tutoring, in which a more expert child tutors another (Foot *et al.*, 1990). Children are certainly able to teach one another in this way, and there may be social, as well as cognitive, advantages to peer tutoring. However, children's ability to provide sensitive scaffolding, such as their ability to detect misunderstandings by their tutees, is limited by their own level of cognitive development (Foot *et al.*, 1997; Shute *et al.*, 1992). The notion of scaffolding has also been used to examine how well computer programs are able to support children's learning (see Box 7.2).

Wood (1988/1998) cited evidence that experts, but not novices, when solving problems, report self-monitoring, self-correction and so forth – known as 'self-explanations'. When the self-explanation aspect is turned off in a computerized problem-solving simulation, the computer model loses flexibility and some powers of generalizability. Wood suggested that this supports the Vygotskian notion that self-talk (aloud or silent) plays a vital role in enabling individuals to solve taxing tasks. As Wood observed, 'Language is not simply *what* we think about but part of the thinking process itself' (Wood, 1988/1998: 108). By then, this had become an extensive area of inquiry in itself, known as 'metacognition', with strong applicability to education (see, for example, Schneider and Artelt, 2010).

BOX 7.2 SCAFFOLDING AND 'EDUCATIONAL' SOFTWARE FOR PRE-SCHOOLERS

Rosalyn Shute and John Miksad (1997) analysed some popular pre-school computer programs to determine the degree of scaffolding they provided for children's learning. Children were allocated to one of three groups: substantial scaffolding; minimal scaffolding; or control (traditional instruction with minimal teacher scaffolding). Maths skills were not improved after eight weekly sessions, regardless of scaffolding. Verbal and general cognitive skills were improved, but only for children who used computer programs incorporating substantial scaffolding, as identified by Wood *et al.* (1976). These findings were seen to 'dispel the myth of computers as magical toys' for teaching young children (Shute and Miksad, 1997: 248). Recent advice on using educational software with pre-schoolers mentions the need for teachers themselves to provide 'cognitive' and 'affective' scaffolding for children's use of computers, and makes some reference to the 'technical scaffolding' inherent in programs (McManis and Gunnewig, 2012). However, the promise of applying a detailed scaffolding framework to educational software for pre-schoolers seems unfulfilled.

The notion of scaffolding has been applied to the social as well as the cognitive sphere (e.g. Kaye, 1977). An interactive social relationship exists between parents and infants from a young age, but initially it tends to be the parent who 'does most of the work'. Later, there is a sharing of responsibility, while as infants grow older they increasingly initiate and manage social interactions. In the course of such interactions, 'shared meaning' develops between adults and infants (Schaffer, 1989).

Cognition and culture

An important feature of Vygotsky's theory, as the earlier quotation from Rogoff illustrates, is that it offers a link between individual cognitive development and the culture in which the individual develops. Whereas the Soviet system was supposed to provide equal chances for everyone's development, Vygotsky and his student Luria found individual differences in cognitive performance between young adults and between those varying in ethnic group and geographical location, and this required explanation (Meacham, 1999). Although Vygotsky did not provide an extensive account of the notion of culture, in broad terms he saw culture as being a product of human social activity over historical time. Such activity produces cultural 'tools' consisting of sign systems, such as language, writing, numerical systems and art. Through social interactions, these sign systems mediate between the culture and the developing individual, becoming incorporated into individual mental functioning. Vygotsky's theory, then, is not a universalist one.

Vygotsky and Luria had a view that various cultures could be ranked in terms of how 'developed' they were. As we shall see in Chapter 9, it has been common practice for western psychologists to perceive their own culture as superior to others. Light is cast on this issue by Joseph Glick's (1975) research with West Africa's farming Kpelle communities, in which people were asked how to classify objects such as an orange, a potato, a hoe and a knife. They classified them functionally (potato and hoe, orange and knife – in the way Vygotsky described children as classifying objects early in development). The Kpelle judged the western, abstract response (classifying the tools together and the food items together) – which would gain more points on a typical IQ test – to be how a fool would classify the objects. Later theorists developed ideas apparent in Vygotsky's own writings to argue that such differences in mental activity are better seen as characteristic of the specific setting in which they develop, and are qualitative differences rather than inherently 'better' or 'worse'. Along these lines, workers such as James Wertsch and Peter Tulviste (1992) proposed that individual mental functioning can best be seen as consisting of a 'cultural tool kit' of mental processes. The link which Vygotsky's theory creates between individual development and culture means that his theory has become especially popular with cross-cultural psychologists (Rogoff and Morelli, 1989).

Although Vygotsky's theory is based on a *dialogue* between the individual and the social world, he placed most emphasis on how social processes shape individual development. More recent researchers have also emphasized the role of the developing individual in influencing the world. Wertsch and Tulviste did not believe the notion of individual agency to be in conflict with Vygotsky's concepts, and united the two perspectives by proposing that the individual uses culturally derived tools to operate upon the world in new ways. Nevertheless, creativity is necessarily constrained by culture to be 'a new use for an old tool' (Wertsch and Tulviste, 1992: 555).

A more radical adaptation of Vygotsky's theory is the suggestion to change the ZPD to the ZCD (zone of collaborative development) in non-western education, where the notion of the individual is less applicable. This idea has been applied to moral education in Malaysia, where there is a challenge to implement this aspect of the national curriculum in multi-ethnic classrooms (Balakrishnan and Claiborne, 2012). Although children's personal reflections on moral dilemmas form part of the process, the emphasis is on reaching a shared moral language with those from other ethnic backgrounds, clans and religions.

Another aspect of Vygotsky's work that has been challenged by more recent work is his view that the cultural aspects of development initially operate separately from 'natural' development, with these two aspects only uniting around the age of two years. As Wertsch and Tulviste (1992) pointed out, much research has clearly demonstrated that, from the earliest days, infants develop under the influence of adult speech. Vygotsky, of course, did not have the benefit of such empirical findings in devising his theory.

How far Vygotsky saw development as being mechanistic rather than organismic is another aspect of his theory that has been given attention. Despite occasional phrases in Vygotsky's writings that suggest a mechanical influence of the social environment on the child's development, Wertsch and Tulviste are in no doubt that Vygotsky did not intend this. Rather, individual agency and social influence are intimately linked, in the sense that individual actions are carried out by socially determined means.

Vygotsky's 'defectology'

Vygotsky's revolutionary work on development in the context of disability has been relatively overlooked in recent years. Although his terminology suggested that a child with a disability is 'lacking' in relation to norms (in line with a typical biomedical perspective), he actually had great insight in viewing such children as 'developing differently' (Bøttcher and Dammeyer, 2012). His view of development as progressing (or even regressing) in the course of an ongoing dialectical exchange between the child and the (socially mediated) environment captures how such differences can come about. Followers of his methods as depicted in *The Butterflies of Zagorsk* provided deaf-blind children with a social environment, in the context of a residential school, that provided them with alternative routes for cognitive development, such as through sign language, touch and use of any residual hearing or sight, always mindful of each child's zone of proximal development. The individualized unfolding of development that he conceptualized, occurring in historical and cultural context, is compatible with more recent understandings gained through a dynamic systems perspective (see Chapter 10) and epigenetics research. Box 7.1 is again useful in illustrating how children's physical abilities affect the way they come to perceive the world. Louise Bøttcher and Jesper Dammeyer (2012) propose that Vygotsky's theory offers a way to break down a dualistic understanding of a person with a disability in relation to the rest of society.

Vygotsky, social constructivism and education

Constructivism has provided an influential perspective in western education since the 1980s, supplanting the more mechanistic behaviourist and information-processing approaches (Liu and Matthews, 2005). It is a postmodern perspective based on the idea that individuals do not perceive an objective world, but create individual subjective constructions of it. While Piaget is seen as the originator of *cognitive* constructivism, Vygotsky is credited with being one of the founding influences on *social* constructivism (Pritchard and Woollard, 2010). Social constructivism has been variously described as a theory, a 'church' of related theories, a paradigm, a metaphor for human learning, a powerful folk-tale and even as akin to a secular religion (Liu and Matthews, 2005). Educational practices based on social constructivism are seen as progressive, and include child-focused learning and the use of one-on-one and small-group learning. However, constructivism has been criticized as having poor empirical foundations, neglecting facts in favour of relativism and leading to a neglect of substantiated teaching methods, such as those based on learning theory (Matthews, 2003).

Educational writings, though, often stray far from Vygotsky's original theory, and he is often misrepresented. There is a lack of appreciation of the philosophical underpinnings of his theory, leading to an individual–cultural dualism that is far removed from his view of these as functionally inseparable (Liu and Matthews, 2005). Furthermore, criticisms of social constructivism (e.g. Matthews, 2003) often reject it in terms of its most extreme relativist versions, which do not reflect Vygotsky's writings (see also Chapter 13).

The reasons for this misunderstanding of Vygotsky are several. They include his early death, unfinished manuscripts, unreliable translations and editing (from *Mind in Society* on), the ban of his works for a time in Soviet Russia and later misinterpretations of his theory in both scholarly and popular accounts. A major project is currently under way to produce a new 'back to basics' collection of Vygotsky's works, to be made available online (Yasnitsky, 2012).

Sergei Rubinstein (1889–1960) and constitutive relationalism

Rubinstein is not a name that is likely to be found in standard textbooks of developmental psychology, yet he was another prominent twentieth-century Soviet psychologist who played an important part in the development of dialectical theory. His cosmopolitan approach to life led him to be denounced as a non-patriot between 1948 and 1953. Particularly influential were books he wrote in 1940 and

1959, which addressed some of the basic questions of psychology, especially the mind–body relationship (Meacham, 1999). He drew together Marxist-Leninist and Pavlovian ideas to create the notion that the mind develops as a result of links between historical or cultural and biological aspects of development. As Jack Meacham (1999) explains, Rubinstein did not envisage this in terms of a mechanistic *interaction* between the separate entities of the brain and the sociohistorical world. Rather, the mind is a reflection of both nervous system activity and the material world, and is always in a *transactional* state with them. Thus, the mind exists only in mutual relationship to these entities. This was his theory of 'constitutive relationalism'. In other words, it is the *relation* that is primary, and the entities in transaction cannot be understood – indeed, do not exist – in the absence of the relationship.

According to John Broughton and Klaus Riegel (1977), Rubinstein saw early development as driven by biological imperatives, with sociohistorical factors later becoming co-determinants. He noted that individuals transform their own environment, thereby creating new conditions for development. A link is apparent here with the later notion of 'niche-picking' (see Chapter 2).

In recent years, relationalism has become regarded as a new metatheory, though prominent writings in the area do not acknowledge Rubinstein. The integrative potential of relationalism will be discussed in Chapter 13.

Some echoes of Rubinstein's ideas (although not attributed to him or any other dialectical psychologist) can be found in a discussion about reductionism by Jane Herlihy and John Gandy (2002). In line with our discussion in Chapter 2, they observe that the modern tendency is to consider neurobiological explanations of phenomena as the 'real' explanations, with an implicit belief that 'to rely on anything but the tangible, like brain matter, somehow implies unworldly and mystical thinking' (Herlihy and Gandy, 2002: 248). They suggest that explanations for any particular phenomenon can be given at different levels, such as biochemical, cognitive or behavioural. However, they suggest, it is wrong to imply that a neurological event *causes* a cognition or behaviour, and it is even misleading to speak of the relationship in terms of correlation. They propose that the biology and the psychology are only separable in the abstract, and are actually two pieces of information about the same event. They conclude that psychologists should not consider neurological explanations as superior to cognitive or behavioural ones, and neither should they lead the public to consider them so; rather, we should think of human beings as 'moving from one psychophysical state to another, describable on different levels by different specialists. Causation flows between these states and not between the levels of description' (Herlihy and Gandy, 2002: 251). Their concerns reflect those of others, such as Bandura, about the 'biologizing' of behaviour.

Klaus Riegel (1925–1977): transactions in historical context

Riegel's contribution to dialectical developmental theorizing has been described by his associate Meacham (1999). Riegel was born in Berlin but later worked as an academic psychologist in the USA. In the years leading up to his comparatively early death he developed a form of dialecticism, disseminated through his university lectures, publications and conferences. Precursors of his theory included the work of Eduard Spranger (who proposed that individuals could only be understood in relation to their historical times), and it was Rubinstein, rather than Vygotsky, who influenced his thinking (*Thought and Language* appeared in English translation in Riegel's lifetime, but *Mind in Society* did not). Riegel's psychological theory was in stark contrast with traditional psychology's concern with stability and the maintenance of equilibrium. Rather, his theory was specifically developmental in nature. Drawing upon Rubinstein's transactional theory, he proposed that aspects of the individual (biological, psychological and sociocultural or historical) are in transactional relationships – each being defined in relation to all the others. A change in one aspect produces a crisis, the resolution of which results in development (which may be positive or negative). His theory was reflexive, in that he recognized that the theory should be applied to theorizing itself, which is therefore influenced by its historical times. Riegel's own times encompassed the Holocaust, the civil rights movement in the USA, and publication of Arthur Jensen's controversial work on genetics and intelligence; in fact, Riegel presented what was probably the first university course in Black psychology. Riegel's concern was therefore not with individuals' stability, but with their development in relation to sociocultural change.

Riegel (1973) commented on Piaget's theory, characterizing it as dialectical, with contradictions in the child's thinking resolved through the processes of assimilation and accommodation. However, he pointed out that Piaget applied these concepts most clearly to the development of early schemas, such as sucking and grasping. As the child develops, these processes fade out of Piaget's discussion, in favour of traditional logic. Riegel argued that dialectical thinking is needed, for mature thought, which does not rely on formal logic. For example, the older child or adult understands that a particular event may be unfortunate from one person's perspective, but fortunate from that of another, so the event can be simultaneously both fortunate and unfortunate, just as an object may be both big and small, depending on the frames of reference applied. Judgements are therefore temporary, in flux, and subject to constant re-evaluation. Further, Riegel noted that although Piaget observed that some individuals 'fail' in formal operational thinking through a lack of relevant experience, he did not carry this through to an acknowledgement that thought develops in relation to the cultural–historical context.

We will take up and expand on the sociocultural theme in Chapter 9, and also mention the place of Riegel's theory in relation to integrative theories of development in Chapter 13. It is of interest that his work is now much less well known than that of Vygotsky. This might be because his emphasis on relativism is more explicit than that of Vygotsky, and therefore presents a greater challenge to traditional positivist developmental psychology. Indeed, Broughton (1987) suggested that the critical perspective on developmental psychology offered by Riegel's dialecticism has been lost in its application to lifespan psychology. He maintained that this field has 'trivialized history ... reducing it positivistically to a variable confounded with psychological change' (Broughton, 1987: 11).

Conclusions

A dialectical approach to children's development was proposed by Vygotsky in the early twentieth century, but not taken up beyond the Soviet Union until much later. The contributions of Rubinstein and Riegel also deserve mention, although it is Vygotsky's theory that has become the best known. However, presentations and understandings of Vygotsky's theory have become distorted.

Three of Vygotsky's original contributions to our understanding of human development are his description of the crisis-like character of development, the importance he placed on the role of speech and his emphasis on the social nature of the young child (van der Veer, 1986). He emphasized the heteronomous, rather than autonomous, nature of children's development. His work has inspired research on the crucial role of adults and (arguably) older peers in cognitive development, with a focus on process rather than structure. Vygotsky's dialectical theory, in providing a link between individual development and the social world, paved the way for a greater consideration of the role of culture and history in individual development. In this way, he provided inspiration for the development of the social constructivist movement. The breadth of his influence stretches even further when we realize that his protégé Luria established the field of neuropsychology (e.g. Luria, 1972). It has also been suggested that the fields of cognitive science and artificial intelligence would benefit from a closer consideration of Vygotsky's theory (Lindblom and Ziemke, 2003).

Dialecticism also represents a move in the direction of more holistic and systemic views of development. In this respect, Rubinstein's and Riegel's notion of constitutive relationalism is worthy of fresh consideration. These issues will be pursued in later chapters.

References

Balakrishan, V. and Claiborne, L.B. 2012. Vygotsky from ZPD to ZCD in moral education: reshaping Western theory and practices in local context. *Journal of Moral Education*. 41 (2): 225–43.

Berk, L. 2000. *Child development*. Boston: Allyn & Bacon.

Bøttcher, L. and Dammeyer, J. 2012. Disability as a dialectical concept: building on Vygotsky's defectology. *European Journal of Special Needs Education*. 27 (4): 433–6.

Bowlby, J. 1975. *Separation*. Harmondsworth: Penguin.

British Broadcasting Corporation. 1990. *The Butterflies of Zagorsk*. London: BBC Education and Training.

Broughton, J.M. 1987. An introduction to critical developmental psychology. In J.M. Broughton (ed.), *Critical theories of psychological development*. New York: Plenum, 1–30.

Broughton, J.M. and Riegel, K.F. 1977. Developmental psychology and the self. *Annals of the New York Academy of Sciences*. 291: 149–67.

Bruner, J. 1962. Introduction. In L.S. Vygotsky, *Thought and language*. Cambridge, MA: MIT Press, v–x.

Bruner, J. and Haste, H. 1987. *Making sense: the child's construction of the world*. London: Methuen.

Doise, W. 1990. The development of individual competencies through social interaction. In H.C. Foot, R.H. Shute and M.J. Morgan (eds), *Children helping children*. Chichester: Wiley, 43–64.

Feibleman, J.K. 1973. *Understanding philosophy: a popular history of ideas*. New York: Horizon Press.

Foot, H.C., Shute, R.H. and Morgan, M.J. 1997. Children's sensitivity to lack of understanding. *Educational Studies*. 23 (2): 185–94.

Foot, H.C., Shute, R.H., Morgan, M.J. and Barron, A-M. 1990. Theoretical issues in peer tutoring. In H.C. Foot, M.J. Morgan and R.H. Shute (eds), *Children helping children*. Chichester: Wiley, 3–17.

Frauenglass, M.H. and Diaz, R.M. 1985. Self-regulatory functions of children's private speech: a critical analysis of recent challenges to Vygotsky's theory. *Developmental Psychology*. 21: 357–64.

Glick, J. 1975. Cognitive development in cross-cultural perspective. In F. Horowitz (ed.), *Review of child development research*. Vol. 4. Chicago, IL: University of Chicago Press, 595–654.

Gredler, M.E. 2012. Understanding Vygotsky for the classroom: is it too late? *Educational Psychology Review*. 24: 113–31.

Harris, J.R. 1995. Where is the child's environment? A group socialization theory of development. *Psychological Review*. 102 (3): 458–89.

Herlihy, J. and Gandy, J. 2002. Causation and explanation. *The Psychologist*. 15 (5): 248–51.

Holaday, B., Lamontagne, L. and Marciel, J. 1994. Vygotsky's zone of proximal development. Implications for nurse assistance of children's learning. *Issues in Comprehensive Pediatric Nursing*. 17: 15–27.

Iossifova, R. and Marmolejo-Ramos, F. 2013. When the body is time: spatial and temporal deixis in children with visual impairments and sighted children. *Research in Developmental Disabilities*. 34: 2,173–84.

Kaye, K. 1977. Toward the origin of dialogue. In H.R. Schaffer (ed.), *Studies in mother-infant interaction*. London: Academic Press, 89–117.

Kozulin, A. 1988. Reality monitoring, psychological tools, and cognitive flexibility in bilinguals: theoretical synthesis and pilot experimental investigation. *International Journal of Psychology*. 23 (1–6): 79–92.

Lindblom, J. and Ziemke, T. 2003. Social situatedness of natural and artificial intelligence: Vygotsky and beyond. *Adaptive Behavior*. 11 (2): 79–96.

Liu, C.H. and Matthews, R. 2005. Vygotsky's philosophy: constructivism and its criticisms examined. *International Education Journal*. 6 (3): 386–99.

Lourenço, O. 2012. Many resemblances, and a crucial difference. *New Ideas in Psychology*. 30: 281–95.

Luria, A.R. 1972. *The man with a shattered world*. Harmondsworth: Penguin.

Matthews, W.J. 2003. Constructivism in the classroom: epistemology, history, and empirical evidence. *Teacher Education Quarterly*. 30 (3): 51–63.

McManis, L.D. and Gunnewig, S.B. 2012. Finding the education in educational technology with early learners. *Young Children*. May: 14–23.

Meacham, J. 1999. Riegel, dialectics, and multiculturalism. *Human Development*. 42 (3): 134–44.

Pritchard, A. and Woollard, J. 2010. *Psychology for the classroom: constructivism and social learning*. London: Routledge.

Riegel, K.F. 1973. *Dialectic operations: the final stage of cognitive development*. Princeton, NJ: Educational Testing Service.

Reeves, J.W. 1965. *Thinking about thinking*. London: Methuen.

Rogoff, B. 1986. Adult assistance of children's learning. In T.E. Raphael (ed.), *Contexts of school based literacy*. New York: Random House, 27–40.

Rogoff, B. 1990. *Apprenticeship in thinking: cognitive development in social context*. Oxford: Oxford University Press.

Rogoff, B. and Gardner, W. 1984. Adult guidance of cognitive development. In B. Rogoff and J. Lave (eds), *Everyday cognition: its development in social context*. Cambridge, MA: Harvard University Press, 95–116.

Rogoff, B. and Morelli, G. 1989. Perspectives on children's development from cultural psychology. *American Psychologist*. 44: 343–8.

Schaffer, R. 1989. Early social development. In A. Slater and G. Bremner (eds), *Infant development*. Hove: Erlbaum, 189–210.

Schneider, W. and Artelt, C. 2010. Metacognition and mathematics education. *ZDM Mathematics Education*. 42: 149–61.

Shute, R. and Miksad, J. 1997. Scaffolding effects of computer-assisted instruction on the cognitive development of preschool children. *Child Study Journal*. 27 (2): 237–53.

Shute, R., Foot, H. and Morgan, M. 1992. The sensitivity of children and adults as tutors. *Educational Studies*. 1 (1): 21–36.

Van der Veer, R. 1986. Vygotsky's developmental psychology. *Psychological Reports*. 59: 527–36.

Vygotsky, L.S. 1930/1978. *Mind in society: the development of higher mental processes*. Cambridge, MA: Harvard University Press.

Vygotsky, L.S. 1934/1962. *Thought and language*. Cambridge, MA: MIT Press.

Wertsch, J.V. and Tulviste, P. 1992. L.S. Vygotsky and contemporary developmental psychology. *Developmental Psychology*. 28 (4): 548–57.

Wood, D. 1988/1998. *How children think and learn*. Oxford: Blackwell.

Wood, D.J., Bruner, J.S. and Ross, G. 1976. The role of tutoring in problem solving. *Journal of Child Psychology and Psychiatry*. 17 (2): 89–100.

Wood, D.J., Wood, H.A and Middleton, D.J. 1978. An experimental evaluation of four face-to-face teaching strategies. *International Journal of Behavioral Development*. 1: 131–47.

Yasnitsky, A. 2012. The complete works of L.S. Vygotsky: PsyAnima Complete Vygotsky project. *Dubna Psychological Journal*. 3: 144–8.

8

THE HISTORIC EVENT

Contextualism

Introduction

Although psychology has tended not to embrace more recent philosophical developments (Teo, 1997), the discipline has certainly acknowledged its philosophical origins: as Howard Gardner observed, 'nearly every field begins as philosophy; and psychology continues to foreground its philosophical origins more faithfully than any other discipline' (Gardner, 1994: 182). John Dewey, one of the theorists covered in this chapter, stated in his *Psychology as Philosophic Method*, 'what else can philosophy in its fullness be but psychology, and psychology but philosophy' (Dewey, 1981: 116). In this chapter, we examine the philosophical underpinnings of contextualism, adopting Kahlbaugh's argument that 'contextualism is based on assumptions fundamentally distinct from those of the dialectical (organismic) paradigm' (Kahlbaugh, 1989: 4). There is, however, some commonality between Stephen Pepper's (1942) organismic and contextualism metaphors, in particular, the idea that 'reality is in constant flux' (Kramer and Bopp, 1989: 4). They also share an emphasis on placing activity in a given time and place. However, organicism places the focus on the developmental process of the organism, while contextualism includes the subjective context of the observer and the observed in a certain social context.

The root metaphor for contextualism is 'The real historic event' (Pepper, 1942: 232). Contextualism is generally associated with the writings of William James, John Dewey and Margaret Mead, and we will consider all three, as well as lifespan developmental psychology. We will touch upon Urie Bronfenbrenner's theory, although his work is given fuller treatment in Chapter 10.

A contextualist approach holds that developmental change involves reciprocal or bi-directional influence whereby an active organism is relating to a responsive context, thus individuals are both products and producers of their contexts (Lerner, 1976). Ralph Rosnow and Marianthi Georgoudi (1986) have identified four themes that are especially important in considering contextualism.

> **BOX 8.1 PARENTAL BELIEFS ABOUT CHILD DEVELOPMENT: THE ROOT METAPHOR OF CONTEXTUALISM**
>
> There is a steadily accumulating body of research regarding cultural differences in parental beliefs about child development. Ideas about appropriate parenting are determined not only by beliefs about childhood, but also by understanding of the psychology of how children grow (Sanson and Wise, 2001). Charles M. Super and Sara Harkness (2003) examined the role of Pepper's (1942) four root metaphors for explaining child-rearing behaviour, finding all four useful for explaining parental child-rearing beliefs. The extent to which parents adopted one metaphor as a general model of child behaviour drew on their broad philosophical views and their exposure to, and experience with, a range of child-rearing behaviours, as well as their education and training. Contextualism, with its focus on multiple determinants and perspectives, was favoured by parents with a higher level of education.

1. The historic event is the basic unit of analysis, with a consequent focus on change and development.
2. The context consists of all the conditions surrounding the event. The socio-cultural context in which the event takes place provides meaning to the event.
3. Variability and chance are an integral part of contextualism, because contexts themselves are ultimately developing and impermanent realities. This point alone differentiates contextualism from mechanism and organicism, which are based on the assumption that the true order and unity of events can be determined probabilistically (Thayer, 1968).
4. Action and knowledge: the purposive and intentional nature of human action is emphasized in contextualism. Development, then, is an active participation in the construction of contexts that in turn impact upon any future action.

Box 8.1 illustrates that having a contextualist outlook influences how one perceives and acts in the world – in that case, in parenting children.

Functionalism: William James (1842–1910) and Charles S. Peirce (1839–1914)

Whether New York-born James was a true contextualist is open to some debate, but his work certainly provides relevant background. As we observed in Chapter 3, James was the founder of 'functionalism'. The brother of novelist Henry James, William James was profoundly influenced by their theologian father, particularly in relation to his indifference to worldly success and his focus on addressing some of the fundamental problems of life. James broke off from his Harvard University studies and spent time in Germany, experiencing bouts of ill health, depression and suicidality. This period confirmed for James his deep and abiding interest in philosophy. He returned to Harvard, completed his medical degree and had an academic career there from 1872 to 1907. In 1878, James began the 12-year task of writing *Principles of Psychology*, which was finally published in 1890 and was a significant marker in the history of psychology. James is sometimes called 'the father of American psychology'.

An undergraduate friend was the philosopher Charles S. Peirce, whose writings focused strongly on the link between theory and practice and particularly the application of philosophy to everyday life. Peirce noted that, '[a]lmost every proposition of ontological metaphysics is either meaningless gibberish – one word being defined by other words, and they still by others, without any real conception ever being reached – or else is downright absurd' (Peirce, 1958: 192). According to Peirce, truth was discovered using the scientific method, and the next step was to apply it to solving everyday problems. Philosophical pragmatism embraced the idea that what is true will work, and highlighted the practical usefulness of discovered truth. At heart it was a 'pragmatic' theory and informed the later writings of both James and Dewey. Peirce argued that pragmatism begins with beliefs that are conscious, deliberate habits of action: 'Our beliefs guide our desires and shape our actions ... The feeling of believing is a more or less sure indication of there being established in our nature some habit that will determine our actions' (Peirce, 1958: 59). Thus, our beliefs cause us to act in a certain way because of the perceived consequences.

James endeavoured to understand and apply Peirce's philosophy. For James, pragmatism was first of all a way to evaluate truth claims, not by looking at the truth or falsity of a primary definition but by evaluating the claim in terms of its moral and aesthetic outcome. Second, it was a way of reconciling conflicting definitions of reality. People could still maintain their individual idiosyncratic beliefs if their outcomes led to common social behaviour agreed as acceptable (James, 1907). The pragmatic outlook appealed to those interested in using science to solve everyday problems. It also appealed to the frontier mentality of some developing western nations, such as the USA, in the early twentieth century. Through Darwinian influence, James argued for adaptive function. According to James, the mind is revealed in habits, knowledge and perceptions:

> Sow an action and you reap a habit;
> Sow a habit and you reap a character;
> Sow a character and you reap a destiny.

(James, 1890/1982: n.p.)

The mind is seen as constantly engaged in interaction with, and adaptation to, the environment. James emphasized the selective function of consciousness, holding that the 'stream of consciousness' includes ideas, as well as relations among them. As a pragmatist, he argued that 'thoughts and feelings exist' (James, 1890/1982, Vol. 1: vi).

A significant component of his *Principles of Psychology* was its trenchant criticism of the structuralist psychology originating in Germany (see Chapter 6). As elaborated by James, his main purpose was the development of a functional psychology whereby the aim was not to reduce psychology to its constituent elements, but rather to study consciousness as an ongoing process or stream. James critiqued the 'mind-stuff' theory, that 'our mental states are composite in structure, made up of smaller states conjoined' (James, 1890/1982, Vol. 1: 145). Mind-stuff theory attempted to explain higher mental states by viewing them as the sum of lower ones:

> All the 'combinations' which we actually know are effects, wrought by the units said to be 'combined', upon some entity other than themselves ... no possible number of entities (call them as you like, whether forces, material particles, or mental elements) can sum themselves together. Each remains in a sum, what it always was; and the sum itself exists only for a bystander who happens to overlook the units and to apprehend the sum as such.
>
> *(James, 1890/1982, Vol. 1: 160–1)*

As noted by Owen Flanagan, 'the mind cannot be identical to the sum of its parts because we need the mind to do the summing and to acknowledge the addition' (Flanagan, 1991: 42). Functionalism required the use of multiple methods to pursue answers to questions in both basic and applied psychological research (Crosby and Viney, 1990). In 'The meaning of truth', James wrote, 'To know an object is to lead to it through a context which the world provides' and 'Owing to the fact that all experience is a process, no point of view can ever be the last one' (James, 1907: 5). For example, he viewed scientific truth as changeable and the product of human perception (James, 1890/1982), and that therefore no one could claim to discover 'Truth'. He believed that the important questions of human behaviour could best be understood holistically. In *Principles*, James saw human perception as central to the understanding of psychological questions (James, 1909/1974, cited in Wozniak, 1995). James argued that people construct the nature of the world in their minds in unique ways on the basis of personal experiences, and that history is shaped by individual constructions of experience.

Both mechanism and organicism assume some causal connection between events across some dimension, either temporal or spatial: 'Events are assumed to be systematically related such that each new state is both an improvement over and a transformation of the previous one' (Kahlbaugh, 1989: 77). James, however, did not advocate a theory of progress, but proposed that history was simply a collection of unrelated facts, without any assumption about what the end state would be, or that it would represent an improvement. In this respect, we can see a connection with dynamic systems theory (see Chapter 12).

In the 1940s, the views and research of a number of psychologists belonging to the functionalist school (such as Ames, 1951) began to gain attention. Perception came to be seen as resulting from the relationship between the observing person

---

BOX 8.2 CAN TEACHERS FIGURE OUT THE FUNCTIONS OF PROBLEMATIC CLASSROOM BEHAVIOUR?

In 1997 it became mandatory in the USA for children's behavioural problems to be addressed using a support plan based on functional behavioural assessment (FBA). This process assumes that behaviour serves some purpose for the child. It involves detailed observations of the child in the environment (typically, the classroom), normally requiring the time and expertise of a psychologist. One of the present authors (RS), with an Australian and a US colleague, examined whether it was possible to train a teacher to undertake this process in an efficient, shortened way within the regular classroom context (Packenham *et al.*, 2004).

We worked with a teacher who nominated two children with problematic behaviours: eight-year-old high achiever Michelle, who caused frequent disruption by calling out and excessive talking; and nine-year-old low achiever Jack, who was often off-task. After brief training in analysing the behaviours, the situations leading up to them (antecedents), and the consequences, the teacher hypothesized that the function of Michelle's behaviour was to seek teacher attention, while Jack's behaviour was aimed at escaping from difficult work. New and appropriate ways of providing attention to Michelle were implemented, while Jack was given easier and more individually supported work tasks. Single case studies showed sustained improvements. Michelle's disruptive behaviour decreased from 34 per cent of observation periods to 10 per cent, while Jack's off-task behaviour dropped from 53 per cent to 24 per cent.

---

and the observed object, with context as the critical functional factor in helping us interpret the world around us (see Chapter 3). Functionalism continues to have a place in addressing children's behavioural difficulties, particularly in the case of children with disabilities and in educational settings (Box 8.2).

John Dewey (1859–1952): active minds in cultural settings

In her review of Dewey's work, Emily Cahan concluded that 'Dewey is not well known to contemporary psychologists, nor did he exert a strong influence on the emergence of a disciplinary psychology' (Cahan, 1992: 213). Any perusal of educational or developmental psychology textbooks would confirm that this claim still holds today. However, in reflecting on the role of history, culture and values in psychology, to redress some of its preoccupation with the collation of facts, there is a significant place for a greater understanding of Dewey's thinking.

Studying under G. Stanley Hall (see Chapter 3), and perhaps influenced by the writings of Jean-Jacques Rousseau (see Chapter 1), Dewey developed a rather idealist philosophy. This was somewhat tempered by Hall, who counselled against its excesses. Cahan noted Dewey's 'personal craving for a philosophical system in which parts related to a whole in a manner consistent with the new evolutionary biology with its emphasis on the organism in interaction with the environment' (Cahan, 1992: 206). To that end, Dewey shared a great deal in common with James. Dewey's thinking capitalized on two significant achievements of his time, namely biology's concepts of the 'organism in the environment' and social psychology's emphasis on observing 'active minds in cultural settings'. Dewey's writings provided a counterbalance to much of the laboratory-based psychology of the time: 'folk-lore and primitive culture, ethnology and anthropology, all render their contributions of matter and press upon us the necessity of explanation' (Dewey, 1884: 57).

In 'The reflex arc concept in psychology' (1896), Dewey argued against the suggestion that human beings are mechanisms made up of separate parts. He also disagreed with a view of consciousness as the simple additive sum of discrete elements such as sensations. In a functional manner, Dewey did not believe that stimulus and response were separate, unrelated entities, instead arguing that they were 'functionally related to each other through purposeful activity' (Cahan, 1992: 208).

For example, a behavioural interpretation of a child learning not to put her hand in a flame would be as follows. The sight of the flame entices the child to reach for it, out of curiosity, and the burning sensation causes the child to withdraw her hand. Any further encounter with the flame would call up the idea of the painful burn and result in the child avoiding the flame. That is, a simple association has formed between the sight of the flame and the burn. Dewey would explain the child's behaviour in a more functional manner. The child would see the attractive dancing flame in a curiosity-arousing way and the flame would not be a passive thing at all. After touching the flame, rather than an 'association' being formed with the pain of the burn, the experience literally changes the flame holistically, to a shining, hot painful object: it is our interaction with objects as a whole that gives them their meaning.

Development, then, is an active participation in the construction of contexts that in turn impact on any future action. As Aaron Schutz notes, 'Dewey was convinced that understanding something involves seeing how it is connected with other things and events' (Schutz, 2001: 269). Authentic learning occurs in the midst of purposeful activity. In this regard he believed that the best learning occurred when instruction was geared to a student's interests and motivations. His approach to education involved student interest, student activity, group work and real-life experience. Thus, Dewey took a child-centred approach to education well before the introduction of open classrooms, discovery learning and the activity-based curriculum.

In 1896 Dewey established and created one of the most important educational experiments of the nineteenth and twentieth centuries – the Laboratory School at the University of Chicago. Dewey believed strongly that it was from our experiences that we develop our theories about the world. As noted by Cahan,

'Dewey warned against the excesses and indicated the limits to the knowledge' gleaned from laboratories – a view later expounded by Bronfenbrenner (Cahan, 1992: 207, see also Chapter 10).

Daniel Fishman and Stanley Messer (2013) have drawn inspiration from the early pragmatism of James, Dewey and Peirce to suggest a 'bottom up', phenomenon-based, approach to applied psychology, rather than a 'top down' approach that applies theories drawn from basic research. Their 'pragmatic' case study method is described in Chapter 13.

Margaret Mead (1901–1978) and cross-cultural research

The American anthropologist Margaret Mead is widely known for her cross-cultural research and writing, heralded by the publication of *Coming of Age in Samoa* in 1928. She was a prolific author and social commentator, and married Gregory Bateson, anthropologist and social historian (see Chapter 4), after they met on a field trip in New Guinea.

Mead's ideas help us to appreciate the role played by culture in shaping our views of children and the family. In her book *Culture and Commitment* (1970) she called upon knowledge she had gleaned from studying children in Manus, Bali and New Guinea, following their lives into adulthood to identify three different kinds of culture: postfigurative, cofigurative and prefigurative.

1. *Postfigurative*: children learn primarily from the collective experience and history of their forebears.
2. *Cofigurative*: children learn from their peers.
3. *Prefigurative*: adults are capable of learning from their children, as well as vice versa.

To make a connection here with Vygotsky, we can see that his theory explicitly focused on the first two types of learning. However, his theory could be applied to the third type if we assume that, in some circumstances, children are more capable than adults (for example, one of the present authors, PS, constantly turns to his children for assistance with computing).

In her 1970 book, Mead mounted a powerful argument, based on years of anthropological research, to suggest that a number of conditions had combined to bring about the revolt of youth around the world. The first was the novel emergence of an identifiable world community, characterized by the sharing of knowledge and an awareness of the dangers of nuclear annihilation. Second, advances in modern technology, while beneficial in some areas, such as food production, were seriously challenging the ecology of the planet. Third, advances in medical knowledge had reduced the pressure for population increase, which in turn freed women from the necessity of devoting themselves entirely to reproduction, thereby changing their role in society and influencing the raising of children. In the light of these momentous changes, Mead believed people were living in a present unprepared for by their understanding of the past: 'In the past there were always some elders who knew more than any children in terms of their experience of having grown up within a cultural system. Today there are none' (Mead, 1970: 61). According to Mead, the young generation felt there must be better ways than those offered by the previous generation to deal with society's problems, and that they must find them; they recognized the crucial need for immediate action on world problems (see also Chapter 12). Mead wrote:

> Now, as I see it, the development of a prefigurative culture will depend on the existence of a continuing dialogue in which the young, free to act on their own initiative, can lead their elders in the direction of the unknown. Then the older generation will have access to new experiential knowledge, without which no meaningful plans can be made. It is only with the direct participation of the young who have that knowledge, that we can build a viable future.
>
> *(Mead, 1970: 73)*

Of course, Mead wrote this in an era of student protests (e.g. against the Vietnam, or American, War), a reminder that her theory, like others, must be historically contextualized. Youth voices became quieter for some years – for example, cuts to public funding of universities obliged students in many countries to take employment as well as studying, leaving little time for civic participation. However, new impetus to youth protest was given by the global financial collapse of 2008, with neoliberal austerity measures galvanizing youth led protests against global capitalism, with social media playing a central role in the formation and activities of movements such as 'Occupy' (Giroux, 2013).

To summarize Mead's contribution, she added a strong voice and some semblance of balance to the nature–nurture debate, which until that time had favoured nature, although there has been considerable debate about the validity of her Samoan research, with suggestions that her adolescent participants 'pulled the wool over her eyes' in describing their sexual adventures (Freeman, 1996). We have presented her significant contribution in this chapter because of her strong focus on culture in explaining differences in development.

Urie Bronfenbrenner (1917–2005) and the ecology of development

During much of the twentieth century, there was an emphasis on childhood as an individual process, to the neglect of social and cultural contexts (Oakley, 1972). During the 1970s, Bronfenbrenner began to address this, famously criticizing developmental psychology as 'the study of the strange behavior of children in strange situations with strange adults for the briefest possible period of time' (Bronfenbrenner, 1977: 513). He modestly claimed that the increasing attention paid to ecological context was not especially due to his work, but rather that his

work represented an idea whose time had come (Bronfenbrenner, 1986). Nevertheless, Bronfenbrenner's name remains the one that developmental psychologists most
closely associate with the shift at the end of the twentieth century towards recognizing the influence of environmental contexts on children's development, a shift that
can be traced to the publication of *The Ecology of Human Development* in 1979.
Bronfenbrenner argued that:

> The ecology of human development involves the scientific study of the
> progressive mutual accommodation between an active, growing human being
> and the changing properties of the immediate settings in which the developing
> person lives, as this process is affected by relations between these settings, and
> by the larger contexts in which the settings are embedded.
>
> *(Bronfenbrenner, 1979: 21)*

He envisaged the child as developing within a nested series of contexts, like a set of
Russian dolls, although students of psychology often recall him as 'the man with the
circles' – a reference to the two-dimensional visual representations of the interacting layers of the environment surrounding the child as a series of mutually
influential concentric circles. With his recognition of the importance of broader
contexts for development, he also advocated a closer connection between child
development research and public policy. We say more about Bronfenbrenner in
Chapter 10.

Lifespan development

Lifespan developmental psychology is a contextually orientated psychology with
the core assumption that development is not completed upon reaching adulthood.
Rather, ontogenesis continues across the entire life course, and the notion of development is adapted and used to encompass the idea of lifelong adaptive learning
(Baltes *et al.*, 1998; Wohlwill, 1973). As noted by Paul Baltes (1987) lifespan developmental psychology is considered to involve flux and change by virtue of the
consideration it gives to the growth and decline of the individual, a focus on the
historical embeddedness of development and its location in cultural context, and
the plasticity it attributes to human development.

Daniel Levinson (1978) believed that Sigmund Freud's Swiss protégé Carl Jung
(1875–1961) should be considered the founder of the modern study of adult
development, though Baltes and colleagues (1998) observed that the German
approach to developmental psychology was always more lifespan orientated than
the approaches of a number of other countries, including the USA, Britain and
some other European countries. Jung disagreed with Freud's emphasis on the early
childhood years and intrapsychic conflicts, and placed more emphasis on the second
half of life as an important period of development, and on the roles of religion,
mythology and culture in shaping our lives. The scene was further set for lifespan
theory by Baltes, when he wrote,

There can be no strong field of lifespan developmental psychology without a solid foundation in and connection to childhood. By the same token, the study of child development does not exist in a vacuum, but is vitally enriched by considering the aftermath of childhood.

(Baltes, 1979: 1)

The lifespan approach, in contrast to the passivity of mechanism, views the individual as actively involved in his or her development, an idea relatively neglected by developmental psychology until recent years (Brandtstadter, 1998), with Michael Lewis and Leonard A. Rosenblum's (1974) proposition that infants affect their own development, and Richard Bell's (1968) milestone paper on infant socialization as a bi-directional process. However, the notion of the 'seasons' of life and the concept of transformation and perfectibility have a long history dating back to Aristotle's idea of action (i.e. when we choose to undertake an action we do so for some purpose), to the 'Renaissance Man' ideal and, latterly, to the German 'understanding psychology' of Wilhelm Dilthey (Brandtstadter, 1998).

Lives of all great men remind us
We can make our lives sublime,
And, departing, leave behind us
Footprints on the sands of time
   (Henry Wadsworth Longfellow, A Psalm of Life, *in Peirce and Andrew, 1982)*

Baltes and colleagues (1998) also suggested that lifespan developmental psychology can be viewed in either a person-centred (holistic) or function-centred fashion. The former focuses on the person as a system and attempts to describe the stages or ages of development of the individual, while the latter focuses on attributes such as memory and tracks the development of those functions across the lifespan.

Writers including Erik Erikson (1968), Daniel Levinson and colleagues (1976) and Bernice Neugarten (1976) have written about the concept of the 'life-cycle'. This term seems to be adopted from biology, where the development of the individual passes through a sequence of stages such as from egg to embryo, birth, sexual development, reproduction and death. It is cyclical, in that it is repeated across generations. Levinson (1986), a colleague of Erikson, in attempting to describe the concept, compared it with 'life course' (the temporal unfolding of life over the years). 'Life-cycle' went beyond this, suggesting the unfolding of an underlying sequence or order of various phases or seasons of life. Other theorists have identified turning points, tasks or, as Neugarten (1976: 1) described it, 'punctuation marks along the life-cycle' that impact on the individual's self-concept, or sense of identity, and usually require adaptation by the individual and surrounding people. Robert Havighurst's task-based approach was described in Chapter 3, while Erikson's life-cycle stages are summarized in Table 8.1 (for further information, see Slee *et al.*, 2012). The concept of the life-cycle emphasizes that the individual grows

TABLE 8.1 Erikson's psychosocial stages

Ages	Stages
Infancy	Basic trust versus mistrust
1½ –3½ years (approx.)	Autonomy versus shame and doubt
3½–5½ years (approx.)	Initiative versus guilt
5½–12 years (approx.)	Industry versus inferiority
Adolescence	Identity versus role confusion
Young adulthood	Intimacy versus isolation
Adulthood	Generativity versus stagnation
Maturity	Ego integrity versus despair

and changes across the lifespan; an individual is not doomed to live out the effects of early childhood experiences.

Levinson (1978) proposed that the life-cycle evolves through a series of 'eras', each lasting approximately 25 years. During each era certain tasks present themselves and the extent to which they are accomplished determines how much satisfaction or turmoil the individual experiences. An era is a time of life in the broadest possible sense, each era using a distinctive character shaped by biological, psychological and social aspects. In moving from one era to the next basic changes occur in the 'fabric of life', and the transition can take as long as six years. The major eras consist of pre-adulthood, early adulthood, midlife transition, middle adulthood and late adulthood. There is a limited amount of research to support the validity of Levinson's scheme of developmental periods, which were largely based on his impressionistic interpretations of his large amount of clinical interview material with men, although he later followed this up by considering with his wife the 'seasons of life' of women (Levinson and Levinson, 1996, published after his death) (see also Sheehy, 1976).

During childhood, major developmental achievements (such as walking and talking), which exert a major influence on the child's relationships with others, occur within a specific age range. In contrast, the developmental landmarks in adulthood (establishing a relationship, bearing children or becoming a grandparent) are less age-linked and not universally experienced. While attaching specific time periods to adult life-events is less important at one level, at another level, the 'timing' of such events is often quite critical. Neugarten (1968) used the term 'social clock' to describe each culture's sense of timing for events such as marriage and child-bearing. Neugarten believed that individuals are sensitive to being 'off-time' in a particular culture by, for example, bearing children later in life than expected.

Recent demographic changes in many industrialized and postindustrial western countries have prompted Jeffrey Arnett (2000) to propose a new phase of life, between adolescence and adulthood (Box 8.3). This acts as a clear reminder of the importance of the historical and sociocultural context in understanding lifespan development.

BOX 8.3 EMERGING ADULTHOOD

'In effect, a new period of life has opened up between adolescence and adulthood as a normative experience for young people in industrialised societies' (Arnett, 2000: 3). In support of his view, Arnett (e.g. 2007) has cited the changing demographics in many western industrialized and postindustrialized countries. These include a rise in the median age of marriage, an increase in age at first childbirth for women and the proportion of young people completing tertiary education. Accordingly, emerging adulthood exists in cultures that postpone the entry into adult roles and responsibilities until well past the late teens. Such countries require a high level of education for entry into the information-based professions and individuals postpone marriage and parenthood until well after schooling is completed.

Arnett's proposal is for a new theory of development from the late teens through the early twenties, since the period between the end of adolescence and the beginning of early adulthood is now long enough to be considered not a 'transition period' but a *life stage* in itself, labelled 'emerging adulthood'. As Arnett has argued, 'it is a period of life characterised for many young people by a high degree of change, experimentation, and instability as they explore a variety of possibilities in love, work, and worldviews' (Arnett, 2000: 3). Arnett proposes there are five characteristics that make emerging adulthood a distinct entity, including that it is:

* the age of identity explorations;
* the age of instability;
* the self-focused age;
* the age of feeling in-between;
* the age of possibilities.

Arnett's views have invoked considerable discussion in the lifespan development literature.

That lifespan approaches need to be culturally contextualized is also highlighted by considering the writing of A. Bame Nsamenang (2005), who proposes that in the African context human ontogenesis comprises three stages of selfhood. The first stage, spiritual selfhood, begins at conception, or before that if the culture believes in reincarnation of an ancestral spirit; it ends when the child is named and thus introduced into the community. This is followed by social selfhood, lasting until biological death, which includes seven phases based on developmental tasks that are intimately linked with culture, social integration and interdependence. An intelligent child, in African terms, is one who shows good social responsibility, with the peer group playing a central role in promoting this.

The third stage of the life-cycle is that of an ancestor, who continues to influence the affairs of the living.

Conclusions

In this chapter we have focused on contextualism as a means for understanding human development, taking Pepper's (1942) idea that the root metaphor for contextualism is the real historic event in all its dynamic activity. To this end, we have examined the contributions of the functionalists, those who highlighted the significance of culture in understanding and interpreting development, and lifespan theorizing. There is no doubt that contextualism has had, and continues to exert, a strong impact on the study of child development. The twin notions of 'constant change' and 'embeddedness' emphasize change as promoting change. Richard Lerner and Imma De Stefanis have argued that 'the regulation by individuals of their relations with their complex and changing context is the process involved in successful development across life' (Lerner and De Stefanis, 2000: 476). Contextualism paves the way for a deeper consideration of cultural issues in children's development, and this is the theme of the next chapter.

References

Ames, A. 1951. Visual perception and the rotating trapezoidal window. *Psychological Monographs.* 65 (7): 234.

Arnett, J.J. 2000. Emerging adulthood: a theory of development from the late teens through twenties. *American Psychologist.* 55 (5): 469–80.

Arnett, J.J. 2007. Emerging adulthood: what is it, and what is it good for? *Child Development Perspectives.* 1 (2): 68–73.

Baltes, P.B. 1979. On the potential and limits of child development: life-span developmental perspectives. *Newsletter of the Society for Research in Child Development.* Summer: 1–4.

Baltes, P.B. 1987. Theoretical propositions of life-span developmental psychology: on the dynamics between growth and decline. *Developmental Psychology.* 23 (5): 611–26.

Baltes, P.B., Lindenberger, U. and Staudinger, U.M. 1998. *Life-span theory in developmental psychology.* New York: Academic Press.

Bell, R.A. 1968. A reinterpretation of the direction of effects in studies of socialization. *Psychological Review.* 75: 81–95.

Brandstadter, J. 1998. Action perspectives on human development. In R.M. Lerner (ed.), *Handbook of child psychology. Theoretical models of human development.* Fifth edn, Vol. 1. New York: Wiley, 807–63.

Bronfenbrenner, U. 1977. Toward an experimental ecology of human development. *American Psychologist.* July: 513–31.

Bronfenbrenner, U. 1979. *The ecology of human development: experiments by nature and design.* Cambridge, MA: Harvard University Press.

Bronfenbrenner, U. 1986. Recent advances in research on the ecology of human development. In R.K. Silbereisen, K. Eyferth and G. Rudinger (eds), *Development as action in context: problem behavior and normal youth development.* New York: Springer-Verlag, 286–309.

Cahan, E.D. 1992. John Dewey and human development. *Developmental Psychology.* 28: 205–14.

Crosby, D.A. and Viney, D.W. 1990. *Toward a psychology that is radically empirical*. Paper presented at the Ninety-Eighth Annual Convention of the American Psychological Association, Boston, August.

Dewey, J. 1884. Kant and the philosophic method. *The Journal of Speculative Philosophy*. 18 (2): 162–74.

Dewey, J. 1896. The reflex arc concept in psychology. *The Psychology Review*. 4: 357–70.

Dewey, J. 1981. The structure of experience. In J.J. McDermott (ed.), *The Philosophy of John Dewey*. Second edn, Vol. 1. Chicago, IL: The University of Chicago Press, 1–325.

Erikson, E. 1968. *Identity, youth and crisis*. New York: Norton.

Fishman, D.B. and Messer, S.B. 2013. Pragmatic case studies as a source of unity in applied psychology. *Review of General Psychology*. 17 (2): 156–61.

Flanagan, O. 1991. *The science of the mind*. Second edn. Cambridge, MA: MIT Press.

Freeman, D. 1996. *Franz Boas and the flower of heaven: coming of Age in Samoa and the fateful hoaxing of Margaret Mead*. Harmondsworth: Penguin.

Gardner, H. 1994. The stories of the right hemisphere. In W.D. Spaulding (ed.), *Integrative views of motivation, cognition and emotion*. The Nebraska Symposium on Motivation. Vol. 41. Lincoln, NE: University of Nebraska Press, 57–69.

Giroux, H.A. 2013. The Quebec student protest movement in the age of neoliberal terror. *Social Identity Journal for the Study of Race, Nation and Culture*. 19 (5): 515–35.

James, W. 1890/1982. *The principles of psychology*. New York: H. Holt and Company.

James, W. 1907. The meaning of truth. In *Pragmatism, a new name for some old ways of thinking: popular lectures on philosophy*. New York: Longmans Green and Co., 1–308.

James, W. 1909/1974. 'The tigers of India'. In *Pragmatism and four essays from the meaning of truth*. New York: New American Library, 227.

Kahlbaugh, P.E. 1989. William James' pragmatism: a clarification of the contextual world view. In D.A. Kramer and M.J. Bopp (eds), *Transformation in clinical and developmental psychology*. New York: Springer-Verlag, 73–88.

Kramer, D.A. and Bopp, M.J. 1989. *Transformation in clinical and developmental psychology*. New York: Springer-Verlag.

Lerner, R.M. 1976. *Concepts and theories of human development*. Reading, MA: Addison-Wesley.

Lerner, R.M. and De Stefanis, I. 2000. The importance of infancy for individual, family and societal development. Commentary on the special section: does infancy matter? *Infant Behaviour and Development*. 22: 475–82.

Levinson, D. 1978. *Seasons of a man's life*. New York: Random House.

Levinson, D. 1986. A conception of adult development. *American Psychologist*. 41: 3–12.

Levinson, D.J., Darrow, C.M., Klein, E.B., Levinson, M.H. and McKee, B. 1976. Periods in the adult development of men: ages 18 to 45. *The Counseling Psychologist*. 6: 21–4.

Levinson, D.J. with Levinson, J.D. 1996. *Seasons of a woman's life*. New York: Alfred A. Knopf.

Lewis, M. and Rosenblum, L.A. 1974. *The effect of the infant on its care-giver*. New York: Wiley.

Mead, M. 1928. *Coming of age in Samoa*. New York: William Morrow & Co.

Mead, M. 1970. *Culture and commitment*. New York: Doubleday.

Neugarten, B.L. 1968. *Middle age and aging*. Chicago, IL: The University of Chicago Press.

Neugarten, B. 1976. Adaption and the life cycle. *The Counseling Psychologist*, 6: 16–20.

Nsamenang, A.B. 2005. Human ontogenesis: an Indigenous African view on development and intelligence. *International Journal of Psychology*. April: 1–5.

Oakley, A. 1972. *Sex, gender and society*. Melbourne: Sun Books.

Packenham, M., Shute, R. and Reid, R. 2004. A truncated functional behavioral assessment procedure for children with disruptive classroom behaviours. *Education and Treatment of Children*. 27: 9–25.

Peirce, C.S. 1958. The fixation of belief. In P.P. Wiener (ed.), *Charles S. Peirce: selected writings*. New York: Dover Publications, 91–112.

Peirce, H.W. and Andrew, J. 1982. moodle.baylorschool.org. Accessed 24 June 2014.

Pepper, S. 1942. *World hypotheses: a study of evidence*. Berkeley, CA: University of California Press.

Rosnow, R.L. and Georgoudi, M. (eds) 1986. *Contextualism and understanding in behavioral science: implications for research and theory*. New York: Praeger.

Sanson, A. and Wise, S. 2001. Children and parenting: the past hundred years. *Family Matters*. 60: 36–45.

Schutz, A. 2001. John Dewey's conundrum. Can democratic schools empower? *Teachers College Record*. 103: 267–302.

Sheehy, G. 1976. *Passages*. New York: Dutton & Co.

Slee P.T., Campbell, M. and Spears, B. 2012. *Child, adolescent and family development*. Third edn. Melbourne: Cambridge University Press.

Super, C.M. and Harkness, S. 2003. The metaphors of development. *Human Development*. 46 (1): 3–23.

Teo, T. 1997. Developmental psychology and the relevance of a critical metatheoretical reflection. *Human Development*. 40: 195–210.

Thayer, H.S. 1968. *Meaning and action: a critical history of pragmatism*. New York: Bobbs-Merrill.

Wohlwill, J.F. 1973. *The study of behavioural development*. New York: Academic Press.

Wozniak, R.H. 1995. Mind and body: Rene Déscartes to William James. Available at: http://serendip.brynmawr.edu/Mind/. Accessed 24 June 2014.

9
SOCIOCULTURAL INFLUENCES ON DEVELOPMENT

Introduction

We saw in the previous chapter how certain theorists acknowledged the importance of environmental contexts in children's development. The total context consists of all the conditions surrounding an event, including the physical and social world. It is the sociocultural context that gives meaning to the event (Georgoudi and Rosnow 1985), and it follows from this that the field of child development is itself culturally bound. Erica Burman (1994/2008) pointed out its bias as a product of western society, mainly the USA, with some influence from other parts of the Anglosphere. This view must be balanced by recognizing highly influential theorists from the non-English-speaking world, such as Sigmund Freud, Jean Piaget and Lev Vygotsky, though it is through translations of their works into English that their ideas have become incorporated into mainstream developmental theorizing (we will see later how important work can be overlooked because of not being available in English).

While Vygotsky's dialectical theory (see Chapter 7) provides a framework for understanding how language-based cognitive processes, especially, are determined by culture, it remains the case that our understanding of child development is based almost entirely on a very narrow sample of the world's children. A striking example of how child development has been viewed through a western (and a psychological) lens has been provided by David Lancy (2007). That mother-child play is essential for children's development is a message often taken from the developmental psychology literature; for example, Lancy notes that Jerome Bruner saw peek-a-boo play as universal and essential for early cognitive development. Yet, historical and current anthropological records show that mother-child play is exceptional, and almost entirely confined to the upper echelons of western societies. It is therefore not appropriate, Lancy argues, for bodies to be proselytizing for mother-child play in societies where it is not culturally appropriate.

Such criticisms of the underlying assumption of universality are gradually gaining influence, and the term Majority World is used to refer to those neglected by developmental psychology (Nsamenang, 2006). Indeed, the very scientific status of the field has been questioned, on the grounds that the discipline neglects the majority of its subject matter and, even when expanding its horizons, applies a particular value system that prizes individualism and cognitive competence above all (Nsamenang, 1999, 2005, 2006). This emphasis places traditional models and methods of developmental psychology at odds with the social interdependence that is central to most cultures of the world, and neglects socio-emotional development in favour of rational thought. As African psychologist A. Bame Nsamenang and others have noted, western writings have often carried the implication that alternative notions of childhood are faulty, leaving them open to accusations of racism. It seems, therefore, that whenever one tries seriously to address questions about culture and development, one becomes inevitably embroiled in philosophical, epistemological, ethical and political issues.

Culture and development

Despite the overwhelming bias towards US samples and values in developmental research, it is nevertheless the case that some very influential work recognizing the role of culture in development has emerged from there, notably from individuals with strong overseas links. We saw in the previous chapter how the anthropologist Margaret Mead identified the characteristics of different kinds of culture that shape children and families. Urie Bronfenbrenner, too, included culture as an overarching environmental influence on development. His 1970 account of the importance of peer influences on children's development in the USA and Russia was greeted with great interest, while the same point had been made by cross-cultural psychologists, but gone unrecognized, for the previous 30 years (Ritchie and Ritchie, 1979).

An important figure in this area is Erik Erikson (see Chapter 5 and Figure. 8.1). He was born in 1902 in Germany, of Danish parents, and moved to the USA as an adult. He was influenced by Freud (Erikson underwent psychoanalysis with Freud's daughter Anna) and by Mead. He is probably best remembered for his emphasis on stages of lifespan development, but he also made an important contribution to under-standing development in relation to culture. In his book *Childhood and Society* (1950), Erikson described his work with the Sioux and Yurok, Indigenous peoples of North America. In contrast to then typical western approaches to Indigenous peoples as primitive or infantile, he recognized that they had their own ways of dealing with the world and bringing up children. He argued that stages of development are marked by the resolution of normative crises resulting from the interaction between the biological plan for the species and the cultural environment.

Another researcher who made a significant contribution to understanding sociocultural influences on development was Vygotsky. Although, like Piaget, his focus was on cognitive development, for Vygotsky this development was insep-arable from the influence of more experienced members of the culture. The

BOX 9.1 LEARNING FROM ELDERS

Within New Zealand's Maori context, the teacher-pupil relationship is an intimate one based on high expectation with both the more learned and the learner working together on a set task. For example, a grandmother teaching her grand-daughter(s) about the mythology and art of finger weaving . . . The pupil(s) and the teacher are in a position jointly to evaluate the ongoing process and development of their efforts. When the pupil proves that she has learned the necessary skills, knowledge and understanding to perform the task on her own, both teacher and pupil are then ready to move on to another task.

(Pere, 1982: 67)

Vygotskian recognition of the importance of learning from others, and the co-construction of learning within the ZPD, is illustrated by Rangimarie Pere's (1982) description of the teaching of cultural tasks to New Zealand's Maori children (Box 9.1).

As we saw in Chapter 7, Vygotsky's theory of thought was that the interpersonal becomes internalized as the intrapersonal, so that the way a person thinks is inculcated through linguistic interaction with others, the nature of which is culturally determined. That cultural differences can operate even at the perceptual level was brought home to him when he discovered that, in Uzbekistan, the visual illusions that fooled city folk did not work. Recently, one of us (RS) heard a non-Indigenous Australian woman interviewed about her time living with a particular Australian Aboriginal group. She reported that she had been forced to abandon her struggles to learn their language; this was because everything they said had to be contextualized in terms of 'where-I-am-in-the-journey-of-the-day', and she found this way of thinking about the world too alien.

While Vygotsky's theory proposed that culture plays an integral role in development, developmental researchers have often seen sociocultural variables as something to be *controlled* in studies, to enable the observation of 'pure process'. A shift from this type of thinking has become apparent, however, in the direction of seeing social environmental variables as something to be *studied* to enable development to be understood. This shift was acknowledged by the later versions of Bronfenbrenner's theory. Bronfenbrenner and Pamela Morris made this point well by referring to a 1995 work by Laurence Steinberg and colleagues:

it made no sense at all to control for ethnicity, social class, or household composition in an attempt to produce 'pure' process. No process occurs outside of a context. And if we want to understand context, we need to take it into account, not pretend to control it away.

(Bronfenbrenner and Morris, 1998: 1,016)

Like Bronfenbrenner, the dialectical psychologist Klaus Riegel developed his theory in the USA in the 1970s (see Chapter 7). Influenced by the earlier Soviet-based work of Sergei Rubinstein rather than Vygotsky, he maintained that it was inappropriate to study the isolated individual as the focus of development; rather, the individual can only be understood in relation to historical and societal changes regarding issues such as demography, political structures and majority–minority group relations. Thus, the individual does not just exist within the boundaries of the body, but within a 'psychological space' that encompasses interactions with family, friends and the broader culture (Meacham, 1999).

In a similar vein, Joan Miller (1999) distinguished between ecological per-spectives and the approach of cultural psychology. The former sees culture as merely providing a context for development: development happens through universal processes and mechanisms, with culture merely providing specific content. The cultural approach, by contrast, is concerned with shared meaning systems, so that psychological notions such as 'mind', 'self' and 'emotion' are themselves culturally created and understood. From the perspective of cultural psychology, cultural practices are not based only on adaptive considerations, but may be nonrational, such as when people refuse to eat certain animals for cultural reasons although they are edible. Psychological explanations therefore need to take account not just of the person and the ecological context, but also of the culture.

Indeed, culture itself can be seen as subject to evolutionary processes: rather than viewing humans as 'biologically complete hominids' who 'suddenly invented culture' (Miller, 1999: 87), the cultural view sees culture itself as a factor contributing to evolutionary selection. So, apart from some innate propensities in infancy and some involuntary responses, development must occur within a cultural setting for most psychological processes to develop. This more radical approach owes much to the views of the dialectical psychologists and, as Miller observed, presents a major challenge to the Piagetian theory that development occurs independently of enculturation. Rather, research indicates that the stages and end-points of cognitive development are dependent upon the provision of culturally specific support. In general terms, Miller pointed out the need to recognize that all research findings are dependent upon the constructs that underlie them, and that these may be culture-specific. She suggested that cultural psychology might be best seen not as a separate area of inquiry, but as a perspective that can inform whatever psychological issue is under consideration.

It is certainly the case that mainstream developmental psychology pays far more attention to cultural influences on development than it did previously. A cross-cultural study of infant temperament (de Vries, 1984) was (by chance) particularly telling about differing perceptions about children that parents in some cultures hold in comparison with western researchers' beliefs. The study was investigating the notion of differences in temperament between infants, researchers in the USA having established that infants vary in how easy or difficult they are to manage. The researchers applied their temperament criteria to infants of Masai parents (people of Kenya and Tanzania). A tragic drought occurred, in which many infants died; it turned out that the survivors were the 'difficult' babies, who had, presumably, demanded more frequent feeding. Furthermore, Masai parents valued more assertive characteristics in children, perhaps the very characteristics that US parents regarded as difficult, but that promoted survival for the Masai. Therefore, a valued characteristic in one culture may not be highly valued, and even detrimental to survival, in another. This illustrates the notion of 'goodness-of-fit' between a child's propensities and the environment in determining development (Thomas and Chess, 1977).

Parental ethnotheories, or parental belief systems, have been proposed as a way of capturing the link between cultural forces and parenting practices (Harkness et al., 2001). Researchers draw upon both anthropology and developmental psychology (following in the footsteps of Mead and Erikson), and note the need for tolerance of research methods coming from different traditions. This cross-cultural approach aims to elicit the often implicit theories that parents have about the correct way to raise children. As Jane and James Ritchie commented,

> socialisation is not conducted in terms of the literature on child development but in terms of cultural goals. Adults everywhere want their children to grow up not simply to be good human beings in universal terms but to be good people in their own cultural terms.
>
> *(Ritchie and Ritchie, 1979: 147)*

David Shwalb *et al.* (2010) examined how mothers in the USA, Japan, South Korea and Indonesia view children's development, in accord with a range of metaphors and images of children (see Chapter 1). All saw children's development as under environmental rather than genetic influences (though not as 'blank slates'), and in unique, rather than universal, terms. Interestingly, they most strongly endorsed Stephen Pepper's formism metaphor – the least considered in this book, as it is not clearly aligned with any strong theoretical tradition. This means that mothers saw children as falling into different 'types', a view that best aligns with theories of temperament and personality. Contextualism was the next most endorsed metaphor. Except for the Indonesian mothers, they saw children as 'pure' rather than 'mischievous', and all endorsed a 'gardening' metaphor for bringing up children. All except the Japanese mothers saw religious influence as important. Japanese mothers also perceived children as lonely. Overall, the results suggested that mothers' views of children's development are multifaceted and show both individual differences and cultural influences.

The question of how young people are growing up in an increasingly globalized world has also been raised. Focusing on Indian youth, Walter Renner *et al.* (2014) have presented this by exploring both risks and opportunities. Drawing upon John W. Berry's (2005) acculturation theory, they point to the importance of preserving cultural identity in the face of westernization, in order to promote optimum development.

With an increasing recognition of such cultural differences, Nsamenang (1999) proposed that editors of textbooks and journals, and scientific panels concerned with children's development, should have multicultural audiences in mind.

Critical psychology

Some workers considering cultural influences on development question the very philosophical basis of psychology, an issue we originally raised in Chapter 1. This view represents a change in epistemology from the modern, positivist tradition in which most psychology students are still educated. The explicit recognition that cultural, historical and political factors are crucial in developmental psychology is part of the broad field of 'critical psychology'. This term covers a variety of areas of endeavour, such as feminist psychology, which have been around for some years, but exist at the margins of the discipline (Ussher and Walkerdine, 2001; see also Chapter 11). From a postmodern perspective, subjectivity, ethical and power issues are central, and qualitative methods provide the major methodological approach.

Burman (1994 / 2008) reviewed developmental psychology from a critical perspective. She observed that, in the mid-nineteenth century, non-western peoples, along with infants and animals, were studied as examples of the 'primitive' mind, thus serving the perspective of European (especially British) imperialists that their own race was superior. This perspective continued into the twentieth century. Even Vygotsky, who did so much to foster understanding of cultural influences on individual thought, regarded some cultures as inferior (Wertsch and Tulviste, 1992). Recent, more subtle and implicit inferences that some cultural achievements are to be valued more highly than others include the observation that 'the development of reading and writing can be regarded as an indication of a culture "coming of age"' (Garton and Pratt, 1998: 68).

Burman observes that US culture is taken as the norm in the organization of child development textbooks – for example, developmental tasks across the lifespan are culture-bound (lifespan theorist Robert Havighurst explicitly acknowledged this, as mentioned in Chapter 3). Textbooks often contain a cross–cultural applications section, but Burman maintains that the underlying message is that the processes and stages described are universal, with only the *content* varying across cultures. She notes, for example, that cognitive development is often linked in texts with physical development, giving it pride of place after the biological, with emotional development seen as secondary (we will pick up the theme of emotional development theories again later).

Patricia Dudgeon and Harry Pickett (2000), writing about psychology and reconciliation between Australia's Indigenous and non-Indigenous communities, have similarly observed that, like anthropology, psychology is based in western culture. While purporting to be objective and apolitical, it is in fact a value-laden discipline, based on individualism and granting only a peripheral role to cultural contexts, largely ignoring historical and social factors. Psychology promotes individualism to the neglect of the community and family welfare, which are central to many Indigenous cultures. Nsamenang (1999, 2006) has similarly observed that developmental psychology is a scientific endeavour rooted in a particular culture and worldview, and as such cannot be divorced from its context. However, alternative psychological perspectives, including community, narrative and discursive psychology, recognize issues such as multiple truths and social justice, and are explicitly concerned with social change and valuing the marginalized (Dudgeon and Pickett, 2000). Rather than speaking of a universal 'psychology', the possibility is raised of the development of specific psychologies.

This recognition of the value of alternative perspectives has extended to calls for psychology not to remain isolated from other relevant disciplines (Gridley *et al.*, 2000) and, from the perspective of critical psychology, that psychology as a discipline should entertain critique based within social, political and cultural analyses of today's world (Bendle, 2001). Such a perspective has implications for the work of mental health professionals: culturally competent practice includes acknowledging and accepting cultural differences and biases, recognizing racism and oppression in society and acknowledging the fact that the mental health professions are unavoidably political.

These views follow from a consideration of the epistemological issues raised by Teo (1997), as discussed in Chapter 1, and also from an acceptance of Vygotsky's theory: if thought is culturally determined, why would a system of thought such as developmental psychology be exempt? Riegel, too, specifically maintained that developmental theorizing must be understood in relation to its sociohistorical context. Such a perspective throws up serious challenges to traditional developmental psychology, which aims not only to produce universal truths about development, but sees the researcher as a neutral observer. Nsamenang commented that western psychologists 'tend to focus more on measuring research participants, they rarely listen to them in their own terms' (Nsamenang, 1999: 164). Nsamenang's perspective is in accord with Taft's (1987) advice that developmental psychology would benefit greatly from taking into account alternative sources of information, including historical, demographic and anthropological. The value of broadening the scope of developmental psychology to include such sources of information has been endorsed by Kojima (1996), who proposed that an 'ethnopsychological pool' of ideas about childrearing has built up over centuries in Japan, and forms a basis from which western ideas may be assimilated.

Nsamenang supports the use of 'participatory and interpretive research that values both qualitative and quantitative methodologies' (Nsamenang, 1999: 164). The developmental psychology literature remains firmly grounded in traditional science and quantitative methods, but postmodern approaches and qualitative methods are slowly gaining ground. For example, in our own area of peer victimization, we have come to value both approaches: quantitative data can capture succinctly differences in types of aggression across ages and gender (e.g. Russell and Owens, 1999), while in-depth qualitative investigations complement this by providing deeper insights into participants' experiences of being victimized (e.g. Shute *et al.*, 2008). However, fence-straddling can be decidedly uncomfortable!

Most psychologists remain firmly quantitative, and the debate between the two sides continues. We will revisit these issues in the following chapters.

Culture, history and developmental theories

Let us at this point examine further the criticism that developmental psychology has tended to neglect historical influences. While Bronfenbrenner observed that culture is more stable than the inner ecosystems, it does change, and this change was central to Riegel's theory of development. Nevertheless, according to David Ho and colleagues (2001), researchers often treat culture as if it is 'frozen in time' – a background variable to be controlled.

Consider the case of parenting in China. There, and in East Asia broadly, Confucianism has been a strong cultural force for centuries. The effects of the environment on human development are seen as dominant, with people viewed as initially similar, but becoming 'wide apart through practice' (Bai, 2005). Moral or character education lies at the heart of Confucianism, transmitted by parents and teachers, and self-improvement is a lifelong aim (Chou *et al.*, 2013). Personal needs are to be suppressed in favour of the family and community. Obligation and acquiescence to elders (filial piety) is a central concept (Canda, 2013), with elders as role models for appropriate behaviour. Men dominate women in a hierarchical system, and 'strict fathers and kind mothers' are the expectation (Chang *et al.*, 2011). Over the past 30 years, China has undergone massive economic and social changes. Using a cultural evolutionary framework, which predicts conformity in socially stable times but innovation in the face of change, Chang and colleagues predicted, and found, that today's attitudes to parenting are non-hierarchical, non-traditional and egalitarian. Although there has been a resurgence in Confucianism in an effort to resist western influence (Chou *et al.*, 2013), Chinese parents have been turning to western-influenced psychology for guidance on raising their children, resulting in a move towards more child-centred, individualistic ideals, with pressure on children to achieve academically causing much distress (Ho *et al.*, 2001; Kaiman, 2014). However, in contrast with the typical western finding that poverty places children at greater risk for poor developmental outcomes, more behavioural problems in China are found among the children of the rich. Finding such a difference within 'the world's largest geopolitical community' makes it much more difficult for western commentators to dismiss such results as anomalies to be found occasionally in small, exotic communities (Goodnow, 2001).

The foregoing discussion clearly implies that there is an important place for a historical perspective in creating a deeper understanding of the field itself. As Elizabeth Valentine observed, although 'psychology par excellence does not occur in a social or political vacuum', history and philosophy are often marginalized, for reasons such as a positivist inheritance and an emphasis on short-term gain (Valentine, 1998: 167). It is certainly the case that child development textbooks, including this one, generally give a brief description of various views of childhood that have existed in previous historical times. This in itself demonstrates that views of childhood are changeable and relative, and yet the implication generally seems to be that, now that we have reached the era of scientific understanding, we are finally on the right track and nearer to the truth. What we generally fail to stop and consider are issues such as why those particular figures became influential, or why certain theories have gained prominence over others (after all, history is written by the winners). We will take as an example theorizing about a specific area of child psychology: emotional development.

Carol Magai and Susan McFadden (1995) observed how the long-held view in western culture that the emotions are inferior to the intellect, and need to be tamed, is reflected in the history of the study of emotional development. For example, John Watson, who performed the famous experiment on conditioned fear with Little Albert in 1920, gave advice to parents on child-rearing which advocated the avoidance of 'mawkish sentimentality' (see Chapter 6). Watson's stance seemed to be influenced not only by prevailing western approaches to emotion, but by his own upbringing, which combined religious fundamentalism with an alcoholic father prone to violent outbursts. The topic of emotional development became increasingly neglected during much of the twentieth century. This was reflected in its being gradually squeezed out of child development textbooks over the years, and in the difficulty reported by researchers on emotion, such as Carroll Izard, to gain funding and become published in the area; Izard reported receiving dismissive reviews of papers he submitted to scientific journals, and having to maintain his academic reputation by undertaking research on cognition. Similarly, one of the present authors (PS) found it impossible to publish papers in psychology journals from his 1983 PhD thesis on mother–infant emotional relationships, and the first major paper from this research was published in a journal of psychiatry.

As well as demonstrating how the western belief in the superiority of cognition over emotion influenced the course of child development research, Magai and McFadden also provided an enlightening analysis of how historical factors influenced twentieth-century theorizing about the development of infant emotions. Watson's proposal that infants express three basic emotions (fear, rage and love) was disputed in the 1930s by Kathryn Bridges, who maintained that the emotions of young infants are initially undifferentiated, and only become differentiated gradually through a process of conditioning. Her work was later criticized for its lack of descriptive detail of infant behaviour and her use of institutionalized infants, who are unusually lacking in emotional expression, as we saw in Chapter 5. Nevertheless, her theory of emotional development was accepted for many years and completely overshadowed research undertaken by another woman, Charlotte Bühler, whose work demonstrated the existence of discrete emotions in infants. Her research included painstaking, detailed observational work and experiments, including one that was, in effect, the first demonstration of object permanence in infants. Yet how many psychology students today have heard of Bühler? The first demonstration of object permanence is firmly ascribed to Piaget, whose work, in terms of experimental rigour, was arguably outstripped by Bühler's.

The influence of these three individuals on child development theory appears to have resulted from historical factors, with Bühler working in the German language and remaining untranslated into English, while Piaget's work was translated from French into English from the 1930s onwards. With English-language publications being the most influential in developmental psychology, Piaget became known as a 'giant' of developmental psychology, Bridges's notion of undifferentiated emotions held sway for many years and Bühler's work has remained little acknowledged, even in German-language accounts of the history of emotional development, which have drawn upon English-language accounts.

An exercise such as Magai and McFadden's is a historical and not a scientific one, but can it be denied that it throws valuable light upon theorizing in developmental psychology? It shows us how certain theories and theorists gain credence and others disappear because of cultural factors such as prevailing views about which topics are worthy of publication, what languages are influential and, as we shall see in the next chapter, the gender of the researcher. To use Bronfenbrenner's language, there may be much value in paying closer attention to the chronosystem as it applies to the development of our discipline.

Indigenous psychology

Interest in Indigenous psychology – especially in the experience of Indigenous people themselves – is quite recent in the history of psychology. Care must be taken that the concept of 'Indigenous psychology' is not used to marginalize non-western perspectives (Nsamenang, 2005). This area of inquiry can only thrive when members of the dominant culture are prepared to recognize the impact of colonialism on Indigenous people. This is consistent with Riegel's perspective that individual development can only be understood in relation to cultural and historical change and the relations between majority and minority groups. As recently as 1988 the International Congress of Psychology, held in Australia, was devoid of Indigenous content, a fact raised by a New Zealand community psychologist at the closing ceremony (Gridley *et al.*, 2000). This galvanized some Australian psychologists into action, so that by the turn of the millennium articles on Indigenous issues were published in journals of the Australian Psychological Society. Furthermore, non-traditional types of journal article and review processes were accepted, guidelines for psychologists working with Indigenous people had appeared and Aboriginal issues and presenters became regularly included in conferences. It also became usual for conferences to include a welcome from local Indigenous elders, although we know of one dispossessed elder from the Kaurna nation who will only 'greet', not 'welcome', visitors onto her traditional land on which our university has been built. The editorial of a special issue on Indigenous issues of the journal *Australian Psychologist* (Sanson and Dudgeon, 2000) noted that in some of the articles the authors had chosen to be explicit about their own background. This recognition of subjectivity (that disclosure of where a writer is coming from personally is relevant to the understanding and interpretation of their writing on psychological matters – and

---

BOX 9.2 IS A 'PURE' INDIGENOUS PSYCHOLOGY POSSIBLE? A LATIN AMERICAN EXAMPLE

Embedded in the social, political, and economic reality of El Salvador, Martín-Baró demanded that psychology should make a contribution to the social development of Latin America and that liberation psychology should free itself from the perspectives of Western Europe and North America. He argued that Latin American psychology should not be concerned about whether it would be recognized in the rich countries, but rather should focus on whether it provided a service to the majority of Latin Americans. In his critique of mainstream Euro American psychology he rejected the idea of value neutral science and the primacy of research in academia. Yet, this example also shows that pure indigenous psychologies, in this case pre-Colombian psychologies, are no longer conceivable. His liberation psychology contains Roman Catholic principles, liberation theology, and socialist ideas as well as local reflections and practices. Any historical reconstruction would have to take such interwoven factors into account.

(Teo, 2013: 13)

---

that journal editors should encourage this) represented a radical, and as yet, rare, shift from the traditions of science.

Teo (2013) maintains that the term 'Indigenous psychology' should not be reserved for minority or less powerful cultures, but refers to the specificities of *all* psychologies, including that of the USA. He argues that German critical psychology can be understood, in part, as a backlash against US psychology and the Americanization of German psychology after World War II, as well as being influenced by the life paths of certain institutions and individuals. Also see Box 9.2 for a Latin American example.

If Indigenous psychology is recent, then the specific area of Indigenous *developmental* psychology barely exists. However, given the various arguments that culture is a crucial influence on children's development, these broader issues are important to consider. Graham Davidson and colleagues (2000) raised the issue of what should be done with a century of psychological research on Indigenous people that those people regard as an aspect of colonial oppression, and question whether social responsibility (a moral precept) is compatible with science. They observe that twentieth-century research on Indigenous Australian people was typically based on identifying 'deficits', which were attributed to genetic and cultural inferiority to the majority culture. Similarly, in New Zealand, considering the educational difficulties of Maori children, 'the dominants assume they are dealing with quirks of personality or ethnic traditions created in pre-European history when most often they are dealing with modern class problems which are largely the creation of the dominants themselves' (Burch, 1967, cited in McDonald, 1973).

In the Australian case, Aboriginal children's cognitive and motivational 'short-comings' with regard to education and the 'incompetence' of Aboriginal parents were identified by western researchers, and gave succour to arguments for the forced removal of Aboriginal children from their parents. Evidence from Aboriginal people and others that many children (predominantly those of mixed ancestry) were indeed removed from their communities and placed in White families as recently as the 1970s, leading to intergenerational social and psychological problems, was presented in a Royal Commission report *Bringing Them Home* (Human Rights and Equal Opportunity Commission, 1997). Yet some (White) influential Australian voices continued to question the existence of 'stolen generations' of Indigenous children (Maiden, 2008). In this regard, the issue of the privileging by the dominant culture of written evidence over oral history has further marginalized the histories of Indigenous people, and although the federal government formally apologized to Indigenous peoples in 2008 for past actions, Australia has ongoing 'culture wars' about what versions of Australian history should be privileged (Manne, 2009).

Researchers working with Indigenous people have been challenged by the constructivist movement to move away from a universalist approach to Indigenous psychology (Davidson *et al.*, 2000). These writers observed a disillusionment with mainstream psychological approaches to Indigenous issues, born of concern that traditional approaches were not delivering benefits to Indigenous communities, together with a growing awareness of ethical obligations to give research participants greater involvement in research aims, processes and outcomes. They took up the issue that psychology's position as a value-neutral science was being challenged by the view that psychology cannot be apolitical and value-free because it is itself a cultural phenomenon.

Despite the assertion referenced in Chapter 2 that developmental psychologists often have melioristic aims, Davidson and colleagues (2000) cited examples from the USA, Australia and South Africa to support the argument that it cannot be assumed that psychology will automatically work towards social justice. Indeed, South Africa's leading advocate of apartheid, Hendrik Verwoerd, was a psychologist, and US psychologists have been involved in torture in the name of the 'war on terror' (Institute on Medicine as a Profession Task Force, 2013). Members of the dominant culture tend to see that culture as being the national culture, ignoring the perspectives of other groups within it.

Nsamenang (1999) suggested that it is necessary to integrate traditional psychology with Indigenous psychologies and to take account of the subjectivity of the researcher. An article by Yvonne Clark (2000) is an example of a study by an Aboriginal person, with Aboriginal participants, using a constructivist framework but also drawing upon mainstream social psychological theory. Participants, who were from the 'stolen generations', were asked about their experiences of being taken away from their families as children. The dominant theme to emerge concerned confusion over identity while growing up, with all participants seeking,

---

BOX 9.3 THE FIVE 'WORLDS' OF ABORIGINAL ADOLESCENTS: CULTURE AND COGNITION CREATING EACH OTHER

[F]ive major worlds . . . are significant for Aboriginal adolescents as they seek to form their personal and cultural identity . . . the family, the Aboriginal community, the wider society, peers and the school . . . Each world has a virtually limitless series of patterns and models for identity and cultural formation, including a range of expectations about values, beliefs, behaviours, and different patterns of control, relationships and communication. Between each world there are real or potential boundaries created by individual and group perceptions of the value and importance of the other worlds and their members. Within each world there are tensions as individuals and groups challenge accepted values and norms, seeking to create their own identities and cultures.

(Groome, 1995: 18–19)

---

recovering and/or maintaining their Aboriginal identities, while also experiencing other identities. This can be viewed in terms of self-categorization theory, which 'emphasises the dynamic and contextual nature of self and identity that are always the outcome of a particular social relational context' (Clark, 2000: 152). See also Box 9.3.

A further example is a study where a remote Australian Aboriginal community wanted non-Indigenous health care providers to have a better understanding of their parenting practices, which proved to have similarities to those of other Indigenous communities both in Australia and elsewhere (Byers *et al.*, 2012). The qualitative methodology used fits culturally with the Aboriginal practice of 'yarning' (discussing, having a say or storytelling). They explained that a central aspect is raising children to 'fit in' to their kinship network and understand to whom they are related and how. This defines the broad family network responsible for raising the child, as opposed to a nuclear family. In accord with critiques of attachment theory (see Chapter 5), they said babies never cry as they have many constant carers. In contrast to the adult control of children in Confucianism, the Aborigines expect children to develop independence and learn through experimentation. They are praised for aspects of development such as starting to sit, but there is no expectation that achievements will occur at a particular age; children are allowed to develop at their own pace and are given responsibility appropriate to their own level of maturity. Stepping out of line socially or getting in harm's way are dealt with by teasing distraction or, occasionally, shaming, not by controlling commands. It was therefore alien to their culture to force children to take prescribed medication, casting light on a problematic health issue in the community. This is not unique to Australian Aborigines. In many traditional cultures children are free to organize their own time and activities and develop self-reliance; the language of the Wintu people of California does not allow for coercion, so that, for example, one does not 'take a baby' somewhere but 'goes with the baby' (Griffiths, 2013).

Another recent example where Indigenous perspectives have been sought is in implementing KidsMatter Early Childhood, an Australian national initiative aimed at fostering wellbeing through early childhood centres. Feedback from communities with high proportions of Indigenous children provided suggestions for cultural adaptations such as the presence of grandparents in the centres (Slee *et al.*, 2012).

Wilhelmina Drummond (unpublished, 1990s) described three models of human development derived from different cultures. Interestingly, she took Bronfenbrenner's ecological theory as an example of a western model, though it is clearly not typical in that it explicitly sets out to encompass a broad range of developmental environments – in other words, to be cross-culturally applicable. The systemic nature of Bronfenbrenner's model, with its dynamically interacting levels of analysis, has parallels in another model described by Drummond, specific to the Maori people of New Zealand and developed by Pere (Figure 9.1). This is based on

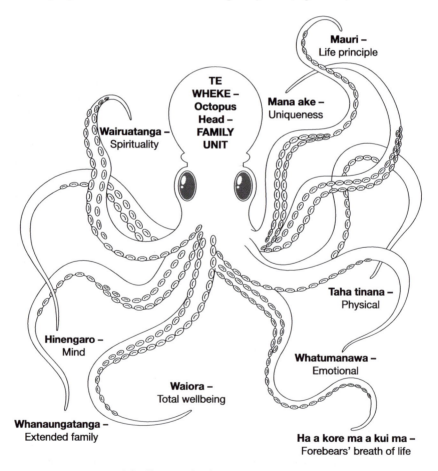

FIGURE 9.1 Maori model of human development

Te Wheke, or the Octopus, with nine tentacles representing various aspects of Maori life, such as spirituality, material and bodily needs and *Mauri* (life principle), which includes respect for the environment. The intertwining tentacles represent connections between these various aspects, and the interconnectedness and mutual reliance of the parts on one another is very reminiscent of systems theory (see Chapter 10).

A major difference can be identified, however, between the Bronfenbrenner and Maori models: Bronfenbrenner's scheme of nested levels places the individual at the centre, whereas the head of the Octopus represents not the individual but the family unit. Factors unique to the individual are placed within a single tentacle; while inseparable from the whole, giving sustenance to the whole and receiving it, the individual is not at the centre. By comparison, we can see how the individual-centred ecological systems model still bears the hallmarks of the western thinking which influenced its development.

Drummond also described a Philippine model of development, centring around Church, family and broader community, and reflecting aspects of both Asian identity and western influence resulting from colonization. To western eyes this model contains many paradoxes, such as the co-existence of strong women and machismo, and of Christianity and belief in spirits. Ritchie and Ritchie (1979) also observed apparent contradictions in Polynesian society, such as admiring individual prowess but also valuing cooperation. They cited Robert Redfield's proposal that the very 'work' of culture might be to reconcile such inconsistencies. Drummond observed that Maori writing on human development has incorporated ideas such as Vygotsky's notion of the zone of proximal development, and Bruner's concept of scaffolding. These notions are clearly consonant with their own cultural experiences, as illustrated by the previous example of how Maori children learn finger-weaving.

Is a universal approach to optimal development possible?

Cigdem Kagitcibasi (2012) acknowledges that the notion of Indigenous psychologies has been valuable in correcting the imposition of western developmental models on Majority World cultures. Nevertheless, he proposes that there may be universal features of optimal development that are important to understand, given that culture is fluid and the world is seeing many changes in contexts for development, such as rapid global urbanization. Devising standards for optimal development across the world is something he believes many developmental psychologists shrink from, for fear of being considered ethnocentric. He proposes that what is needed is an integration of both the contextual and the global.

One approach he puts forward is through the 'autonomous-related self'. Rather than seeing autonomy and relatedness as at opposite ends of a continuum, he proposes the existence of two dimensions: agency (ranging from autonomy to heteronomy) and interpersonal distance, or connectedness (ranging from separateness to relatedness). He proposes that a healthy model for children's development might be to aim for a good balance between these dimensions: promoting greater relatedness in societies that value autonomy, and greater autonomy in societies that value relatedness. This more balanced self he sees as better adapted to sociocultural change. Similarly, he proposes that a better balance between cognitive competence (valued by the West) and social competence (valued by the Majority World) is adaptive in a changing world. Kagitcibasi (2012) cites longitudinal early enrichment work, based on these principles, with Turkish families who moved from rural to urban environments. For those children in whom autonomy was promoted, while still reinforcing relatedness, there were long-term gains, compared with control groups, in areas relevant for urban living. These included autonomy, self-concept, vocabulary, school grades, likelihood of attending university, being in a high-status occupation and even likelihood of holding a credit card.

Conclusions

Teo puts forward the philosophical position that, '[b]ecause psychological theories and concepts are of a human and not a natural kind, they reflect the culture and history from which they emerge' (Teo, 2013: 14). Nsamenang considered the notion of culture so central that he defined developmental psychology as 'the science of human development in context' (Nsamenang, 1999: 163). We have observed in this chapter an increasing recognition by western psychologists of the centrality of cultural influences on development through theorists such as Vygotsky and Bronfenbrenner. This has involved a shift towards attending to cultural influences rather than simply controlling for them. We have also attempted to outline some of the very fundamental challenges to traditional developmental psychology put forward by postmodern, critical and Indigenous perspectives. While theories and knowledge gained through the traditional scientific method are very valuable, they provide only a fragmentary picture of development. While there is evidence that western developmental psychology is influencing Indigenous psychologies, it is heartening to observe that this is not a one-way street representing yet another aspect of colonialism: western developmentalists are increasingly willing to recognize alternative perspectives, which come from listening to, rather than simply experimenting on, peoples from various cultures. It is to be hoped that such cross-fertilization of ideas will be enriching to all.

References

Bai, L. 2005. Children at play: a childhood beyond the Confucian shadow. *Childhood*. 12: 9–32.

Bendle, M.F. 2001. Being critical in a globalised world. *Australian Psychologist*. 36 (1): 81–3.

Berry, J.W. 2005. Acculturation: living successfully in two cultures. *International Journal of Intercultural Relations*. 29: 697–712.

Bronfenbrenner, U. and Morris, P.A. 1998. The ecology of developmental processes. In R.M. Lerner (ed.), *Handbook of child psychology. Theoretical models of human development*. Fifth edn, Vol. 1. New York: Wiley, 993–1,027.

Burman, E. 1994/2008. *Deconstructing developmental psychology*. London: Routledge.

Byers, L., Kulitja, S., Lowell, A. and Kruske, S. 2012. 'Hear our stories': child-rearing practices of a remote Australian Aboriginal community. *Australian Journal of Rural Health.* 20: 293–7.

Canda, E.R. 2013. Filial piety and care for elders: a contested Confucian virtue reexamined. *Journal of Ethnic and Cultural Diversity in Social Work.* 22 (3–4): 213–34.

Chang, L., Chen, B-B. and Ji, L.Q. 2011. Attributions and attitudes of mothers and fathers in China. *Parenting: Science and Practice.* 11 (2–3): 102–15.

Chou, M-J., Tu, Y-C., and Huang, K-P. 2013. Confucianism and character education: a Chinese view. *Journal of Social Sciences.* 9 (2): 59–66.

Clark, Y. 2000. The construction of Aboriginal identity in people separated from their families, community and culture: pieces of a jigsaw. *Australian Psychologist.* 35 (2): 150–7.

Davidson, G., Sanson, A. and Gridley, H. 2000. Australian psychology and Australia's indigenous people: existing and emerging narratives. *Australian Psychologist.* 35 (2): 92–9.

De Vries, M.W. 1984. Temperament and infant mortality among the Masai of East Africa. *American Journal of Psychiatry.* 141: 1,189–94.

Drummond, W. 1990s, unpublished. Three models of human development. Massey University, New Zealand.

Dudgeon, P. and Pickett, H. 2000. Psychology and reconciliation: Australian perspectives. *Australian Psychologist.* 35 (2): 82–7.

Erikson, E. 1950. *Childhood and society.* New York: Norton.

Garton, A. and Pratt, C. 1998. *Learning to be literate: the development of spoken and written language.* Second edn. Oxford: Blackwell

Georgoudi, M. and Rosnow, R.L. 1985. The emergence of contextualism. *Journal of Communication.* 35: 76–88.

Goodnow, J. 2001. Commentary: culture and parenting. Cross-cultural issues. *International Society for the Study of Behavioural Development Newsletter.* 1 (38): 13–14.

Gridley, H., Davidson, G., Dudgeon, P., Pickett, H. and Sanson, A. 2000. The Australian Psychological Society and Australia's Indigenous people: a decade of action. *Australian Psychologist.* 35 (2): 88–91.

Griffiths, J. 2013. Why parents should let kids roam at will. *Guardian Weekly.* 31 May: 26–9.

Groome, H. 1995. Towards improved understandings of Aboriginal young people. *Youth Studies Australia.* Summer: 17–21.

Harkness, S., Super, C.M., Axia, V., Eliasz, A., Palacios, J. and Welles-Nystrom, B. 2001. Cultural pathways to successful parenting. *International Society for the Study of Behavioural Development Newsletter.* 1 (38): 9–13.

Ho, D.Y.F., Peng, S. and Lai, A.C. 2001. Parenting in mainland China: culture, ideology and policy. *International Society for the Study of Behavioural Development Newsletter.* 1 (38): 7–9.

Human Rights and Equal Opportunity Commission. 1997. *Bringing them home: the report of the National Inquiry into the Separation of Aboriginal and Torres Strait Islander Children from their Families.* Sydney: Commonwealth of Australia.

Institute on Medicine as a Profession Task Force. 2013. *Ethics abandoned: medical professionalism and detainee abuse in the 'War on Terror'.* New York: IMAP.

Kagitcibasi, C. 2012. Sociocultural change and integrative syntheses in human development: autonomous-related self and social-cognitive competence. *Child Development Perspectives.* 6 (1): 5–11.

Kaiman, J. 2014. Nine-hour tests and lots of pressure. *Guardian Weekly.* 7 March (originally in the *Observer*).

Kojima, H. 1996. Japanese childrearing advice in its cultural, social, and economic contexts. *International Journal of Behavioral Development.* 19: 373–91.

Lancy, D. 2007. Accounting for variability in mother-child play. *American Anthropologist.* 109 (2): 273–84.

Magai, C. and McFadden, S.H. 1995. *The role of emotions in social and personality development: history, theory and research.* New York: Plenum.

Maiden, S. 2008. Lib MP denies Stolen Generations exist. *The Australian.* 13 February. Available at: www.theaustralian.com.au/news/nation/lib-mp-denies-stolen-generations-exist/story-e6frg6nf-1111115544009?nk=73978ca522529be00b6ec689f8032b19. Accessed 30 June 2014.

Manne, R. 2009. The history wars. *The Monthly.* November. Available at: www.themonthly. com.au/issue/2009/november/1270703045/robert-manne/comment. Accessed 4 May 2014.

McDonald, G. 1973. *Maori mothers and pre-school education.* Wellington, New Zealand: Council for Educational Research.

Meacham, J. 1999. Riegel, dialectics, and multiculturalism. *Human Development.* 42 (3): 134–44.

Miller, J.G. 1999. Cultural psychology: implications for basic psychological theory. *Psychological Science.* 10 (2): 85–91.

Nsamenang, A.B. 1999. Eurocentric image of childhood in the context of the world's cultures. *Human Development.* 42: 159–68.

Nsamenang, A.B. 2005. Human ontogenesis: an indigenous African view on development and intelligence. *International Journal of Psychology.* April: 1–5.

Nsamenang, A.B. 2006. Cultures in early childhood care and education. Paper commissioned for the EFA Global Monitoring Report 2007, Strong Foundations: Early Childhood Care and Education. Available at: http://unesdoc.unesco.org/images/0014/001474/147442e.pdf. Accessed 6 May 2014.

Pere, R.R. 1982. Concepts and learning in the Maori tradition. Working paper No. 17, Dept of Sociology, University of Waikato Hamilton, New Zealand.

Renner, W., Ramalingam, P. and Pirta, R.S. 2014. Moral universals, ancient culture and Indian youth. Part II: facing the challenge of westernization. *Journal of the Indian Academy of Applied Psychology.* 40 (1): 9–19.

Ritchie, J. and Ritchie, J. 1979. *Growing up in Polynesia.* Sydney: Allen and Unwin.

Russell, A. and Owens, L. 1999. Peer estimates of school-aged boys' and girls' aggression to same- and cross-sex targets. *Social Development.* 8: 364–79.

Sanson, A. and Dudgeon, P. 2000. Guest editorial: psychology, indigenous issues, and reconciliation. *Australian Psychologist.* 35 (2): 79–81.

Shute, R., Owens, L. and Slee, P. 2008. Everyday victimization of adolescent girls by boys: sexual harassment, bullying or aggression? *Sex Roles.* 58: 477–89.

Shwalb, D.W., Shwalb, B.J., Hyun, J-H., Chen, S-J., Kusanagi, E., Satiadarma, M.P., Mackay, R. and Wilkey, B. 2010. *Maternal beliefs, images, and metaphors of child development in the United States, Korea, Indonesia, and Japan.* Hokkaido: Research and Clinical Center for Child Development, Hokkaido University.

Slee, P., Skrzypiec, G., Dix, K., Murray-Harvey, R. and Askell-Williams, H. 2012. *KidsMatter Early Childhood Evaluation in services with high proportions of Aboriginal and Torres Strait Islander children.* Adelaide: SWAPv, Flinders University.

Taft, R. 1987. Presidential address: cross-cultural psychology as psychological science. In C. Kagitcibasi (ed.), *Growth and progress in cross-cultural psychology.* Berwyn, PA: Swets North America, 3–9.

Teo, T. 1997. Developmental psychology and the relevance of a critical metatheoretical reflection. *Human Development.* 40: 195–210.

Teo, T. 2013. Backlash against American psychology: an Indigenous reconstruction of the history of German critical psychology. *History of Psychology*. 16: 1–18.

Thomas, A. and Chess, S. 1977. *Temperament and development*. New York: Bruner / Mazel.

Ussher, J.M. and Walkerdine, V. 2001. Guest editorial: critical psychology. *Australian Psychologist*. 36: 1–3.

Valentine, E. 1998. Out of the margins. *The Psychologist*. 11 (4): 167–8.

Wertsch, J.V. and Tulviste, P. 1992. L.S. Vygotsky and contemporary developmental psychology. *Developmental Psychology*. 28 (4): 548–57.

10

SYSTEMS THEORIES

Introduction

A 'system' can be broadly understood as an integrated whole whose essence or essential properties arise from the relationships amongst the components. Furthermore, systems thinking emphasizes that the properties of the system are properties of the whole which none of the parts possesses. This point takes us back to the early dichotomy between matter and form, and Aristotle's belief that all around us is a combination of substance (e.g. matter) and form (e.g. pattern): form is immanent in matter.

There is no specific 'systems theory', but a family of theories that constitutes a very broad field of inquiry (Bausch, 2003), with the influence of organicism, Gestaltism and functionalism apparent (see Chapter 3). Ludwig von Bertalanffy's general systems theory (GST) can perhaps be considered to have the status of a fundamental metatheory that encompasses numbers of more specific theories, including various family therapy theories, ecological systems theory, dynamic systems theory and critical state theory.

An important feature of systems theories is their transdisciplinary nature. This is at odds with the tendency towards neatly compartmentalizing the understanding of a phenomenon, and instead proposing that understanding necessitates the embracing of complexity. We begin this chapter with a broad description of the nature of systems thinking, placing it in historical context and linking it to other theoretical approaches. This accords with von Bertalanffy's comment that, 'In order to evaluate the modern systems approach, it is advisable to look at the systems idea not as an ephemeral fashion or recent technique, but in the context of the history of ideas' (von Bertalanffy, 1972: 407).

Early systems thinking

Systems thinking has been informed by a long and distinguished group of philosophers, writers and scientists. The early Greek philosopher Hesiod, writing in *The Theogony*, spoke strongly to the idea of order, and the world for Hesiod was an interconnected place.

> From Chaos came forth Erebus and black Night; but of Night were born Aether and Day, whom she conceived and bare from union in love with Erebus. And Earth first bare starry Heaven, equal to herself, to cover her on every side, and to be an ever-sure abiding-place for the blessed gods. And she brought forth long Hills, graceful haunts of the goddess-Nymphs who dwell amongst the glens of the hills. She bare also the fruitless deep with his raging swell, Pontus, without sweet union of love. But afterwards she lay with Heaven and bare deep-swirling Oceanus . . .
>
> *(Hesiod,* The Theogony, *in Evelyn-White, 1914)*

Somewhat later in the era of classical Greece, Aristotle's writings alerted us to the purpose of all things. The son of a physician to the Macedonian king Alexander the Great, Aristotle's interest in biology led him to advance the notion that all living things exist for a reason and have a purpose (*telos*) or direction to their life. His dictum that the 'whole is more than the sum of its parts' (*Metaphysica*, 10f–1,045a) is well known and serves to highlight the reductionism inherent in behavioural approaches to psychology.

Stoicism added yet another dimension. Roman stoicism (developed from earlier Greek thinking), informed by the thinking of Seneca, Epictetus and Marcus Aurelius, highlighted the need to live according to our ideals rather than reflect upon them. Stoic epistemology rejected reductionist thinking that focused on a single part of nature and instead emphasized the interconnected nature of things and the need for an overarching 'cataleptic impression' (knowledge about the world arising from the gathering together of perceptions, memories and experiences).

The twentieth-century contribution of Ilya Prigogine (1917–2003)

A significant contributor to the development of systems thinking was Moscow-born Belgian chemist, Prigogine. Winning the 1997 Nobel Prize, his research into dissipative structures arising out of the non-linear processes in non-equilibrium systems provided a comprehensive theory of change. The theory (Prigogine and Stengers, 1984) is underpinned by a number of key concepts:

1. *Systems and sub-systems.* All systems are composed of sub-systems, which are in a continual state of fluctuation or change that may not be reversible. At any one time the fluctuation may be so strong as to shatter the pre-existing order.

2. *Chaos and order.* At any 'singular moment' or 'bifurcation' the system may descend into 'chaos' or transcend to a higher level of organization or 'order', known as a 'dissipative structure' because it requires more energy to sustain it than the previous structure.
3. *Equilibrium.* In Newtonian thermodynamics all systems run down to disorder, with energy dissipating over time. In the natural world, many systems are 'open', exchanging energy, matter or information with the environment. Prigogine discovered that entropy (running to disorder) in a chemical system could be prevented by introducing energy into the system. He argued that a deterministic approach to unstable systems is not possible, and that prediction can only be made in terms of probabilities, not absolutes.

General systems theory

It was Austrian-born Ludwig von Bertalanffy (1901–1972) who proposed the seminal idea of *Allgemeine Systemlehre* (general theory of systems, i.e. general systems theory – GST). Although a biologist, he was no stranger to psychology, counting among his close friends the developmental psychologist Charlotte Bühler (Weckowicz, 2000; see also previous chapter). In the 1930s he wrote that:

> Since the fundamental character of the living thing is its organization, the customary investigation of the single parts and processes cannot provide a complete explanation of the vital phenomena. This investigation gives us no information about the coordination of parts and processes. Thus the chief task of biology must be to discover the laws of biological systems (at all levels of organization).
>
> *(von Bertalanffy and Woodger, 1933: 64)*

His writings as part of the famous 'Vienna Circle' of philosophers proposed that understanding the biological nature of things necessitated new ways of thinking that went beyond the traditional methods of science, which had been dominated by a mechanistic view. This notion of entropy was sharply at odds with the evolutionary view that the living universe was in fact evolving from disorder to increasing levels of complexity. To resolve this impasse, von Bertalanffy proposed the idea of 'open systems', in which entropy may not apply. He noted that:

> The 19th and first half of the 20th century conceived of the *world as chaos*. Chaos was the oft-quoted blind play of atoms, which, in mechanistic and positivistic philosophy, appeared to represent ultimate reality, with life as an accidental product of physical processes, and mind as an epi-phenomenon. It was chaos when, in the current theory of evolution, the living world appeared as a product of chance, the outcome of random mutations and survival in the mill of natural selection. In the same sense, human personality, in the theories of behaviorism as well as of psychoanalysis, was considered a chance product

of nature and nurture, of a mixture of genes and an accidental sequence of events from early childhood to maturity.

(von Bertalanffy, 1968, cited in Lilienfeld, 1978: 7–8)

The following characteristics of GST provide an understanding of the underlying principles.

- *Natural systems.* A natural system is a system that does not degrade over time, has emerged over time and has been able to reorganize itself and manage challenges to its integrity.
- *Reduction to dynamics vs reduction to components.* Scientists typically attempt to understand complex systems by reducing them to their components and understanding their inter-relationships. This contrasts with the reduction to dynamics, where the attempt is to understand how a system reacts when it is exposed to a complex set of influences.
- *Emergent properties.* An emergent property becomes apparent only when its components are assembled. Emergence ceases when the component is removed from the system – e.g. an eye ceases to 'see' when removed from the body.

In further writings (1968, 1972) von Bertalanffy suggested that some of the problems in implementing GST would be answered more fully in the future in four ways:

- with the application of dynamic systems theory and control theory to general systems theory (von Bertalanffy, 1968);
- through development of a mathematics of systems theory, which could further expand explanations and understanding of processes of change within systems (von Bertalanffy, 1972);
- with increased understanding of the development and function of the brain and nervous system, which von Bertalanffy held would be the key to understanding individual humans as systems (von Bertalanffy, 1968);
- with recognition that GST would provide a basis for unity in science.

Gregory Bateson (1904–1980) and family systems

During the 1950s, the English anthropologist Bateson (husband of Margaret Mead) extended systems thinking to social phenomena, in researching schizophrenic families in association with the 'Palo Alto group'. Adopting many of the ideas associated with GST they identified several characteristics of families.

- Families are systems, having properties that are more than the sum of the properties of their parts.
- Families are open systems, which nonetheless are governed by rules.
- A family is a cybernetic system, incorporating the important notion of feedback to family members.

Bateson and colleagues identified a feature of schizophrenic families that they called 'the double bind'. They argued that schizophrenia was not a disturbance within the individual, but a result of interactions and feedback loops. He provided the following example, of a son receiving contradictory messages from his mother:

> A young man who had fairly well recovered from an acute schizophrenic episode was visited in the hospital by his mother. He was glad to see her and impulsively put his arm around her shoulders, whereupon she stiffened. He withdrew his arm and she asked 'Don't you love me any more?' He then blushed, and she said, 'Dear, you must not be so easily embarrassed and afraid of your feelings'. The patient was able to stay with her only a few minutes more and following her departure he assaulted an aide and was put in the tubs.
>
> *(Bateson, 1972: 217)*

Double-bind theory has not been extensively researched, and today schizophrenia is considered to have more complex causation (and in any case, Bateson may often have been dealing with patients who would later be more appropriately considered to have war-induced post-traumatic stress disorder). Nevertheless, his ideas have been taken up strongly in the field of family counselling. According to Harold Goolishian and Harlene Anderson (1987: 529), 'The family could now be described as a system that had characteristics and organizing principles that were independent of the psychic structures of the individuals comprising the family'. The same principles can be applied to schools; Box 10.1 explains how a systemic approach can be applied to school bullying.

Bateson further contributed a number of significant concepts to contemporary systems thinking. One was that communication can occur across different levels, and that unhealthy communication often involves this, as in the double-bind example. Also, with a consuming interest in biology as well as human behaviour, Bateson wrote about connecting patterns: 'What pattern connects the crab to the lobster and the orchid to the primrose and all four of them to me? And me to you? And all six of us to the amoeba ...?' (Bateson, 1979: 16). He went on to describe the connecting patterns in terms of meta-patterns – patterns of patterns.

A significant line of family counselling based on Batesonian ideas was developed by the 'Milan group' of psychologists, in their work with the families of people with anorexia nervosa (Selvini Palazzoli *et al.*, 1978). In Adelaide, South Australia, the family counsellor Michael White developed an influential narrative approach to family therapy based on a unique blend of ideas drawn from Batesonian theory. Bateson's ideas were also influential in emerging thinking about constructivism (see Chapter 4).

Patricia Minuchin noted commonalities between family counselling and developmental psychology: 'Both disciplines regard the family as a primary focus for understanding human behavior and must find some way of conceptualizing the

BOX 10.1 THE APPLICATION OF SYSTEMS THINKING TO SCHOOL BULLYING

Viewing bullying as a phenomenon that is 'collective in its nature, based on social relationships in the group' (Sutton *et al.*, 1999: 97), one can apply many of the principles of systemic thinking to it. Thus, it can be argued that bullying is not a problem located solely within a particular individual (Pepler, 2006). Conventional western mechanistic and causal ways of thinking direct us to search for the faulty or broken part – or problematic individual – in order to fix the 'problem'. Schools are, however, also based around systems, and systems within systems (e.g. community, home, school, year level, classroom and peer groups). The various systems interact, and within the systems individuals are viewed as active agents in construing their own world. From a systemic perspective, people are viewed in terms of their relationships with one another, rather than simply being understood principally on the basis of their individual development. A child's misconduct in school (e.g. bullying others) is understood to serve some purpose within the system or to reflect something about the system itself. The behaviour is not just the result of some inner psychic disturbance or carried out for a reward. The student's behaviour is, in a sense, a window through which we can look to understand his or her place in the system, and provides an important insight into the various roles and relationships within the system.

relationship between the family and the individual' (Minuchin, 1985: 289). She went on to observe:

> Family therapy is based on systems theory. Although the field is character-ized by theoretical argument and a diversity of alternative techniques for creating change the systems view of human functioning is well established. It shapes the nature of clinical work and generates data about children and families from a different perspective than that of developmental psychologists.
> *(Minuchin 1985: 289)*

She summarized the principles of systems theory that are also relevant to developmental psychology.

- A system (e.g. a family) is an organized whole with each part of the system interdependent with the other parts.
- Patterns are circular, not linear. That is, the basic unit is the cycle of interaction, not a search for causation.
- A system has some stability of patterns.

- Evolution and change are a part of open systems whereby information is exchanged.
- Complex systems are made up of sub-systems, e.g. mother–father, child–child.
- There are boundaries between sub-systems.

From a systems perspective, the individual is an interdependent, contributing part of the system that controls his or her behaviour. The emphasis is on studying the functioning of the individual as part of the system rather than on internal or intrapsychic processes. Such an approach emphasizes understanding the individual's functioning within context (Minuchin, 1985).

Urie Bronfenbrenner (1917–2005) and ecological systems theory

The notion of context brings us to Bronfenbrenner's theory. Ann Oakley noted that 'the emphasis on childhood as an individual process unfolded from within has tended to neglect the impact on children and childhood of social and cultural contexts' (Oakley, 1972: 22). Socio-ecological models were introduced to urban studies by sociologists associated with the 'Chicago School' after World War I, as a reaction to the narrow scope of most research conducted by developmental psychologists. Members of this school included the philosopher George Herbert Mead, with later writing and thinking associated with symbolic interactionists such as Herbert Blumer. Social ecology pays explicit attention to the social, institutional and cultural contexts of people-environment relationships, and these considerations lie at the heart of Bronfenbrenner's theorizing.

Bronfenbrenner's early move from the newly formed Soviet Union to the USA gave him his appreciation of how different environmental contexts affect children's development, and in 1970 he published *Two Worlds of Childhood: U.S. and U.S.S.R.* Later, in *The Ecology of Human Development* (1979), he proposed that:

> The ecology of human development involves the scientific study of the progressive mutual accommodation between an active, growing human being and the changing properties of the immediate settings in which the developing person lives, as this process is affected by relations between these settings, and by the larger contexts in which the settings are embedded.
>
> *(Bronfenbrenner, 1979: 21)*

These settings and contexts are as follows.

- *Microsystem.* This is made up of the individual characteristics of the child and the various settings within which the child is embedded, such as family, school and neighbourhood.
- *Mesosystem.* Here the focus is on the inter-relationships between elements of the microsystem and contexts, for example, how a family responds to the school system and experiences it.

- *Exosystem.* Elements of the exosystem do not impinge on the child directly but influence the child through one of the microsystems.
- *Macrosystem.* This is composed of settings that refer to the much larger cultural or sub-cultural environment in which the child lives, and refers to the values and mores that are part of the broader environment.
- *Chronosystem.* Across the lifespan, how do events such as parental divorce or separation impact on the way a child develops?

Two important features of Bronfenbrenner's theory need to be taken into account in considering any evaluation or application. First, the foregoing description represents the child as a rather passive organism shaped and moulded by the environment. This was not Bronfennbrenner's view, and is countered by the notion of the 'developmental niche' (see Chapter 2), whereby the child assumes an active role in their development. For example, a child who enjoys reading at school shapes her or his own experiences by seeking out like-minded individuals. Second, Bronfenbrenner later broadened his theory to be inclusive of biological aspects of development and to give more emphasis to the chronosystem (Bronfenbrenner and Morris, 1998). This version is therefore even more holistic than the original theory, and so we will discuss it in considering theoretical integration in Chapter 13.

Bronfenbrenner regarded his theory as suitable for research in 'discovery mode' rather than 'verification mode', with propositions for testing being drawn (at least initially) more from theory than from research findings. This implies that one should be less concerned about falsely claiming to have found an effect (Type I error) than overlooking a 'real' effect (Type II error), since even a marginal finding may in fact be a useful pointer towards new discoveries. This is especially important given that, in development, small initial influences may become magnified over time and, ultimately, powerful predictors of outcome. Thus, as with systems approaches in general, Bronfenbrenner's theory challenges traditional hypothesis testing and the use of linear statistics in developmental psychology, and critiques of his theory often refer to the difficulty of empirically testing his ideas.

Bronfenbrenner was a founder of the USA's *Headstart* programme, aimed at supporting the development of pre-school children from low-income families. His 1979 book is frequently cited and his work continues to have great influence. For example, his theory has been applied to assist social workers in the USA to provide for the healthy development of children from immigrant families (Paat, 2013). However, a shortcoming of his theory is that 'the precise relationships of systems to one another remain elusive' (Neal and Neal, 2013: 723). Jennifer Watling and Zachary Neal maintain that the typical depiction of his theory in terms of nested concentric circles is misleading and disguises the fact that the various contexts actually overlap and network with each other. They draw attention to the work of Georg Simmel (1858–1918) on social networks, which held that the circles should be juxtaposed, not concentric. The Neals' re-theorizing of ecological systems theory turns the settings on their head, defining them in terms of interacting relationships rather than spatial features. This new formulation, they argue, has an improved potential to guide research based on ecological systems theory, by enabling better operationalization and measurement, through the use of social networking methodology.

This relationships-based approach has something in common with 'social systems theory' as advanced by Niklas Luhmann (1997). This emphasizes that the basic element of all social systems is *communication*, or the synthesis of utterance (including physical movements as well as speech or writing), information and understanding. Communication is a social (and, as proposed by Luhmann, the only genuinely social) operation, which cannot be causally reduced to individual action. Social systems for Luhmann are not, therefore, systems of action, structured in terms of the thoughts and behaviours of individual actors, but systems of communications in which the communications themselves determine what further communications occur.

Esther Thelen (1941–2004) and dynamic systems theory

In the fifth edition of the *Handbook of Child Psychology*, edited by William Damon, Lerner commented that the focus in theoretical development had become '... a burgeoning interest not in structure, function, or content per se, but in change, in the process through which change occurs, and thus in the means through which structures transform and functions evolve over the course of human life' (Lerner, 1998: 1). This understanding captures significant features of dynamic systems theory (DST).

The founder of DST was Esther Thelen, a US zoologist and professor of psychology. Described as a 'maverick', she established a research programme on motor development that gave rise to a new theory of child development and promoted the notion of 'embodied cognition' (refer back to Box 7.1; see also Smith, 2006). Her theory drew upon the insights provided by systems thinking in a range of scientific disciplines, including Prigogine's and von Bertalanffy's work: 'What we invoke here are the principles for the global properties of complex systems ...' (Thelen and Smith, 1994: 49).

Thelen and Linda Smith aimed to meet six requirements for a developmental theory:

- biological plausibility;
- to understand the origins of novelty;
- to reconcile global regularities with local variability, complexity and context-specificity;
- to integrate developmental data at many levels of explanation;
- to understand how local processes lead to global outcomes;
- to establish a theoretical basis for generating and interpreting empirical research.

Further:

> [T]he new science that can extract common principles in the behavior of chemical reactions, clouds, forests, and embryos is variously called the study

of dynamic, synergetic, dissipative, nonlinear, self-organizing, or chaotic theories. (We adopt here dynamic systems as the descriptor to emphasize that these are systems that change continuously over time.)

(Thelen and Smith, 1994: 50)

As such, a dynamic system is any system whose behaviour at one point in time depends in some way on its state at an earlier point in time (Elman, 1998), and which therefore emerges from the interplay of many factors over time and is self-organizing (Clarke, 1997). Ideas of non-linearity may be used to explain how apparently small transformations result in significant changes in the organism. DST shares a common origin with, and is an extension of, GST. Jean Piaget's organismic theory also fits well with this perspective, but Thelen and Smith noted that much research inspired by his theory has been more concerned with structure than process. Other important theories that influenced their work include Gerald Edelman's (1992) theory of neuronal group selection and Eleanor Gibson's work in ecological psychology and the notion of affordance (see Chapter 3).

Thelen and Smith observed that a number of developmentalists, including Arnold Sameroff (1983), had recognized the implications of Prigogine's theorizing: 'Adoption of such a systems model, with its assumptions of wholeness, self-stabilization, self-organization, and hierarchical organization, has implications for every aspect of developmental psychology' (Thelen and Smith, 1998: 575). To illustrate this point Thelen and Smith cited the need for development to be contextualized, because the concept of open systems necessitates an interchange between the organism and the environment.

Drawing on the writings of numbers of researchers and clinicians, such as van Geert (1998), it is possible to identify a number of general assumptions that underpin DST. The first is that development is a transaction between the person and their environment, where the emphasis is on the dynamic interplay between them, producing change in both the individual and the environment.

The second assumption challenges the deterministic assumptions underpinning development, particularly the idea that a single or a few factors shape development. This is replaced with 'the new synthetic concept that unites determinism and indeterminism . . . the concept of complex order, emerging out of self-organization' (van Geert, 1998: 272).

The third assumption goes to the heart of challenging genetic determination. The latest research in molecular biology questions the very nature of what we might understand to be a 'gene'. Evelyn Fox Keller and David Harel have noted that 'the concept of the gene has begun to outlive its usefulness. Among the reasons generally given is the great difficulty that we encounter today in trying to reach any sort of consensus about what a gene actually is' (Fox Keller and Harel, 2007: 1). The suggestion is that in looking at a DNA sequence there is no locatable gene but rather a series of protein chains, which, while separated spatially, operate in concert with the rest of the cell chemistry to influence development (Clarke, 1997).

The fourth assumption is that dynamic systems are seen as having properties of self-organization, resulting from the transactions within the system. As such, there is no one driving external factor or combination of factors that shapes development. To illustrate, early understandings of how infants learn to walk generally concluded that it was the result of the maturation of the nervous system. DST shed new light onto the process, emphasizing that, rather than the nervous system instructing the muscles in learning to walk, it is the dynamics of the movement of walking that instruct the nervous system.

A fifth assumption is that development, while subject to external and internal constraints, will settle into a preferred state called an 'attractor state', described as a set of physical properties towards which a system is attracted. As described by van Geert (2008), while a significant range of patterns is possible in a self-organizing open system, the system settles into or prefers only a limited range of behaviours. (This can be linked to Annette Karmiloff-Smith's conceptualization of how brain modules develop – see Chapter 2.)

Thelen and Smith (1994) maintained that the appearance of development as being orderly, progressive, incremental and directional, giving the impression of a predetermined plan, is illusory. For example, the development of infants' ability to walk has long been regarded as a series of invariant stages determined by maturation, as described by Arnold Gesell (see Chapter 3); Thelen and Smith presented evidence that, on closer inspection, development is much 'messier' than this, with component processes moving along in fits and starts, and sometimes regressing rather than progressing. On closer investigation, then, the grand plan disappears, as it does also if one examines cognitive development. Effectively, group averages mask individual differences that are important for understanding the true nature of development, a point also made by Robert Hinde (1992). Thelen and Smith observe that descriptions of typical developmental stages have become mistaken for explanations.

Increasingly, DST is being applied in the field of developmental psychology (Pepler and Craig, 2000; Slee, 2001; Thelen and Smith, 1994, 1998). At its heart DST is a mathematical theory; conventional linear equation modelling does not adequately address the complex and changing patterning of relationships.

Overall, DST has drawn on a rich and broad history of thought with regard to systems. As von Bertalanffy predicted for GST, it has been significantly informed by advances in neuroscience (Slee *et al.*, 2012); as new breakthroughs occur, the interaction between the brain, developing behaviour and the environment presents new challenges in terms of model building and empirical research. It is here that pivotal concepts of dynamic systems thinking, such as self-organization, provoke new ways of reasoning about how the growing child develops and changes. We consider further the integrative nature of DST in Chapter 13.

Critical state theory

As we have seen, in adopting systems thinking, developmental psychology has drawn upon insights from other disciplines, such as chemistry and biology. We speculate here that some recent advances in theoretical physics may in the future impinge upon our understanding of human development and behaviour as we increasingly take a systemic approach.

Science is traditionally concerned with predictability of events, yet, as we have seen, Prigogine warned that unstable systems create a difficulty here. Theoretical physicists carried out a wide range of studies during the 1980s and 1990s, showing that many natural events within complex systems are unpredictable (Buchanan, 2000). Catastrophic events, such as earthquakes, major forest fires and species extinctions, are not events that can be predicted and controlled, although the likelihood of occurrence of a particular-sized event can be calculated mathematically. The larger an event, the less likely it is to happen, but at any time the interacting factors underlying the event may reach a critical state of hidden instability such that an additional, minor change to the system can trigger a catastrophic event (in accord with the notion of emergence). For example, an extensive and intricate pattern of fault lines in the earth's crust may be balanced on the edge of instability, but this only becomes apparent when one small movement of the earth triggers a shift in the entire system; like a house of cards tumbling down as one card is placed slightly carelessly, the result is a massive earthquake.

Evidence is accumulating that these laws of non-equilibrium physics apply not just to events in the physical world but also to human activities such as stock market crashes and world wars. There seems no reason to suppose that these laws might not also apply to aspects of the developing individual, family or community. Indeed, if we take a broad systemic view of development that includes cultural, historical and even evolutionary change, we can say that there is already strong evidence that development is subject to these influences. The challenge that this new approach presents is addressed in Box 10.2.

Since we put these ideas forward in the first edition of this book, it has been proposed that critical state theory might be applicable to brain functioning. Gerhard Werner (2009) has suggested that, just as cooling water 'suddenly' becomes ice, so abrupt transitions in brain states may occur. Taking the example of consciousness, he observes that a subjective state of awareness may happen suddenly, but the groundwork for it has been laid below the level of consciousness, with processing occurring at different levels of hierarchical organization. He likens activity in widely dispersed areas of the brain to a 'bucket brigade', whereby, if a state transition occurs at one level, the contents of the bucket (neural messages) are passed up to the next level, until a critical state is reached and consciousness emerges. The existence of such processes is consistent with patterns of brain activity found in EEG studies. The well-known 'cocktail party effect' perhaps affords an example here, whereby an overheard mention of one's name pops into consciousness out of an undifferentiated background hum of voices. Werner cites vision research that similarly suggests that activity in widely dispersed parts of the brain comes together to produce a response that takes account of the needs, goals and history of the whole system. Such an approach, combined with the principles of DST and an increasing understanding of

---

BOX 10.2 TWENTY-FIRST-CENTURY CHALLENGES FOR DEVELOPMENTAL PSYCHOLOGY

The following extract comes from a section of a textbook headed 'The emerging challenge to causal thinking'.

> All the sciences of Western industrialized society are based on a traditional mode of thought that can be traced back to Aristotle, at least, but was codified and established within the scientific enterprises of the seventeenth, eighteenth and nineteenth centuries ... This mode of thinking, amounting to a world-view, an article of faith in the way the world works, assumes direct linearity in causation ... Whether from the perspective of 'normal' science or the new sciences of complexity, the advantages of multidisciplinary studies of complex systems are impressive. The compartmentalized disciplines of modern science have each special strengths for investigating a circumscribed range of phenomena. None can exhaust the complexities of any aspect of the world, but each can specify the likely states of some variables, and the relationships between variables within parts of a given system.
>
> *(Dincauze, 2000: 35)*

After reading the present chapter, these ideas should sound familiar. However, this passage comes not from a developmental psychology text, but from a book on environmental archaeology. Issues concerning systems, complexity and the value of multidisciplinary collaboration have come to the forefront in many sciences concerned with change, such as meteorology, geology and epidemiology. In these respects, developmental psychology may find that it has more in common with these sciences than with other fields of psychology.

---

epigenetics, holds considerable promise for our understanding of neural development and functioning.

Conclusions

We have suggested that general systems theory constitutes a metatheory, the principles of which are drawn upon by a range of other theories, including family therapies, ecological systems theory, dynamic systems theory and critical state theory. Model building and empirical research in this field is a dynamic and ongoing process, and we have attempted to capture some of the vibrancy of current developments. Systems thinking provides a challenge to the positivism of traditional developmental psychology, but there is now an established strong focus on the application of systems theories to the study of children and the family (Carr, 2014).

Systems thinking is best viewed in the context of the history of ideas. It became influential in various fields in the middle of the twentieth century; as Admiral 'Amazing' Grace Murray Hopper (1906–1992) said, 'Life was simple before World War II. After that we had systems' (see Wikiquote, n.d.). While systems thinking shares with organicism a focus on the individual as an active participant in his or her own development, it overcomes some limitations of organismic theories by focusing on the processes of change and the complexity and diversity of individuals' development. This focus on complexity, change and plasticity is moving developmental science beyond dualistic debates such as 'nature versus nurture' (Lerner, 2012). Systems thinking has also given a new prominence to the role of culture in human development, as no longer a mere backdrop, but as *part of the very fabric of human development*, operating in a co-constructive fashion. Systems thinking has also played a part in promoting the idea of embodied cognition – that cognition is not a brain-only phenomenon, but extends into the body and beyond, into the technological and cultural worlds of the individual (Overton, 2013).

References

Bateson, G. 1972. *Steps to an ecology of mind*. London: Ronald Press Ballantine.

Bateson, G. 1979. *Mind and nature*. London: Flamingo.

Bausch, K.C. 2003. *The emerging consensus in social systems theory*. Dordrecht: Kluwer Academic Publishers.

Bronfenbrenner, U. 1970. *Two worlds of childhood: U.S. and U.S.S.R*. New York: Russell Sage Foundation.

Bronfenbrenner, U. 1979. *The ecology of human development: experiments by nature and design*. Cambridge, MA: Harvard University Press.

Bronfenbrenner, U. and Morris, P.A. 1998. The ecology of developmental processes. In R.M. Lerner (ed.), *Handbook of child psychology: Theoretical models of human development*. Fifth edn, Vol. 1. New York: Wiley, 993–1,028.

Buchanan, M. 2000. *Ubiquity: the science of history or why the world is simpler than we think*. London: Weidenfeld & Nicolson.

Carr, A. 2014. The evidence base for family therapy and systemic interventions for child-focused problems. *Journal of Family Therapy*. 36: 107–57.

Clarke, J.E. 1997. A dynamical systems perspective on the development of complex adaptive skill. In C. Dent-Read and P. Zukow-Goldring (eds), *Evolving explanations of development: ecological approaches to organism-environment systems*. Washington, DC: American Psychological Association, 383–406.

Dincauze, D. 2000. *Environmental archaeology*. Cambridge: Cambridge University Press.

Edelman, G.M. 1992. *Bright air, brilliant fire: on the matter of the mind*. New York: Basic Books.

Elman, J.L. 1998. Generalization, simple recurrent networks, and the emergence of structure. In *Proceedings of the Twentieth Annual Conference of the Cognitive Science Society*. Mahwah, NJ: Erlbaum.

Evelyn-White, H.G.E. 1914. *The Theogony of Hesiod*. Available at: www.sacred-texts.com/cla/hesiod/theogony.htm. Accessed 3 June 2014.

Fox Keller, W. and Harel, D. 2007. Beyond the gene. *PLoS ONE*. 2 (11): e1231.

Hinde, R.A. 1992. Developmental psychology in the context of other behavioral sciences. *Developmental Psychology*. 28 (6): 1,018–29.

Lerner, R.M. 1998. Theories of human development: contemporary perspectives. In R.M. Lerner (ed.), *Handbook of child psychology. Theoretical models of human development.* Fifth edn, Vol. 1. New York: Wiley, 1–24.

Lerner, R.M. 2012. Developmental science: past, present, and future. *International Journal of Developmental Science.* 6: 29–36.

Lilienfeld, R. 1978. *The rise of systems theory: an ideological analysis.* New York: Wiley.

Luhmann, N. 1997. *Die Gesellschaft der Gesellschaft.* Frankfurt: Suhrkamp.

Minuchin, P. 1985. Families and individual development: provocations from the field of family therapy. *Child Development.* 56: 289–302.

Neal, J.W. and Neal, Z.P. 2013. Nested or networked? Future directions for ecological systems theory. *Social Development.* 22 (4): 722–37.

Oakley, A. 1972. *Sex, gender and society.* Melbourne: Sun Books.

Overton, W.F. 2013. A new paradigm for developmental science: relationism and relational-developmental systems. *Applied Developmental Science.* 17 (2): 94–107.

Paat, Y-F. 2013. Working with immigrant children and their families: an application of Bronfenbrenner's ecological systems theory. *Journal of Human Behavior in the Social Environment.* 23 (8): 954–66.

Pepler, D. 2006. Bullying interventions: a binocular perspective. *Journal of the Canadian Academy of Child & Adolescent Psychiatry.* 15 (1): 16–20.

Pepler, D.J., and Craig, W.M. 2000. Making a difference in bullying. *LaMarsh Research Report No. 60.* Toronto, ON: York University.

Prigogine, I. and Stengers, I. 1984. *Order out of chaos.* London: Flamingo.

Sameroff, A.J. 1983. Developmental systems: contexts and evolution. In W. Kessen (ed.), *Handbook of child psychology. History, theory and methods.* Vol. 1. New York: Wiley, 237–94.

Selvini Palazzoli, M., Boscolo, L., Cecchin, G. and Prata, G. 1978. *Paradox and counter-paradox.* New York: Jason, Aronson.

Slee, P.T. 2001. *The P.E.A.C.E. Pack: a program for reducing bullying in our schools.* Adelaide: Flinders University.

Slee P.T., Campbell, M. and Spears, B. 2012. *Child, adolescent and family development.* Third edn. Melbourne: Cambridge University Press.

Smith, L.B. 2006. Movement matters: the contributions of Esther Thelen. *Biological Theory.* 1: 87–9.

Sutton, J., Smith, P.K. and Swettenham, J. 1999. Bullying and 'theory of mind': a critique of the 'social skills deficit' view of anti-social behaviour. *Social Development.* 8: 117–27.

Thelen, E. and Smith, L.B. 1994. *A dynamic systems approach to the development of cognition and action.* Cambridge, MA: MIT Press.

Thelen, E. and Smith, L.B. 1998. Dynamic systems theories. In R.M. Lerner (ed.), *Handbook of child psychology. Theoretical models of human development.* Fifth edn, Vol. 1. New York: Wiley, 563–630.

Van Geert, P. 1998. A dynamic systems model of basic developmental mechanisms: Piaget, Vygotsky, and beyond. *Psychological Review.* 105: 634–77.

Van Geert, P. 2008. The dynamic systems approach in the study of L1 & L2 acquisition: An introduction. *The Modern Language Journal,* 92: 179–99.

Von Bertalanffy, L. 1968. *General systems theory.* New York: Braziller.

Von Bertalanffy, L. 1972. The history and status of general systems theory. *The Academy of Management Journal.* 15 (4): 407–26.

Von Bertalanffy, L. and Woodger, J.H. 1933. *Modern theories of development: an introduction to modern biology.* London: Oxford University Press.

Weckowicz, T.E. 2000. Ludwig von Bertalanffy (1901–1972): a pioneer of general systems theory. *University of Alberta Center for Systems Research Working Paper No. 89-2.* Available at: www.richardjung.cz/bert1.pdf. Accessed 18 May 2014.

Werner, G. 2009. Viewing brain processes as critical state transitions across levels of organization: neural events in cognition and consciousness, and general principles. *Biosystems.* 96: 114–19.

Wikiquote, n.d. http://en.wikiquote.org/wiki/Grace_Hopper. Accessed 22 January 2015.

11

LISTENING TO DIFFERENT VOICES 1

Feminism and developmental psychology

Introduction

> My five-year-old granddaughter was visiting us in Australia when I happened upon a website called Pinkstinks (www.pinkstinks.co.uk). In response to my granddaughter's query, I briefly explained that this UK-based website was opposed to the marketing of certain toys and activities for girls only or boys only, with girls' things in soft shades, but boys' things bright, noisy and exciting. I said I thought this was wrong and that anyone can do anything. A week or so later, Skyping from London to say the family had arrived home safely, her first comment was, 'Hey, Nanna, guess what. I looked in the airport shops and I saw lots of those Pinkstinks things!'
>
> *(Anecdote by RS)*

First-wave feminism achieved the vote for women (in some countries and at different times). The second wave, beginning in the 1960s, broke down further barriers to sex equality, at a time when it was possible for well-known Austrian-American child psychologist Bruno Bettelheim to write that 'as much as we want women to be good scientists or engineers, they want first and foremost to be womanly companions of men and to be mothers' (cited in Eagly *et al.*, 2012: 211). The third wave, from the 1980s onwards, acknowledged a range of complexities regarding gender. Some western scholars came to believe that equality had been achieved and spoke of post-feminism. Why, then, did Australia's first female prime minister, Julia Gillard (2010–2013), suffer a barrage of public sexist insults experienced by no previous occupant of that high office (Delahunty, 2013)? (This culminated in her 'misogyny speech' in Parliament, which went viral on the Internet (Julia Gillard's Misogyny Speech, n.d., or see Parliament of Australia's Hansard, 2012).) Why did the (male, conservative) addressee of that speech, when himself elected as prime Minister, select only one woman to serve in his 20-strong Cabinet? Why are there 150 (known) rapes a day in South Africa, driven by conceptions of manhood (Jacobson, 2009), and why does Saudi Arabian law oblige every woman to have a male guardian to make decisions for her (Human Rights Watch, 2008)? How can an entire school of Nigerian girls be kidnapped on the grounds that girls should not receive an education (*Independent*, 2014)? This book is not the place to answer these questions, but the fact that they can be raised demonstrates the ongoing need for feminism. Just as developmental psychologists often aim to improve the lot of the world's children, so feminist psychologists have a political goal: to increase women's power in the direction of equality with men.

After a brief historical note, we discuss feminist views on research methods, metaphors, theories of gender development, and the theorizing behind clinical practice, and also explore whether feminist theorizing might benefit from a consideration of the work of developmental psychologists.

A historical perspective

Having challenged the portrayal of Charles Darwin as the father of the field of child development (see Chapter 2), his pre-eminent position as the writer of the first child study can also be questioned by the fact that there were many earlier such observational diary studies, including many by women, which have been overlooked by history (Bradley, 1989, cited in Burman, 1994/2008). Indeed, a gendered approach to child study was soon apparent, with fathers, but not mothers, believed to have the emotional detachment necessary to carry out proper scientific studies of their children (Burman, 1994/2008).

According to Sigmund Freud's Oedipal theory (see Chapter 5), the young girl believes she has lost her penis, the ultimate compensation being to produce a baby (the penis-baby equation). Seymour Fisher and Roger Greenberg suggested that this is about the female being obliged to 'construct an illusory maleness' (Fisher and Greenberg, 1996: 165) in order to orientate herself in a male-centric, phallically defined world.

These two examples illustrate that the field of child development 'is associated with the rise of science and modernity, subscribing to a specific, gendered model of scientific practice' (Burman, 1994/2008: 10). Until very recently, girls' and women's values and experiences were missing, with the notable exception of the emphasis on mothers, rather than fathers, as parents. Indeed, it has been claimed that the focus of developmental psychology has shifted from children to mothers, resulting in regulation of women's lives through placing on them responsibility for providing what is 'best' for their children (Burman, 1994/2008).

Feminists argue that women's experiences, values and contributions have been sidelined historically, and have raised some very fundamental questions about the androcentric approach taken to theory, research and practice in developmental psychology. However, it is our experience (supported by Rosser and Miller, 2000) that feminism is given, at best, a marginal place in the teaching of developmental psychology, and unless they have taken topics in fields such as women's studies or sociology, many of our readers will not be familiar with it. We therefore outline the common themes of feminist theories, followed by an overview of the different kinds of theories and their relationship to developmental psychology. All question patriarchal assumptions about what should be studied and how, and what the underlying mechanisms are, with profound implications for theorizing and research.

Common themes of feminist theories

Feminist scholars come from a wide range of disciplines, and there is no single feminist theory (DeKeseredy, 2011; Griffin, 1995). Feminism has been described as having the status of a metatheory, or broad perspective within which more specific theories can be developed and tested (Tate, 2013). Some common feminist themes can be discerned with relevance for developmental psychology. We have drawn here upon Judith Worrell and Claire Etaugh's (1994) analysis, which identified six such themes.

1. Almost all feminist theories challenge the tenets of traditional scientific inquiry. For example, science is challenged as failing to be objective and value-free, and a broad range of data-gathering methods are seen as valuable. Qualitative methods are especially valued.
2. There is a focus on the lives and experiences of women. For example, women are seen as worthy of study apart from the standard of male norms, gender differences are examined from the perspective of socialized power differentials and research questions relevant to women's lives are explored.
3. There is a view of power relations as the basis of patriarchal political social arrangements. For example, women's social status is seen as resulting from unequal power distribution and not their deficiencies.
4. Gender is seen as something to be analysed, rather than an explanation of difference in itself. For example, the situational contexts of gender as actively structuring social interactions should be examined. We can also add that gender itself is now often seen as something that is *constructed* through discourse.
5. There is concern with the role of language, including explicit 'naming' of otherwise hidden phenomena (such as sexual harassment), restructuring language to be inclusive and reducing the (western) public–private polarity in women's lives.
6. Finally, there is a common concern with social activism, such as reconceptualizing theories, methods and goals, in the interests of promoting gender justice.

The very notion of 'empowerment' is not unproblematic. For example, with the rise of 'raunch culture' in the West, a differentiation has been made between subjective sexual empowerment of adolescent girls and 'actual' constraints on their power (although this does raise the question of who makes that judgement). Sharon Lamb (2010) maintains that feeling sexually emboldened is not the same as being empowered, while Rosalind Gill warns that 'empowerment' is difficult to identify in cultures that use this notion 'to sell everything from liquid detergents to breast augmentation surgery' (Gill, 2012: 736).

Furthermore, characteristics of feminism vary across the world. Although there is a global feminist movement, a question that has been raised is, 'Global according to whom?' There is a danger that theories emanating from privileged, western parts of the world may act as a new colonizing force elsewhere (Spurlin, 2010: 11). For example, the 'three waves' of feminism do not reflect the interlocking nature of periods of historical change in women's position in Southern Africa (Spurlin, 2010). In China, feminism has been seen in the context of traditional Chinese values of harmony and complementarity between the sexes, creating 'feminism with a smiley face' (Schaffer and Xianlin, 2007).

Specific feminist theories and developmental psychology

Despite these common themes, there are important differences between various feminist standpoints. Sue Rosser and Patricia Miller (2000, 2003) have examined their relationship to developmental psychology, although only one of the theories (psychoanalytic feminism) is specifically developmental.

Liberal feminism is the variation that developmental psychologists have been most open to, presumably because it does not question the positivist approach but rather seeks to make it more inclusive. An example is the extension of Lawrence Kohlberg's research on moral development by Carol Gilligan to include notions of care and responsibility (Gilligan, 1982). Gilligan's groundbreaking work was triggered by dissatisfaction with Kohlberg's male-based model of moral development, derived from a longitudinal study of Chicago boys. Indeed, Kohlberg proposed that women's moral development was limited by their inability to see beyond personal relationships (Kohlberg, 1971). Gilligan's research indicated that women's view of moral dilemmas lay in a consideration of conflicting responsibilities rather than rights, although later research suggested that care and justice perspectives are not the exclusive preserve of either gender. Gilligan's contribution is well accepted in mainstream developmental psychology and her work regularly gains a prominent place in developmental texts. Her broader importance lies in the fact that she alerted psychologists to the neglect of female experiences in developmental psychology.

Types of feminism other than liberal feminism question positivism and scientific objectivity. Developmentalists appear to be either less familiar with, or less receptive to, these more radical ideas (Rosser and Miller, 2000). Feminism's concern with social justice takes on different emphases in different approaches. *Marxist* and *socialist feminism* are concerned with the oppression of women on the grounds of both class and gender, drawing attention to a covert value system that privileges certain topics and interpretations in developmental psychology over others. For example, the negatively toned finding that sons of single mothers were 'less masculine' than those raised with fathers actually reflected the fact that they were less aggressive, which can be seen as positive (Rosser and Miller, 2000). Socialist feminism is consistent with Vygotskian concepts of development – indeed, Lev Vygotsky's interest in the social origins of cognitive development reflected his Soviet background.

Other forms of feminism, such as *African American feminism*, place more emphasis on race and ethnic issues, while *postcolonial feminism* maintains that patriarchy continues to influence countries that were previously colonized by western oppressors. Developmental psychology has given little consideration to such cultural changes, however (see Chapter 9).

Essential feminism, which emphasizes biological differences, does not appear to have a strong place in developmental psychology. Most feminists do not support such a difference-based approach because of its potential use by sociobiologists and evolutionary psychologists to provide a rationale for female inferiority and keeping women in their place.

Existentialist feminists, by contrast, argue for the social construction of gender: that it is not biological differences, but societies' interpretations of them, that lead to women being defined as 'the other' in contrast to male norms. Many examples exist in the developmental literature, such as the concept of 'mastery' (achievement of a skill, see Rosser and Miller, 2000) and Freud's Oedipal theory. Feminists often fought against Freudian notions of biology as destiny, but there has been some interest in object relations (see Chapter 5) in regard to the construction of gender and sexuality.

Radical feminists maintain that women's oppression is the deepest and most widespread kind, with men dominating most institutions, including science. The historical privileging of baby biographies by men is an example and, despite the pre-eminent role of mothers in bearing and rearing offspring, the field of developmental psychology has identified a father, rather than a mother, figure as its originator. Radical feminists usually reject existing scientific and theoretical frameworks and focus upon women's experiences in women-only groups, and support education in all-female environments, although Campbell Leaper (2000) draws upon much 'standard' developmental research in proposing what he identifies as a radical feminist approach to gender development. Little developmental research has taken female experiences as a starting point, Gilligan's work being a notable exception (Rosser and Miller, 2000). On the contrary, Jean Piaget's theory privileged masculine, as well as rational and western, forms of reasoning; this is illustrated by his more favourable view of boys' rule-based understanding of their games of marbles, compared with the relational nature of girls' games (Burman, 1994/2008). Box 11.1 addresses another suggested link between Piaget's research and masculine values.

Postmodern feminism rejects the idea of female universality so as to appreciate the diversity of experiences. It also challenges the assumption of 'progress' towards a defined end-point (e.g. adult standards of functioning) and emphasizes instead discontinuities, regressions and diverse pathways and achievements. Coming from a very different perspective, these ideas are also reflected in dynamic systems theory (Chapters 10 and 13).

Rosser and Miller (2003) later added to this list *cyberfeminism*, which is concerned with how information technologies and the Internet liberate or oppress women. While some see these technologies as providing new outlets for women's creativity, as well as job opportunities, others point to how various issues, including the

BOX 11.1 DID THE SPACE RACE INFLUENCE DEVELOPMENTAL PSYCHOLOGY?

The socialist-feminist focus on the power of the dominant group raises the question of why, in developmental psychology, certain topics, subject groups and interpretations of data are privileged over others . . . Does this privileging reflect the interests and values of a dominant class of middle-class white males? In the 1960s and 1970s, developmental psychologists' receptivity to Piaget's focus on children's scientific concepts may in part have reflected anxieties about the position of the United States in the cold war, including the space race with the Soviet Union. Concerns about the effects of working mothers (but not working fathers) and 'cocaine mothers' (but not 'cocaine fathers') on development imply blame on only part of the population. Day care and latchkey children are seen as a problem of working mothers but not working fathers . . . These examples suggest that a covert social value system steers developmental psychology.

(Rosser and Miller, 2003: 294)

proliferation of pornography and access to 'mail-order brides' from developing countries, further entrench pre-existing power relations.

Liberal feminism provides the least challenge for traditional developmental psychology, and postmodern and radical feminism the greatest (Rosser and Miller, 2000). Rosser and Miller also suggest that feminist theories could well take a more developmental perspective, an idea we expand on later. For example, radical feminism could take the experiences of girls as well as women as their starting point. An example of such an approach is our own qualitative work with Larry Owens in exploring teenage girls' experiences of social aggression (e.g. Owens *et al.*, 2000) and sexual victimization (Shute *et al.*, 2008).

Methodology

As we have seen, most versions of feminism challenge the epistemological under-pinnings of traditional scientific inquiry. For example, the dichotomy between the objective observer and the research subject breaks down into a concern with inter-subjectivity between researcher and participant (Griffin, 1995). What has been called feminist-standpoint research is concerned with reducing any power differen-tial that favours the researcher. It acknowledges that no research is value-free and explicitly considers the effect of the researcher on the participant. In ensuring that participants' voices are heard, qualitative methods such as interviews, focus groups and discourse analysis have been particularly favoured, as they provide the opportu-nity for more open-ended data gathering and interpretation than quantitative methods do. Christine Griffin suggests that it would be beneficial to focus more on the political aims of research in empowering women, rather than expending too much energy debating the nuances of various qualitative methods.

In any case, feminism in general has focused on women rather than children and, clearly, such methods have their limitations when working with children. Try holding a focus group with one-year-olds! Obviously, other methods, such as observation, must be used in some circumstances. The concern with intersubjectivity still holds true, however, and researchers must be conscious of their impact upon the child. This lesson was learned through Margaret Donaldson and colleagues' now classical demonstrations (such as the 'Naughty Teddy' study) that how a young child performs on cognitive (Piagetian) tasks depends upon the child's understanding of the social context surrounding the task (Donaldson, 1978; see Chapter 4).

While not arguing with the general feminist push favouring qualitative methods, Janet Hyde (1994) pointed out that no research method is in itself sexist or feminist, and that quantitative methods can also serve feminism. What matters is the research's theoretical framework, the questions posed, the interpretations made and the application of the findings. Numbers of researchers (e.g. Hyde, 2005) have undertaken meta-analyses of results of studies in a number of areas that support the 'gender similarities hypothesis', which holds that males and females are alike on most, but not all, psychological variables; for example, they showed that boys' 'maths superiority' and girls' 'verbal superiority' were of small extent, dropping to non-existent in more recent research. Hyde queries how such shifts could occur if the differences were biologically determined (see also Box 11.2). This kind of analysis is extremely valuable for demonstrating biased synthesis and reporting of research

---

BOX 11.2 THE PRENATAL BRAIN AND NEUROSEXISM

Cordelia Fine coined the word 'neurosexism' for practices such as overinterpretation of marginal or spurious findings of sex differences in the brain, and has been described as having a biology-free theory of sex differences. Accused of such 'extreme social determinism', she replied:

> I reject all charges! . . . My conception of development is one in which the developmental path is constructed, step by step, out of the continuous and dynamic interaction between brain, genes and environment . . . I struggled to reconcile a conception of brain development as the emergence of experience-dependent neural structures with the idea that prenatal hormones permanently organise a 'male type' or 'female type' brain. What exactly is organised? The concept of prenatal brain organisation acknowledges 'a bit of both', sure. But I'm not sure it embraces the inextricability of the two.

> (Fine, 2010: 900–3)

findings, but of course it cannot address bias in other areas, such as selection of research questions, selection of studies for publication or, as we discuss below, the metaphors used in publications.

Psychologists in the quantitative tradition are often highly suspicious of qualitative methods, seeing them as providing an undisciplined approach to research. It is possible, however, to adopt qualitative methods that meet standards of rigour analogous to those applied to quantitative research, such as reliability and validity, although many postmodernists would reject such an approach. In our own qualitative research on school peer victimization (e.g. Owens *et al.*, 2000) we drew upon a paper by Margarete Sandelowski (1986) that outlined this approach. This served a very practical purpose in enabling us to get our research accepted in forums that normally reject qualitative approaches. We therefore succeeded in getting young people's voices heard in arenas where they are generally silenced. However, we acknowledge that Sandelowski herself has since rejected the approach as being too driven by positivist assumptions about rigour, rather than wholeheartedly embracing a postmodern outlook (Sandelowski, 2006).

Metaphors

Ellin Scholnick and Miller (2000) have discussed the notion of metaphor in developmental theorizing, on the basis that metaphors reflect choices about what aspects of development are to be highlighted. They describe four metaphors used in developmental theory, arguing that these reflect masculine values, such as rationality, conflict and hierarchy.

Two of these metaphors concern how change occurs. The first is 'argument' – that development occurs through a series of confrontations between different perspectives, one of which wins following a tussle. Examples include Kohlberg's view that moral development arises from engagement in moral disputes, and the Piagetian notion that new, higher-order schemas are formed through resolving the contradictions between clashing schemas. The second metaphor for developmental change is 'survival of the fittest'. An example is the connectionist view of neural pruning as 'competition' in early brain development, whereby weaker, underused nodes (or neurons) in interconnecting neural networks are wiped out in favour of the stronger ones.

The other two metaphors concern the direction of change. One is the 'arrow' metaphor of development as launched (like a military attack) from a starting point, passing through consecutive points until it reaches the target of maturity. Scholnick and Miller suggest that this metaphor reflects three modern concerns of developmental theory: biology (the launcher); ideal cognitive solutions; and linearity. The fourth metaphor is that of 'building', with lower-order functions providing the platform for building higher-order ones. Again, this implies linear progression, with obstacles being overcome to reach a superior position. Scholnick and Miller maintain that the traditional, masculine metaphors produce a picture of 'an abstract, timeless, universal child' (Scholnick and Miller, 2000: 40).

They propose some alternative, feminine metaphors for covering the same developmental ground. One is 'friendship' rather than antagonism, reflecting respectful negotiation between parties who come from different perspectives. They claim that such notions are creeping into developmental writing, with a breakdown of the notion of warring dichotomies such as nature *versus* nurture and an increasing recognition of mutuality and cooperation.

The second metaphor, related to the first, is 'conversation', as both a means of creating cultural meanings and as a way of conceiving of development. This term has increasingly permeated everyday usage. Unlike arguments, which are about conquering through seeking vulnerabilities, conversations promote growth through intersubjectivity. Perhaps this is what the focus group students who discussed our original book proposal meant when they said they were frustrated with being told only what was *wrong* with developmental theories. Those students are not alone in their concerns about the university culture of critique (Tannen, 2000).

Scholnick and Miller's third metaphor is 'apprenticeship', as used by feminist theorists, Vygotsky and later cultural developmental psychologists. Rather than the fittest surviving in a given environment, the apprenticeship picture proposes the novice who is encouraged by experts to succeed in their field.

Scholnick and Miller's final metaphor is the 'narrative' or storytelling metaphor, which acknowledges that narratives take roundabout paths and regressions and do not just proceed linearly. It also permits metaquestions, such as who is the listener or the narrator (whose 'voice' is speaking).

Despite initial appearances, Scholnick and Miller do not fall into the trap of setting up yet more false dichotomies (masculine *versus* feminine metaphors), but suggest that both may have a place and create balance in what has, until now, been a very unbalanced field of inquiry. The value of presenting alternative metaphors is in inviting reflection about how knowledge is acquired, understood and valued, both in terms of the field of inquiry itself (developmental psychology) and in our understanding of the development of children's own knowledge. It enables us to stand back from our traditional positivism and see things we normally overlook, about how the field of developmental psychology came to be as it is and how it might be different and richer.

Theories of gender development

Introductory psychology texts often describe sex differences found in research, without offering possible explanations for such differences (Eagly *et al.*, 2012), despite the fact that (or perhaps because) the nature of such explanations is hotly contested. Theorizing about gender development brings into sharp relief two opposing camps, both of which have been described as metatheories. On the one hand is evolutionary developmental psychology, which holds that evolutionary pressures for division of labour earlier in our evolutionary history predispose males and females to behave differently. Observed differences are therefore seen to have a biological origin, and the term 'sex differences' is used to reflect this. On the other hand are those, including feminist scholars, who emphasize similarity between the sexes, and maintain that gender (which is often seen as something that is 'performed') results from social forces such as sex-based differences in status and power. We discussed this issue in the first edition of this book and, if anything, disagreement between these two perspectives has intensified further since then, although, as we shall see, there have been some recent efforts at rapprochement.

From the feminist side, Alice Eagly and Wendy Wood (2013) have demonstrated that many studies have failed to support the predictions of sexual strategies theory about male and female mating preferences. For example, the majority of studies used to support the notion that men want more sexual variety and extramarital sex than women come from educated self-report samples from postindustrial societies such as the USA; by contrast, cross-cultural anthropological studies show that in pre-industrial societies women's extramarital sex is widespread or even culturally accepted, with differences across societies related to male and female roles. More broadly, Eagly and Wood have accused some evolutionary psychologists of confirmatory bias in their interpretation of the evidence base, while Charlotte Tate (2013) has highlighted the fact that, although sexual strategies theory is a gene-based theory, it is limited in that it relies on self-reported gender as a proxy.

Such bias is not limited to human studies. Biological studies of the evolution of genitalia are strongly biased towards studying males. An examination of the literature indicates that this is not accounted for by easier access to male organs for study, but by 'enduring assumptions about the dominance of males in sex', who are therefore seen to 'lead' the evolutionary process (Ah-King et al., 2014: n.p.). This bias has actually strengthened since it was pointed out in 2000, despite evidence of co-evolution of male and female genitalia. This research base provides a biased grounding for evolutionary psychologists seeking guidance from animal studies.

From the evolutionary psychology side, Anne Campbell (2012) has taken feminists to task for ignoring strong evidence for differences between male and female minds that must have an evolutionary origin. For example, a hormonal basis for sex-typed behaviour is suggested by the finding that women's empathy, trust and fear are reduced when testosterone is administered to them. Campbell has also accused feminists of focusing too closely on the construction of bodies and brains, and therefore wrongly characterizing evolutionary psychology as promoting biological determinism; she points out that evolutionary psychologists highlight the existence of plasticity and epigenetic effects in building upon evolved modules of the mind. Also, as other evolutionary psychologists have done, Campbell objects to feminist political critique of evolutionary psychology, and draws a distinction between what 'is' and moral judgements about what 'ought to be'.

Is it possible to reconcile evolutionary and feminist approaches to gender development? Eagly and Wood (2013) have identified a need to bridge the evolutionary/nature–feminism/nurture divide and move towards a 'biosocial interactionist' theory of gender (see Chapter 13). Campbell (2012) suggests a number of areas of evolutionary psychology, such as the effects of the so-called 'bonding hormone' oxytocin, which may be of mutual interest. The theory that post-menopausal grandmothers play a central role in human evolution is also of interest to feminist scholars (see Chapter 2, Box 2.2). This continues to be controversial, with a tendency for female researchers to study the menopause and male researchers to focus on sexual selection theory, which views males as the main drivers of evolution (Saini, 2014).

By and large, the feminism–evolutionary psychology debate (which does not really have the feel of a 'conversation!') has not focused on children's development. Leaper (2000), however, has proposed a theory of gender development that brings feminism together with numbers of other developmental theories. He acknowledges evolution, but in the sense that what has evolved is *adaptability* to different environments. At a broad level, these environments constitute the macrosystem (as in Urie Bronfenbrenner's ecological theory), and include cultural values and practices such as patriarchy or egalitarianism, which provide constraints and opportunities for development. The macrosystem links to the home microsystem. To illustrate the fact that western norms for the division of labour in parenting are not biologically determined, Leaper cites the work of Barry Hewlett with the Aka people in Central Africa: in this egalitarian culture, mothers and fathers share child care and subsistence tasks, and infant care is seen not as a 'feminine' task but as an 'adult' one. The microsystem provides the context in which children construct their understanding of gender, in accord with Vygotsky's sociocultural theory. While it has been found that children tend to demonstrate similar behaviours in similar situations, in reality the early microsystems of boys and girls differ, with access to different toys and play activities (Lytton and Romney, 1991), through which children construct gender schemas and internalize gender norms (Bem, 1993). Insofar as these create asymmetrical representations of masculinity and femininity, they limit people's opportunities throughout life. As such, Leaper regards the promotion of early gender stereotyping as a form of discrimination. An example is that the television advertising of toys to children in the USA is heavily gendered, with girls depicted indoors playing with toys concerned with 'family, friendship, and romance', but boys shown in diverse locations that suggest 'more opportunities, action, and life chances' (Kahlenberg and Hein, 2010: 844). An apparent trend towards further 'pinkification' of children's toys (including little girls' make-up) and clothing is of concern, not least because 'self-objectification', or a focus on how one looks to others, leads to greater adolescent body shame, appearance anxiety and disordered eating, with girls more affected than boys (Slater and Tiggemann, 2010), although western boys are increasingly displaying concerns about body image, and feeling pressure to match up to a muscular male 'ideal' (Field *et al.*, 2014).

One recent attempt to reduce gender discrimination in the early years draws upon feminist-informed 'queer theory' (Blaise and Taylor, 2012), which is premised on the idea that there is no one way to 'perform' gender. This approach considers children's gender stereotypes to be constructed by societal norms of heterosexuality, dominant masculinity and subservient femininity, as reflected in the games (including romantic games) of even small children. Queer theory understands power differences to be created through gender discourses, and advocates believe that early childhood educators can change stereotypes by encouraging competing discourses in children's play and stories. This would be a dramatic change from prevailing attitudes in the recent past: the daughter of one of us (RS) reported that, during a wet lunchtime in the 1980s, her class had been provided with paper and told that the girls should draw houses and the boys should draw rockets!

Feminist theorizing and psychotherapy with children and families

Feminist critiques have had a significant effect on clinical theorizing and practice with regard to women. One example is the defeat of attempts in the 1980s to include 'masochistic personality disorder' in the *DSM-III-R* – a psychiatric diagnosis that would have pathologized women trapped in abusive relationships (Butler, 1999; Franklin, 1987). Feminist critiques also drew attention to the blaming of mothers for children's problems, such as attributing schizophrenia to 'refrigerator mothers'. Something of a reversal has been observed more recently, with (absentee) fathers being held responsible around the world for the problematic behaviour of their offspring, and the USA passing laws to promote responsible fatherhood (Cobb–Clark and Tekin, 2011).

Feminist theorizing has also had a profound influence on family therapy, by introducing the important notions of power and gender hierarchy, as well as insisting that women's experiences should be heard (Gladding, 1998). According to Douglas Breunlin and colleagues (1992), the lack of credit given to family therapist Virginia Satir for her pioneering theoretical work in the mid-twentieth century, particularly in comparison with her male colleagues, illustrates the wider undervaluation of women's contributions to society. It was as late as 1975 before a feminist critique appeared (by Frederick Humphrey) of family therapy, and 1978 before a paper by Rachel Hare-Mustin had a major impact on theorizing about family problems. Since then there have been numerous further critiques.

The central issue raised by feminists was that, in emphasizing reciprocal relationships between family members, family therapists had assumed that all parties had equal options for changing the relationships, ignoring the gender inequality in society. As a result of clinical experience and research, including work on domestic violence, the US behavioural marital therapist Neil Jacobson came to realize that this power differential could not be ignored:

> Marital therapists come face to face on a daily basis with the products of an antiquated, patriarchal marital structure which manifests itself in a power differential almost always favoring men ... when a therapist knows that they are observing a structure which oppresses women, they can not help but either contribute to the perpetuation of that oppression or ally themselves with its removal.
>
> *(Jacobson, 1989: 32)*

It might be expected that the feminist influence would have trickled down from a therapeutic interest in women's issues to an interest in the application of feminism to clinical work with girls, but this does not seem to be common. Author PS's response to RS's first draft of this section was that 'the child' was largely missing! He had hit the nail on the head. While this absence seemed to result less from some omission by his colleague than from a paucity of applications of feminism to child psychology, on reflection we felt that we needed to address this issue more directly.

While feminist theory has certainly influenced professional practice with children and adolescents in the education system (e.g. Gilbert and Gilbert, 1998; Mills, 2001), clinical child psychology has not been similarly affected. A search of abstracts in the psychological literature using terms such as 'clinical child psychology', 'child psychology' and 'child psychotherapy' in association with 'feminism' or 'feminist' produced practically nothing. Despite the history of feminist influence on family therapy, further searches in the psychological and sociological literatures again revealed an absence of scholarly feminist literature with regard to psychotherapeutic work with girls, as individuals or as members of families. This paucity is in accord with Miller's (2006) observation that feminist theorizing ignores the formative years. One can find occasional exceptions, such Marianne Walters and colleagues' 1988 book *The Invisible Web*, in which they include a consideration of mother-daughter relationships as part of their feminist approach to family therapy (although the basis for their practice in theory and research was rather weak, see Travis, 1991), and Margo Maine and colleagues' (2009) feminist approach to treating anorexia nervosa.

The tendency in clinical psychology practice to take a relatively individualistic approach (as observed in Chapter 2), together with an adherence to positivism, has perhaps contributed to this relative neglect of considering how patriarchy may be contributing to girls' psychological problems. Even those who favour systemic and multisystemic approaches to children's clinical problems may not consider gender-related cultural issues; for example, Alan Carr's (2014) excellent summary of the evidence base for such therapies for a broad range of children's psychological problems makes no mention of gender issues. Surely this is something that needs to be considered more deeply, given that problems with teenage girls' wellbeing can be considered to be of epidemic proportions. Research repeatedly shows that, across the teenage years, girls' wellbeing drops in comparison with boys. For example, a recent Australian report found that girls aged between 14 and 16 are more likely than boys and younger girls to be 'languishing' rather than 'flourishing' (Skrzypiec et al., 2014). Similarly, recent UK research shows a decline in measures including girls' life-satisfaction, self-esteem, emotional wellbeing and resilience, with boys' measures declining a little or remaining stable. As that report's authors state, the data show 'something deeply worrying about girls' wellbeing' (Finch et al., 2014: 8). They suggest that invidious sexism, exacerbated by new technologies, may be an important contributory factor.

One aspect of this may be the sexual harassment that is commonplace in schools in many countries, which affects girls more deeply than boys (e.g. Shute et al.,

2008), and gives rise to a sociological view that 'sexual bullying' arises from a culture of misogyny (Duncan, 1999). Concerns about body image and eating disorders are much more common among girls, with anorexia nervosa having a high death rate (Sullivan, 1995). Some of these issues have been subject to feminist analysis (e.g. Edwards, 2007), including, as noted earlier, the treatment of anorexia nervosa (Maine *et al.*, 2009) – perhaps because this condition requires multidisciplinary attention, opening up its treatment to a range of perspectives. Generally, though, the clinical psychology literature does not suggest the existence of a strong push to apply a feminist framework to interventions for girls' psychological problems.

One might expect to see a greater feminist consideration of girls' issues in family therapy, which has a stronger sociological influence, but this is not obvious in the literature; most feminism-inspired articles focus on women rather than girls, and even those critiques faded out during the 1990s in favour of a greater focus on multiculturalism (Goodrich and Silverstein, 2005). There has been a broadening of the original feminist agenda to produce 'gender-sensitive' family therapy, which is inclusive of those with gay, bisexual, lesbian and transgender orientations and gives attention to relevant issues, such as 'coming out' (e.g. Winek, 2010). A blending of cultural and gender issues can be seen in the adaptation of family therapy to the Japanese context, which considers issues such as Japanese fathers' tendency to emotionless presentation in therapy and the pressure parents place on young couples to produce grandchildren quickly (Nakamura, 2008). Such blending of gender and multicultural issues is not common, however (Goodrich and Silverstein, 2005).

It may be that feminism has been so successful in getting women's issues onto the agenda that its influence on family therapy has become taken for granted. This is also apparent in much research into women's and girls' issues that is clearly inspired by feminism but lacks an explicitly feminist agenda (Eagly *et al.*, 2012). Miller (2006) observes that the 'booming' research into girls' issues such as aggression and body image is often atheoretical, non-developmental and only loosely linked to feminism. Concern has been raised that ceasing to 'name' the issues risks making them invisible, and that therapist training programmes may be failing to give appropriate attention to such matters (Goodrich and Silverstein, 2005). Certainly, the prevalence of psychological problems among teenage girls today seems to call out for more thoroughgoing feminist attention.

A developmental perspective on feminism

While we have discussed some ways in which feminism might affect developmental psychology, it is clear that the reverse – the potential for developmental psychology to inform feminism – has been given even scantier attention. Indeed, the contributions of Carol Gilligan and of psychoanalytic theory are the only ones regularly mentioned in feminist writings (Scholnick and Miller, 2000).

Miller (2006) bemoans this situation, given that feminism and developmental psychology share common ground. For example, both are concerned with cultural differences, gender socialization and the construction of identity. Gender schema theory could contribute by explaining why individuals are biased to select information consistent with the stereotypes they have learned (Martin and Halverson, 1981). Vygotsky's theory (see Chapter 7) could also be helpful in explaining how children are socialized by more experienced members of the culture, such as parents, and how they internalize culturally defined social prescriptions, such as gender roles, in the process. Miller encourages greater dialogue between feminist scholars and developmental psychologists to explore such issues.

A personal note

Our conversations with young people today suggest that they often fail to appreciate how much, and how recently, feminism has transformed women's positions in many western societies. We saw in Chapter 4 how Eleanor Maccoby was obliged to take a rear entrance to her university's faculty club in the mid-twentieth century. Many young women today reject the feminist label and seem to take for granted the position they now have. At this point, therefore, one of us (RS), as the female half of our writing team, would like to provide a personal story that illustrates some gendered aspects of academic life in the final part of the twentieth century and demonstrates the context within which academic women and developmental psychology have been operating (in the UK and Australia) in the recent past. Readers are also referred to Sue Wilkinson's (1990) account of a British Psychological Society working party report on gender representation in psychology; the report's suggestion that women's experiences of psychology might differ from those of men was especially contentious.

We mentioned above the importance that feminists place on language. Today, our professional organizations and universities have guidelines on gender-appropriate language. This has only been the case since the late 1980s. As a student and earlier in my academic career, every hypothetical person was referred to as 'he' unless there was a very specific reason to state otherwise (this can be observed in some of the pre-1990 quotations used in this book). Around 1970, I became aware that the focus of psychological research was on males, noting in an undergraduate assignment that a particular published study had only male subjects, and that this might have affected the results; however, I felt very uncertain about making such a comment, never before having seen this issue raised during my studies.

Radical feminists would have approved of my education at an all-girls school, followed by a university college that had formerly been exclusively female, and that therefore still had a good representation of women academics. Given my educational background, I had been socialized to expect teachers of either gender. On attending a staff (faculty) meeting in my first university post in 1972, I was shocked to realize that I was the only woman in the room; I later understood that my earlier exposure to women academics was atypical for the time. From the 1990s I worked in departments with a good staff gender balance, including at senior levels of appointment, and I was appointed as a professor (in the UK and Australian sense) and head of psychology. By contrast, a predecessor in one department of the 1970s (the first female staff member) had received an invitation for 'Dr K. and Mrs K.' to attend an official university function (she replied that, unfortunately, her mother-in-law was unable to attend!). In a previous position during the 1980s I had discovered that the only woman staff member, who was of mature years, lived in rented accommodation, unlike her male colleagues who owned their homes; the reason was that women were not granted mortgages in those days.

During that decade, I was heavily involved in the British Psychological Society. I once sent my apologies to a departmental staff meeting, as I was attending a meeting of the Society's top executive committee, which was several hours' journey away (where, incidentally, I was the only woman and the only non-professorial member). I later discovered how masculine social constructions could influence the lack of recognition of women's professional contributions when I discovered that the reason for my absence had not been reported, and one of my male colleagues had assumed I must have been at home because 'one of the kids must have had a cold or something'.

I had previously taken several years out of paid employment to raise my young family, but when I later wished to mention this in the biographical 'blurb' for a book, I was prevented from doing so on the grounds that it was irrelevant and would place my biography out of step with those of my colleagues, thus forcing my personal story into the same mould as male and childless female academics and preventing my attempt to close the public–private gap.

I faced a re-run of some earlier professional experiences in the early 1990s, when I served as the only woman (and only non-medic) on the committee of a research funding body. As a university sexual harassment officer in the twenty-first century I was still observing (and intervening in) some concerning gender-related situations, but overall the position of women was improving. The rate of change seems glacial, however, when one realizes that, more than 40 years after I found myself the only female academic in that faculty meeting, men still outnumber women by three to one in that particular department, especially at senior levels, despite the 'feminization' of the field of psychology (itself a contested issue – see Ostertag and McNamara, 2006).

I hope this personal note will enhance younger readers' appreciation of the social landscape in which developmental theorizing, research and practice were occurring during the late twentieth century, and foster an appreciation of the changes the feminist movement has brought about. However, as we noted at the start of this chapter, there is still a long way to go in many places around the world, including the authors' own back yard.

Conclusions

Feminists have argued that developmental psychology is an overwhelmingly gendered, androcentric undertaking, which we have illustrated through examples from the literature and personal experience. We have outlined a variety of feminist theories, which in recent years have influenced theory, research and practice in developmental and family psychology, though this influence is not always explicit. There has been success in shifting psychology away from the male as norm and creating a greater interest in sex role socialization (Eagly *et al.*, 2012; Jacklin and McBride-Chang, 1991), though the shift from explicit mother-blaming may have been replaced by a more hidden agenda of regulating women's (and sometimes men's) lives (Burman, 1994/2008). Some varieties of feminism, such as liberal feminism, are more easily accommodated by traditional developmental psychology than others, such as radical feminism. All, however, have some common aims and issues, such as the adoption of a social justice perspective. In this respect, links with socio-cultural theories of development are especially apparent. The field of developmental psychology in turn has the potential to inform feminist theory. To date, however, such mutual exchange has barely begun.

Finally, the greatest achievement of feminism in the twentieth century was to create a broad shift in thinking, such that gender has increasingly been seen as socially constructed rather than a 'fact of nature' (Gardiner, 2005). This has opened up new possibilities for human development in some countries, not only for girls and women but also for boys, men and those with a range of sexual and gender identities.

References

Ah-King, M., Barron, A.B. and Herberstein, M.E. 2014. Genital evolution: why are females still understudied? *PLOS Biology*. 12 (5): e1001851.

Bem, S. 1993. *The lenses of gender: transforming the debate on sexual inequality*. New Haven, CT: Yale University Press.

Blaise, M. and Taylor, A. 2012. Using queer theory to rethink gender equity in early childhood education. *Young Children*. January: 88–98.

Breunlin, D.C., Schwartz, R.C. and Kune-Karrer, B.M. 1992. *Metaframeworks: transcending the models of family therapy*. San Francisco, CA: Jossey-Bass.

Burman, E. 1994/2008. *Deconstructing developmental psychology*. London: Routledge.

Butler, P. 1999. Diagnostic line-drawing, professional boundaries, and the rhetoric of scientific justification: a critical appraisal of the American Psychiatric Association's *DSM* project. *Australian Psychologist*. 34 (1): 20–9.

Campbell, A. 2012. The study of sex differences: feminism and biology. *Zeitschrift für Psychologie*. 220 (2): 137–43.

Carr, A. 2014. The evidence base for family therapy and systemic interventions for child-focused problems. *Journal of Family Therapy*. 36: 107–57.

Cobb-Clark, D.A. and Tekin, E. 2011. Fathers and youth's delinquent behaviour. Discussion paper no. 6042. Bonn: Institute for the Study of Labor (IZA). Available at: http://papers.ssrn.com/sol3/papers.cfm?abstract_id=1943292. Accessed 7 May 2014.

DeKeseredy, W.S. 2011. Feminist contributions to understanding woman abuse: myths, controversies and realities. *Aggression and Violent Behavior*. 16: 297–302.

Delahunty, M. 2013. Julia Gillard's uphill battle against sexism. Available at: www.crikey.com.au/2013/05/01/mary-delahunty-julia-gillards-uphill-battle-against-s-xism/. Accessed 18 October 2013.

Donaldson, M. 1978. *Children's minds*. Glasgow: Fontana.

Duncan, N. 1999. *Sexual bullying*. London: Routledge.

Eagly, A.H. and Wood, W. 2013. Feminism and evolutionary psychology: moving forward. *Sex Roles*. 69: 549–56.

Eagly, A.H., Eaton, A., Rose, S.M., Riger, S. and McHugh, M.C. 2012. Feminism and psychology: analysis of a half-century of research on women and gender. *American Psychologist*. 67 (3): 211–30.

Edwards, E. 2007. Are eating disorders feminist? Power, resistance, and the feminine ideal. Paper presented at the Perspectives on Power Conference. *Quest*. 4. Available at: www. qub.ac.uk/sites/QUEST/JournalIssues/. Accessed 28 May 2014.

Field, A.E., Sonneville, K., Crosby, R., Swanson, S., Eddy, K., Camargo, C. Jnr, Horton, N. and Micali, N. 2014. Prospective associations of concerns about physique and the development of obesity, binge drinking, and drug use among adolescent boys and young adult men. *Journal of the American Medical Association Pediatrics*. 168 (1): 34–9.

Finch, L., Hargrave, R., Nichols, J. and Van Vliet, A. 2014. Measure what you treasure: well-being and young people, how it can be measured and what the data tell us. New Philanthropy Capital. Available at: www.thinknpc.org/publications/measure-what-you-treasure/. Accessed 28 May 2014.

Fine, C. 2010. The battle of the sex differences: Jon Sutton interviews Cordelia Fine about neurosexism and more. *The Psychologist*. November: 900–3.

Fisher, S. and Greenberg, R.P. 1996. *Freud scientifically reapraised: testing the theories and therapy*. New York: Wiley.

Franklin, D. 1987. The politics of masochism. *Psychology Today*. 21 (1): 52–7.

Gardiner, J.K. 2005. Men, masculinities and feminist theory. In M.S. Kimmel, J. Hearn and R.W. Connell (eds), *Handbook of studies on men and masculinities*. Thousand Oaks, CA: Sage, 35–50.

Gilbert, R. and Gilbert, P. 1998. *Masculinity goes to school*. St Leonards, NSW: Allen and Unwin.

Gill, R. 2012. Media, empowerment and the 'sexualization of culture' debates. *Sex Roles*. 66: 736–45.

Gilligan, C. 1982. *In a different voice: psychological theory and women's development*. Cambridge, MA: Harvard University Press.

Gladding, S.T. 1998. *Family therapy: history, theory and practice*. Second edn. Upper Saddle River, NJ: Prentice Hall.

Goodrich, T.J. and Silverstein, L.B. 2005. Now you see it, now you don't: feminist training in family therapy. *Family Process*. 44 (3): 267–81.

Griffin, C. 1995. Feminism, social psychology and qualitative research. *The Psychologist*. 8 (3): 119–21.

Hare-Mustin, R. 1978. A feminist approach to family therapy. *Family Process*. 17 (2): 181–94.

Human Rights Watch. 2008. *Perpetual minors: human rights abuses stemming from male guardianship and sex segregation in Saudi Arabia*. New York: Human Rights Watch.

Humphrey, F.G. 1975. Changing roles for women: implications for marriage counselors. *Journal of Marriage and Family Counseling*. 1 (3): 219–28.

Hyde, J.S. 1994. Can meta-analysis make feminist transformations in psychology? *Psychology of Women Quarterly*. 18: 451–62.

Hyde, J.S. 2005. The gender similarities hypothesis. *American Psychologist*. 60 (6): 581–92.

Independent. 2014. Editorial: the Nigerian girls are still missing. *Independent*. 29 June.

Jacklin, C.N. and McBride-Chang, C. 1991. The effects of feminist scholarship on developmental psychology. *Psychology of Women Quarterly*. 15: 549–56.

Jacobson, C. 2009. In South Africa, rape is linked to manhood. Available at: www.mg.co.za/article/2009-07-09-in-south-africa-rape-is-linked-to-manhood. Accessed 16 February 2014.

Jacobson, N.S. 1989. The politics of intimacy. *The Behavior Therapist*. 11: 1–4.

Julia Gillard's Misogyny Speech. n.d. www.youtube.com/watch?v=SOPsxpMzYw4. Accessed 22 January 2015.

Kahlenberg, S.G. and Hein, M.M. 2010. Progression on Nickelodeon? Gender role stereotypes in toy commercials. *Sex Roles*. 62: 830–47.

Kohlberg, L. 1971. From is to ought: how to commit the naturalistic fallacy and get away with it in the study of moral development. In T. Mischell (ed.), *Cognitive development and epistemology*. New York: Academic Press, 151–235.

Lamb, S. 2010. Feminist ideals for a healthy female adolescent sexuality: a critique. *Sex Roles*. 62: 294–306.

Leaper, C. 2000. The social construction and socialization of gender during development. In P.H. Miller and E.K. Scholnick (eds), *Toward a feminist developmental psychology*. New York: Routledge, 127–52.

Lytton, H. and Romney, D.M. 1991. Parents' differential socialization of boys and girls: a meta-analysis. *Psychological Bulletin*. 109: 267–96.

Maine, M. with Davis, W. and Shure, J. (eds). 2009. *Effective clinical practice in the treatment of eating disorders: the heart of the matter*. New York: Routledge.

Martin, C.L. and Halverson, C.F. 1981. A schematic-processing model of sex typing and stereotyping in children. *Child Development*. 52: 1,119–34.

Miller, P.H. 2006. Contemporary perspectives from human development: implications for feminist scholarship. *Signs*. 31 (2). Available at: www.jstor.org/stable/full/10.1086/491680. Accessed 18 June 2014.

Mills, M. 2001. *Challenging violence in schools*. Buckingham: Open University Press.

Nakamura, S.-I. 2008. Gender-sensitive family therapy in Japan. *World Cultural Psychiatry Research Review*. 3 (4): 216–18.

Ostertag, P.A. and McNamara, J.R. 2006. 'Feminization' of psychology: the changing sex ratio and its implications for the profession. *Psychology of Women Quarterly*. 15 (3): 349–69.

Owens, L., Shute, R. and Slee, P. 2000. 'Guess what I just heard . . .' Indirect aggression among teenage girls in Australia. *Aggressive Behavior*. 26: 67–83.

Parliament of Australia. 2012. Hansard. Available at: http://parlinfo.aph.gov.au/parlInfo/search/display/display.w3p;query=Id%3A%22chamber%2Fhansardr%2F5a0ebb6b-c6c8-4a92-ac13-219423c2048d%2F0039%22. Accessed 23 January 2015.

Rosser, S.V. and Miller, P.H. 2000. Feminist theories: implications for developmental psychology. In P.H. Miller and E.K. Scholnick (eds), *Toward a feminist developmental psychology*. New York: Routledge, 11–28.

Rosser, S.V. and Miller, P.H. 2003. Viewing developmental psychology through the lenses of feminist theories. *Anuario de Psycología*. 34 (2): 291–303.

Saini, A. 2014. Menopause: nature's way of saying older women aren't sexually attractive? *Observer*. 30 March 2014. Available at: www.theguardian.com/society/2014/mar/30/menopause-natures-way-older-women-sexually-attractive. Accessed 30 March 2014.

Sandelowski, M. 1986. The problem of rigor in qualitative research. *Advances in Nursing Science*. 8 (3): 27–37.

Sandelowski, M. 2006. In response to: de Witt L. and Ploeg J. (2006) Critical appraisal of rigor in interpretive phenomenological nursing research. *Journal of Advanced Nursing*. 55 (2): 215–29.

Schaffer, K. and Xianlin, S. 2007. Unruly spaces: gender, women's writing and Indigenous feminism in China. *Journal of Gender Studies*. 16 (1): 17–30.

Scholnick, E.K. and Miller, P.H. 2000. Engendering development: metaphors of change. In P.H. Miller and E.K. Scholnick (eds), *Toward a feminist developmental psychology*. New York: Routledge, 241–54.

Shute, R., Owens, L. and Slee, P. 2008. Everyday victimization of adolescent girls by boys: sexual harassment, bullying or aggression? *Sex Roles*. 58: 477–89.

Skrzypiec, G., Askell-Williams, H., Slee, P. and Rudzinsky, A. 2014. *IB middle years programme (MYP): student social-emotional well-being and school success practices*. Adelaide: Flinders University Centre for Student Well-being and Prevention of Violence.

Slater, A. and Tiggemann, M. 2010. Body image and disordered eating in adolescent girls and boys: a test of objectification theory. *Sex Roles*. 63: 42–9.

Spurlin, W.J. 2010. Resisting heteronormativity/resisting recolonisation: affective bonds between Indigenous women in southern Africa and the difference(s) of postcolonial feminist history. *Feminist Review*. 95: 10–26.

Sullivan, P.F. 1995. Mortality in anorexia nervosa. *American Journal of Psychiatry*. 152: 1,073–4.

Tannen, D. 2000. Rites of demolition. *The Australian*. 12 April: 41.

Tate, C.C. 2013. Addressing conceptual confusions about evolutionary theorizing: how and why evolutionary psychology and feminism do not oppose each other. *Sex Roles*. 69: 491–502.

Travis, C.B. 1991. Reviews: *The invisible web: gender patterns in family relationships*. *Psychology of Women Quarterly*. 15: 179–80.

Walters, M., Carter, B., Papp, P. and Silverstein, O. 1988. *The invisible web: gender patterns in family relationships*. New York: Guilford Press.

Wilkinson, S. 1990. Gender issues: broadening the context. *The Psychologist*. 3 (9): 412–14.

Winek, J.L. 2010. *Systemic family therapy: from theory to practice*. London: Sage.

Worrell, J. and Etaugh, C. 1994. Transforming theory and research with women. *Psychology of Women Quarterly*. 18: 443–50.

12

LISTENING TO DIFFERENT VOICES 2

The voices of children

Introduction

As we noted in our discussion of feminism, postmodern critiques of psychology question its claim to objectivity. '[P]sychology, so far from being objective and value-free, has traditionally silenced and marginalised the perspective and voice of those without power and has promoted the worldview and interests of white, Western, middle-class, heterosexual adult males' (Greene, 2006: 8). In developmental research specifically, the voices of children are even more silent than those of women. Vicki Coppock (2011) sees a similarity between these situations, with feminism influencing critical thinking about childhood: just as femininity is understood as the opposite of, and inferior to, masculinity, so childhood is understood in opposition to adulthood. In this chapter we look at some recent changes to this view, on a number of fronts. These include: the 'new sociology of childhood' and social constructivism; increasing views of children as active rather than passive; seeing children as 'being' and not just as 'becoming'; increasing concern with children's rights and empowerment; and the effects of the digital age. We provide some examples where children's voices have been heard, including as research partners. Finally, we express some words of caution.

The 'new sociology of childhood' and social constructivism

While childhood has long been considered a topic worthy of scholarly attention within the field of psychology, it has only become a prominent area within sociology since the 1990s (Matthews, 2007). That discipline has, however, been much more progressive in taking seriously the notion that children have voices that should be heard. This perspective has gained increasing traction, under the rubric of 'the new sociology of childhood' (NSC) (Matthews, 2007). It has been argued that in both sociology and psychology children have been seen as passive and vulnerable beings, acted upon by others rather than being social actors, and considered 'in the process of becoming' rather than 'being' (Heary and Guerin, 2006; Wyness, 2006). The very use of the term 'the child' in scholarly literature has been criticized as objectifying children and implying that development takes a universal course (Greene, 2006). The field of anthropology has taken a similar critical track; although US anthropology in particular has a long-standing research interest in childhood in different cultures, a commitment to listening to children's voices is more recent (James, 2007).

Such critiques adopt a social constructivist perspective. Although forerunners of social constructivism can be identified among some early thinkers, including the Buddha (Pritchard and Woollard, 2010), it was a number of twentieth-century writers who were especially influential. Foremost was Lev Vygotsky, with his dialectical theory emphasizing how an individual's constructions of reality develop within cultural contexts (see Chapter 7). George Kelly's (1955) Personal Construct Theory, although not a child development theory, was also influential (see Chapter 4). Others credited with promoting social constructivism are the philosophers G.H. Mead in the 1930s and John Macmurray in the 1950s and 1960s (Lock *et al.*, 1989). Adopting a social constructivist position means accepting that children in different cultures experience childhood differently. A universal view of childhood is not possible, and children's experiences are bound to differ in terms of how they view their relationships, rights and responsibilities. The fact that views of childhood have changed over time (Ariès, 1962) reinforces the difficulty of producing universal truths.

If we subject the very notion of children's voices to such analysis, the complexity becomes apparent:

> Voice is a social construct operating in a cultural context where shared meaning is negotiated. This immediately raises problems for children's voice because in order to have influence, their voice has to transcend the cultural boundaries of childhood and negotiate a shared understanding in the adult world, yet much of children's voice is not expressed in words – least of all adult words – and the rich tapestry of their non-verbal communication frequently goes unheard.
>
> *(Kellett, 2010: 196)*

Active and passive views of children

The argument that children have been wrongly viewed as passive beings is not without its problems. From a biological perspective, humans are certainly altricial mammals, coming into the world dependent upon the care, nurturing and protection of older members of society. While the sociological concern with 'socialization' of youngsters into the ways of their culture did have an 'acted-upon' emphasis, it has long been recognized in child psychology that children, despite their dependence, have agency from infancy. Greene (2006) suggests that some critics of developmental psychology have not appreciated this history. Jean Piaget's view of the child as a little scientist experimenting upon the world is a prime example of an approach that sees children as actors (see Chapter 4), although his interest was in epistemology rather than children themselves (Greene, 2006). Infant cognition has been an important area in which the competence, rather than inferiority, of children has been highlighted. The phrase 'the competent infant' gained currency in the 1970s as new research methods enabled infant capabilities to be examined. This field continues to surprise with its revelations about the abilities of babies. For example, it has been demonstrated that from 10 months of age, babies show surprise when a big animated block (with an eye and mouth) bows and gives way to a smaller one, showing that by this age babies understand how social dominance normally plays out when two actors have conflicting goals (Thomsen *et al.*, 2011). Research on temperament was another influence in dispelling perspectives of passivity in infants, as it became clear that they contribute their own steps to the interactive dance between parent and child (e.g. Thomas and Chess, 1977). Such research findings emanating from child psychology gave strong impetus to the development of the NSC.

An important contribution of the NSC is in drawing attention to the fact that children do not simply accept passively and ape the attitudes and behaviours of their elders (as the 'socialization' approach suggested), but instead can transform them. William Corsaro (2005) has proposed the term 'reproductive interpretation' for this process. One example is the contribution of children to the development of creole languages. These arise in situations where speakers of different languages are brought together as a new community and form a new language adapted from elements of their mother tongues; although children's role in the creation of creoles may have been overplayed, it does appear that they are the ones primarily responsible for regularizing the grammar as the creole develops (Hudson Kam and Newport, 2005).

Becoming or being?

> Childhood is not preparation for life. It is life.
>
> *(James, aged nine, quoted at Generation Terrorists, n.d.)*

Like the notion of socialization in traditional sociology, it is undeniable that the field of child development – arising as it did in mainstream western society – is about 'becoming', with the adult form seen as the pinnacle. An example is Piagetian theory, with the child passing through several stages of cognitive development until the capacity for abstract reasoning (formal operations) is attained. Another example is that the main concern in child abuse has been about what kind of adult an abused child will become (Wyness, 2006). This future focus has been especially prevalent in the USA, which is more inclined than many other countries to take a lifespan approach to development (Matthews, 2007).

The NSC draws us back to the notion of being interested in, and valuing, children for what they are, not just what they may become. A focus on the future may lead us to neglect the here and now and children's current wellbeing. For example, in many societies academic pressure on children to compete for places in the best schools and universities has become intense. In some countries, regular school is supplemented by cram schools. Among these, the youth of South Korea has the lowest rate of subjective happiness in the OECD, citing schoolwork as their main source of stress (*Chosunilbo*, 2010). A future focus is also relevant in considering children with disabilities, who may never reach the milestones that most children, or their parents, typically hope for. Among parents of children with severe disabilities, the most contented are those who focus on enjoying their child in the here and now (Zschorn, 2005). And what about children who die? A major concern of bereaved parents is to make meaning of their child's life and death, which entails keeping alive the memory of an important family member who never had the chance to reach adult status (Darbyshire *et al.*, 2013).

Children's rights and empowerment

Another spur to the development of the NSC was the adoption by the United Nations of the Convention on the Rights of the Child in 1989. The only countries that have failed to ratify it are Somalia, the USA and the new country of South Sudan. The Convention recognizes children's right to be counted as persons (and not property), to express their views and to contribute to decisions that affect them. Karabelle Pizzigati (2010) considers the USA's failure to ratify to be a product of concern about international interference in US affairs and the potential compromise of states' rights. Sarah Matthews (2007), however, is inclined to accept that the USA's reluctance points to a cultural difference, whereby the USA is less receptive to the idea of children's rights than other western countries. She points to its ongoing attachment to the 'socialization' perspective, which is reflected in US research and its particular tendency to take a lifespan perspective. Matthews notes a greater research emphasis in the USA than in other western countries on peer relationships rather than on how the adult–child power differential affects children's development. The greater European focus on recognizing the effect of 'relations of constraint' – even in the cognitive work of Piaget – can perhaps be traced back to the influence of the great French sociologist Emile Durkheim at the start of the twentieth century (Doise, 1990). This acts as a reminder that the overwhelmingly large body of US-based research on child development must be interpreted in its cultural context – and, according to Timothy Teo (2013), this research should be regarded as an Indigenous psychology in itself. One might add that one would expect a range of Indigenous psychologies in such a culturally diverse country as the USA.

The translation of the Convention on the Rights of the Child into practice has been weak, and has varied across and within countries (Grugel, 2013). For example, Ireland established a national Children's Parliament while also threatening children's rights by promoting the use of anti-social behaviour orders (Greene, 2006). The authors' own home state of South Australia does not yet have a children's commissioner (it is the only state without one), with a bill before Parliament as we write. A positive example comes from Namibia, where, in 2013, members of the Children's Parliament heard presentations about the Special Olympics and signed a pledge to promote the rights of those with intellectual impairments (Mashuga, 2013).

The Convention itself has been criticized for taking a universal, westernized, approach to children's needs, but the universalism–relativism debate, as applied to children's rights, has been seen as creating an impasse that is not helpful for improving children's lives on the ground (Twum-Danso, 2008). Afua Twum-Danso proposes that what is needed is a localized understanding of global discourse about children's rights, derived from research with children as well as adults. Research in Ghana illustrates this point: there, younger relatives are always perceived as children, even if they are grown up, married and living separately with their own children, while Ghanaian children understand their position in terms of respect and obedience to elders – indeed, they see the ability to respect and obey as children's rights.

Such attempts to understand children's experiences from their own perspectives are not common, with others, especially mothers, frequently speaking on their behalf (Mayall, 1999). The NSC recognizes that children have less power than adults, 'who control institutions that justify and support the type of dependency that children experience' (Matthews, 2007: 327). One illustrative area is that of children's experiences of chronic conditions (Wallander et al., 2003); here, preadolescent children in particular have been neglected in terms of research into their views about their condition and its management. There may be a range of pragmatic reasons for this, as well as a paternalistic neglect of children's views (Garth and Aroni, 2003; Shute, 2005). The absence of children's voices from the educational literature has been similarly noted (Kinash and Hoffman, 2008). However, in keeping with the Convention on the Rights of the Child, and promoted by postmodern perspectives, there is increasing advocacy in clinical practice and research for child-client empowerment and participation (Davis, 1998; Garth and Aroni, 2003).

The concept of empowerment has gained increasing importance in the social work field, being described as a new paradigm; it is taking over from a problem-solving approach that views clients as having deficits that need to be 'fixed' (Rankin, 2006/2007). The empowerment perspective is in accord with the positive psychology movement, which seeks to emphasize and work from people's strengths rather than pathologizing them (e.g. Seligman, 2002). Empowerment has been conceptualized in various ways, such as differentiating between having a subjective sense of power and an actual ability to influence (Rankin, 2006/2007); this is similar to the point made in the previous chapter with regard to adolescent girls' sexuality. In considering the various ways in which adults might empower children through collaboration, Harry Shier (2001) has drawn upon Vygotskian theory, with listening to children as the lowest level, and sharing decision-making power and responsibility with them as the highest.

In psychology, the term 'child-centred research' has been used to refer to children's greater involvement, though this approach remains uncommon (Heary and Guerin, 2006). One promising novel method includes using photographs ('photovoice') to elicit children's perceptions (Epstein *et al.*, 2006), in place of formal interviews. One example is a study that asked 8–12-year-old Irish children to take photographs that represented their wellbeing, while another group was responsible for categorizing them and identifying missing elements (Gabhainn and Sixsmith, 2006); the themes were loved people, activities, food and drink and animals and pets, all of which they saw in an integrated fashion as 'the way I live'. One of us (PS) is currently using photovoice to study bullying and school violence in India.

While qualitative methods are often the choice, quantitative methods can also be child-centred in ensuring that questionnaires, for example, are child-appropriate in their language and content (Heary and Guerin, 2006). Naturally, this should always have been the case in the interests of developing reliable and valid instruments. Margaret Donaldson's research (see Chapter 4) also reminds us that children's understanding of the social context is crucial in determining the validity of any clinical, educational or research assessment.

Children's voices in the digital age

Today's children and adolescents grow up in a world transformed by the Internet and the digital age more broadly. While research has to some degree examined the opportunities this affords, the main focus has been on risks, such as online sexual exploitation, cyberbullying and Internet addiction (see Livingstone and Smith, 2014, for a review). Sonia Livingstone (2008) has combined the two aspects, writing of 'risky opportunities'. She uses the concept of 'affordance' (see Chapter 3) to view information technologies as offering – not determining – possibilities for constructing a social self, arguing that the Internet simply offers a new format through which young people negotiate the risks and opportunities of adolescence that have always existed (see Chapter 4, Box 4.3). Indeed, we have not seen evidence that the digital age has led to radical new ways of conceptualizing children's development, except for the introduction of a cybernetic, information-processing approach to cognition in the early days of computing (see Chapter 6).

What is of interest, though, in the context of the present chapter, is the potential of the Internet to empower children. Margaret Mead (1970) identified the existence of 'prefigurative' cultures, where 'reverse socialization' of adults by children occurs when a society is faced with new challenges to which children adapt more readily than their parents (see Chapter 8). In this way, the view of adults as experts and children as learners is turned on its head. To draw upon Mead's analogy, the 'natives' of the digital age (the children) educate the 'immigrants through time' (parents who grew up in a pre-digital, or earlier digital, age), so that children become adults' 'Internet brokers' (Grossbart *et al.*, 2002). This idea has been used by Barbara Spears and colleagues (2011) to promote the concept of working collaboratively with young people as co-researchers to address cyberbullying, drawing upon their lived experiences of the phenomenon and the wisdom they have developed in the process.

Some words of caution

Of course, determining how to involve children in research and important life decisions, and how to act upon their input, is not straightforward. Allison James (2007) raises the risk that children will be 'listened to' in a way that simply confirms old prejudices. Children's 'voices' quoted in research, for example, have still been edited and contextualized by the adult researchers, and she suggests that this is not sufficiently acknowledged (in her field of anthropology, at least). She also cautions that, paradoxically, the very use of the term 'children's voices' runs the risk of universalizing children. For another note of caution, see Box 12.1.

A situation with profound consequences for children, which raises issues about hearing their voices, is in the making of custody and parenting plans in the case of family breakdown. For signatories to the UN Convention, the child must have separate legal representation and the child's opinions must be heard. Although the USA is not a signatory, how to involve children in the process is nevertheless of concern, and Richard Warshak (2003) has criticized the most radical type of 'empowerment' of children in making this important decision – which lies at a much higher order of responsibility than simply being 'heard' (Shier, 2001). Warshak sees the attempt to seek and honour children's preferences in this context as flawed, as children may not have the maturity to make a considered decision. For example, children's expressed preferences (to live primarily with one parent or the other) may be based upon pressure from a parent, or upon transient issues, such as a recent argument with a parent with whom a child actually has a warm long-term relationship. A child may also express a preference for a permissive parent who allows behaviours such as late bedtimes or alcohol consumption, which are not *in the best interest of the child*. We can note here that some postmodernists criticize this

---

BOX 12.1 A NOTE OF CAUTION ABOUT CHILDREN AS CO-RESEARCHERS

Given the current level and extent of anxiety about children and 'childhood' manifest in many Western nation states, the recent obsession with 'listening to children' in research, policy and practice may in fact represent the political management of children's rights claims and children's opposition through the illusion of participation; meanwhile keeping fundamental structural relations intact. In this sense, participatory approaches may, inadvertently, be contributing to a different form of colonisation of childhood by adults – research as a process of socialisation.

(Coppock, 2011: 444)

very phrase for its potential to being abused in order to maintain adult oppression of children (Coppock, 2011). Warshak's caution, though, suggests that a critical approach to children's welfare needs to be tempered by taking account of insights gained from research that focuses on longer-term outcomes. Warshak suggests that listening to the *collective* voices of children, as expressed through research, is one appropriate path, though it is unlikely that many postmodernists would accept such a solution as it sounds suspiciously like the status quo. A more personalized method he approves is to appoint a guardian who listens to a child's perspectives and speaks in the child's best interest, especially in contexts where parenting plans may be trialled and the child provides feedback on the experience.

Examples of hearing children's voices

We end this chapter by giving examples from paediatric psychology and education where children's voices have been heard, and which may serve as inspiration for the further incorporation of children's perspectives into research, policy and practice (see also Box 12.2).

Psychological studies of children have rarely used a qualitative approach that allows children's experiences to emerge, but one of the present authors took such an approach in seeking to solicit the views of pre-adolescent children and young adolescents with chronic illnesses, as well as their parents, about what Max van Manen (1990) called their 'lived experiences' (Gannoni and Shute, 2010). The children were able to provide rich material about their lives with their chronic illnesses, whether cancer, renal failure or diabetes. In many respects, parents and children gave similar perspectives, but new insights emerged from the children. Those with cancer mentioned the effect of treatment on their sense of taste, but their parents did not mention this; also, children (but not mothers) described the helpful support they received from their fathers. It also emerged that children were

---

BOX 12.2 'MALALA YOUSAFZAI'S WELL SICK, INNIT?'*

These words, from the conversation of some 16-year-old boys from London, translate as an expression of admiration for Malala Yousafzai. She is the Pakistani girl who was shot in the head by the Taliban in 2011, at the age of 14, because of her public stance favouring girls' education – the ultimate attempt at silencing a child's voice. With her survival and continued advocacy for her cause, she earned a nomination for the 2013 Nobel Peace Prize and won it in 2014. Yousafzai may be exceptional in her drive and articulateness, but more than anyone else in recent times she has drawn the world's attention to the true potential of children when their voices are heard.

*Sanghani, 2013: n.p.

BOX 12.3 A CHILD RESEARCHER'S REFLECTIONS

My peers were very excited for me and they said that they were excited for themselves as well because I was both writing for myself and speaking for them as well. It matters to all of us that children are better represented . . . this research project is a bright green and orange Australian banner being waved around the world and saying, 'Look out, because kids can do anything!' This project has given more insight into how a howling classroom full of regular kids can become real-life phenomenologists and researchers.

(Kinash and Hoffman, 2008: 87 and 90)

---

not merely recipients of support: they gave emotional support to their parents (mainly reassurance about their health and capacity to function independently with treatment tasks). Children's attempts to cope competently with their illness demands also served as a coping model for parents. For example, a father of a boy with diabetes noted, 'I figure that if he can get on with life . . . I do get a lot of strength from him'. Such findings refute perceptions of children as passive victims of chronic illnesses that must be managed by parents and the medical profession.

In the educational field, there has been a shift from teacher-centred dissemination of information to student-centred inquiry methods (Kinash and Hoffman, 2008). We can pause at this point to note that the author Madison Hoffman, just cited, was a 12-year-old girl who was a student at a school where an educational study occurred. The student was fully included in the research process, the first author endeavouring to 'create empowering conditions such that children are invited into the research process as full and authentic partners' (Kinash and Hoffman, 2008: 78). Some of the girl's reflections on the process are shown in Box 12.3.

Mary Kellett (2010) has taken this further in proposing that children, with age-appropriate education about research methods and ethics and facilitation by adults, can be capable of driving and carrying out their own research projects. She provides an example of a study by an 11-year-old girl of a child's public transport difficulties when travelling with a wheelchair-using father.

Conclusions

Psychological theories were influential in promoting social constructivism, while developmental research findings further contributed to changing sociological views of children in the direction of understanding them as competent beings. Ironically, it is from those quarters that developmental psychology is now critiqued for silencing children's voices. Psychology as a field remains reluctant to shift from its positivist stance, though much could be gained from taking complementary approaches (Greene, 2006; Mey, 2000; see also Chapter 13). Coppock (2011), although strongly advocating for children's empowerment, has sensibly warned against replacing one kind of essentialism with another: the new sociology of childhood should not lead us to abandon the notion that children are incompetent in favour of a view that they are competent. Adults with decision-making power over children need to balance consideration of both children's vulnerabilities and competencies, and their immediate wellbeing with their long-term prospects.

References

Ariès, P. 1962. *Centuries of childhood*. New York: Vintage Books.

Chosunilbo. 2010. Korean kids unhappiest in the OECD. Available at: http://english.chosun.com/site/data/html_dir/2010/05/06/2010050600355.html. Accessed 25 October 2013.

Coppock, V. 2011. Children as peer researchers: reflections on a journey of mutual discovery. *Children & Society*. 25: 435–46.

Corsaro, W. 2005. *The sociology of childhood*. Second edn. Thousand Oaks, CA: Pine Forge Press.

Darbyshire, P., Cleghorn, A., Downes, M., Elford, J., Gannoni, A., McCullagh, C. and Shute, R. 2013. Supporting bereaved parents: a phenomenological study of a telephone intervention programme in a paediatric oncology unit. *Journal of Clinical Nursing*. 22 (3–4): 540–9.

Davis, J.M. 1998. Understanding the meanings of children: a reflexive process. *Children and Society*. 12: 325–35.

Doise, W. 1990. The development of individual competencies through social interaction. In H.C. Foot, M. Morgan and R.H. Shute (eds), *Children helping children*. Chichester: Wiley, 43–64.

Epstein, I., Stevens, B., McKeever, P. and Baruchel, S. 2006. Photo elicitation interview (PEI): using photos to elicit children's perspectives. *International Journal of Qualitative Methods*. 5 (3): 1–11.

Gabhainn, S.N. and Sixsmith, J. 2006. Children photographing well-being: facilitation of participation in research. *Children & Society*. 20 (4): 249–59.

Gannoni, A. and Shute, R.H. 2010. Parental and child perspectives on adaptation to childhood chronic illness: a qualitative study. *Clinical Child Psychology and Psychiatry*. 15 (1): 39–53.

Garth, B. and Aroni, R. 2003. 'I value what you have to say.' Seeking the perspective of children with a disability, not just their parents. *Disability and Society*. 18 (5): 561–76.

Generation Terrorists. n.d. www.generationterrorists.com/quotes/kids.html. Accessed 23 January 2015.

Greene, S. 2006. Child psychology: taking account of children at last? *Irish Journal of Psychology*. 27 (1–2): 8–15.

Grossbart, S., Hughes, S.M., Pryor, S. and Yost, A. 2002. Socialization aspects of parents, children, and the Internet. In S.M. Broniarczyk and K. Nakamoto (eds), *Advances in consumer research 29*. Valdosta, GA: Association for Consumer Research, 66–70.

Grugel, J. 2013. Children's rights and children's welfare after the Convention on the Rights of the Child. *Progress in Development Studies*. 13: 19–30.

Heary, C. and Guerin, S. 2006. Research with children in psychology: the value of a child-centred approach. *Irish Journal of Psychology*. 27 (1–2): 6–7.

Hudson Kam, C.L. and Newport, E.L. 2005. Regularizing unpredictable variation: the roles of adult and child learners in language formation and change. *Language Learning and Development*. 1 (2): 151–95.

James, A. 2007. Giving voice to children's voices: practices and problems, pitfalls and potentials. *American Anthropologist.* 109 (2): 261–72.

Kellett, M. 2010. Small shoes, big steps! Empowering children as active researchers. *American Journal of Community Psychology.* 46: 195–203.

Kelly, G. 1955. *The psychology of personal constructs.* New York: Norton.

Kinash, S. and Hoffman, M. 2008. Child as researcher: within and beyond the classroom. *Australian Journal of Teacher Education.* 33 (6): Article 6, 75–93. Available at: http://ro. ecu.edu.au/ajte/vol33/iss6/6. Accessed 23 January 2015.

Livingstone, S. 2008. Taking risky opportunities in youthful content creation: teenagers' use of social networking sites for intimacy, privacy and self-expression. *New Media and Society.* 10 (3): 393–411.

Livingstone, S. and Smith, P.K. 2014. Annual research review. Harms experienced by child users of online and mobile technologies: the nature, prevalence and management of sexual and aggressive risks in the digital age. *Journal of Child Psychology and Psychiatry.* 55 (6): 635–54.

Lock, A., Service, V., Brito, A. and Chandler, P. 1989. The social structuring of infant cognition. In A. Slater and G. Bremner (eds), *Infant development.* Hove: Lawrence Erlbaum, 243–71.

Mashuga, T. 2013. Special Olympics Namibia is invited to Children's Parliament. Available at: www.specialolympics.org/Stories/General/Special_Olympics_Namibia_is_invited_to_ Children_s_Parliament.aspx. Accessed 6 June 2014.

Matthews, S.H. 2007. A window on the 'new' sociology of childhood. *Sociology Compass.* 1: 322–34.

Mayall, B. 1999. Children and childhood. In S. Hood, B. Mayall and S. Oliver (eds), *Critical issues in social research: power and prejudice.* Philadelphia, PA: Open University Press, 10–24.

Mead, M. 1970. *Culture and commitment: a study of the generation gap.* New York: Natural History Press and Doubleday.

Mey, G. 2000. Qualitative research and the analysis of processes. Considerations towards a 'qualitative developmental psychology'. *Qualitative Social Research.* 1 (1). Available at: www.qualitative-research.net/index.php/fqs/index. Accessed 30 October 2013.

Pizzigati, K. 2010. Companion piece: the education landscape and the Convention on the Rights of the Child. *Child Welfare.* 89 (5): 91–102.

Pritchard, A. and Woollard, J. 2010. *Psychology for the classroom: constructivism and social learning.* London: Routledge.

Rankin, P. 2006/2007. Exploring and describing the strength/empowerment perspective in social work. *IUC Journal of Social Work Theory and Practice.* 14. Available at: www. bemidjistate.edu/academics/publications/social_work_journal/issue14/articles/rankin. htm. Accessed 31 May 2014.

Sanghani, R. 2013. 'Malala Yousafzai's well sick, innit?' *Telegraph* online. Available at: www.telegraph.co.uk/women/womens-life/10396038/Malala-Yousafzais-well-sick-innit.html. Posted 22 October. Accessed 23 January 2015.

Seligman, M. 2002. *Authentic happiness.* New York: Free Press.

Shier, H. 2001. Pathways to participation: openings, opportunities and obligations. *Children & Society.* 15 (2): 107–17.

Shute, R.H. 2005. Adaptation to chronic physical conditions: why should we ask the children, and how? Past Reflections, Future Directions: Proceedings of the Fortieth APS Annual Conference, 28 September–2 October, Melbourne, 293–7.

Spears, B., Slee, P., Campbell, M. and Cross, D. 2011. Educational change and youth voice: informing school action on cyberbullying. Centre for Strategic Education, Seminar Series Paper 208. Melbourne, VIC: CSE.

Teo, T. 2013. Backlash against American psychology: an Indigenous reconstruction of the history of German critical psychology. *History of Psychology.* 16: 1–18.

Thomas, A. and Chess, S. 1977. *Temperament and development.* New York: Brunner/Mazel.

Thomsen, L., Frankenhuis, W.E., Ingold-Smith, M. and Carey, S. 2011. Big and mighty: preverbal infants mentally represent social dominance. *Science.* 331: 477–80.

Twum-Danso, A.O. 2008. Searching for the middle ground in children's rights: implementing the Convention on the Rights of the Child in Ghana. PhD thesis, Centre of West African Studies, University of Birmingham. Available at: http://core.kmi.open. ac.uk/display/77112. Accessed 18 April 2014.

Van Manen, M. 1990. *Researching lived experience.* London, ON: The University of Western Ontario.

Wallander, J.L., Thompson Jr, R.J. and Alriksson-Schmidt, A. 2003. Psychosocial adjustment of children with chronic physical conditions. In M.C. Roberts (ed.), *Handbook of pediatric psychology.* New York: Guilford, 141–58.

Warshak, R.A. 2003. Payoffs and pitfalls of listening to children. *Family Relations.* 52 (4): 373–84.

Wyness, M. 2006. *Childhood and society: an introduction to the sociology of childhood.* New York: Palgrave Macmillan.

Zschorn, M. 2005. Cognitive appraisal in parents who have a child with a physical disability. Unpublished PhD thesis, School of Psychology, Flinders University, South Australia.

13

PUTTING IT ALL TOGETHER

Towards theoretical integration

Introduction

The focus group of psychology students advising on our first edition said that learning developmental psychology was like going into a dark room with a torch (flashlight, for our US readers) – one only ever sees bits and pieces and cannot put the whole picture together. They hoped that the book might be able to act like a switch to illuminate the whole room. While it would be overambitious to claim that we have achieved this, we do see the present chapter as particularly important since it addresses recent attempts to provide more integrative approaches to understanding child and adolescent development.

In this chapter we will take a fresh look at a number of theoretical approaches with claims to holism. They include family therapy and biopsychosocial theories, dynamic systems theory, evolutionary developmental psychology, lifespan psychology and relationalism. We refer readers back to general systems theory in Chapter 10, as this has provided the metatheoretical basis for numbers of integrative approaches (see also Box 13.1). We will see efforts that have been made to bring together different schools of thought, including considering whether a rapprochement is possible between positivism and postmodernism.

The Tower of Babel

Students of psychology frequently lament for 'just one theory which will explain everything' but, as Mark Antley has said, 'There is no "Big Bang" theory of human development to form the basis of a general consensus' (Antley, 2010: 175). Figure 1.1 (Chapter 1) was developed to facilitate our understanding of links between various theoretical schools of thought. The traditional (meta)theoretical orientations have each in their own right contributed some unique insight into the

BOX 13.1 AESOP'S FABLE OF MUTUAL INTERDEPENDENCE

The members of the Body once rebelled against the Belly. 'You,' they said to the Belly, 'live in luxury and sloth, and never do a stroke of work; while we not only have to do all the hard work there is to be done, but are actually your slaves and have to minister to all your wants. Now, we will do so no longer, and you will have to shift for yourself for the future.' They were as good as their word, and left the Belly to starve. The result was just what might have been expected: the whole Body soon began to fail, and the Members and all shared in the general collapse. And then they saw too late how foolish they had been.

(Aesop, 1979: 128)

corpus of our understanding regarding human nature and human behaviour (Lewis, 2000). Mechanistic theories have been 'valuable for modeling the rule-based regularities in development, especially those that are common to human and non-human information-processing' (Lewis, 2000: 37). Learning theories have helped us better understand the nature of the transfer of knowledge from the world to the child, and the organization of that knowledge. Organismic theories have promoted understanding of the concept of stages of development, while contextualism has helped our understanding regarding interaction and 'goodness of fit' between children and their environments. Nativist theories are enlightening about species-specific cognitive and emotional development. It is nevertheless true that the various schools of thought produce diverse accounts of development (Lewis, 2000).

Within the various schools of thought, further diversity can be identified. The ethologist Robert Hinde (1992) noted that although psychology gained respectability as a science by 'aping physics', the strengths of the standard scientific approach could also be weaknesses. Science proceeds by analysis, to the neglect of synthesis. There has been a gradual breaking up of the discipline of psychology into subdisciplines, which has tended to divorce developmental psychology from other relevant areas, such as social and clinical psychology, and has also isolated it from other relevant fields of inquiry, such as biology. This tendency has been called 'regressive fragmentation' (Bevan, 1994), although, as Robert Sternberg and Elena Grigorenko (2001) observed, some have considered this to be inevitable and a healthy state of affairs.

R.K. Sawyer (2000) too bemoaned the isolation of psychology from other fields, reflecting the reductionist paradigm of methodological individualism – the study of mental activity in isolation from social or cultural context (see Chapter 9). Sawyer suggested that this approach would ultimately render psychology redundant, reducing explanations of human behaviour to a biomedical level, an issue we raised in Chapter 2 (but provided an argument against in Chapter 7). Indeed, attempts to reduce explanations of human development and behaviour to genetics had already occurred, in the field of sociobiology – paradoxically, this form of reductionism had been claimed as a unifying force, since all aspects of human activity and development are seen as ultimately being aimed towards the single end of gene reproduction (Lerner and von Eye, 1992). However, this is an example of an explanation of behaviour in terms of ultimate function, whereas most of the theories we have encountered in this book offer explanations of development in terms of *mechanisms*, which rarely span different levels of analysis.

Concerns continue to be expressed about developmental psychology's fragmentation and isolation, both from other relevant disciplines, such as biology and sociology, and from other areas within psychology (Leaper, 2011). Furthermore, over the years there has been a move within developmental psychology itself away from 'grand theories' and towards many mini-theories. For example, Marion Underwood and colleagues expressed concern that the field of aggression was in danger of going the same way as observed by Carleton Watkins in memory research – into a stage of 'personalized theorizing', 'in which theories become much like toothbrushes in that everyone must have one of her own' (Underwood *et al.*, 2001: 275). Franz and Sabine Weinert appeared resigned to this situation, stating that 'The time of the "large theories" and broad theoretical controversies is past. Micromodels and microtheories have dominated the field for some time' (Weinert and Weinert, 1998: 25). While they saw an advantage here, because this diversity accommodates a wide variety of phenomena and empirical data, they also believed that comprehensive accounts are unlikely to emerge. Similarly, in her book on child development theories, Patricia Miller concluded that, 'Although it is tempting to tidy up the assortment of theories presented here by offering an orderly set of conclusions, that aim is unrealistic' (Miller, 1993: 426). Marc Lewis noted the difficulty experienced even by developmental psychologists in making sense of the proliferation of theoretical approaches, which he describes as constituting a 'Tower of Babel' (Lewis, 2000: 36). Little wonder, then, that students of psychology are equally perplexed!

Campbell Leaper (2011) has taken a critical, reflexive approach in considering the psychological issues standing in the way of theoretical integration. For example, in accord with social identity theory (Tajfel and Turner, 1979), a developmental psychologist may hold a social identity, and derive self-esteem, as an advocate of a particular theory; this would create a bias against 'outgroups', such as advocates of alternative theories, and lead to a highlighting of differences, rather than similarities. This would clearly favour theoretical fragmentation. Other factors include a tendency to focus on a few studied explanatory variables as offering a complete explanation of phenomena, the burgeoning literature that causes information overload and makes it impossible to keep up, organizational pressures to specialize, the use of different linguistic terms for similar phenomena and a lack of incentives to act in an integrated manner (for example, thesis examiners and journal reviewers are likely to favour their own perspectives over novel attempts to broaden theories).

Despite the apparent surrender of some to the dominance of microtheories, as the twentieth century gave way to the twenty-first, there was also a discernible thrust in the direction of integration. Sternberg and Grigorenko (2001) called for a 'unified psychology', citing the well-known parable of the blind men touching various parts of an elephant and each conceiving of it as a very different creature. They cited work from the 1950s by Isaiah Berlin, which drew upon another animal analogy in the words of the Greek poet Archilochus: 'The fox knows many things, but the hedgehog knows one big thing'. Sternberg and Grigorenko called for a more hedgehog-like approach to psychology. Like Hinde, they endorsed the suggestion that this need not be through the old 'grand theory' approach, but through interlevel and interfield theories. Interlevel theories seek to bridge more fundamental levels of analysis (such as basic learning principles) with more molar levels (such as language learning). Interfield theories adopt a combination of approaches, such as biological and psychological, to problems. Sternberg and Grigorenko advocated a 'converging operations approach', in which psychology operates on the basis of phenomena under investigation, rather than separate fields of inquiry, with varieties of perspectives and methodologies applied. They acknowledged the difficulty of achieving this given that the status quo values narrow specialization in psychology, a point also made by one of the present authors in calling for an integrative approach to developmental psychology almost a quarter of a century ago (Shute and Paton, 1992).

Research and theories based on narrow perspectives can be especially frustrating for practitioners, who do not work with 'children doing strange things in strange situations' (to paraphrase Urie Bronfenbrenner), but with real, whole children, with their physical endowment, cognitions, emotions and behaviours, within their families, peer groups, schools and broader cultures. It is perhaps not surprising, then, that some of the thrust towards more holistic and integrative approaches to child development has come from those concerned with applied issues, which we address in the next chapter.

Reciprocalism and holism in developmental psychology

That this is a crucial issue in developmental psychology has become increasingly acknowledged. Particularly influential in this acceptance was the notion of infant temperament, with Alexander Thomas and Stella Chess (1977) suggesting that how an infant's temperament influences later development depends on the 'goodness of fit' between the child's temperament and the physical and social environment. We can observe a connection here with Vygotskian and neo-Vygotskian concepts: the zone of proximal development, which represents the child's potential level of development when operating in collaboration with a more capable member of the culture, will be greater if the child is interacting with a person who is sensitive to his or her level of development and who therefore provides the appropriate level of scaffolding. These are examples of a growing appreciation within developmental psychology that children's social relationships are *transactional*. This concept of mutual influence has provided a bridge between mechanistic and organismic theories of development.

The notion of reciprocal influence can be applied not just within a single level of analysis but also between levels. Hinde (1992), in his expression of concern about the fragmentation and isolation of areas of inquiry, commented that the child's physiology and psychology are embedded in a network of immediate social relationships, broader society, the physical environment, sociocultural values and so forth. These levels of analysis have their separate properties but interact dynamically. Although Hinde did not specifically mention either general systems theory or Bronfenbrenner's ecological theory, elements of both are apparent in his description. As an example of the limitations of existing theories, Hinde mentioned the inadequacy of modelling and reinforcement to explain the finding that early experiences of parenting are translated into later long-term behaviour changes, such as how a child interacts with peers; cognitive intermediaries, such as 'internal working models' of the self, as well as others and the broader world, can help to bridge the gap. This approach is integrative, in bringing together research from cognitive psychology, developmental psychology and psychopathology, and is couched in terms of mutually influential systems.

Contemporaneously with Hinde, one of the present authors was also drawing attention to trends in psychology towards greater integration between subfields, in relation to childhood chronic illness (Shute and Paton, 1992). For example, evidence was accumulating that cognitive development could be promoted through social interaction and also that cognitive performance was influenced by social context (neither of these findings would have surprised Lev Vygotsky). Also, not only were biological factors seen to affect the child psychologically (e.g. illness might have emotional effects), but psychological factors were also starting to be seen as capable of influencing biology (as when the course of a chronic illness is affected by stress). In addition, links between physical health and social relationships were being found, such as children's diabetic control being related to the parental marital relationship. Evidence was therefore accumulating for important causal and reciprocal linkages between various facets of development (e.g. Johnson, 1985; Kazak, 1992).

In considering evidence for reciprocity within and between different levels of analysis, we can also revisit the theme of gene-environment interactions discussed in Chapter 2. Not only has it been shown that genes can influence the environment in which the child develops (for example, through niche-picking), but we now know that the environment can change gene expression, through epigenetic processes. G. J. Vreeke (2000) and Urie Bronfenbrenner and Pamela Morris (1998) took issue with the suggestions of those such as Sandra Scarr and Robert Plomin that genes are the major determinants of developmental outcome, maintaining instead that an interactive, or dynamic, developmental view best accords with the evidence. Vreeke proposed that the distance between a genotype and the ultimate phenotype grows larger, because the phenotype is reached via a network of epigenetic, nonlinear processes. Finding correlations between genotype and phenotype should not be interpreted as providing information about development – rather, they result from the statistical methods used, which assume separateness of the variables. Vreeke proposed that alternative statistical methods need to be applied – non-linear statistics that do not make this assumption.

These examples illustrate the rising acceptance of notions of interaction and transaction in developmental theorizing. Similar trends have also occurred in other fields of psychological inquiry; for example, the social psychologists Willem Doise (1986) and Michael Hogg (1992) called for integration of different levels of explanation in order to understand social phenomena fully. In comparison with earlier ideas of one-way causality, ideas about interaction and transaction certainly represent considerable progress; Esther Thelen and Linda Smith described these terms as 'everyone's comfortable buzzwords, and the proffered "solution" to the nature-nurture dichotomy' (Thelen and Smith, 1994: xv). However, as we shall explain further, these writers, and others, maintain that these ideas in fact provide no such solution.

Family therapy and beyond

The above examples demonstrate that the notion of reciprocal, non-linear influences on development, within and between levels of analysis, was slowly taking hold in developmental psychology research towards the end of the twentieth century. The applied field of family therapy must also be credited with taking up, at an even earlier stage (from the 1940s), notions of mutual influence, within the specific area of the family (see Chapter 10). Various schools of family therapy were developed by a range of professionals, including psychologists, psychiatrists and social workers (Gladding, 1998). They vary in many ways, such as whether emphasis is placed on historical family factors or present symptoms, the length of therapy, the nature and strength of their theoretical basis and the specific therapeutic emphases and techniques. They are all, however, to a greater or lesser degree, based on addressing psychological problems by considering reciprocal influences between family members, rather than focusing on factors within the individual. The notion that repetitive patterns of interaction develop over time is crucial to family therapy, which is aimed at identifying and changing such patterns when they are dysfunctional. The term 'circularity' is often used to refer to these patterns, but the term 'recursion' may be preferable as this better captures the notion that repeated patterns within systems are never actually identical (Breunlin et al., 1992).

While those who devised family therapy took pride in their breadth of vision, later clinical developments saw even family therapy as too narrowly focused. Douglas Breunlin and colleagues (1992) developed a 'metaframework' approach. They pointed out that most family therapy models ignored the intrapsychic aspects of family members, yet at times these needed addressing. Furthermore, systems beyond the family (such as the peer group) sometimes need to be considered to understand their role in the presenting problem. They observed that it is especially ironic that, although claiming to be anti-reductionist, family therapy gave a reductionist account of the environmental context, as consisting of just the family.

Similarly, under the influence of Bronfenbrenner's theory, 'multisystemic therapy' has been devised, based on a consideration of the broader ecological systems in which children and adolescents develop (Henggeler *et al.*, 1998). Multisystemic therapy has been shown to be effective in especially difficult clinical situations, such as working with youth involved with the juvenile justice system.

Some family therapists are now taking on board recent knowledge to create an even more encompassing view, which is also developmental in nature. It takes into account recent knowledge in epigenetics and neuroscience, such as the effect of early stressors on the developing brain (see Chapter 2). This has been called an 'ecobiodevelopmental' view of mental health, and emphasizes the importance of early detection and prevention of mental health problems, especially through addressing the quality of parent-child relationships (Patterson and Vakili, 2013).

Before leaving this section, we can note that the field of psychotherapy more broadly, like developmental psychology, has experienced fragmentation, and significant interest in integrative theories has occurred. Attachment theory has been proposed as a strong contender, not only in its ability to provide a framework for understanding relationship issues from a developmental perspective, but by considering the therapeutic relationship itself as a safe exploratory base for the client (Gold, 2011).

Lifespan psychology as an integrative force

From the 1970s, lifespan psychology extended the study of development from childhood into the adult years. Willis Overton has defined lifespan development as 'the scientific study of systematic intraindividual changes – from conception to the end of life – of an organism's behavior, and of the systems and processes underlying those changes and that behavior' (Overton, 2010: 4). Precursors earlier in the twentieth century included Erik Erikson, Charlotte Bühler and Carl Jung. The influence of lifespan approaches is reflected in an increasing trend towards research that is longitudinal and that examines developmental trajectories. For example, Richard Tremblay and colleagues (2004) followed the development of children's physical aggression from 5 months up to 42 months of age, finding that children fell into three groups: those who displayed little or no aggression, those who increased their aggression modestly over time and those who had a high and rising trajectory. Such research paves the way for addressing early risk factors to prevent poor developmental outcomes later in life.

At its simplest, the lifespan approach expanded interest in development from childhood into the adult years, but it also represented a move towards a unifying metatheoretical developmental framework. Among its foremost exponents were the late Paul and Margret Baltes. Paul Baltes did not believe that one single developmental theory was correct, but identified the lifespan approach as a family of theories with common elements (Baltes, 1987; see Chapter 8). Broadly, development is seen as a change in adaptive capacity, whether positive or negative. Baltes described the approach as complex and pluralist. It is holistic in its multidisciplinarity, its

contextualism and its view of the individual's life course as an unfolding and connected narrative.

Biopsychosocial models

While lifespan psychology was encouraging a longer-term perspective on development, Bronfenbrenner's ecological systems theory was promoting a consideration of
greater breadth. Ironically, though, Bronfenbrenner was coming to accept that his
original theory was too narrow: while it emphasized the nested environmental
contexts in which children develop, it neglected the characteristics of the developing person, including biological and psychological aspects (Bronfenbrenner and
Ceci, 1994; Bronfenbrenner and Morris, 1998). In the field of medicine, George
Engel (1977) had earlier proposed that a comprehensive 'biopsychosocial' approach
should be taken, and during the 1980s health psychologists increasingly advocated
this approach, which recognizes reciprocal interactions between the person's
biology, psychology and social contexts. Consistent with this were the trends we
noted above towards comprehensive and systemic approaches coming from those
with applied interests in child development, especially child health, where a major
concern was to promote good adjustment in children faced with challenges over
and above the usual ones.

   While there was general recognition of the need to acknowledge such linkages
between different levels of analysis, a broad holistic model of child development was
still absent in the late 1980s, when one of the present authors (RS) was addressing
the role of peers in the development of children with chronic illnesses. We were
unaware of any broad theoretical framework for understanding development and
adjustment that explicitly linked peer relationships and cognitive development
(Shute and Paton, 1990). Taking up an earlier suggestion by George Butterworth
(1982) that systems theory might offer a way of integrating social and cognitive
aspects of development, blended with Vygotskian notions of social cognitive links,
we outlined a theoretical framework by which a process of 'social cognitive monitoring' provides a reciprocal link between the child's cognitive-emotional systems
and social world, which consists of environmental systems including home, school
and hospital (similar to Bronfenbrenner's microsystems, although we were then
unfamiliar with his work). Within each, the child experiences relationships with
both adults and peers. These are differentially involved in cognitive development,
given that age-peer relationships are based on equality (which Piaget said was
necessary for certain aspects of development, such as moral understanding), while
relationships with adults (and older peers) are asymmetrical, influencing cognitive
development in the way proposed by Vygotsky (Foot *et al.*, 1990; Hartup, 1980).

   However, we also acknowledged that cognition could interact with non-social
features of the world, in the way proposed by Piaget (and in accord with Vygotsky's
notion of early infant development). The importance of development over time was
also acknowledged, with 'adjustment' being defined in general terms as 'the degree
to which he or she functions at age-appropriate levels in the social, cognitive and

academic spheres, while maintaining good disease management and high self-esteem' (Shute and Paton, 1990: 332). The concern with adjustment, rather than just development, reflected the clinical thrust of the work.

Even more comprehensive was the later version of Bronfenbrenner's theory. This evolved over time from the ecological model (described in Chapter 10) into his 'bioecological model' (Bronfenbrenner and Morris, 1998). The original theory corrected previous neglect of contexts of development, but what it prompted were many studies of 'context without development' (Bronfenbrenner and Morris, 1998: 994). Bronfenbrenner came to place much more emphasis on developmental *processes*, giving pride of place to proximal processes – interactions between the organism and environment that are the primary mechanisms for development (similar to our notion of social-cognitive monitoring). However, as in our framework, Bronfenbrenner also allowed for development through interaction with the non-social world, and saw proximal processes varying as a function of aspects of the developing *person*, his or her *environmental contexts* and *time*. Bronfenbrenner and Morris further categorized person characteristics into *dispositions*, *resources* and *demand characteristics*, concepts that they also applied to the nested environmental systems, such as the microsystem.

The notion was also introduced that features of the environment may not just foster but also interfere with the development of proximal processes. While we were specifically concerned with adjustment of the child with chronic illness, Bronfenbrenner and Morris incorporated the notion that developmental outcomes for all individuals represent competency or dysfunction, something which reflects a growing interest in the idea that factors both internal and external to the child contribute to risk for, or resilience against, poor developmental outcomes. In keeping with the trend towards lifespan approaches, an increased concern with time (the chronosystem) was apparent, as reflected in their definition of development as 'stability and change in the biopsychological characteristics of human beings over the life course and across generations' (Bronfenbrenner and Morris, 1998: 995). A link with evolutionary theory was made, in that it was assumed that biological and evolutionary factors both set limits to, and provide imperatives for, development.

Dynamic systems theory

As discussed in Chapter 10, the term 'dynamic systems theory' was introduced to describe a new and well-articulated theory of development (Thelen and Smith, 1994). It is strongly based upon the principles of general systems theory, which means, of course, that, despite its name, it is not unique in its dynamic emphasis. As with Bronfenbrenner's later (bioecological) theory, central notions are holism, mutual influence within and between traditionally separate levels of analysis, and a focus on process rather than structure. However, the two theories differ markedly in the emphasis placed upon biology. Although Bronfenbrenner came to acknowledge the biological (specifically, the genetic) contribution to development, he did not detail biological processes at all. On the contrary, Thelen and Smith set out deliberately to create a theory that was biologically valid, to the extent that they explicitly rejected models of development that used machine or computer analogies, and used biologically appropriate terminology instead. They questioned the common usage of the term 'biological' to refer exclusively to genes, neurology, hormones, etc. – the things that psychologists call 'biological bases' of behaviour. They argued that aspects of the environment, such as social environments that enable language to develop, are no less biological.

Thelen and Smith also argued that the notion that there is a 'plan for the adult' encapsulated in the genes is illogical, as is any 'plan' encoded in the environment. Both these extreme views, they maintained, lead to an impossible infinite regress of coded instructions for development, which is not solved by interactionism: a theory of development must explain how novelty and complexity in structure and function arise, and simply claiming that the answer is 'through gene-environment interactions' does not explain *how* new forms and behaviours come about. Their answer is that one has to explain development from the bottom up, not from a top-down plan. Various factors interact to create novelty in the way described for general systems theory – so that new properties emerge, rather than being predetermined. An important feature of this is that some abilities may be present but hidden, only coming into play when other aspects of development catch up and enable them to operate. For example, infants can step with alternate legs on a treadmill from early infancy, if their weight is supported; normally, this ability is not apparent until they can also support their own weight and balance in order to walk (Thelen *et al.*, 1984). This conception helps to address one of developmental psychology's perennial questions: does development happen in discrete stages or is it continuous? The answer may be that it is both, with continuity in sub-abilities or attributes leading to relatively sudden change as the sub-abilities operate together to form an emergent property.

From the perspective of their theory, Thelen and Smith said that one of the questions that has so vexed psychologists over the years – what is innate and what is learned? – is uninteresting. This echoes earlier comments by the aptly named Jeffrey Gray (1985) that the fondness psychologists have of (false) dichotomies often stands in the way of understanding the phenomena at hand (see also Chapter 11). Psychologists are as fond of linear causality and traditional research and analytic methods as they are of dichotomies; such approaches do not lend themselves well to investigations in the mould of dynamic systems, and this presents some real challenges for developmental psychology.

In a tribute to Thelen, Smith summed up the integrative power of dynamic systems theory:

> Traditionally, psychologists have considered action, learning, and development as distinct processes. Thelen ... argued and showed us in her work how this conceptualization is wrong. For action, for mind, there is but one dimension of time.

(Smith, 2006: 89)

Evolutionary developmental psychology

As mentioned in Chapter 2, it has been proposed that evolutionary developmental psychology is another approach that has the potential to act as an integrating force. David Geary and David Bjorklund describe it as an emerging interdisciplinary field, a sister discipline to evolutionary developmental biology, with the goals of identifying:

> the social, psychological, cognitive, and neural phenotypes that are common to human beings, and to other species, and to identify the genetic and ecological mechanisms that shape the development of these phenotypes and ensure their adaptation to local conditions.
>
> *(Geary and Bjorklund, 2000: 57)*

This definition makes it clear that the field is inclusive of all aspects of development traditionally studied as separate subdisciplines. Geary and Bjorklund (2000) proposed a hierarchically organized system of modules and submodules of the mind, which enables the individual to manage the social environment (e.g. theory of mind) and the natural environment (e.g. spatial representation). These modules have evolved to subserve survival and reproduction, and one issue for evolutionary developmental psychology is to relate to modern environments mechanisms that evolved under past evolutionary pressures. This level of explanation is, of course, like genetic determinism, concerned with ultimate functions of behaviour and development, rather than with mechanisms, understanding of which must draw upon other theoretical frameworks. In making this point, Robin Dunbar applauded the potential of evolutionary psychology to 'weld together the innumerable cracks that threaten to tear psychology apart' (Dunbar, 2001: 421).

We discussed in Chapter 2 the criticism that evolutionary psychology creates post hoc explanations. As noted by Timothy Ketelaar and Bruce Ellis (2000), critics observe that it accounts for an endless range of phenomena, and when the phenomena change, the explanations change: essentially, evolutionary-derived hypotheses are unfalsifiable. While Ketelaar and Ellis accept that the field was indeed open to such charges in the past, they argue that it has matured to a stage where it can produce surprising and testable new hypotheses. The essence of their argument rests upon adopting the philosophy of science articulated by Imre Lakatos, as outlined in Chapter 1. They suggest that evolutionary theory constitutes a 'metatheoretical research program' based on certain core assumptions. This core is surrounded by a 'protective belt' of middle-level theories, such as attachment theory, parental investment/sexual selection theory and reciprocal altruism theory. Rather than experimental results leading to all-or-none acceptance or rejection of the basic metatheory, they should contribute to making a decision about whether the metatheory in general is progressive or degenerative. Thus, even if the weight of evidence were, say, to destroy attachment theory, provided the weight of evidence still favoured other middle-level theories, the basic evolutionary metatheory would still stand. Ketelaar and Ellis argue that evolutionary theory has the status of a progressive metatheory, in being able both to accommodate major anomalous findings and to generate novel predictions and explanations. An example of the former is altruism, which was initially considered a major threat to evolutionary theory, but was later accommodated within it (see Chapter 2). An example of the latter was a challenge to the accepted 'fact' that males are superior to females in spatial ability: it was predicted, and supported by various studies (e.g. McBurney *et al.*, 1997), that males would tend to be superior on mental rotation tasks, based on the assumption that ancestral males needed such skills to hunt and kill animals, while females would be superior in remembering static locations of objects, based on an ancestral role in gathering food from static sources.

In adopting an evolutionary approach, it will be important for psychologists to ensure that their theories about the operation of ancient societies do not become outdated. Also, postmodern approaches to scientific inquiry should lead us to maintain a healthy scepticism about taken-for-granted archaeological assumptions; for example, a feminist approach might lead us to inquire closely into the truth of tales of strong, brave (male) hunters. Research has shown that archaeological sites with large animal bones are more highly valued and researched than those without them; there has thus been a privileging, in research, of carnivory and hunting over other nutritional strategies, such as gathering plant materials or trapping small animals (Dincauze, 2001). Bones from Czech Upper Palaeolithic sites indicate that mammoth meat was largely scavenged or came from weak animals, while hares and foxes were commonly eaten, together with plants, fruits, seeds and starchy tubers; evidence of cord and other woven materials indicates that the technology for making net traps was available (Stringer, 2012). One might therefore question just how much evolutionary pressure really came from hunting. It has also been proposed that where hunting of large animals did occur, it served the purpose of achieving and validating male status. If so, a hunt-based explanation of male spatial rotation superiority would have to posit a cultural rather than a nutritional selection pressure.

If the overall position that evolutionary theory acts as a metatheory is accepted, this adds philosophical weight to the argument that it has the potential to act as a unifying force across many diverse areas of psychology. We began this book with the suggestion (not unchallenged) that Darwinian theory can be taken as the starting point for the various schools of developmental theory that have arisen. It is fascinating, therefore, that the wheel has turned full circle and the evolutionary approach is now being proposed as a means of reunifying the field.

Uniting evolutionary theory and feminism

As we discussed in Chapter 11, evolutionary theory and feminism have often been ranged against one another, but there have been some recent attempts, from the feminist side, to unite these seemingly oppositional perspectives. One comes from Alice Eagly and Wendy Wood (2013), who have put forward a 'biosocial constructionist' theory of gender. On this theory, ancient ecological and social selection processes have acted on the female–male division of labour, which is constrained, but not determined, by major bodily sex differences, such as females' bearing of children and males' greater body size and strength. The division of labour forms the basis for the social construction of gender roles that in turn reinforces division of labour. Complex neural and hormonal systems underlying male–female behavioural differences are assumed to have evolved to fit societal demands. These systems have built on more ancient mammalian systems, but have become adapted to life in complex social groups where understanding of the self and others is crucial. These evolved abilities allow an understanding of gender expectations and permit the cumulative development of culture. The feminist aspect of the theory is that it allows for human appreciation of the possibility of social change towards greater gender equality.

Charlotte Tate (2013) has also attempted to integrate evolutionary psychology and feminism. She has drawn attention to confusion between metatheories and research theories by some prominent evolutionary psychologists, who have argued that studies that do not support sexual strategies theory do not invalidate the broad thrust of supportive research. Tate says this treats sexual strategies theory as a metatheory rather than the research theory that it is. Metatheories are not falsifiable, but more or less useful, and provide a 'trellis' for research theories and operational definitions. She sees evolutionary psychology and feminist metatheories as not incompatible, with genes seen as providing the first step and experiential variables as providing the second step in a developmental process (as in stepwise statistical analyses); it is therefore possible to analyse the separate contributions of the steps to gender similarities and differences. This provides a framework for the development and empirical testing of specific research theories that straddle the steps. This attempt at integration, however, like Eagly and Wood's, is at a very early stage. A book that sets out to initiate exchanges of ideas on these issues is *Evolution's Empress*, edited by Maryanne Fisher and colleagues (2013).

Theory bridging

In Chapter 11 we outlined Leaper's (2000) theory of gender development, which pulls together a number of theories to offer a fuller explanatory framework than any single theory could do alone. Leaper (2011) has continued to advocate for the integration of theories of social and cognitive development, while also acknowledging the many obstacles to it. He believes that attempts at 'bridging' or 'knitting' theories together should be encouraged, and provides a number of examples of theories with common or complementary elements that could potentially be drawn together to offer more complete explanations of behavioural development. One example is Albert Bandura's social cognitive theory (e.g. Bandura and Bussey, 2004) and gender schema theory (a form of cognitive-developmental theory; see Martin and Halverson, 1981). Advocates of these two theories have fiercely defended their side against the other, yet both highlight observational learning and both hold that people's interpretations of events are influenced by their beliefs. They are also complementary, with social cognitive theory, for example, able to add to gender schema theory by explaining how social sanctions against cross-gender behaviour impact differentially upon boys and girls. While focusing on social and cognitive theories, Leaper also suggests that similar efforts at integration could happen that incorporate different levels of analysis (biological and cultural approaches). He notes that, for example, while social and cognitive theories acknowledge a role for biological dispositions, they do not articulate the links.

Relational metatheory

While Leaper's suggestions for theory bridging are at the level of specific theories, Overton has taken a metatheoretical approach, blending a lifespan perspective with relationalism and dynamic systems theory to present a holistic view of development (Overton and Ennis, 2006; Overton, 2010). According to this view, 'the whole' is not a sum of its parts, but an organized system, within which the parts are seen in relation to one another and to the whole. The metatheoretical concept of 'splitting' the world into pure, incompatible elements, such as pitting nature against nurture or genes against the environment, with no place for reciprocal causality, is rejected. Just as the vase and the faces in the famous Rubin illusion do not exist independently, mental events and behaviours are seen as different poles of the same event:

> the principles of social constructivist or strict behavioral approaches that elevate the environment – particularly the cultural environment – to a privileged primary position, or biological reductionists who elevate biology – particularly the brain – to a privileged primary position lead to seriously incomplete approaches to inquiry.
>
> *(Overton and Ennis, 2006: 148)*

Interaction must be seen not as cooperation between separate parts, but rather as 'interpenetration'. We have met these ideas before, in the 'constitutive relationalism' of Sergei Rubinstein (see Chapter 7), although he is not cited by Overton and Michelle Ennis. Linear views of development must then give way to complex, dynamic ones, in accord with dynamic systems theory. Seeking understanding by analysis into parts is not precluded, but sight must not be lost of the interrelationships between them. It is a question of what 'standpoint' is adopted. When biology, the person and culture are seen as 'interpenetrating' parts, then a biopsychosocial lifespan approach can be said to exist. These three aspects co-evolve, or co-construct one another, with the psychological emerging from relatively undifferentiated biological and cultural beginnings, then also playing its part in the development of the organism into increasingly complex systems over the lifespan. Taking this perspective, the reductionism of the positivist era is replaced with multidisciplinary and multimethod approaches to understanding, which offer complementary, not privileged, perspectives.

The idea of 'standpoints' can be traced back to Renaissance philosopher Nicholas of Cusa, who drew upon Plato's philosophy to suggest that we can see the world from various standpoints that are not in opposition to one another, but complementary. This he referred to as *coincidentia oppositorum*, an idea that so appealed to Ludwig von Bertalanffy that he wrote a book about Cusa (Weckowicz, 2000).

Overton and Ennis (2006) have put relational metatheory forward as a way of uniting cognitive-developmental and behaviour-analytic approaches to development. They have done this by addressing the incompatibility of the underlying metatheoretical assumptions, of organicism on the one hand and mechanism on the other. They begin by re-casting modern behaviour-analytic theory as contextual, rather than mechanistic, in nature. Then they apply the notion of standpoints that are different, but not mutually exclusive. Hence, cognitive-developmental theory focuses on action-in-the-world through the person who acts, while behaviour-analytic theory focuses on the environmental contingencies affecting those acts, offering complementary views of the same event. Some of Leaper's (2011) suggestions for theory-bridging in the specific area of gender development would fit comfortably within this metatheoretical framework. For a different attempt at metatheoretical integration, see Antley (2010).

Can postmodern and scientific approaches be reconciled?

At first sight, the answer to this question might seem to be an obvious no. Throughout this book we have contrasted positivist and postmodern (critical) notions of inquiry, and observed that they have arisen from different philosophical approaches. A postmodern perspective such as that articulated by Kenneth Gergen (2001) holds that all knowledge is relative; there is no such thing as reality, but only individuals' constructions of reality. Thus, any perspective on child development, including those derived from scientific inquiry, would be no better than any other. The result would appear to be an unhelpful descent into anarchy and nihilism. Indeed, as Jack Martin and Jeff Sugarman (2000: 400) have observed, if one takes such views of postmodernism literally, psychology and education are not only problematized, they are liquidated! Yet it is hard to ignore the fact that, without the critique offered by postmodernism, developmental psychology would be even more ethnocentric and androcentric, more ignorant of its history and more disempowering to its research participants than it already is.

In an earlier chapter we described ourselves as 'fence-sitters' on the science and postmodernism issue, acknowledging, for example, the value of both quantitative and qualitative research methods, and suggesting that a reconciliation between the two might be possible. It seems that we are not alone in seeking such a solution. Martin and Sugarman have observed that some psychologists:

> resonate to postmodern themes of difference, plurality, peculiarity and irregularity as refreshing changes from past adherence to sameness, regularity and strict rationalism . . . in effect, having labored within the straightjacket of

modernity, they enjoy the full ludic romp of postmodernism's radical problematizing without really believing its full social constructionist and deconstructive implications for themselves and their everyday and professional practices.

(Martin and Sugarman, 2000: 398)

They suggest that attempting to have the best of both these worlds is a rather sensible approach. It is helpful to note that the term 'postmodernism' does not cover a single approach, and that there are philosophical debates within the field. Gergen's version, which seems so irreconcilable with a scientific approach to child development, is an extreme one. Martin and Sugarman resist a forced choice between 'the unsustainable myths of modernity on the one hand and some of the more excessively radical medicine of postmodernism on the other' (Martin and Sugarman, 2000: 400). They propose a middle-ground philosophical perspective that draws upon the work of Vygotsky and Margaret Mead, as well as other scholars.

According to this view, the non-human world of physical and biological objects ('natural kinds') really exists, independently of the humans who study it. 'Human kinds' also exist, but are themselves heavily implicated in this reality: as humans are aware and reflective, their actions and ways of being are affected by the classification of societies and cultures and by their own reactions to these classifications. Thus, their actions are influenced not only by the culture of which they are a part, but also by their own unique experiences within it. Their reflections and actions may in turn change the available societal classifications. An example provided by Martin and Sugarman is that of changes to *DSM* classifications resulting from the activities of advocacy groups, as we discussed in Chapters 2 and 11. The implications of Martin and Sugarman's position for a rapprochement between reality-based science and postmodern constructivism is captured in the following extract:

> In the dynamic, developmental scenario we have painted, the possibility of reflexive subjectivity is developmentally emergent within human embeddedness in real and preexisiting physical, biological and sociocultural contexts. Although precise forms of emergent subjectivity are necessarily historically and contextually contingent and thus variable, some such emergence (given the physical, biological, and sociocultural conditions of human existence) is existentially inevitable.

(Martin and Sugarman, 2000: 403)

In deciding how to respond to postmodern critiques, readers may find Box 13.2 helpful.

From a practical perspective, Daniel Fishman and Stanley Messer (2013) regard the 'culture wars' between positivist/modern and constructivist/postmodern approaches as undermining unity in applied psychology and unhelpful for dealing with pressing social issues. They propose a 'third way' that draws upon pragmatism (see Chapter 8). According to this view, applied knowledge is seen as constructed by

---

BOX 13.2 HOW SHOULD WE RESPOND TO NON-TRADITIONAL THEORETICAL APPROACHES?

Teo has performed a valuable service in bringing to our attention the diversity of theoretical traditions that address the contexts, phenomena and issues that are central to developmental psychology. In particular, Teo has identified the three extended theoretical families that include the critical-theoretical approaches, the postmodern, post-structuralist, deconstructionist approaches, and the feminist and multicultural approaches . . . there are several alternative visions of the relationships among families of theoretical traditions that might guide us in our reading, understanding, and evaluation of Teo's article. From the exclusivist perspective, we would finish reading the article and ask, What can I do to demonstrate how these alternative theoretical perspectives are wrong? From the inclusivist perspective, we would ask, What can I borrow from these alternative theoretical traditions to strengthen my own? From a detached perspective, we would merely dismiss the article and not return to it again. And from a caring perspective, we would now be asking, What can traditional developmental psychology offer to strengthen these alternative theoretical traditions?

(Meacham, 1997: 211–15)

---

humans in specific contexts to solve particular problems, in line with Sternberg and Grigorenko's (2001) converging operations approach, mentioned previously. Fishman and Messer propose that this can be operationalized through an accumulation of systematic single-case studies, whether quantitative or qualitative, from any theoretical background. They can be built into a large database, which can be interrogated in various ways, or combined with group-based studies such as randomized control trials, to build new integrated knowledge from the 'bottom up'. Integration can be further achieved, they propose, using case studies with alternative aims, such as theory-building and gaining the narrative experiences of participants.

A move towards a more unified psychology may have synergy with greater acceptance of postmodern perspectives that are more open to alternative views of the world than is typical in western theorizing. Western thinking is seen as 'piecemeal' by many cultures, as exemplified by the holism of traditional Indian thought (Box 13.3). The Ngarrindjeri people of South Australia see children as developing in communities where 'Our Lands, Our Waters, Our People, All Living Things are connected', and where there is an 'essential link between the wellbeing of Ngarrindjeri individuals, families, communities, and the place-based consciousness/pedagogy through connection to lands and waters' (Hemming and Rigney, 2011: 352). We can note here international concerns that many children today are growing

---

BOX 13.3 HOLISM IN INDIAN THOUGHT

Western trends in psychology over the years have led Indian scholars to make connections with ancient Indian thought. For example, many Indian scriptures emphasize personal growth, which fitted well with 1960s western psychological theory, such as Abraham Maslow's self-actualization theory (Mathew, 2001). Recently, western psychological practice has in turn been powerfully influenced by the Buddhist notion of 'mindfulness'. V.G. Mathew has suggested that a western move towards more integrative psychological theories may enable a greater exchange of ideas:

> Indian theories of linguistics, social behavior, crime, etc. are all based on the holistic approach and the broad-based intuitive understanding of behavior in contradistinction to Western theories which are piece-meal, analytic and situation specific. The increasing importance given to the holistic approach and need for synthesis makes it possible to integrate modern Western Psychology with ancient Indian thoughts as well as methods.
>
> *(Mathew, 2001: n.p.)*

---

up divorced from connection with nature (Nebraska Department of Education, 2008).

Finally, we raise the question of how children's voices can become better integrated into the theories we have been exploring. As discussed in the previous chapter, there is a need to consider the extent to which young people can genuinely engage in the research endeavour. A genuine 'about face' in child development research that attempts to address matters of participation and power imbalance must involve a great deal more than superficially changing terms such as 'subject' into 'participant'!

Conclusions

We have observed some dissatisfaction with fragmentary approaches to child and adolescent development, with some strong recent moves apparent in the direction of more integrative and holistic approaches. The implication is that developmental theories at a purely psychological (or any other) level of analysis will necessarily be incomplete. As Richard Lerner observed,

> in contemporary developmental theories, the person is not biologized, psychologized or sociologized. Rather the individual is 'systemized' – that is his or her development is embedded within an integrated matrix of variables derived from multiple levels of organization, and development is

conceptualized as deriving from the dynamic relations among the variables in this multi-tiered matrix.

(Lerner, 1998: 1)

Despite the intriguing trends noted in this chapter, we often find psychologist colleagues much more comfortable with small models that are directly testable by standard research methods – in line with the world of mini-theories that encapsulates most psychological research. While we believe that this approach has an important place, as practitioners we are much more excited by the current thrust towards holism and integration, and are appreciative of the enormous intellectual effort that goes into developing such approaches, which can provide the big picture into which the smaller models fit. As with postmodernism, these newer approaches certainly present significant challenges for traditional scientific methods. We leave it to our readers to determine which of the possible paths they believe most worthy of pursuit. Finally, we would do well to recall George Kelly's view that each theory not only has its own limited 'range of convenience', but that all theories are ultimately expendable (Kelly, 1963: 11).

References

Aesop. 1979. *Aesop's fables*, trans. V.S. Vernon Jones. London: Heinemann.

Antley, M. 2010. Toward a metatheoretical integration of developmental paradigms. *Integral Review*. 6 (3): 175–89.

Baltes, P.B. 1987. Theoretical propositions of life-span developmental psychology: on the dynamics between growth and decline. *Developmental Psychology*. 23 (5): 611–26. Available at: www.mpib-berlin.mpg.de/volltexte/institut/dok/full/Baltes/theoreti/index.htm. Accessed 23 January 2015.

Bandura, A. and Bussey, K. 2004. On broadening the cognitive, motivational, and sociocultural scope of theorising about gender development and functioning: comment on Martin, Ruble, and Szkrybalo (2002). *Psychological Bulletin*. 130: 691–701.

Bevan, W. 1994. Plain truths and home cooking: thoughts on the making and remaking of psychology. *American Psychologist*. 49: 505–9.

Breunlin, D.C., Schwartz, R.C. and Kune-Karrer, B.M. 1992. *Metaframeworks: transcending the models of family therapy*. San Francisco, CA: Jossey-Bass.

Bronfenbrenner, U. and Ceci, S.J. 1994. Nature–nurture reconceptualized in developmental perspective: a bioecological model. *Psychological Review*. 101: 568–86.

Bronfenbrenner, U. and Morris, P.A. 1998. The ecology of developmental processes. In R.M. Lerner (ed.), *Handbook of child psychology. Theoretical models of human development*. Fifth edn, Vol. 1. New York: Wiley, 535–84.

Butterworth, G. 1982. A brief account of the conflict between the individual and the social in models of cognitive growth. In G. Butterworth and P. Light (eds), *Social cognition: studies of the development of understanding*. Brighton: Harvester, 3–16.

Dincauze, D. 2001. *Environmental archaeology*. Cambridge: Cambridge University Press.

Doise, W. 1986. *Levels of explanation in social psychology*. Cambridge: Cambridge University Press.

Dunbar, R. 2001. Darwinising ourselves. *The Psychologist*. 14 (8): 420–1.

Eagly, A.H. and Wood, W. 2013. Feminism and evolutionary psychology: moving forward. *Sex Roles*. 69: 549–56.

Engel, G.L. 1977. The need for a new medical model. *Science*. 196 (4,286): 129–36.

Fisher, M.L., Garcia, G.R. and Chang, R.S. 2013. *Evolution's empress: Darwinian perspectives on the nature of women*. New York: Oxford University Press.

Fishman, D.B. and Messer, S.B. 2013. Pragmatic case studies as a source of unity in applied psychology. *Review of General Psychology*. 17 (2): 156–61.

Foot, H.C., Shute, R.H., Morgan, M.J. and Barron, A-M. 1990. Theoretical issues in peer tutoring. In H.C. Foot, R.H. Shute and M.J. Morgan (eds), *Children helping children*. Chichester: Wiley, 3–17.

Geary, D.C. and Bjorklund, D.F. 2000. Evolutionary developmental psychology. *Child Development*. 71 (1): 57–65.

Gergen, K. 2001. Psychological science in a postmodern perspective. *American Psychologist*. 56 (10): 803–13.

Gladding, S.T. 1998. *Family therapy: history, theory and practice*. Second edn. Upper Saddle River, NJ: Prentice Hall.

Gold, J. 2011. Attachment theory and psychotherapy integration: an introduction and review of the literature. *Journal of Psychotherapy Integration*. 21 (3): 221–31.

Gray, J. A. 1985. A whole and its parts: behaviour, the brain, cognition and emotion. *Bulletin of the British Psychological Society*. 38: 99–112.

Hartup, W. 1980. Peer relations and family relations: two social worlds. In M. Rutter (ed.), *Scientific foundations of developmental psychiatry*. London: Heinemann, 280–91.

Hemming, S. and Rigney, D. 2011. Ngarrindjeri *Ruwe/Ruwar*: wellbeing through caring for country. In R.H. Shute, P.T. Slee, R. Murray-Harvey and K.L. Dix (eds), *Mental health and wellbeing: educational perspectives*. Adelaide: Shannon Research Press, 351–4.

Henggeler, S.W., Schoenwald, S.K., Borduin, C.N., Rowland, M. and Cunningham, P.B. 1998. *Multisystemic treatment of antisocial behavior in children and adolescents*. New York: Guilford.

Hinde, R.A. 1992. Developmental psychology in the context of other behavioral sciences. *Developmental Psychology*. 28 (6): 1,018–29.

Hogg, M. 1992. *The social psychology of group cohesiveness: from attraction to social identity*. New York: New York University Press.

Johnson, S.B. 1985. Psychosocial factors in juvenile diabetes: a review. *Journal of Behavioral Medicine*. 3 (1): 95–116.

Kazak, A.E. 1992. The social context of coping with childhood chronic illness: family systems and social support. In A.M. LaGreca, L.J. Siegel, J.L. Wallander and C.E. Walker (eds), *Stress and coping in child health*. New York: Guilford, 262–78.

Kelly, G. 1963. *A theory of personality: the psychology of personal constructs*. New York: Norton.

Ketelaar, T. and Ellis, B.J. 2000. Are evolutionary explanations unfalsifiable? Evolutionary psychology and the Lakatosian philosophy of science. *Psychological Inquiry*. 11 (1): 1–21.

Leaper, C. 2000. The social construction and socialization of gender during development. In P.H. Miller and E.K. Scholnick (eds), *Toward a feminist developmental psychology*. New York: Routledge, 127–52.

Leaper, C. 2011. More similarities than differences in contemporary theories of social development? A plea for theory bridging. *Advances in Child Development and Behavior*. 40: 337–78.

Lerner, R.M. 1998. Theories of human development: contemporary perspectives. In R.M. Lerner (ed.), *Handbook of child psychology. Theoretical models of human development*. Fifth edn, Vol. 1. New York: Wiley, 1–24.

Lerner, R.M. and von Eye, A. 1992. Sociobiology and human development: arguments and evidence. *Human Development*. 35: 12–33.

Lewis, M.D. 2000. The promise of dynamic systems approaches for an integrated account of human development. *Child Development.* 71 (1): 36–43.

Martin, C.L. and Halverson, C.F. 1981. A schematic-processing model of sex typing and stereotyping in children. *Child Development.* 52: 1,119–34.

Martin, J. and Sugarman, J. 2000. Between the modern and the postmodern: the possibility of self and progressive understanding in psychology. *American Psychologist.* 55 (4): 397–406.

Mathew, V.G. 2001. A short history of Indian psychology. Available at: www.psychology4all. com/HistoryI.htm. Accessed 18 May 2014.

McBurney, D.H., Gaulin, S.J.C., Devineni, T. and Adams, C. 1997. Superior spatial memory of women: stronger evidence for the gathering hypothesis. *Evolution and Human Behavior.* 18: 165–74.

Meacham, J. 1997. Relationships among theoretical traditions. *Human Development.* 40: 211–15.

Miller, P.H. 1993. *Theories of developmental psychology.* New York: Freeman.

Nebraska Department of Education. 2008. Reconnecting the world's children to nature. Available at: www.worldforumfoundation.org/wf/nacc/call_to_action.pdf. Accessed 30 June 2014.

Overton, W.F. 2010. Life-span development: concepts and issues. In W.F. Overton (ed.), *The handbook of life-span development. Part 1. Cognition, biology and methods.* Wiley online library.

Overton, W.F. and Ennis, M.D. 2006. Developmental and behavior-analytic theories: evolving into complementarity. *Human Development.* 49: 143–72.

Patterson, J.E. and Vakili, S. 2013. Relationships, environment, and the brain: how emerging research is changing what we know about the impact of families on human development. *Family Process* (online).

Sawyer, R.K. 2000. Connecting culture, psychology and biology: essay review on Inghilleri's *From subjective experience to cultural change. Human Development.* 43: 56–9.

Shute, R. and Paton, D. 1990. Chronic childhood illness: the child as helper. In H.C. Foot, M.J. Morgan and R.H. Shute (eds), *Children helping children.* Chichester: Wiley, 327–52.

Shute, R. and Paton, D. 1992. Understanding chronic childhood illness: towards an integrative approach. *The Psychologist: Bulletin of the British Psychological Society.* 5: 390–4.

Smith, L.B. 2006. Movement matters: the contributions of Esther Thelen. *Biological Theory.* 1: 87–9.

Sternberg, R.J. and Grigorenko, E.L. 2001. Unified psychology. *American Psychologist.* 56 (12): 1,069–79.

Stringer, C. 2012. *The origin of our species.* London: Penguin.

Tajfel, H. and Turner, J. 1979. An integrative theory of intergroup conflict. In W.G. Austin and S. Worchel (eds), *The social psychology of intergroup relations.* Monterey, CA: Brooks-Cole, 94–109.

Tate, C.C. 2013. Addressing conceptual confusions about evolutionary theorizing: how and why evolutionary psychology and feminism do not oppose each other. *Sex Roles.* 69: 491–502.

Thelen, E. and Smith, L.B. 1994. *A dynamic systems approach to the development of cognition and action.* Cambridge, MA: MIT Press.

Thelen, E., Fisher, D.M. and Ridley-Johnson, R. 1984. The relationship between physical growth and a newborn reflex. *Infant Behavior and Development.* 7: 479–93.

Thomas, A. and Chess, S. 1977. *Temperament and development.* New York: Brunner/Mazel.

Tremblay, R.E., Nagin, D., Séguin, J., Zoccolillo, M., Zelazo, P., Boivin, M., Pérusse, D. and Japel, C. 2004. Physical aggression during early childhood: trajectories and predictors. *Pediatrics*. 114: e43–e50.

Underwood, M.K., Galen, B.R. and Paquette, J.A. 2001. Hopes rather than fears, admirations rather than hostilities: a reply to Archer and Bjorkqvist. *Social Development*. 10 (2): 275–80.

Vreeke, G.J. 2000. Nature, nurture and the future of the analysis of variance. *Human Development*. 43: 32–45.

Weckowicz, T.E. 2000. Ludwig von Bertalanffy (1901–1972): a pioneer of general systems theory. University of Alberta Center for Systems Research Working Paper 89–2. Available at: www.richardjung.cz/bert1.pdf. Accessed 18 May 2014.

Weinert, F.E. and Weinert, S. 1998. History and systems of developmental psychology. In A. Demetriou, W. Doise and C. van Lieshout (eds), *Life-span developmental psychology*. Chichester: Wiley, 1–33.

14

THE THEORY-PRACTICE NEXUS

Introduction

Throughout this book we have seen real-life applications of child development theory. For example, children's behavioural problems have been approached from a range of perspectives, including medical diagnosis, family systems and social information processing. Theories such as those of John Dewey, Jean Piaget and Lev Vygotsky have been applied educationally, and attachment and learning theories have been implicated in debates about how to raise children. Such theory-informed practice is sometimes referred to as 'praxis'. Equally, we have seen that policy decisions concerning children can fly in the face of what theory and research suggest will promote children's positive development, as when Australian Aboriginal children were removed from their attachment figures. Alternatively, practice that promotes positive development can sometimes occur without a theoretical basis, as in the case of the South Australian infants who were fostered rather than institutionalized in the nineteenth century.

In this final chapter we turn to a more in-depth discussion of the links between child development theory and practice, against a backdrop of the contribution of the philosophy of science to psychology. We briefly address several terms that have been used in the psychology and educational literatures in recent years, including 'scientist-practitioner', 'applied developmental science' and 'developmentally appropriate practice'. These ideas issue some interesting challenges to researchers and writers enmeshed in the world of theory. As witnessed in the preceding chapters, developmental psychology is almost embarrassed by an excess of riches in relation to theoretical development, with new understandings emerging apace. The application of this knowledge to practice and as a means of informing policy development is, to some extent, uncharted territory (Dodge, 2011). In a reciprocal fashion, there is a challenge to improve understanding of how practice can inform theory development.

We will explore a range of barriers to the application of the 'bench to bedside' notion in the social sciences, and suggest some ways forward through the emerging field of 'translational research', particularly as applied to wellbeing programmes delivered to children through schools. We illustrate this with a case study.

Applied psychology and the nature of knowledge

Notions such as 'evidence-based practice' and 'best practice' have become commonplace in western public policy discourse, but this raises questions about what counts as 'good' evidence on which practice should be based. For example, while researchers in psychology may devise mental health prevention programmes based on child development theories and empirical studies, schools and teachers may not value their scientific basis and select programmes using other criteria (Shute, 2012).

Reflecting Plato's distinction between beliefs and knowledge, a researcher may see a teacher's opinions about 'best practice' as inferior to the knowledge gained from supposedly dispassionate scientific study. The empiricists, such as John Locke, George Berkeley and David Hume, drew upon Stoic philosophy (strongly aligned with that of Aristotle) to posit that reliable knowledge exists outside the individual and that humans acquire knowledge through the senses. Locke argued that 'The senses at first let in particular ideas, and furnish the yet empty cabinet, and the mind by degrees growing familiar with some of them, they are lodged in the memory' (Locke, 1690/1947: 22). Berkeley argued that ideas are the objects of human knowledge – with ideas imprinted on the mind by sensations. In contrast, the rationalists, such as René Descartes, Baruch Spinoza and Immanuel Kant, argued that reason is more important than experience. For example, Kant, while not denying the existence of experience, identified two elements of knowledge: what is given, principally through the senses, and what is posited by the thinking subject. Rationalists argue that we can be deceived by our senses, as in the case of perceptual illusions, and so the senses cannot be trusted to provide reliable knowledge. Such ideas continue to shape western philosophy, and form the basis for the scientific approach that there is knowledge 'out there' in the world waiting to be discovered.

Postmodern views of knowledge propose a very different outlook, entertaining multiple forms of knowledge that are not discoverable, but constructed. The implications of this worldview for practice are exemplified in approaches to family therapy. Alan Carr has noted that 'Among family therapist practitioners, narrative and social constructionist approaches informed by a postmodern ideology have become increasingly popular in informing a vibrant and creative approach to conducting therapy' (Carr, 2009: 3). Narrative therapy essentially embodies such an approach, viewing clients (including children) as experts in their own lives; various techniques have been developed to 'distance' people from their problems (sometimes in a playful way – as when a child with faecal soiling works on the idea of *Beating Sneaky Poo*, see Heins and Ritchie, 1988). It is assumed that people have many skills that they can draw on to address their problems. The approach attempts to understand how the client construes the world in order to facilitate change. In classroom settings, activating students' prior knowledge is considered important to enable scaffolding of their learning of new content; however, there is reasonably heated debate about the value of prior knowledge and whether it facilitates or hinders the acquisition of new knowledge (e.g. McInerney, 2006; Nuthall, 2000).

Writers such as Timothy Teo (1997) and Elizabeth Valentine (1998) suggested that, while developmental psychology draws upon disciplines such as biology, anthropology and sociology, it has been rather reluctant to consider developments in the philosophy of knowledge. Teo suggested that the primary reason concerns the rise and dominance of empiricism, particularly as reflected in mainstream US psychology (see Chapter 6). The focus on the *individual's* development in the majority of theories is perhaps related to this, and is essentially consistent with mainstream western political democratic development. Developmental psychology, with few exceptions, is not a socially or politically critical enterprise; therefore much mainstream theorizing reflects dominant hegemonic thought. In the postmodern context we have elaborated on some contemporary influences on child development theory, including Indigenous and feminist theories (see Chapters 9 and 11). These new understandings have considerably enriched our understanding of human development, with significant implications for practice. For example, the Council of Australian Governments' National Action Plan for Mental Health 2006–2011 (COAG, 2012a) and the recent Roadmap for National Mental Health Reform 2012–2022 (COAG, 2012b) documents step outside mainstream empirical theorizing that focuses on linear causal explanations; they accommodate more systemic, multifactorial explanations for the development of protective factors influencing young people's mental health. This approach is consistent with the more recent, integrative approaches to development outlined in the previous chapter. Implications for western–trained practitioners working in the Majority World are also significant (Box 14.1).

BOX 14.1 APPLYING PSYCHOLOGY IN THE MAJORITY WORLD

[M]ost cross-cultural psychology . . . seems to be more interested in variables than in human problems . . . the first move toward [Majority World] involvement by Western-trained behavioural scientists must be a self-purging of individualistic and scientistic thinking . . . This would entail a shift from 'pure' research focusing on individual behaviour to applied research/intervention of the sort normally associated with primary prevention programs, public health education, family systems approaches, community mobilization strategies, program evaluation, and even world systems analysis.

(Sloan, 1990: 3, 16)

A related and important issue in considering links between theory and practice is the role of universities in creating knowledge, with particular reference to the type of knowledge created. Western universities have generally engaged in the conduct of science to develop and test theories and hypotheses. William Tierney (2001) has summarized the modernist paradigm as encapsulating linear, causal reasoning with an overarching search for theories and universal truths. Consistent with a positivist view of science, the university has generally been represented as a community of scholars dispassionately engaged in the conduct of science and in the pursuit of knowledge unfettered by political or social constraints. As Tierney notes, 'A modernist stance on knowledge production proceeds from the belief that objective scientists from particular disciplines undertake neutral investigations' (Tierney, 2001: 355; see also Chapter 1). The right of the scholar to speak independently has been, and still is, a jealously guarded one although, as we discuss further later, this may be under threat.

The role of the university as the sole repository of knowledge is also being challenged in a postmodern context in which the term 'knowledge society' (Stehr, 1994) implies that knowledge is produced by and across society. Moreover, the type of knowledge so prized by universities, namely 'contemplative knowledge', which seeks to 'describe the world, to represent the world' (Barnett, 2000: 410) is increasingly being understood as only one of *many* types of knowledge. Tierney has noted that 'proponents of modernism have assumed that rational, objective knowledge discovered by scientific inquiry ultimately will set humanity free, or at least improve the lives of men and women' (Tierney, 2001: 353; authors' note – what about children?). This view is under challenge from emergent forms of knowledge, identified as 'performative knowledges' (Gibbons *et al.*, 1994) or 'forms of action and engagement with and in the world' (Barnett, 2000: 410). The implications are that, while theory can inform practice, greater consideration is needed of the possibility that practice (representing a form of knowledge in its own right) can also inform theory.

It has further been argued that knowledge generated by universities has less status now and simply takes its place alongside a range of other 'knowledges' (Gokulsing and DaCosta, 1997). The privileging of knowledge generated by universities, perceived as representing the sectional interests of a small group of academics, is now being questioned in some quarters, although the issue of the existence of other forms of knowledge outside the university research setting is still a debate largely waiting to be had. The outcome is that universities are being challenged to take their knowledge to the marketplace and compete with other forms of knowledge (Barnett, 2000). Laurens Hessels and Harro van Lente (2008) have highlighted this shift in their summary of Modes 1 and 2 of knowledge production, with Mode 2 supplementing Mode 1. As can be seen from Table 14.1, Mode 1 conforms to traditional university modes for knowledge production, while Mode 2 involves transdisciplinary collaborations and reflexivity, with evaluations using different quality criteria.

This brief description of the philosophical background to developmental psychology, the nature of knowledge and links with practice, helps set the scene for

TABLE 14.1 Attributes of Mode 1 and Mode 2 knowledge production

Mode 1	Mode 2
Academic context	Context of application
Disciplinary	Transdisciplinary
Homogeneity	Heterogeneity
Autonomy	Reflexivity/social accountability

Source: Hessels and van Lente, 2008.

the following discussion regarding the manner in which theory has been linked (or not!) with practice. In order to facilitate this discussion we describe three rather disparate models of theory-practice links relevant to developmental psychology: the scientist-practitioner model, developmentally appropriate practice and applied developmental science.

Models of theory-practice links

The scientist-practitioner model

In 1950 the formulation of this model (Raimy, 1950) was facilitated by funding from the US government to provide rehabilitation and other services for service-men and servicewomen returning from duty in World War II. The Boulder Conference in 1949 had preceded Victor Raimy's publication and essentially produced a model of education and training rather than a model of professional practice. As a result, there was a call for clinical psychologists to be trained as both scientists and practitioners (Shapiro, 2002). At the time, the body of psychological knowledge resided principally with academics working in university settings. The scientist-practitioner model is not without its critics: 'one of the bottom-line issues is whether it is viable to train students to be scientists generally and researchers specifically when, at the core, these students enter training to be practitioners and not researchers' (Gelso, 2006: 3).

In the field of developmental psychology, we can hear these sentiments echoed in Urie Bronfenbrenner's concern that research efforts have mainly concentrated on the decontextualized child. Ian John argued that the prevailing positivist influence at the time of the Boulder Conference 'enabled academic psychologists, the exponents and self-declared custodians of these procedures, to position themselves as the arbiters of psychological knowledge claims of any kind' (John, 1998: 25). The implications for scientific practice were almost self-evident and reflected in 'a form of instrumental or technical rationality that proceeds by rigorous deduction of prescriptions for practice from these generalizations' (John, 1998: 26). Furthermore, as we discussed in the previous chapter, the current diversity of incompatible theories provides a daunting challenge not only to developmentalists but also to educators and other practitioners working with children (Lewis, 2000).

Those such as John (1994, 1998) who have criticized the grounding of the scientist-practitioner model in 'a naive empiricist conception of science' (Cotton, 1998: 31) have drawn attention to the issue of the range of 'knowledges' jostling for a voice in the postmodern dawn. Debate is now turning to a consideration of how sociocultural forces influence psychological research and practice (e.g. Slee and Murray-Harvey, 2007). Given that the fostering of free inquiry is the very business of universities, John (1998) regarded as ironic the fact that universities train psychologists through a dominant positivist outlook.

Despite such postmodern critiques, the scientist-practitioner model remains a strong force in clinical psychology. In Australia, for example, university clinical psychology course accreditation depends upon espousal of the model. There is also a strong push towards the further development of the scientist-practitioner model, with calls for the further integration of science with practice and greater recognition of the need for contextually relevant practice (Shapiro, 2002). Nancy Pachana and colleagues have noted that 'a significant feature of the scientist-practitioner model is the value attached to the intellectual and scientifically based stance, which protects against an uncritical acceptance of knowledge' (Pachana et al., 2011: 68). In support of their argument, they cite the words of Cal Stoltenberg and Terry Pace that 'if students don't learn to directly apply scientific method in their clinical practice (e.g. identify a problem, gather relevant data, develop hypotheses, and systematically test those hypotheses)' they will have difficulty applying acquired knowledge to their clinical practice (Stoltenberg and Pace, 2007: 196).

In considering the scientist-practitioner model, it is noteworthy that the practice of clinical child psychology did not arise from developmental psychology theory, but from applied work in child mental health and education (child psychiatry and child guidance). An important aspect of the application of the scientist-practitioner model has been the forging of stronger links between developmental theory or knowledge and clinical applications. For example, learning theory, social learning theory and research on parenting styles have all been very influential in the development of parenting programmes. Nancy Murdock (2006) has called for a greater appreciation of the critical role of theory – whether at a 'grand' level or at a middle-theory level – in the integration of science and practice; at its most basic, when a practitioner faces a specific concrete problem, she or he must be able to conceptualize it in more abstract terms in order to connect the issue with a broader body of knowledge. Nevertheless, in clinical practice with children, the influence of diagnostic systems can detract from the application of theory (see Chapter 2). Alternative methods to diagnosis in formulating an understanding of children's behavioural and emotional problems include functional behavioural analysis (derived from learning theory – e.g. Sonuga-Barke, 1994; also refer back to Chapter 8, Box 8.2) and the use of empirically devised classificatory systems, such as those developed by Achenbach and colleagues (Achenbach, 1991, 2001). Some ways in which various theories have underpinned peer-based interventions for children with social and emotional difficulties are outlined in Box 14.2.

BOX 14.2 THEORY INTO PRACTICE: CHILDREN'S SOCIAL SKILLS

Children with social and emotional difficulties often face peer conflict and rejection, which exacerbate their mental health problems. Peer-based interventions that have been developed include anger management, peer tutoring and social skills training (SST) (Kaya *et al.*, 2013). These draw upon a number of theoretical approaches, as described in Chapter 6, including information processing, behaviourism and social learning theory. For example, following an information-processing approach, children are coached or instructed in steps such as interpreting social cues appropriately and selecting suitable responses. Behaviourism may be used, as when children are reinforced for demonstrating appropriate social skills, and social learning theory may be drawn upon, as when adults or other children model appropriate social behaviours for children to imitate. Children might also be taught to give themselves instructions aloud, then to whisper them and finally just to think them, in the manner of Vygotskian theory about private speech (see Chapter 7). Barry Schneider (2000) reported that an important aspect of effective SST is that the children should feel fully engaged with the process and have a sense of ownership concerning the programme; this is in accord with the theoretical move promoted by Albert Bandura, from the more mechanistic versions of learning theory to a consideration of personal agency. However, these methods are not universally useful: in a review of SST with children diagnosed with Asperger's and high functioning autism (HFA), Patricia A. Rao and colleagues (2008) were highly critical of a lack of agreement about the definition of social skills training, and identified significant implementation problems when they were used in the classroom setting, concluding that '. . . despite their widespread clinical use, empirical support for SST programs for children with AS/HFA is minimal at this time' (Rao *et al.*, 2008: 353).

Developmentally appropriate practice (DAP)

DAP was introduced in 1987 and revised in 1997 and 2009 by the National Association for the Education of Young Children (NAEYC) in the USA (Bredekamp, 1987; Bredekamp and Copple, 1997; Copple and Bredekamp, 2009).

> Developmentally appropriate practice is grounded in the research on child development and learning and in the knowledge base regarding educational effectiveness. From this knowledge base, we know a great deal about how children develop and learn at various ages and what approaches and conditions tend to work best for them.
>
> *(Copple and Bredekamp, 2009: 33)*

It was introduced mainly in response to increased academic pressures in early child-hood centres (Kim, 2013), where the term is generally used to refer to children's meaningful engagement in learning activities using 'hands-on' support material; children are seen as actively constructing their own knowledge, in accordance with Piagetian theory (see Chapter 4). Teachers or child care workers in DAP classrooms utilize research on child development and learning, and knowledge of an individual child's strengths, needs and cultural and social background to inform their practice. DAP has been subject to some critical evaluation, in particular concerning the underlying assumption that knowledge and theory generated through research directly informs 'best practice' in working with children. In defending their position, advocates of DAP have noted that, in order to develop a DAP curriculum, it is necessary to address three areas: age appropriateness; individual appropriateness; and social and cultural appropriateness (Aldwinckle, 2001). That is, DAP practice is best understood as being informed by a broad range of theoretical and research insights into child development. It has been criticized as failing to cater well enough for diverse cultural perspectives and allow for capacity to accommodate what constitutes 'ideal practice' from culture to culture and country to country. For example, research indicates that Korean and US pre-service teachers differ with regard to the value they place on the role of music and the aesthetics of music in educating young children (Kim, 2013). At this point it appears that the direction of influence is largely one way and it is difficult to see how knowledge gained from DAP informs theory and research.

Applied developmental science (ADS)

The establishment of ADS began with a meeting of delegates at Fordham University in New York in 1991 (Fisher and Lerner, 1994). In keeping with the melioristic values of developmental psychology, the purpose of ADS is to utilize descriptive and explanatory knowledge about human development in the interests of pursuing interventions of a preventative or enhancing nature. Since its origins, the field has expanded considerably.

Richard M. Lerner and colleagues (2000) identified three characteristics of ADS: it has direct implications for the behaviour and actions of individuals, families and policy-makers; it has a focus on change across the lifespan; and finally, it stresses the utilization of a diversity of research methods to capture information regarding the phenomena under study. Lerner and Celia Fisher (2014) express optimism that ADS can be used to enhance the development and wellbeing of all individuals across the lifespan. In large part they attribute their optimism to recent advances in understanding biology, including evolution and epigenetics, which they believe have significant implications for human health and welfare. This is of importance given that public anxiety about many social problems affecting children and families became apparent as the twentieth century progressed (Lerner *et al.*, 2000), with the health and wellbeing of young people becoming a global concern (Fisher *et al.*, 2013).

ADS and the scientist-practitioner model share some interesting parallels. Both aim to address significant social issues for young people such as the impact of violence, crime and poor mental health, while also raising challenges for the traditional keepers of knowledge – the universities – regarding better understanding of the nature and type of knowledge they are pursuing. Universities are also being asked to address the ability of such knowledge to successfully address the various and immediate problems facing the world. As Fisher and colleagues have noted, 'One of the defining characteristics of applied developmental science (ADS) is that theory, research, and its application in the real world are interwoven, each informing and enriching the other' (Fisher *et al.*, 2013: 54). This perspective has created a burgeoning interest in linking scholarship and outreach (i.e. in fostering 'outreach scholarship'; see Gonzales-Kruger *et al.*, 2000). An important focus is that of contextualized knowledge (Lerner *et al.*, 2000). The idea that all knowledge is related to its context has promoted a change in the typical ontology within current scholarship (i.e. a focus on 'relationism' or 'relationalism') and has helped to advance the view that all existence is contingent on the specifics of the physical and social conditions that exist at a particular moment of history, as acknowledged by theorists such as Klaus Riegel (Overton, 1998; Pepper, 1942; see also Chapter 7). Contrast this view with the idea of the pursuit of knowledge in a context-free, value-free situation. Alvin Toffler critiqued the mechanistic worldview that had dominated understanding of science and scientific inquiry for so long, instead conceiving of science as 'an open system embedded in society and linked to it by very dense feedback loops. It is powerfully influenced by its external environment, and, in a general way, its development is shaped by cultural receptivity to its dominant ideas' (Toffler, 1984: xii–xiii). It follows, then, that knowledge separated from its context is not basic knowledge.

ADS, like DAP, tends to be unidirectional in nature, with theory and research informing fieldwork practice and application, whereas the scientist-practitioner model represents a more bi-directional relationship between theory and practice.

Current challenges in applying developmental psychology

As we observed earlier, in this postmodern era there has been a significant challenge to the idea that science, driven by its own laws, is somehow conducted in isolation from the world around it. Rather, as we discussed in Chapter 9 and elsewhere, it is argued that scientists conceive of and conduct research within a broader social context that determines the nature and fate of their work (Fabes *et al.*, 1994, 2000). R.A. Fabes and colleagues (2000) have described a model of developmental research in terms of Bronfenbrenner's ecological model. The researcher is at the centre of the organizational system, driven to research by interests and motivation. The microsystem includes those who impact directly on the researcher, including family, colleagues and professionals. The exosystem encompasses community interests and funding agencies, while the macrosystem taps into cultural practices and beliefs, including the politics of the particular time and place that impact on the research process. Looked at in this way, the research endeavour is understood to reflect the forces to which it is subject, as it is integrally linked to the context in which it is conducted (see again Box 14.1).

Various writers have observed that researchers are being challenged to apply their knowledge in addressing some of the ills faced by children and adolescents in the world today (Fabes *et al.*, 2000; Fisher *et al.*, 2013; Lerner *et al.*, 2000; McCall and Groark, 2000; Shonkoff, 2000). There is an imperative to use knowledge to inform practice and policy in order to improve the development and delivery of services to address social, economic, environmental and health problems. On the basis of both the scientist-practitioner model and a postmodern perspective, it can be argued that there should be a broader exchange of knowledge, with the opportunity for fieldwork practice to inform research and theory. Indeed, this is already happening in the case of Indigenous psychologies, following from disillusionment with the ability of traditional services to deliver benefits to Indigenous peoples. There is no doubt that the discipline of developmental psychology faces significant challenges if it is to achieve this end more broadly:

> Put simply, a scholar's knowledge must be integrated with the knowledge that exists in communities in order to understand fully the nature of human development and, based on this constructed knowledge, to develop and sustain ethical actions that advance civil society.
>
> *(Lerner et al., 2000: 27)*

The starkness of this challenge is highlighted in the writing of Jack Shonkoff (2000), who has drawn our attention to three related and separate cultures working to address issues facing children and adolescents. In the culture associated with science, practitioners are engaged in theory building, hypothesis testing and research. The culture of policy is a separate world, whose practitioners are driven by political, economic and social imperatives, and where science is just one point of view, often not the most influential. Finally, the 'culture of practice' refers to domains where clinical judgement or professional experience is valued; these may or may not be based on scientific evidence, as we observed earlier, and may not bear any relationship to policy imperatives. There are significant tensions among these three separate but related cultures, neatly summarized as follows:

> Science is focused on what we do not know. Social policy and the delivery of health and human services are focused on what we should do. Scientists are interested in questions. Scholars embrace complexity. Policy makers demand simplicity. Scientists suggest that we stop and reflect. Service providers are expected to act.
>
> *(Shonkoff, 2000: 528)*

The gap between theory, research and practice has been a long-standing concern (Dodge, 2011). As Shonkoff has put it, 'The transmission of knowledge from the academy (science) to the domains of social policy and practice is a formidable task' (Shonkoff, 2000: 101). Nevertheless, universities and researchers are increasingly being challenged to bridge this gap. This imperative is reflected in practical ways through collaborative research and funding involving industry and universities, a move that is also being urged by reductions in public funding for universities in many countries. A number of writers have issued significant warnings against an uncritical acceptance of this link, maintaining that the universities and the academic community have been 'largely silenced as a source of dissent and independent critical thought' (Miller and Philo, 2002: 44). These authors call our attention to the fact that, as the linkage between universities and government and corporate bodies strengthens, such external forces will exert increased control over research findings and the research agenda itself.

In relation to this danger, one of us (PS) is directly involved in a number of university-industry collaborative grants. In the finalization of the contracts keen attention is given to the issue of 'intellectual property'; in particular, the ability of the university researchers to publish their findings (in some cases adverse ones) is an issue. Happily enough, this has been resolved in every instance, but the article by Shonkoff (2000) resonates with this personal experience. We are similarly aware that researchers with young people in the USA have been constrained by some funding bodies not to focus upon findings that would offend the gun lobby. David Miller and Gregory Philo commented that, 'If academics are to give any lead or guidance on such pressing social issues, the universities and research councils must assert their independence from the state' (Miller and Philo, 2002: 45). Corporate sponsorship must not allow corporations to suppress publications or findings, especially where the findings are not supportive of their product or service. George Albee took an editorial stand on this, declaring, 'The integrity of psychological science is based on the academic freedom to explore fundamental questions about the nature of human behaviour, thoughts, feelings, and social process' (Albee, 2002: 161). In the same article, the ability of psychological research to impact on both policy and programme development was alluded to. In this age of globalization and the demise of nation-states, there are some significant issues still to be addressed.

In light of the current emphasis on evidence-based policy and practice, what can be done, in practical terms, to address the challenge of how theory relates to the effective application of developmental science for promoting a civil society (Lerner *et al.*, 2000; Shonkoff and Bales, 2011)? A starting point is the concept of quality assurance, as this will provide the foundation for understanding the notion of 'translational research', which links in turn to the emerging field of implementation science.

Defining quality assurance

The increasing demand for evidence-based practice means an increasing need for more practice-based evidence. Social scientists recognize that developing effective interventions is only the first step towards improving the health and wellbeing of

FIGURE 14.1 A quality assurance process

populations. Transferring evidence-based programmes into real-world settings, consolidating and maintaining them there is a complex process that requires ·dealing effectively with the challenge of programme diffusion (Durlak and DuPre, 2008).

Quality assurance is a widely used term across the physical and behavioural sciences. It has significant implications for the delivery of knowledge-informed practice across the broad field of child development. It is argued here that quality assurance is deeply grounded in the notion that theory gives rise to essential research, which then informs the development of programmes and practice – all designed to enhance the optimal development of children and young people. This process is anything but linear, involving continuous feedback loops. To assist the reader we have developed a simple representation of the process, highlighting its interconnected nature (see Figure 14.1).

As the field of evaluation has matured, the call for quality assurance has strengthened. The development of evaluation standards is one part of a move towards evidence-based practice. The focus on quality is also evident in attempts to define, describe and improve meta-evaluations. Overall, improving, ensuring and monitoring evaluation quality are significant concerns: 'At the strategic level, quality has to do with articulating a vision for clients of what the profession promotes as quality service' (Schwandt, 1990: 187).

Other literature indicates that defining the term 'quality assurance' is not straightforward (Cuttance, 1995). Stephen Murgatroyd and Colin Morgan defined it as 'the determination of standards, appropriate methods and quality requirements by an expert body, accompanied by a process of inspection or evaluation that examines the extent to which practice meets the standards' (Murgatroyd and Morgan, 1993: 45). Their definition captures significant elements pertinent to the current chapter. In summary, quality assurance – with its focus on process – is beginning to be seen as a necessary component of interventions. In particular, the intention of quality assurance is to monitor and assess the practice and process of programme implementation in order to ensure that the effective standards of the programme are being maintained. Quality assurance must be interwoven with child development theory in informing standards for the delivery of optimal child development practices.

Translational research

A not unrelated field of study to that of quality assurance is translational research, which refers to how best to transfer knowledge regarding effective programmes and practice into real-world settings. Steven Sussman and colleagues see it as 'an extended process of how research knowledge that is directly or indirectly relevant to health behavior eventually serves the public' (Sussman *et al.*, 2006: 18). This reflects the fact that the term is most prevalent in the context of the medical sciences, but is increasingly being applied to the behavioural sciences. In no small part, the impetus for the increasing focus on translational research is driven by economic modelling that highlights the cost to society of the burden of health problems such as mental illness. Jeremy Grimshaw and colleagues (2012) have noted that billions of dollars are spent globally in the public and private sectors on biomedical, clinical and health services research, and yet the single biggest concern is the failure to translate research into policy and practice. Shonkoff's (2000) theory of the different cultures of research, policy and practice offers one possible explanation for translation failures. Unfortunately, the resultant evidence–practice gap provides less than optimal delivery of care, services and programmes to children and young people.

Grimshaw and colleagues (2012) have identified five central questions relating to translational research:

1. What should be transferred (e.g. research papers or systematic reviews)?
2. To whom should research knowledge be transferred (e.g. consumers, professionals, policy makers)?
3. Who should transfer research knowledge (e.g. an individual, group or organization)?
4. How should research knowledge be transferred (taking into account the barriers and facilitators)?
5. With what effect should research knowledge be transferred (e.g. to inform or educate)?

At another level the focus is on the barriers that exist to effecting translational research. Shonkoff and Susan Bales have given many reasons why scholars and researchers are reluctant to be part of translational research, including 'differences in opinion about when the science is ready for translation, challenges associated with conveying discrepant findings, concern over maintaining appropriate boundaries between scholarship and advocacy, and a desire to avoid charges from peers of publicity seeking' (Shonkoff and Bales, 2011: 17).

Peter Greenwald and Joseph Cullen (1985) have developed a useful five-phase model for translational research:

1. basic research;
2. methods development;
3. efficacy trials;
4. effectiveness trials;
5. dissemination trials.

We suggest that it is at the level of basic research that theory is important – whether theory drives the research, as in in the standard scientific method, or whether research gives rise to theory, as in some postmodern approaches. Furthermore, as we shall mention later, programme trials can in themselves feed back into theory. Dissemination is the phase concerned with implementation, and it is to this issue that the discussion now turns, focusing on mental health interventions through schools.

Implementation

> If we keep on doing what we have been doing, we will keep on getting what we have been getting.
>
> *(Wandersman et al., 2008: 171)*

Joseph Durlak and Emily DuPre (2008), in reviewing the literature on preventative mental health studies, found that only a minority (5–24 per cent) report on their implementation process. The same authors, in a meta-analytic review, concluded that, 'the magnitude of mean effect sizes [is] at least two to three times higher when programs are carefully implemented and free from serious implementation problems than when these circumstances are not present' (Durlak and DuPre, 2008: 340). More recent research has confirmed that the quality of the implementation of mental health programmes in primary schools impacts significantly on their effectiveness in bringing about change (Dix *et al.*, 2011; Slee *et al.*, 2009, 2012).

It is increasingly recognized that interventions are influenced by ecological factors, such as the socioeconomic and cultural environment in which they are situated (Slee and Murray-Harvey, 2007). These factors affect people's responses to an intervention and ultimately its success. In relation to organizations such as schools, Celene Domitrovich and colleagues (2008) described contextual factors influencing the implementation of new programmes at three levels – policy, school and individual – arguing that these have a significant impact on the quality with which evidence-based interventions are implemented. One way to accommodate the influence of contextual factors is to collect qualitative information. For example, Domitrovich and Mark Greenberg urge that when 'schools consider program adoption, they should talk with other schools already using the program to gain local insights into the practical issues associated with its implementation' (Domitrovich and Greenberg, 2000: 208).

A case study: KidsMatter Primary mental health programme

A consortium based in the Flinders Centre for Student Wellbeing and the Prevention of Violence evaluated the two-year pilot of KidsMatter Primary mental health programme in 100 schools across Australia during 2007 and 2008. KidsMatter (KM) is a primary school mental health promotion, prevention and early intervention initiative developed in collaboration with the Australian government Department of Health and Ageing, the national depression initiative *beyondblue*, the Australian Psychological Society and the Australian Principals Associations Professional Development Council.

The KM initiative was theoretically derived and broadly based on Bronfenbrenner's ecological theory (see Chapter 10). It is underpinned by four components (mental health promotion, parenting support, early intervention and a positive school community) and aims to strengthen those factors that protect students from developing mental health problems. Some of these factors reside within the student (e.g. being socially and emotionally competent), some occur within the school context (e.g. creating a climate in which students feel that they are safe and that they belong) and others reside within the family context (e.g. having supportive and caring relationships with family members). The programme suggests that it is particularly important to strengthen these protective factors in students who are at risk or who are experiencing mental health problems. The initiative is based on the understanding that protective factors can be enhanced, that early signs of mental health problems can be detected in young children and that such problems are more effectively treated at an early age, before they become entrenched. The evaluation examined the impact of KM on student mental health, engagement with and implementation of KM and influences on schools, teachers, parents and students, primarily through questionnaires. These were gathered on four occasions over two years from teachers and on three occasions from parents, for up to 76 students (target age of 10 years) per school. The first survey was completed by the parents and teachers of 4,980 students. Student voice was incorporated through interviews and focus groups, which indicated that students had an improved sense of self-efficacy and self-management, both at school and at home. They reported becoming empowered to express their feelings, problem-solve and generate alternative ways of coping when situations were difficult or confronting.

KM impacted upon schools in multiple ways, and was associated with a systematic pattern of positive change to schools, teachers, parents and students (Slee *et al.*, 2009). These included changes associated with school culture and approaches to mental health difficulties, as well as changes that served to strengthen protective factors within the school, family and child. Importantly, KM was associated with significant improvements in measured mental health, especially for those with higher existing levels of mental health difficulties, consistent with earlier research reported by Durlak and colleagues (2011).

The implementation and rollout of KM Primary on a national basis

As a result of the positive evaluation of KM (Slee *et al.*, 2009) and the growing recognition of the importance of wellbeing as an essential component of students' positive development, socially, emotionally and academically, the Australian government allocated considerable federal funding towards the national rollout (Graetz, 2009). The extension of KM challenged the way it was delivered in schools after the pilot study, particularly with the training of external staff to deliver it to schools. In upscaling from 100 to 1,700 schools by 2017, challenges arose related to quality assurance and transference of the programme. Slee and colleagues (2011) undertook a review of the international literature to develop a quality assurance framework for the national rollout (see Figure 14.2). Durlak and DuPre's informative (2008) review concluded that there are eight different aspects of implementation, which could be considered as part of a quality assurance system.

1. *Fidelity:* the extent to which the innovation corresponds to the originally intended programme (adherence, compliance, integrity, faithful replication).
2. *Dosage:* how much of the original programme has been delivered (quantity, intervention strength).
3. *Quality:* how well different programme components have been conducted (are the main programme elements delivered clearly and correctly?).
4. *Participant responsiveness:* the degree to which the programme stimulates the interest or holds the attention of participants (e.g. are staff attentive during professional learning?).

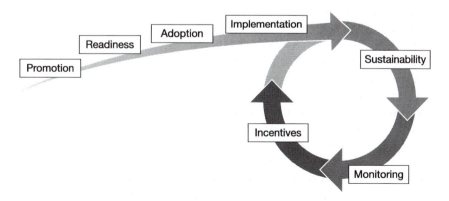

FIGURE 14.2 The seven-step model of KidsMatter quality assurance (adapted from Slee *et al.*, 2011)

5. *Programme differentiation:* the extent to which the programme's theory and practices can be distinguished from other programmes (programme uniqueness).
6. *Control monitoring:* involves comparing differences to non-participating schools and their outcomes.
7. *Programme reach:* (participation rates, programme scope) refers to the rate of involvement and representativeness of programme participants.
8. *Adaptation:* refers to changes made to the original programme during implementation (programme modification, reinvention).

As argued by Slee and colleagues (2011) and Helen Askell-Williams and colleagues (2013), the quality assurance concept incorporates a number of stages and feedback loops. These are designed to ensure that the introduction of any programme in complex organizations such as schools takes into account a range of factors, including the uptake, adoption, implementation and ongoing review of the programme, as described in more detail here.

1. *Promotion:* how well is information about the existence and value of the programme promoted to new schools and the broader service community (e.g. an email or letter introducing the programme)?
2. *Readiness:* school readiness to undertake the initiative is a significant step; it refers to the extent to which the school recognizes that there is a problem to be addressed, is willing to address it and, importantly, has the capacity to do so.
3. *Adoption:* a key person such as the school principal may take the initiative to drive the adoption of an intervention; this may be undertaken through a whole-school decision-making process.
4. *Implementation:* how well the programme is conducted during the start-up period; the initiative must meet the local needs of the community in which the intervention is taking place and must be responsive to local conditions and local needs.
5. *Sustainability:* this refers to whether fidelity, dosage and programme quality are maintained over time across all programme components in the manner intended.
6. *Monitoring:* central to quality assurance, an accurate monitoring and feedback system should be integrated into the operation of the programme.
7. *Incentive:* infrastructure that provides incentives or recognition to schools and individuals within schools for achieving implementation milestones is important.

Domitrovich and colleagues (2008) found that, outside highly controlled research studies, prevention programmes are not well implemented in schools, given the complexity of the school environments in which they are delivered. Lower-quality implementation leads to poorer programme effectiveness (Askell-Williams *et al.*, 2013; Dix *et al.*, 2011). The fidelity of an implementation, broadly described as whether a programme was delivered in a comparable manner to all participants true to its underlying theory, is a significant, if under-researched, component of intervention programmes, and only a minority of intervention studies have attended to it. Traditionally, research has paid more attention to other key methodological issues (such as experimental design, reliability of measurements and statistical power), with the assumption that the participants received the intervention(s) they were supposed to receive.

In this case study, consideration was given to the quality of the implementation assessed in relation to the key parameters of 'fidelity', 'dosage' and 'quality of delivery'. A series of indicators was collated from all the various data sources in the evaluation to create an innovative 'Implementation Index' (Slee *et al.*, 2009), suitable for classifying schools according to the quality of their implementation. The interest lay in identifying the particular features of schools categorized into the 'performing well group', in order to report indicators of exemplary practice. In order to identify schools as being 'low' or 'high' implementers, a framework was developed based on Domitrovich and colleagues' (2008) recommendations to ensure that aspects of fidelity, dosage and quality of delivery were gauged by those implementing the intervention and those providing the support (Slee *et al.*, 2009). Evaluations of the implementation index clearly demonstrated its utility, highlighting links between the quality of the implementation and outcomes associated with the level of change in mental health functioning of the students (Askell-Williams *et al.*, 2013; Dix *et al.*, 2011).

Overall, in describing this case study of a wellbeing programme implemented in Australian schools, it has been argued that such programmes cannot be successfully implemented in complex organizational settings such as schools without a continuous cycle of quality assurance designed to ensure the sustainability of the programme.

Can programme evaluation inform theory?

> [E]valuations of parenting programmes, if well conducted, can serve a dual aim: (1) to enhance children's and family functioning; and (2) to elucidate important developmental processes and mechanisms. The first aim is immediately obvious, but the second aim tends to get somewhat 'forgotten'.
>
> *(Deković* et al., *2011: 64)*

The basic question one asks when evaluating any programme is, 'Does it work?' (Deković *et al.*, 2011). However, as the above quote suggests, so much more can be achieved if we also ask, 'Why does it work?' Taking parenting programmes as an example, Maja Deković and colleagues emphasise the value of programme evaluations for testing theory. Often it is not clear what the crucial aspects of a complex programme are, though numbers might be suggested by previous theory. Initially, the programme must be both theory-based and well implemented, or its value for theory-testing is useless. Theory-testing can be done by measuring process variables and assessing their mediating role in determining outcomes. Preferably, one mediator would be evaluated against another. For example, if children's emotional or behavioural problems improve after a parenting programme, is it because parents have become less harsh, more supportive, more confident or less stressed? By designing programmes in ways that enable such questions to be answered, theory is refined and future programmes can be tailored better. Hence, theory, research and practice are intimately entwined and mutually informative.

Conclusions

We began this book with a consideration of ways of knowing children, as beings in philosophical, historical and cultural contexts. We then traced various theoretical frameworks that offer a range of ways of understanding children's development. In this final chapter we returned to issues of knowledge: how it is created and used by various parties with an interest in promoting children's wellbeing. We have seen how the scientist-practitioner model, developmentally appropriate practice and applied developmental science variously act as guides for attempting to put theoretical knowledge into practice. We have also seen that practice can feed back into theory. However, from a more postmodern perspective, we have also seen how differences in professional cultures can create a barrier to effective translation of theory and research into policy and practice with children, within the complexities of the real world.

It has been suggested that developmental research will increasingly be judged in terms of new kinds of validity concerned with pragmatics and social relevance (McCall and Groark, 2000) and, in that spirit, we have examined the issue of quality assurance in relation to how theory and research can be transformed into effective programmes and policy that advance the health and wellbeing of young people. In view of the billions of dollars spent worldwide in the field of child development, there is a growing demand to see how the knowledge created is translated into practice. From a consumer's perspective the demand is for standards that inform the quality of evidence-based practice. Through the KidsMatter case study, we have illustrated some principles of translational research, implementation science and quality assurance, whereby a theoretically based programme is applied to the real world as effectively as possible. In the medical sciences the 'bench to bedside' debate has a long and rich history, but in the behavioural sciences such discussions are just now emerging in the literature and are yet to be widely applied in the consideration and design of research programmes.

We close with this eloquent reflection on the links between theory and practice by systems researchers Peter Checkland and Jim Scholes:

> Theory which is not tested out in practice is sterile. Equally, practice which is not reflective about the ideas upon which it is based will abandon the chance to learn its way steadily to better ways of taking action. Thus, theory must be tested out in practice; and practice is the best source of theory. In the best possible situation the two create each other in a cyclic process in which neither is dominant but each is the source of the other.
>
> *(Checkland and Scholes, 1990: xiv)*

References

Achenbach, T.M. 1991. Manual for the child behavior checklist. Vermont, CT: Dept of Psychiatry, University of Vermont, 4–18.

Achenbach, T.M. 2001. Challenges and benefits of assessment, diagnosis, and taxonomy for clinical practice and research. *Australian and New Zealand Journal of Psychiatry*. 35: 263–71.

Albee, G.W. 2002. Exploring a controversy. *American Psychologist*. 57: 161–4.

Aldwinckle, M. 2001. The DAP debate: are we throwing the baby out with the bath water? *Australian Journal of Early Childhood*. 26: 36–9.

Askell-Williams, H., Slee, P. and van Deur, P. 2013. Social and emotional wellbeing programs: the nexus between sustainability and quality assurance. *The Psychology of Education Review*. 37 (2): 48–56.

Barnett, R. 2000. University knowledge in an age of supercomplexity. *Higher Education*. 40 (4): 409–22.

Bredekamp, S. (ed.). 1987. *Developmentally appropriate practice in early childhood programs serving children from birth through age 8*. Washington, DC: National Association for the Education of Young Children.

Bredekamp, S. and Copple, C. (eds). 1997. *Developmentally appropriate practice in early childhood*. Washington, DC: National Association for the Education of Young Children.

Carr, A. 2009. The effectiveness of family therapy and systemic interventions for child-focused problems. *Journal of Family Therapy*. 31: 3–45.

Checkland, P. and Scholes, J. 1990. *Soft systems methodology in action*. Chichester: Wiley.

Copple, C. and Bredekamp, S. (eds). 2009. *Developmentally appropriate practice in early childhood programs*. Washington, DC: National Association for the Education of Young Children.

Cotton, P. 1998. The framing of knowledge and practice in psychology: a response to John. *Australian Psychologist*. 33: 31–8.

Council of Australian Governments. 2012a. National action plan on mental health 2006–2011. COAG, Commonwealth of Australia. Available at: www.health.gov.au/coagmentalhealth. Accessed 10 April 2013.

Council of Australian Governments. 2012b. Roadmap for National Mental Health Reform (2012–2022). COAG, Commonwealth of Australia. Available at: www.coag.gov.au/node/482. Accessed 10 April 2013.

Cuttance, P. 1995. Quality assurance and quality management in education systems. In C. Evers and J. Chapman (eds), *Educational administration: an Australian perspective*. St Leonards: Allen and Unwin, 296–316.

Deković, M., Stolz, S., Schuiringa, H., Manders, W. and Asscher, J.J. 2011. Testing theories through evaluation research: conceptual and methodological issues embedded in evaluations of parenting programmes. *European Journal of Developmental Psychology*. 9 (1): 61–74.

Dix, K.L., Slee, P.T., Lawson, M.J. and Keeves, J.P. 2011. Implementation quality of whole-school mental health promotion and students' academic performance. *Child and Adolescent Mental Health*. 17 (1): 45–51.

Dodge, K. 2011. Context matters in child and family policy. *Child Development*. 82: 433–42.

Domitrovich, C.E. and Greenberg, M.T. 2000. The study of implementation: current findings from effective programs that prevent mental disorders in school-aged children. *Journal of Educational and Psychological Consultation*. 11(2): 193–221.

Domitrovich, C.E., Bradshaw, C.P., Poduska, J.M., Hoagwood, K., Buckley, J.A., Olin, S. and Ialongo, N.S. 2008. Maximising the implementation quality of evidence-based preventive interventions in schools. A conceptual framework. *Advances in School Mental Health Promotion*. 1 (3): 6–28.

Durlak, J.A. and DuPre, E.P. 2008. Implementation matters: a review of research on the influence of implementation on program outcomes and factors affecting implementation. *American Journal of Community Psychology*. 41: 327–50.

Durlak, J.A., Weisberg, R.P., Dymnicki, A.B., Taylor, R.D. and Schellinger, K.B. 2011. The impact of enhancing students' social and emotional learning: a meta-analysis of school-based universal interventions. *Child Development*. 82: 405–32.

Fabes, R.A., Martin, C.L. and Smith, M.C. 1994. Further perspectives on child development research: a reconsideration and recall. *Journal of Family and Consumer Sciences*. 23: 42–54.

Fabes, R.A., Martin, C.L., Hanish, L.D. and Updegraff, K.A. 2000. Criteria for evaluating the significance of developmental research in the twenty-first century: force and counterforce. *Child Development*. 71: 212–21.

Fisher, C.B. and Lerner, R.M. 1994. Foundations of applied developmental psychology. In C.B. Fisher and R.M. Lerner (eds), *Applied developmental psychology*. New York: McGraw-Hill, 2–20.

Fisher C.B., Busch-Rossnagel, N.A., Jopp, D.S. and Brown, J.L. 2013. Applied developmental science, social justice, and socio-political well-being. *Applied Developmental Science*. 16 (1): 54–64.

Gelso, C.J. 2006. On the making of a scientist-practitioner model: a theory of research training in professional psychology. *Training & Education in Professional Psychology*. 1: 3–16.

Gibbons, M., Limoges, C., Nowotny, H., Schwartzman, S., Scott, P. and Trow, M. 1994. *The new production of knowledge: the dynamics of science and research in contemporary societies*. Thousand Oaks, CA: Sage.

Gokulsing, K. and DaCosta, C. 1997. *University knowledges as the goal of university education*. Lampeter: Edwin Mullen.

Gonzales-Kruger, G., Zamboanga, B.L., Carlo, G., Raffeli, M., Carranza, M., Hansen, D.J., Cantarero, R. and Gajardo, J. 2000. The Latino Research Initiative: a multidisciplinary and collaborative community-university outreach and scholarship model. *Great Plains Research*. 10: 359–85.

Graetz, B. 2009. Mental health reality in our primary schools. *The Advertiser Newspaper*. 13 October.

Greenwald, P. and Cullen, J. 1985. The new emphasis in cancer control. *Journal of the National Cancer Institute*. 74 (3): 543–51.

Grimshaw, J.M., Martin, P., Eccles, M.P., Lavis, J.N., Hill, S.J. and Squires, J.E. 2012. Translation of research findings. *Implementation Science*. 7: 2–17.

Heins, H. and Ritchie, K. 1988. *Beating Sneaky Poo*. Adelaide: Dulwich Centre. Available at: www.dulwichcentre.com.au/beating-sneaky-poo-2.pdf. Accessed 27 June 2014.

Hessels, L.K. and van Lente, H. 2008. Re-thinking new knowledge production: a literature review and a research agenda. *Research Policy*. 37: 740–60.

John, I.D. 1994. Constructing knowledge of psychological knowledge: towards an epistemology for psychological practice. *Australian Psychologist*. 2: 174–7.

John, I.D. 1998. The scientist-practitioner model: a critical examination. *Australian Psychologist*. 33: 24–30.

Kaya, C., Blake, J. and Chan, F. 2013. Peer-mediated interventions with elementary and secondary school students with emotional and behavioural disorders: a literature review. *Journal of Research in Special Educational Needs*. 1: 1–9.

Kim, H.K. 2013. A comparison of early childhood preservice teachers' beliefs about music and developmentally appropriate practice between South Korea and the US. *Australasian Journal of Early Childhood*. 38 (2): 122–8.

Lerner, R.M. and Fisher, C. 2014. Evolution, epigenetics, and application in developmental science. *Applied Developmental Science*. 17 (4): 169–73.

Lerner R.M., Fisher, C.B. and Weinberg, R.A. 2000. Toward a science for and of the people: promoting civil society through the application of developmental science. *Child Development*. 71: 11–20.

Lewis, M.D. 2000. The promise of dynamic systems approaches for an integrated account of human development. *Child Development*. 71 (1): 36–43.

Locke, J. 1690/1947. *An essay concerning human understanding*. London: Tegg & Son.

McCall, R.B. and Groark, C. 2000. The future of applied child development research and public policy. *Child Development*. 71: 197–204.

McInerney, D.M. 2006. *Developmental psychology for teachers*. Crows Nest, NSW: Allen & Unwin.

Miller, D. and Philo, G. 2002. Silencing dissent in academia. The commercialisation of science. *The Psychologist*. 15: 44–6.

Murdock, N.L. 2006. On science-practice integration in everyday life: a plea for theory. *The Counselling Psychologist*. 34: 548–69.

Murgatroyd, S. and Morgan, C. 1993. *Total quality management and the school*. Philadelphia, PA: Open University Press.

Nuthall, G. 2000. The anatomy of memory in the classroom: understanding how students acquire memory processes from classroom activities in science and social studies units. *American Educational Research Journal*. 37: 247–304.

Overton, W.F. 1998. Developmental psychology: philosophy, concepts, and methodology. In R.M. Lerner (ed.), *Handbook of child psychology. Theoretical models of human development*. Fifth edn, Vol. 1. New York: Wiley, 107–89.

Pachana, N.A., Soffronoff, K., Scott, T. and Helmes, E. 2011. Attainment of competencies in clinical psychology training: ways forward in the Australian context. *Australian Psychologist*. 46: 67–76.

Pepper, S. 1942. *World hypotheses: a study of evidence*. Berkeley, CA: University of California Press.

Raimy, V. 1950. *Training in clinical psychology*. Englewood Cliffs, NJ: Prentice Hall.

Rao, P.A., Beidel, D.C. and Murray, M.J. 2008. Social skills interventions for children with Asperger's syndrome or high-functioning autism: a review and recommendations. *Journal of Autism and Developmental Disorders*. 38 (2): 353–61.

Schneider, B.H. 2000. *Friends and enemies: peer relations in childhood*. London: Arnold.

Schwandt, T.R. 1990. Path to inquiry in the social disciplines: scientific, constructivist and critical theory methodologies. In E.G. Guba (ed.), *The paradigm dialog*. London: Sage, 258–76.

Shapiro, D. 2002. Renewing the scientist-practitioner model. *The Psychologist*. 15: 232–4.

Shonkoff, J.P. 2000. Science, policy, and practice: three cultures in search of a shared mission. *Child Development*. 71: 181–7.

Shonkoff, J.P. and Bales, S.N. 2011. Science does not speak for itself: translating child development research for the public and its policymakers. *Child Development*. 82 (1): 17–32.

Shute, R.H. 2012. Promoting mental health through schools: is this field of development an evidence-based practice? *The Psychologist*. 25 (10): 752–5.

Slee, P.T. and Murray-Harvey, R. 2007. Disadvantaged children's physical, developmental and behavioural health problems in an urban environment. *Journal of Social Services Research*. 33: 57–69.

Slee, P.T., Murray-Harvey, R., Dix, K. and van Deur, P. 2011. Kidsmatter Quality Assurance System for KidsMatter Primary. A scoping paper. Flinders University, Adelaide.

Slee, P.T., Murray-Harvey, R., Dix, K.L., Skrzypiec, G., Askell-Williams, H., Lawson, M.J. and Krieg, S. 2012. KidsMatter Early Childhood evaluation. Available at: www.kidsmatter.edu.au. Accessed 18 May 2013.

Slee, P.T., Lawson, M.J., Russell, A., Askell-Williams, H., Dix, K.L., Owens, L., Skrzypiec, G. and Spears, B. 2009. KidsMatter Primary Evaluation Final Report. KidsMatter and the Centre for Analysis of Educational Futures. Available at: www.kidsmatter.edu.au. Accessed 18 May 2013.

Sloan, T.S. 1990. Psychology for the Third World? *Journal of Social Issues*. 46 (3): 1–20.

Sonuga-Barke, E.J.S. 1994. Annotation: on dysfunction and function in psychological theories of childhood disorder. *Journal of Child Psychology and Psychiatry*. 35: 801–5.

Stehr, N. 1994. *Knowledge societies*. London: Sage.

Stoltenberg, C.D. and Pace, T.M. 2007. The scientist–practitioner model: now more than ever. *Journal of Contemporary Psychotherapy*. 37: 195–203.

Sussman, S., Valente, T.W., Rohrbach, S., Skara, S. and Pentz, M.A. 2006. Translation in the health professions converting science into action. *Evaluation and the Health Professions*. 29: 17–32.

Teo, T. 1997. Developmental psychology and the relevance of a critical metatheoretical reflection. *Human Development*. 40: 195–210.

Tierney, W.G. 2001. The autonomy of knowledge and the decline of the subject: postmodernism and the reformulation of the university. *Higher Education*. 41: 353–72.

Toffler, A. 1984. *Future shock*. London: Random House.

Valentine, E. 1998. Out of the margins. *The Psychologist*. 11 (4): 167–8.

Wandersman, A., Duffy, J., Flaspoler, P., Noonan, R., Lubell, K., Stillman, L., Blachman, M., Dunville, R. and Saul, J. 2008. Bridging the gap between prevention research and practice: the interactive systems framework for dissemination and implementation. *American Journal of Community Psychology*. 41: 171–81.

STUDENT RESOURCES

This part of the book provides an array of supplementary materials for both students and lecturers to accompany the new edition of *Child Development: Theories and Critical Perspectives*. These include:

* a list of historical milestones relevant for developmental psychology;
* discussion questions, activities and relevant websites for each chapter.

In addition, there is a separate glossary on p. 280.

Some historical milestones relevant for developmental psychology

Nineteenth century

Charles Darwin publishes *On the Origin of Species* (1859)
Wundt opens first experimental psychology laboratory (1879)
William James publishes *Principles of Psychology* (1890)
Karl Pearson develops statistical theory of correlation (1896)
James McKeen Cattell influential in development of mental tests (1896)
Edward Thorndike performs experiments on animal learning (1898)
Edward B. Titchener establishes 'structuralism' (1890s)

Early twentieth century

Sigmund Freud presents his ideas on psychoanalysis (1900)
Charles Spearman proposes his theory of intelligence (1904)
G. Stanley Hall publishes *Adolescence* (1905)

Alfred Binet and Theodore Simon devise first intelligence test for children (1905)
Ivan Pavlov publishes his findings on classical conditioning (1906)
Catherine Helen Spence writes history of child care in South Australia (1907)
John Dewey publishes his ideas on problem-solving (1910)
William Stern presents his concept of IQ (1911)
Gestalt psychology presented by Max Wertheimer (1912)
John B. Watson publishes on behaviourism (1913)
Binet intelligence test revised as Stanford–Binet by Lewis M. Terman (1916)
Wolfgang Köhler publishes studies on problem-solving by apes (1917)
John B. Watson and Rosalie Rayner publish their study on 'Little Albert' (1920)
Jean Piaget publishes his theory of language and thought in children (1926)
Ivan Pavlov's work on the conditioned reflex is published in English (1927)
Margaret Mead publishes *Coming of Age in Samoa* (1928)
Edward C. Tolman presents his ideas on purposive behaviourism (1929)
Mary Cover Jones lays foundations for behaviour therapy (1920s)
Melanie Klein is influential in the object relations school (1920s)
Lev Vygotsky presents sociocultural theory (1930)
Louis Leon Thurstone develops factor analysis (1935)
B.F. Skinner publishes on operant conditioning in *The Behaviour of Organisms* (1938)
Kathryn Bridges and Charlotte Bühler (independently) work on infant emotion
    (1930s)
Sergei Rubinstein writes on the mind–body question (1940)
Steven Pepper writes on metaphors for developmental psychology (1942)
Heinz Werner elaborates the orthogenetic principle (1948)
Family therapy is developed (1940s)

Later twentieth century

Erik Erikson publishes *Childhood and Society* (1950)
The scientist-practitioner model is formulated (1950)
Konrad Lorenz publishes on ethology (1952)
Diagnostic and Statistical Manual of Mental Disorders (*DSM*) is first published (1952)
John Bowlby publishes *Child Care and the Growth of Love* (1953)
Robert J. Havighurst writes about developmental tasks (1953)
George Kelly publishes on personal construct theory (1955)
'Birth' of artifical intelligence (1956)
James and Eleanor J. Gibson establish work on infant perception and 'affordance'
    (1950s)
Philippe Ariès writes about views of childhood (1962)
Lev Vygotsky's *Thought and Language* is translated into English (1962)
Abraham Maslow publishes on self-actualization (1962)
Alexander Luria establishes the field of neuropsychology (1962)
Karl Popper proposes that 'falsification' is central to science (1963)
Virginia Satir publishes on family therapy (1964)

Imre Lakatos presents his ideas on the philosophy of science (1965)

Ulric Neisser establishes cognitive psychology (1967)

Ludwig von Bertalanffy applies general systems theory to biology (1968)

Lawrence Kohlberg applies Jean Piaget's theory to moral development (1960s)

Nicholas Blurton Jones promotes the ethological study of children (1972)

Michael Rutter critiques the notion of maternal deprivation (1972)

Eleanor E. Maccoby and Carol N. Jacklin publish *The Psychology of Sex Differences* (1974)

Robert Hinde publishes on biological bases of behaviour (1974)

Frederick G. Humphrey provides a feminist critique of family therapy (1975)

E.O. Wilson establishes sociobiology (1975)

Richard Dawkins publishes *The Selfish Gene* (1976)

Albert Bandura publishes on social learning theory (1977)

Notion of child–environment 'goodness-of-fit' introduced (1977)

The biopsychosocial perspective on health is introduced (1977)

Margaret Donaldson publishes *Children's Minds* (1978)

The theory of mind is introduced (1978)

Richard Q. Bell proposes that socialization is two-way process (1978)

Gregory Bateson publishes on systems theory (1979)

Urie Bronfenbrenner founds ecological systems theory (1979)

Mary Ainsworth develops the 'Strange Situation' (1970s)

Klaus Riegel develops transactional theory (1970s)

The notion of the 'competent infant' is promoted (1970s)

Paul B. Baltes founds Centre for Lifespan Psychology in Berlin (1981)

Carol Gilligan's *In a Different Voice* published (1982)

Humberto Maturana and colleagues publish ideas on constructivism (1988)

Adoption by United Nations of Convention on the Rights of the Child (1989)

Connectionism emerges (1980s)

Esther Thelen and Linda B. Smith publish on dynamic systems (1994)

Timothy Teo provides a postmodern critique on the philosophy of knowledge (1997)

The new sociology of childhood (NSC) takes off (mid-1990s)

Increasing fragmentation of developmental psychology (1990s)

Calls for theoretical integration (1990s)

Postmodern/critical perspectives on psychology are offered (1990s)

Behaviour genetics gains currency (1990s)

Critical state and complex systems theories gain momentum (1990s)

Evolutionary developmental psychology gains increasing prominence (1990s)

Indigenous psychology begins to gain recognition (2000)

Twenty-first century

The human genome sequence is announced (2003)

Epigenetics research increases (2000s)

Children's voices, child-centred and collaborative research is advocated (2000s)
Translational research is highlighted (2011)
Greater focus on change processes and plasticity (2012)
Willis Overton highlights relationalism (2013)

Discussion questions, activities and selected websites*

*All websites cited in this section were last accessed 27 January 2015.

Chapter 1

1. Consider the various 'views' of children in Figure 1.1; identify and discuss their key distinguishing features.
2. Identify the significant characteristics of the terms 'development', 'maturation' and 'growth', distinguishing between them.

Activities

1. Form small groups. Each group draws an outline of a child on a large sheet of paper, approximately 90 cm x 30 cm. For 10–15 minutes, members write on the outline words that they associate with the word 'child'. Each person then explains the words he or she has contributed and the views they are based on.
2. In this chapter we suggested readers consider the following questions throughout the text. Workshop the questions in small groups:
   • How do children change as they develop?
   • What factors influence the developmental changes?
   • What individual differences exist in growth and development?

Websites

Australian Institute of Family Studies: www.aifs.gov.au.
Child/adolescent psychological and educational resources: www.caper.com.au.
Child Research Net (CRN): www.childresearch.net/.
Philosophy of childhood: http://plato.stanford.edu/entries/childhood/.

Chapter 2

1. Is evolutionary psychology just a politically correct version of sociobiology?
2. How far has Darwin influenced theorizing about children's development?

Activity

Find some Internet or newspaper articles about ADHD. How far do they reflect a biological perspective?

Websites

Evolutionary developmental psychology: www.epjournal.net/articles/an-introduction-to-evolutionary-developmental-psychology/.

Epigenetics: www.epigenome.eu/en/1,1,0.

Adolescent brain development: www.ted.com/talks/sarah_jayne_blakemore_the_mysterious_workings_of_the_adolescent_brain.

Chapter 3

1. Identify the characteristics of the root metaphor of 'organicism' and discuss.
2. Debate the usefulness or otherwise of 'stages' in describing development.

Activity

Find a policy document (such as a government document) related to children's health or education. Discuss how far 'stages' of development are implicitly or explicitly used as a guiding framework. Present your findings in class.

Website

Child Development Institute: http://childdevelopmentinfo.com/ages-stages/.

Chapter 4

1. After reading Chapters 4 and 7, review the videos below describing Jean Piaget's and Lev Vygotsky's theories, and compare and contrast the views of the developing child that they provide.
2. Research and present the identifying features of Jerome Bruner's constructivist understanding of development.

Activity

Search the library shelves or the Internet for journal reviews regarding the nature of the child as an 'active participant' in development. What evidence can you find that contemporary theories of development consider the child from this perspective?

Websites

Piaget: www.youtube.com/watch?v=TRF27F2bn-A.

Vygotsky: www.youtube.com/watch?v=0BX2ynEqLL4.

Transcript of interview with Eleanor Maccoby: www.srcd.org/sites/default/files/documents/maccoby_eleanor_interview.pdf.

Theory of mind in different cultures: www.hindawi.com/journals/cdr/2014/893492/.

Chapter 5

1. Can attachment theory be supported by empirical evidence?
2. What are the advantages and disadvantages of the Strange Situation as a measure of attachment?

Activity

Explore and discuss the status afforded to Freudian theory in some standard child development textbooks.

Websites

Object relations therapy: www.psychotherapy.net/interview/otto-kernberg.
Freud's enduring contributions: www.yorku.ca/dcarveth/freudtoday.
Beyond attachment: www.psychologytoday.com/blog/freedom-learn/201307/beyond-attachment-parents-children-need-community.

Chapter 6

1. To improve your understanding of the contemporary relevance of Watson's work, take and critically examine an article utilizing a behavioural framework in terms of the challenge that it is not really a theory of development.
2. Identify the key elements of Albert Bandura's social learning theory, as reflected in his review article 'Social cognitive theory: an agentic perspective' (2001), *Annual Review of Psychology* (52: 1–26).

Activity

Draw up a table comparing and contrasting the theories of Ivan Pavlov, John Watson, B.F. Skinner and Albert Bandura.

Websites

Social cognitive theory: www.education.com/reference/article/social-cognitive-theory/.
Self-efficacy: http://p20motivationlab.org.
Mary Cover Jones: www.feministvoices.com/mary-cover-jones/.

Chapter 7

1. Discuss the notion of constitutive relationalism. Explain how the 'Rubin vase' and Overton's 'hands' drawing illustrate this (the latter is shown in several of Overton's articles).
2. How do Lev Vygotsky's and Sergei Rubinstein's theories differ?

Activity

Observe parents and children engaged in activities together. Look for examples of scaffolding.

Websites

Lev Vygotsky: http://home.mira.net/~andy/works/soviet-psychology.htm.
Scaffolding: www.education.com/reference/article/scaffolding/.

Chapter 8

1. Corey A. Kahlbaugh has argued that 'contextualism is based on assumptions fundamentally distinct from those of the dialectical (organismic) paradigm' (Kahlbaugh, 1989: 4). Debate this argument.
2. Identify the key features of Urie Bronfenbrenner's ideas regarding human development, comparing and contrasting them to the ideas encompassed in lifespan development theory.

Activity

Examine the 'Milestones' in the previous section, identifying the main philosophical, cultural and historical influences shaping recent understandings in developmental theory.

Websites

William James: http://video.about.com/psychology/Profile-of-William-James.htm.
John Dewey: www.biography.com/people/john-dewey-9273497#awesm=~oIeq 1sfwyNpsZu.
Margaret Mead: www.interculturalstudies.org/Mead/biography.html.
Functionalism in therapy: http://contextualscience.org/functional_contextualism_0.

Chapter 9

1. Research and discuss the notion of 'cultural evolution'.
2. How might 'folk wisdom' differentially influence the development of a Chinese child and one from the USA?

Activity

Examine a standard textbook on child development. How far does it reflect a western perspective on children's development?

Websites

Mothering Japanese newborns: www.theatlantic.com/health/archive/2013/05/the-lasting-influence-of-mother-infant-attachment/275428/.

Memes (cultural evolution): www.ted.com/talks/susan_blackmore_on_memes_and_temes.

Human development in Africa: www.thehdrc.org/index.html.

Research with Indigenous communities: http://cds.web.unc.edu/files/2012/12/Markstrom_Allen_Mohatt_2012.pdf.

Chapter 10

1. Systems thinking has been informed by a long and distinguished group of philosophers, writers and scientists. Provide an overview of the various influences and their particular contributions to the metatheory of systems thinking.
2. Dynamic systems theory (DST) has emerged as a force in child development theory. Describe its particular focus and identifying features.

Activities

1. Select a research paper from a child development journal or journal of family therapy and identify, critique and present in class the key elements that distinguish its basis in systems theory.
2. Divide into small groups. Each group draws a large diagram of Urie Bronfenbrenner's ecological systems model and chooses a specific situation: an eight-year-old child diagnosed with diabetes; a teenager offered a cigarette for the first time by a friend; a child who migrates with his or her family to a new country. Add to the diagram as many specific examples as you can of the various aspects of the subsystems relevant for the child's development.

Websites

Outline of Bronfenbrenner's theory: www.youtube.com/watch?v=me7103oIE-g.

Dynamic Systems Theory: http://psysc613.wikispaces.com/Dynamic+Systems+Theory.

Dynamic systems theory and cerebral palsy: www.canchild.ca/en/canchildresources/dynamic_systems_theory.asp.

Chapter 11

1. Are women and girls morally underdeveloped compared with men and boys?
2. Research and discuss how feminism inspired notions of 'masculinities'.

Activity

Watch a children's cartoon programme on television and the commercials associated with it. Observe any differences between the portrayal of boys and girls (e.g. activities, dress, values, music, toys, voice overs).

Websites

Freud and femininity: http://scandalousthoughts.wordpress.com/2010/02/18/some-notes-of-my-reading-on-freuds-femininity/.

Pinkstinks: www.pinkstinks.co.uk/.

One teenage girl's view of feminism: www.ted.com/talks/tavi_gevinson_a_teen_just_trying_to_figure_it_out#t-36147.

Chapter 12

1. Discuss the notion of 'affordance' with respect to young people's use of information technologies.
2. What challenges does the notion of children's 'being' (as compared with 'becoming') pose for developmental theorizing?

Activity

Discuss how 'photovoice' could be used to examine the views of children (in a culture other than your own) about children's rights.

Websites

A South Sudanese child speaks: www.voicesofyouth.org/en/posts/all-i-want-is-peace---a-child-s-testimony-from-south-sudan.

Children's voices: www.everychild.sa.gov.au/docs/Childrens_Voices_booklet_web.pdf.

Photovoice: http://ctb.ku.edu/en/table-of-contents/assessment/assessing-community-needs-and-resources/photovoice/main (then click on Section 20 in a search).

Chapter 13

1. Of the various theoretical schools, which do you find most compelling, and why?
2. What holds the most promise as an integrative theory of development?

Activity

Consider the possible reactions to postmodern theories discussed by J. A. Meacham (Box 13.2). In groups, draw up checklists of advantages and disadvantages of each kind of response.

Websites

Integrative potential of evolutionary psychology: www.epjournal.net/wp-content/uploads/EP08284296.pdf.
Multisystemic therapy for troubled youth: http://mstservices.com/.

Chapter 14

1. Identify the characteristics of the 'scientist-practitioner' model, 'developmentally appropriate practice' and 'applied developmental science' and compare how they each link theory with scientific practice.
2. What are the implications for developmental theory of the notion that there is more than one 'type of knowledge'?
3. Discuss the notion of 'quality control' and its importance for school-based programmes to promote children's wellbeing.

Activities

1. Take Jack P. Shonkoff's (2000) three cultures of 'science', 'policy' and 'practice' and interview a practitioner regarding how they impact on psychological practice.
2. The terms 'scientist-practitioner', 'applied developmental psychology' and 'developmentally appropriate practice' are all described in this chapter. Select one of the terms related to your field of interest and provide a class presentation summarizing its main features and critiquing its role and the contribution it makes to child development theory.

Websites

Scientist-practitioner model set to music: www.youtube.com/watch?v=823ydlMwZAU.

Center on the Developing Child, Harvard (Shonkoff, etc.): http://developingchild.
harvard.edu/resources/articles_and_books/.
Developmentally appropriate practice: www.naeyc.org/DAP.

References

Kahlbaugh, P.E. 1989. William James' pragmatism: a clarification of the contextual world
view. In D.A. Kramer and M.J. Bopp (eds), *Transformation in clinical and developmental
psychology*. New York: Springer-Verlag, 73–88.
Shonkoff, J.P. 2000. Science, policy, and practice: three cultures in search of a shared mission.
Child Development. 71: 181–7.

GLOSSARY

accommodation in Jean Piaget's theory, the modification of mental structures to incorporate new knowledge

adolescence a term for teenagers derived from the Latin *adolescere*, meaning 'to grow to maturity'

affective processes processes regulating emotional states and elicitation of emotional reactions

agency the idea that people are active in making decisions about their lives

assimilation in Piaget's theory, the incorporation of new information into the child's existing patterns of thought and behaviour

associationism the view that all knowledge derives from associating one small item of information with another

attachment the primary social bond between one individual and another

attachment behaviour behaviour that promotes contact and/or proximity of an infant to the caregiver

BCE before the common era (equivalent to BC)

behaviourism a reductionist approach that focuses entirely on the overt and visible

biological determinism the idea that all human behaviour is determined by biology

canalization the idea that there are decision points in development and that proceeding down certain 'channels' makes it difficult or impossible to 'backtrack' into alternative channels

Cartesian dualism René Descartes's idea that the mind and body are entirely distinct and separate

CE common era (equivalent to AD)

classical conditioning learning in which a neutral stimulus elicits a certain response by repeated association with another stimulus that already elicits the response

cofigurative Margaret Mead's description of a culture in which children learn from their peers

cognition the way we know about the world through the use of thinking, reasoning, learning and remembering

cognitive processes thinking processes involved in the acquisition, organization and use of information

concrete operations period according to Jean Piaget, the stage between 7 and 11 years old when children begin to understand the relationship between things in the world but still cannot think in abstract terms

conditioned reflex occurs when a previously neutral stimulus acquires the ability to produce a response through association with an unconditioned stimulus (a stimulus that evokes a response that has not been learned)

conservation in Piagetian theory, the retention by an object or substance of certain properties, regardless of changes in shape and arrangement

constitutional present at birth

constructive development occurs when a child actively participates by finding personal meaning in a situation, making decisions and sharing viewpoints with peers

constructivism a school of thought in psychology that emphasizes the subjectivity of experience and the role of individuals in actively construing their world.

constructivist emphasizing the subjectivity of our experience and the role of individuals in actively construing meaning in their world

contextualism the idea that an action only has meaning in relation to its context

development increase in the functional complexity of an organism; changes that take into account the effect of experience on an individual (compare with maturation)

developmental psychology the study of the individual from conception to death (but see African perspective in Chapter 3)

developmental tasks in Robert J. Havighurst's theory, tasks that must be completed during certain periods of a person's life

dialectical proceeding by debate between conflicting viewpoints

ego in Freudian theory, the conscious self, the realistic rational part of the personality that mediates between the instinctual demands of the id and the superego

empiricism the approach to understanding the world that assumes only information that can be detected physically and measured should count as valid knowledge

epigenetics broadly, the interplay between genetic and ecological conditions to determine the phenotype; narrowly, environmentally induced genetic changes that do not alter the DNA sequence and can be passed on to subsequent generations

epistemological development development of the child's knowledge base

epistemology the study of the theory of how we acquire knowledge

existentialism a philosophy emphasizing the importance and value of the individual and the role of freedom, responsibility and choice in determining behaviour

experiential child refers to the concept that children develop solely as a product of their experience

feminism advocacy for women's experiences, values and contributions, aimed at achieving equality between males and females

formal operations period Jean Piaget's name for the fourth stage of cognitive development, from about 11 years of age onwards, during which individuals acquire the ability to think in abstract terms

functionalism the idea that the mind functions to adapt the individual to the environment

genes biological units of heredity involving self-reproducing DNA

genetics the scientific study of heredity

genotype the genetic composition of the organism

Gestalt a school of thought in psychology that suggests that the perceived organized whole is more than the sum of its parts

id in Freudian theory, that part of the personality containing all of the basic impulses or drives

information processing the taking in, storing and using of information by humans and animals

iniquitous child John Wesley's view that children are inherently sinful

Lamarck, Jean–Baptiste (1744–1829) French naturalist who theorized that acquired characteristics could be inherited

maturation the changes that occur in an organism as it fulfils its genetic potential (compare with development)

mechanism the idea that organisms are like complicated machines, the whole being the sum of the individual parts

méthode clinique the method of interviewing adopted by Jean Piaget to help him understand the child's thought processes

organicism the idea that development is significantly shaped by mutual influence and the patterning of its parts

organismic emphasizing the contribution individuals make to their own development

perceived self-efficacy people's beliefs about their capabilities to produce effects

phenotype the physical or behavioural traits in an individual that reflect both genetic and environmental factors

positivism a branch of philosophy advocating the use of the methods and principles of the natural sciences in the study of human behaviour

postfigurative Margaret Mead's description of a culture in which children learn from their forebears

preformist refers to the view that a miniature adult exists in the egg or sperm

pre-operational period Jean Piaget's name for the stage between two and seven years of age, during which children acquire the ability to represent the world using symbols, such as language

reaction range the broadest possible expression of a genotype

reinforcement any stimulus that increases the likelihood of a behaviour recurring

relationalism the idea that entities only exist in relation to one another

scaffolding Lev Vygotsky's term for the way in which a person skilfully encourages a learner to acquire a new skill or understand a concept

schema in Piagetian terms, a pattern of action or a mental structure (plural: schemes or schemata)

scientism the idea that all true knowledge arises from the use of empirical scientific method

self-regulation exercise of influence over one's own motivation, thought processes, emotional states and patterns of behaviour

sensori-motor period Jean Piaget's first cognitive development stage, in which infants use their senses and motor skills to explore their environment

structuralism Edward B. Titchener's idea that the mind can be analysed into components

superego in Freudian theory, that part of the personality incorporating the internalized values held by the individual and corresponding to the internalized injunctions of the parent

temperament behaviours that comprise relatively stable characteristics of a person's personality (generally thought to be constitutional)

theory of mind the ability to impute mental states to self and others

transactional view of development the view that development is a two-way interaction between child and environment; strictly, that the entities concerned do not exist independently

transivity in Jean Piaget's theory, the ability to recognize relationships between things in serial order (e.g. increasing in size)

translational research making findings from basic science useful in an applied sense

virtuous child refers to Jean-Jacques Rousseau's notion that the child is inherently good

zone of proximal development (ZPD) the 'gap' between what individuals can achieve alone and what they can achieve with the help of a more knowledgeable person

INDEX